Designing
AppleTalk Network Architectures

Network Frontiers Field Manual Series

LIMITED WARRANTY AND DISCLAIMER OF LIABILITY

ACADEMIC PRESS, INC. ("AP") AND ANYONE ELSE WHO HAS BEEN INVOLVED IN THE CREATION OR PRODUC-
TION OF THE ACCOMPANYING CODE ("THE PRODUCT") CANNOT AND DO NOT WARRANT THE PERFORMANCE
OR RESULTS THAT MAY BE OBTAINED BY USING THE PRODUCT. THE PRODUCT IS SOLD "AS IS" WITHOUT
WARRANTY OF ANY KIND (EXCEPT AS HEREAFTER DESCRIBED), EITHER EXPRESSED OR IMPLIED, INCLUD-
ING, BUT NOT LIMITED TO, ANY WARRANTY OF PERFORMANCE OR ANY IMPLIED WARRANTY OF MER-
CHANTABILITY OR FITNESS FOR ANY PARTICULAR PURPOSE. AP WARRANTS ONLY THAT THE MAGNETIC
DISKETTE(S) ON WHICH THE CODE IS RECORDED IS FREE FROM DEFECTS IN MATERIAL AND FAULTY WORK-
MANSHIP UNDER THE NORMAL USE AND SERVICE FOR A PERIOD OF NINETY (90) DAYS FROM THE DATE THE
PRODUCT IS DELIVERED. THE PURCHASER'S SOLE AND EXCLUSIVE REMEDY IN THE EVENT OF A DEFECT IS
EXPRESSLY LIMITED TO EITHER REPLACEMENT OF THE DISKETTE(S) OR REFUND OF THE PURCHASE PRICE,
AT AP'S SOLE DISCRETION.

IN NO EVENT, WHETHER AS A RESULT OF BREACH OF CONTRACT, WARRANTY OR TORT (INCLUDING NEGLI-
GENCE), WILL AP OR ANYONE WHO HAS BEEN INVOLVED IN THE CREATION OR PRODUCTION OF THE PROD-
UCT BE LIABLE TO PURCHASER FOR ANY DAMAGES, INCLUDING ANY LOST PROFITS, LOST SAVINGS OR
OTHER INCIDENTAL OR CONSEQUENTIAL DAMAGES ARISING OUT OF THE USE OR INABILITY TO USE THE
PRODUCT OR ANY MODIFICATIONS THEREOF, OR DUE TO THE CONTENTS OF THE CODE, EVEN IF AP HAS
BEEN ADVISED OF THE POSSIBILITY OF SUCH DAMAGES, OR FOR ANY CLAIM BY ANY OTHER PARTY.

Any request for replacement of a defective diskette must be postage prepaid and must be accompanied by the original defective
diskette, your mailing address and telephone number, and proof of date of purchase and purchase price. Send such requests, stating the nature of the problem, to Academic Press Customer Service, 6277 Sea Harbor Drive, Orlando, FL 32887, 1-800-321-
5068. APP shall have no obligation to refund the purchase price or to replace a diskette based on claims of defects in the nature
or operation of the Product.

Some states do not allow limitation on how long an implied warranty lasts, nor exclusions or limitations of incidental or consequential damage, so the above limitations and exclusions may not apply to you. This Warranty gives you specific legal rights,
and you may also have other rights which vary from jurisdiction to jurisdiction.

THE RE-EXPORT OF UNITED STATES ORIGIN SOFTWARE IS SUBJECT TO THE UNITED STATES LAWS UNDER
THE EXPORT ADMINISTRATION ACT OF 1969 AS AMENDED. ANY FURTHER SALE OF THE PRODUCT SHALL BE
IN COMPLIANCE WITH THE UNITED STATES DEPARTMENT OF COMMERCE ADMINISTRATION REGULATIONS.
COMPLIANCE WITH SUCH REGULATIONS IS YOUR RESPONSIBILITY AND NOT THE RESPONSIBILITY OF AP.

Designing AppleTalk Network Architectures

Network Frontiers Field Manual Series

Dorian J. Cougias • Tom Dell • E.L. Heiberger

Foreword by Garry Hornbuckle

AP PROFESSIONAL

Boston   San Diego   New York
London   Sydney   Tokyo   Toronto

AP PROFESSIONAL
1300 Boylston Street, Chestnut Hill, MA 02167
World Wide Web site at http://www.apnet.com

An Imprint of ACADEMIC PRESS, INC.
A Division of HARCOURT BRACE & COMPANY

United Kingdom Edition published by
ACADEMIC PRESS LIMITED
24–28 Oval Road, London NW1 7DX

ISBN 0-12-192566-8

Printed in the United States of America
96 97 98 99   IP   9 8 7 6 5 4 3 2 1

DEDICATIONS

Dorian Cougias's Dedication:

To my mother, **Elsie M. Cougias**, *a.k.a Mrs. Koscho*

Mrs. Koscho was a real person who lived next door to my father on Van Buren Street in Gary, Indiana back in the 1920s and 1930s. Mrs. Koscho was from the old country and was a do-it-your-selfer. She would probably make Tim the Toolman blush with envy. Whenever my mother would start a new building project, my father, who wasn't into that sort of thing, would say, "Uh-oh, Mrs. Koscho's at it again."

My mother and I built the back room on our house. We spent a summer waiting for dribs and drabs from the local cement guys to build our driveway. We built fences, rock gardens, and reroofed the house. We built everything there was to build, and usually built it better than if we had paid someone to build it for us. It was Mom who taught me the joy in building something you could be proud of, something that worked better than anything you had previously built, something that might last a heck of a lot longer than you would.

It is to my mother, then, that I dedicate the book that includes all my best knowledge about building networks. I hope it earns her respect.

Elisabeth L. Heiberger's Dedication:

Dedicated to my mother—Thanks for believing in me

CONTENTS

FOREWORD

by Garry Hornbuckle
Product Line Manager for Communications and Collaboration
Apple Computer, Inc.

A note from Dorian, first: Here is the "official stuff" about Garry. Garry Hornbuckle is currently the Product Line Manager for Communications and Collaboration at Apple Computer. Garry is responsible for the direction of networking and communications technologies in the Macintosh OS, including AppleTalk, TCP/IP, Open Transport, and PowerTalk. Now in his ninth year with Apple, Garry has also worked in N&C Evangelism and spent five years with Apple USA as a consulting engineer specializing in networking. Before joining Apple, Garry managed a cross-platform software development startup company for two years, and began his professional life as a software development engineer and manager in a mainframe environment.

Now here is "my stuff" about Garry. Garry is a great guy. His offering to write the foreword for this book was a very pleasant surprise. First, he's incredibly busy. He's probably one of the hardest working folks I know. Second, he's up to his ears in moving Open Transport out the door. Third, he has Copeland and the migration of PowerTalk from a proprietary system to an Internet-based system to worry about. So, while he's doing all that and reviewing this book during vacation, he offered us the foreword. What a guy! If you ask me, this is one of those folks in the industry to watch. He not only knows where the communications of AppleTalk and Macintoshes/Mac OS clones are going, he's one of the primary architects of their movement one way or the other. So, if you want to know where AppleTalk and Open Transport are heading, you need only to listen to Garry for a while. I know. I listen. Intently.

A wise man once said, "Knowledge is power." But an even wiser man said, "A little bit of knowledge is a dangerous thing." Sometimes I wonder if they were both thinking of AppleTalk.

The AppleTalk Networking System, designed and introduced by Apple Computer, Inc. in 1984, is one of the most elegant, ahead-of-its-time—and yet misunderstood—information systems technologies of the last ten years.

Originally envisioned as an inexpensive way to share an expensive laser printer peripheral, AppleTalk was enhanced and grew to become one of the world's top three installed networking technologies in less than ten years. It expanded dramatically beyond its Apple Macintosh and Mac OS roots to almost every mainstream computing hardware and OS platform including IBM, VAX, Sun, SGI, Novell, and Windows.

AppleTalk pioneered technologies for the support of mobile users, such as dynamic addressing and naming, years ahead of protocols like DHCP and WINS. It offered a rich foreign-protocol transport architecture before PPP was even a glimmer in a designer's eye. All that, and it still sets the standard for ease of use in regard to the end-user's networking experience.

But unlike its protocol and architectural counterparts—such as SNA, DECnet, NCP/SPX/IPX—AppleTalk most frequently "just appeared" on networks, often as Macintosh systems and LaserWriters were introduced into an organization. It wasn't typically planned in advance, and it often was deployed in spite of an IS organization, rather than with their help and support. In these earlier days, the idea of a professionally trained AppleTalk Network Administrator or an Apple-Talk Network Designer was almost unthinkable. Many of us found ourselves being forced to learn about networks and zones; tagged because we were the one person that demonstrated some interest, knowledge, or willingness to learn.

But the introduction of AppleTalk Phase 2 in 1989 changed things. While it made AppleTalk scalable to enterprise proportions, it also made the historical practice of the "accidental enterprise network" much less effective, much less reliable, and much less practical. Suddenly (it seemed) you now had to know the details to manage this thing called the Phase 1-to-Phase 2 transition. As we de facto network administrators began to deal with this issue, IS organizations (also suddenly, it seemed) came to realize how important AppleTalk had become to their organizations. Truly mission-critical applications were being built and deployed, and almost no one really understood how this AppleTalk stuff worked.

The AppleTalk industry began to change; to see a real demand for formal training, consulting, and reference materials. As a result we began to see the emergence of a new breed of professional, technically knowledgeable AppleTalk administrators and network design engineers. Robust Mac OS-based network troubleshooting and planning tools came to market including "low-level" tools, like protocol analyzers, and "high-level" tools, like router management software and system profilers.

But still, overall, there were and are too few professionals with the level of knowledge to be powerful. "AppleTalk is a chatty protocol," "AppleTalk doesn't scale," and "AppleTalk networks can't be managed" are examples of the half-truths and misstatements that I suspect all of us have heard, and many of us have come to expect, when it comes to AppleTalk.

The reality is, of course, more complex. AppleTalk does shift many of the housekeeping tasks required to manage routing and name space data structures to protocols that run on the network, rather than leave them as clerical tasks for an administrator. AppleTalk can scale to hundreds of networks and tens of thousands of nodes, but only if properly designed, implemented, and managed. And AppleTalk can be managed, if the proper tools and training are applied.

This book (actually the first of two) provides *excellent* information about the design and planning of AppleTalk networks: small ones, big ones, LANs, WANs, bridged, routed, switched, and more. It is the kind of information that, as you read and apply it in your work environment, can bring you to realize that "knowledge is power" when it comes to AppleTalk. These books will be very valuable, regardless of where you are in your learning curve. You may have just found yourself thrust into the role of AppleTalk network administrator, kicking furiously to keep your head above water. You may have been working with AppleTalk for a while, but are now facing the expansion of your network, perhaps needing to connect remote locations or to integrate Internet connectivity. Or you may even be a seasoned professional, looking for a reference work. The collected knowledge and experience of the authors, found in these two volumes, will be a valuable asset.

Introduction to the Design Books

This was supposed to be the only book in the series on network design, but it just kept growing and growing and growing. We wanted to provide the complete guide to designing an AppleTalk network. Therefore, we wanted to put as much as we knew into this book. At about the 600th page, we knew one more thing—the publisher was going to kill us if we didn't do something drastic. Our solution was to completely reorganize the book (again) and split it into two parts. Part one, the one you are reading right now, is about designing a structured system. It is about cabling, hubs, bridges and switches, routers, and gateways. It is about 10BaseT, Category 5, and Fast Ethernet. It is about ISDN and Frame Relay. It is about the basics of TCP/IP addressing, as well as AppleTalk addressing, and how the two can coexist on your network.

What is *not* in this book are the services that run on top of your structured networking system—not that they shouldn't be here, but hey, we ran out of pages. The one thing we couldn't agree on was how to best split the book with some services in the first book and some services in the second book. Therefore, we took this approach. If you want to know how to pick a server, if you want to know how to set up a DNS (or even what one is), go to the second book, *AppleTalk Network Services,* for that. If you want to know the best configuration for your Web server, that too is in the second book. However, if you want to know which is the best router for your needs, you can find that here. Here is the way it works:

- Use this book, *Designing AppleTalk Network Architectures,* as a reference guide when designing the physical and logical structure and architecture of your network. Use it as a reference for how the devices work and as a design guide for both wiring and hardware.

- Then, use the second book, *AppleTalk Network Services,* so that you can incorporate services into your network designs, integrating the service into the architecture.

As always, fax us at (415) 896-1573 or send us e-mail if you need help. Our e-mail addresses are:

Dorian Cougias:	dorian_cougias@netfrontiers.com
Lynn Heiberger:	lynn_heiberger@netfrontiers.com
Tom Dell:	tom_dell@netfrontiers.com

Acknowledgments

Wow. There are *so* many people to acknowledge for this book, it's incredible. I now know what it means when they say that a writer merely puts into words what others are helping him or her to say.

First and foremost, I'd like to thank Garry Hornbuckle—not only for his introduction to the book, but also for pushing Apple to move Open Transport from an idea to a reality. It's going to make a huge difference in the way computers operate on a network. It *truly* makes the Macintosh Operating System one of the best networking citizens in the world.

Second, I'd like to thank both Michael Swan and Dwight Barker at Neon Software. I bugged them continually throughout the writing of this book.

A really heartfelt thanks goes to two guys who I probably rubbed the wrong way more than a few times and drove entirely crazy many times: Clint Bogard from Asanté and Tom Ver Ploeg from Engage Communications. I'm a hard guy to make happy, and while I sometimes praised their products, at other times I ate them for lunch. These are the two front men—the best guys each company has—who had to deal with me. For me it was a pleasure. For them . . . well, I'm sorry . . . I'll be nicer next time.

Also, I really have to thank Tom Skoulis and the wonderful folks at Farallon. I call it "Tom's company," because that's how he treats it — like it's his own. He nurtures it, works it, and helps it more than a normal "employee." Hey, you folks at Farallon, give him some ownership! Anyway, Tom helped a lot with their products, and without him, I don't think I would have gotten anywhere.

While I'm at it, Georganne Benesch at Farallon is a supporter from *way* back. Without Georganne we wouldn't have *squat* with which to train or on which to learn. She saw the value in our training and writing before most others did. Thanks, Georganne, I really appreciate it.

A special thanks to all the readers of the first draft of this book: Dean White, Dale Youri, Kathy Rose, Vernon Rose, Allan Crump, David Burk, Michelle Koblas, Paul Shields, Roger Wilde, and Walter Fry. Further, thanks to all of you who taught us that "parts is *not* just parts": Rich Willis of AT&T, Mary Beth Beckford of MicroTest, Marc Cooper of Kalpana, John Ward of Tut; Trevor, Dan, and Tom at Compatible Systems; and Charlie O., Dean, and Mike of Global Village.

Thanks to all the vendors who gave us something to write about, like the ones we have just mentioned and also Bay Networks, Cisco, and Tribe. Thanks to AG Group, Santorini, Wave Research, and Caravelle for giving us the tools to poke in the network and peek at the packets.

As always, thanks to Monty Lewis, our cover artist, and to our indexer, Steve Rath. No one is better.

Thanks to Maizie Gilbert and Felix Barrientos for all their foot and phone work. Without their rounding up pictures and reader's comments, this book couldn't have been produced.

A special personal thanks to Randy Matamoros for his infinite wisdom.

Finally, thanks from Dorian to Kee Nethery for reading the book. Yes, there were a lot of readers of this book, but Kee's comments were the most appreciated by yours truly. Why? He's one of the guys I look up to.

PART 1:
CABLING YOUR NETWORK

While most network design books don't focus much on cabling, we have made it the heftiest part of the book. If the cabling doesn't meet the same exacting standards used for the rest of the system, you will find yourself with a Bozo No-No network. You don't want a Bozo No-No network.

What's a Bozo No-No network? First, I'll tell you the origin of the term Bozo No-No, which made me famous to Miss Kelley's second grade class in the 1960s. I was on the Bozo show in Chicago, and was picked—from a "cast of thousands," mind you—to play the grand prize game. In this game, you and another kid throw ping pong balls into these six small buckets on the floor. As you hit buckets that are farther and farther away, your prize becomes better and better, bucket six being nirvana: a Schwinn five-speed Stingray bicycle with banana seat! Wow! As a kid from Chicago in the '60s, that was just unbelievable. I didn't reach bucket six and went home with a giant Tootsie Roll. But that wasn't what made me famous. I was famous because I was on the show with the *other kid.* He made it all the way to bucket five, but when he reached bucket six, he, gasp, *missed!* As he missed, he yelled out on the *live* televised show, "Aw, shit!" Bozo—aka Larry Harmon—came over and said, "That's a Bozo No-No." To that, the kid turned around, and before the cameras could cut, he said, "Cram it, clown!" At that, my second grade class told me that they went to a commercial. I won't tell you what happened to the kid—it was ugly. You can buy me a beer someday and then I'll tell you.

I told you this story for two reasons. First, I want you to know the severity of a Bozo No-No. After the incident, the worst thing you could do was cause a Bozo

No-No. Second, and more important, I had to fill up some space. I wanted to show you a couple of network Bozo No-No pictures, and they wouldn't fit on the previous page.

Take some time and look at these two pictures. Do these look familiar? Unfortunately, they probably do. I have seen this far more often than I've seen well-implemented networks. Look at the computer on the top right. I wonder why the LocalTalk network might not be visible? Why is the LocalTalk connector just hanging there? In this section, I want to stress to you that even though you are building a relatively simple network, build it so that you don't have cable bedlam. Look at all those cables by the power protector! Ouch!

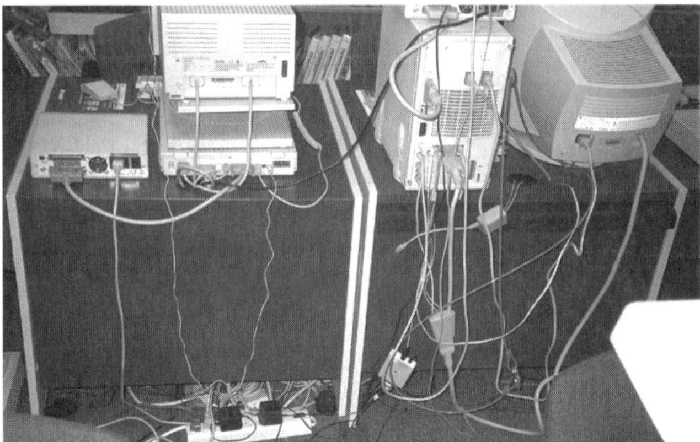

HOW TO USE THIS SECTION

In this section of the book, we will teach you the fundamentals and more of wiring a local area network. We will briefly walk you through some of the basics for both LocalTalk and Ethernet cabling, and then we will discuss, in depth, what you need to know about the different options for cabling both of these networks.

We will discuss daisy chains, trunks, infrared, and radio frequency networks. We will then focus our attention on structured wiring systems and what you need to know about them from the basics through the planning and implementation phases of your cabling design. If you don't know me well enough yet, you will learn rather quickly that I favor a structured wiring system over any other type of wiring system. Hence, we will spend most of our time learning about the structured wiring system.

Chapter 1: Overviews of LocalTalk and EtherTalk Physical Layer Specifications

First, the basics. There are a few characteristics you need to understand about AppleTalk's media capabilities. I know that some of you have a good grasp of these specifications, but others of you have no clue.

First of all, there is no such thing as "AppleTalk cabling." A long time ago there was a type of LocalTalk cabling that was marketed as "AppleTalk cabling." In some of the cabling catalogs, such as those from Anixter and GraybaR, you will sometimes find "AppleTalk cabling" advertised. What they mean by that is the original, shielded, twisted pair cabling with two-port transceivers and other such paraphernalia that went along with it. We don't discuss that stuff in this book because nobody really uses it. The only time I've even *seen* it in the real world in the last couple of years was at a client site—in a box with a lot of dust on it.

So, what then are we going to talk about? We are going to explore the different LocalTalk and Ethernet cabling issues that are applicable to AppleTalk. It will be the structured wiring systems that this section will focus most heavily upon, as with these, you can go up to 100 Mbps!

QUICK REVIEW OF LOCALTALK

First of all, if you don't know what LocalTalk is, or the options for LocalTalk connectivity, I suggest you put a marker on this page and go read about LocalTalk in our primer book on AppleTalk and Open Transport. Then come back here and begin the design process in earnest. If, however, you know more about LocalTalk than you care to know (like most of us), and you want to look at how to design connectivity into your network with LocalTalk, you are in the right place.

Every Macintosh and Macintosh clone comes with LocalTalk on board and the AppleTalk protocols built-in. If you are a PC user, you will need PhoneNET PC from Farallon, Apple's AppleShare for Windows software, or Miramar's AppleTalk product for Windows devices. PhoneNET PC is a hardware/software combination that includes a PC LocalTalk Network Interface Card (NIC) and PhoneNET PC software that allows the PC to access the LocalTalk network to print and share files from other computers. Honestly, though, if you are going to buy an NIC for your PC, you may as well buy an Ethernet card. Why pay so much for something so slow? If you are buying separate cards anyway, look at Apple's or Miramar's solutions as well. Anyway, on each Macintosh or clone, you will find both a printer and a modem port. Contrary to some people's belief (including my own, until Kee Nethery set me straight. Thanks, Kee—much appreciated), you cannot use either port for LocalTalk, because the computer is set up to automatically recognize the printer port as being the LocalTalk port. Only in special circumstances can applications like the Apple Internet Router use the modem port for LocalTalk, and that is because a special driver was written for that purpose.

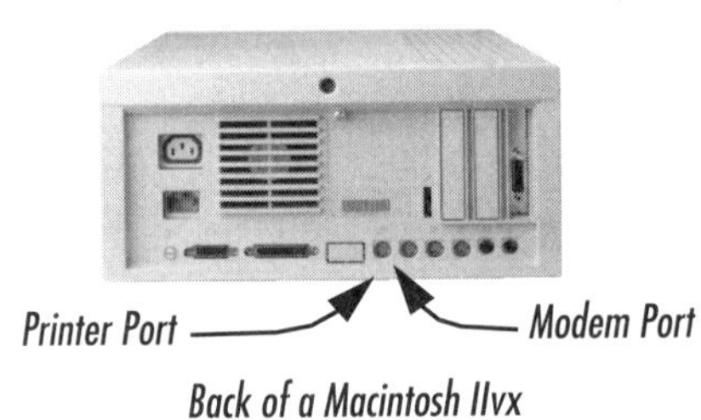

Back of a Macintosh IIvx

Review of the Rules

Let's start with a quick review of LocalTalk connection rules. First, LocalTalk is built into every Macintosh, Macintosh clone, and Apple LaserWriter that rolls off the assembly line. It is *not,* however, built in to PCs. You need some additional equipment for PCs to connect with LocalTalk. We will cover that in the section "Building a PhoneNET Daisy Chain" on page 19.

Twisted Pair for LocalTalk

LocalTalk networks over shielded or unshielded twisted pair wire require only one pair of wires. The wire type can be the exact same as your general telephone wiring—22 American Wire Gauge (AWG) or 24 AWG. Although 26 AWG can also be used, it is not recommended.

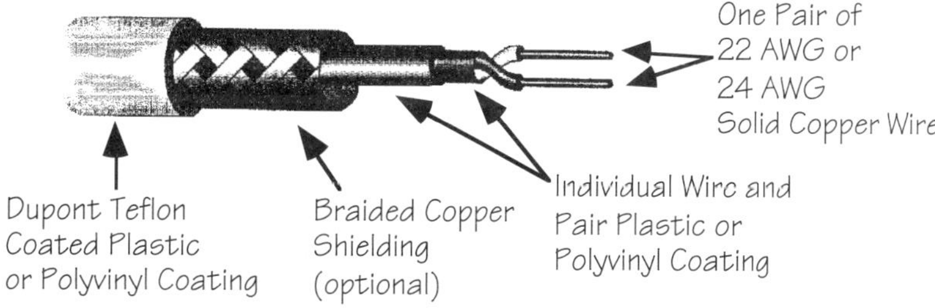

Single Twisted Pair Cable

Even though the LocalTalk design calls for *twisted* pair cables, most LocalTalk cabling systems don't use twisted pair. They use the flat wiring that comes with the Farallon PhoneNET connectors. It is sometimes solid copper, sometimes stranded copper, or sometimes the wiring is not pure copper at all, but a mix of alloys called silver satin cable.

LocalTalk is also designed to work with infrared (IR) networking technology, such as the Photonics GameNET and Cooperative connectors, and the new IR technology found on the PowerBook 5000 series computers and Farallon AirDocks.

Speed

LocalTalk runs at 230.4 kilobits per second. That roughly translates into about 0.48 megabytes of data moving from point A to point B per minute.

Topologies

LocalTalk can use daisy chain, trunk, passive star, and active star topologies as well as infrared's free-form topology.

Number of Devices per Network

Theoretically, there can be up to 254 networked devices on a LocalTalk network. Realistically, the number should be somewhere around 32–64 networked devices per LocalTalk network, if you are using the Tribe LocalSwitch.

Summary Information

This table consolidates some of the information we just covered.

Medium	Topology	Max. # Nodes	Max. Length
Shielded Twisted Pair	Bus	32	1000 ft.
Unshielded Twisted Pair	Bus	20–40	2000 ft.
Unshielded Twisted Pair	Passive Star	4	750 ft.
Unshielded Twisted Pair	Active Star	254	2000 ft.

Common LocalTalk Topologies and Their Wiring Distances

QUICK REVIEW OF ETHERTALK (APPLETALK OVER ETHERNET)

When I first started building networks, LocalTalk was the prevalent networking system for Macintoshes, and Ethernet was very expensive. You put your *servers* up on Ethernet. Just so that you geeks know, Ethernet was originally developed by the Xerox corporation at their Palo Alto Research Center, known as Xerox PARC, in the 1970s. In 1980, Xerox, Intel Corporation, and Digital Equipment Corporation jointly published their first specification for the Ethernet Local Area Network. By 1985, the IEEE standards committee released the 802.3 10Base5 specification (ThickNet), which was similar to the Ethernet specification but called for a different packet composition. The 802.3 specification replaced the Xerox "type" information with "packet length" information. Following the 10Base5 specification, the IEEE also released another relevant specification, the 10Base2 (ThinNet) specification. In 1991, the 10BaseT or 802.3i specification was finalized, and now in 1995, the Fast Ethernet specification has been finalized.

These days almost every Macintosh computer comes with Ethernet on board. The PowerComputing clones *all* come with Ethernet on board, as do most printers. I say *most printers* because many cross-platform printers, like those from Hewlett Packard, have Ethernet as an extra add-on. Before we go any farther, let's review some of the rules to make sure we are all on the same track.

Review of the Rules

If you are wondering what all the "base" stuff means, here is how it works. In each of the cases, the *10* refers to the transmission rate of 10 megabits per second. The *base* describes the fact that the baseband transmission method is used. The *5* ($\times$ 100) and the *2* ($\times$ 100) represent the maximum cable distance that the signal can be carried. For example, 10Base5 can go a distance of 500 meters. The *T* in 10BaseT represents the twisted wires or unshielded twisted pair cable specified for that network.

Ethernet NIC and Connectors

Each computer or printer has to have an Ethernet Network Interface Card (NIC) and an appropriate connector. There are basically four different types of connectors on the market today. The connector types are AUI, BNC, AAUI, and 10BaseT. If you have a Macintosh computer or Apple LaserWriter, then you have an AAUI connector. If you have any other type of device, you could have any one of these connectors or a variety of them. In the following picture, two Ethernet NICs are shown with the different types of connectors. Note that the one on the left has three of the four types of connectors.

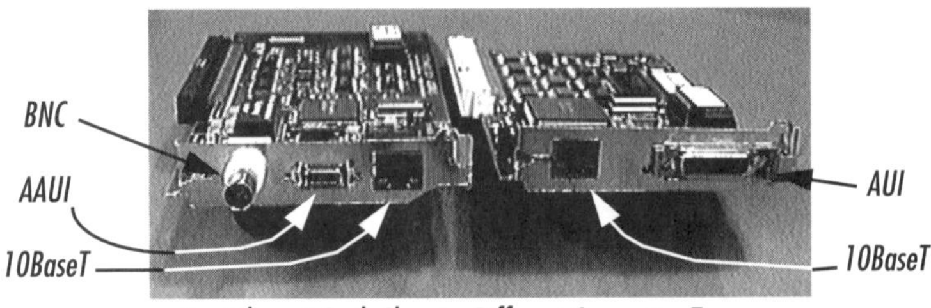

Two Ethernet Cards Showing Different Connection Types

For the NICs that don't have the BNC connector or the 10BaseT connector, you will need an external transceiver. (By the way, BNC stands for Bayonet Niell Concelman, supposedly after the names of the two inventors and the bayonet connection type.) The transceivers are either for ThinNet or for 10BaseT. In the next picture, there are four transceivers. The top two are from Apple; one for ThinNet (A) and one for 10BaseT (B). Transceiver D is for AUI to ThinNet, and transceiver C has *both* ThinNet and 10BaseT connectors.

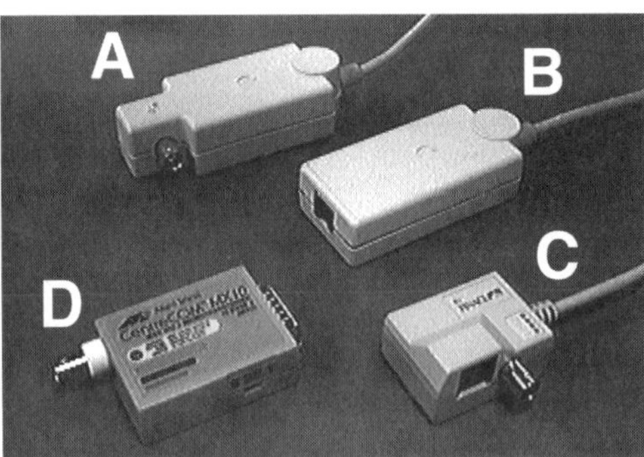

Four Different Transceiver Types

In addition to the Ethernet NIC and transceiver, each computer has to have the appropriate Ethernet driver installed into the system. This software contains the following: control panel software, LAP Manager, an INIT resource, AppleTalk

Address Resolution Protocol (AARP) implementation, and the Ethernet driver. Although their operations are explained in detail in our primer on AppleTalk and Open Transport, we will explain them briefly here.

Control Panel Software

There are two types of control panel software for the Macintosh and its networking environments. For all computers using System 7.5.1 or *earlier,* AppleTalk networking information and connectivity can be changed via the Network control panel. For all computers using System 7.5.2 or *later,* AppleTalk networking information is found and changed via the AppleTalk control panel. Why the shift? System 7.5.2 is the demarcation point for Apple's Open Transport system of interconnectivity. Where straight AppleTalk or TCP/IP gave users a good deal of flexibility but not much control or management, Open Transport offers *more* flexibility and *a lot* of network management options.

Because most of us are still used to straight AppleTalk, we'll cover that first. Then we'll go back and show the same windows for Open Transport. Hopefully we won't lose any of you along the way.

Straight AppleTalk Connectivity The Network control panel displays the icons for all alternative AppleTalk connection files (adevs), such as EtherTalk, TokenTalk, and Apple Remote Access. The computer can only use one connection type at a time, and the method of connecting to the network, represented by the icons, must be selected in the Network control panel. The computer can only send and receive data via the selected network connection.

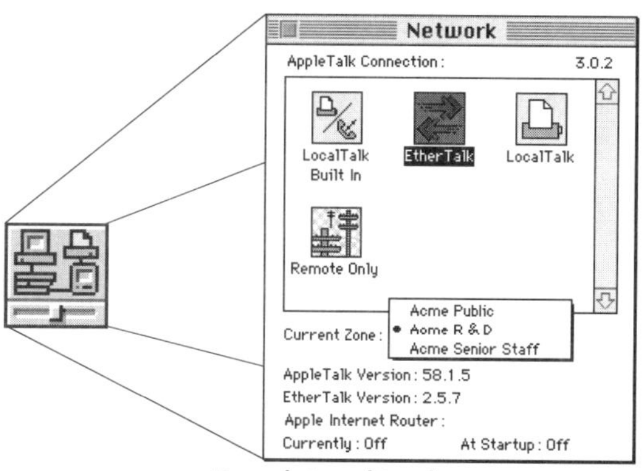

Network Control Panel

If you are wondering, the Apple Internet Router *does* use more than one connection type at a time, but it still has to have a single *home* network registered for other networking connections, such as printing and file sharing. This Network control panel does not give the user any flexibility in assigning AppleTalk node addresses, nor does it give the administrator the ability to set and then *lock down* any of the available settings.

Apple Open Transport's AppleTalk Control Panel

The AppleTalk control panel used with Open Transport is a bit different from the Network control panel. First, both the connection type and the zones are accessed via pop-up menus instead of picture fields and pop-up menus.

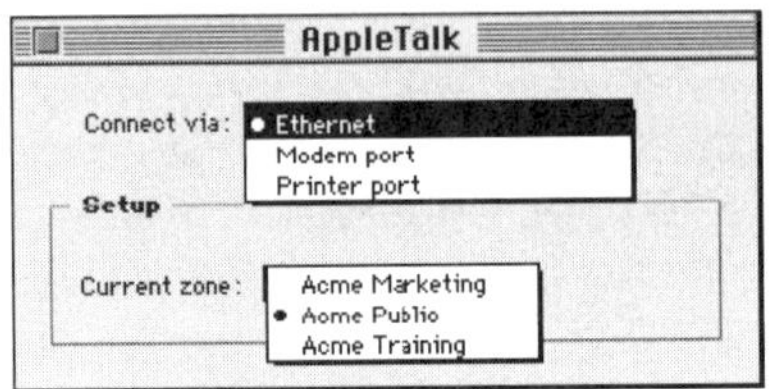

AppleTalk Control Panel

When using Open Transport, there are two more layers of administration, other than the standard user view. The standard view is called the **Basic** view. The more in-depth views are the **Advanced** view and the **Administrator** view. The only difference between the **Administrator** view and the **Advanced** view is that the **Administrator** view allows you to lock down the settings. Both views give the user the ability, through the **Info** button, to query the computer's address and the router it last heard from, as well as driver versions. Through the **Options...** button the user can make AppleTalk active or inactive. Both views automatically show the node's address, network, and range.

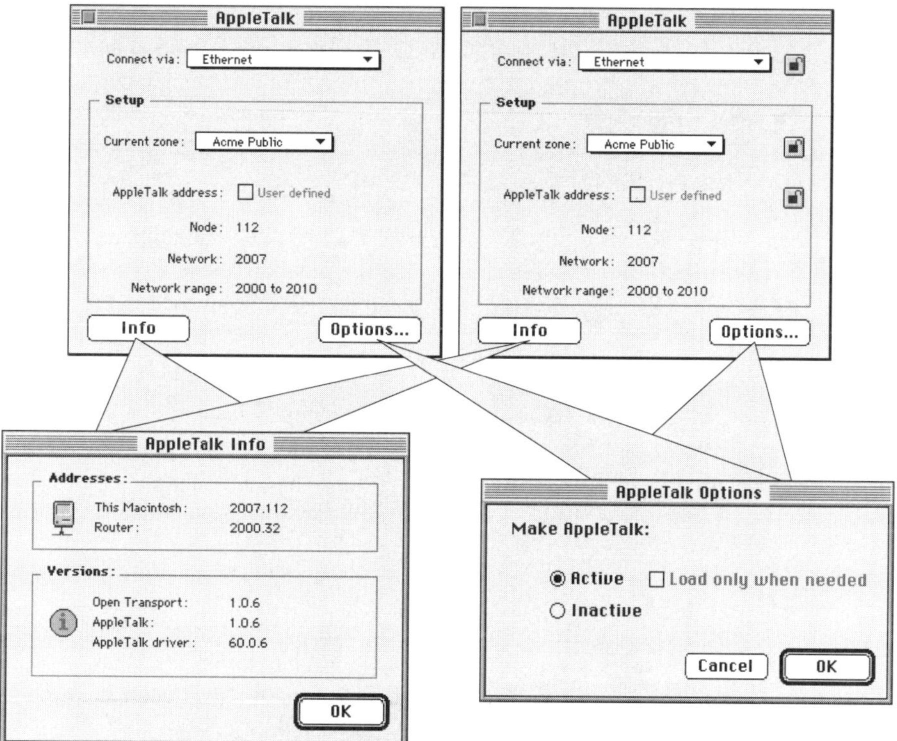

Advanced (top left) and Administrator (top right) Views

LAP Manager and INIT Resource

The LAP Manager is an interface between the Physical layer—the hardware connecting the computer to the network—and the Data Link layer—the software that sends the data. It sends the network packets to the connection you selected in the Network control panel.

AARP

AppleTalk networks are dynamically addressed through software in the Macintosh's operating system. This address is called a *protocol address.* Ethernet networks are addressed through "burned in" addresses in the Ethernet interface cards used to access the networks. To allow the two to work together, Apple came up with the AppleTalk Address Resolution Protocol (AARP), which creates a map between the hardware address of Ethernet and the AppleTalk protocol address.

Ethernet Driver

The Ethernet driver is software installed into the System file itself. This driver acts as an interface and controls the hardware transmitting and receiving packets on the Ethernet network.

Wiring

There are four basic types of wires that Ethernet can use: thin or thick coaxial cable, twisted pair wires, and fiber optic cable. We are going to cover the coaxial and twisted pair cables in this section. We are *not* going to cover fiber cables because as of the writing of this book, they are not commonly used.

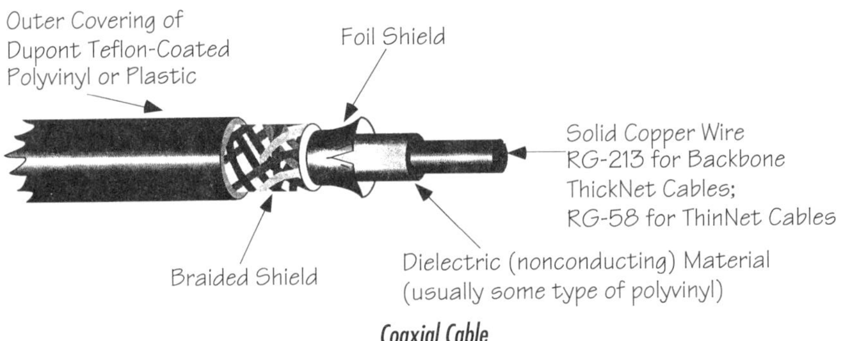

Coaxial Cable

Coaxial cable has several layers of material surrounding its center, or co-axis. The center conductor of solid copper wire is surrounded by nonconducting material. This is in turn covered by a shielding material, usually a wire braid or foil jacket. Everything is then covered with a polyvinyl or plastic coating. These 0.50-ohm cables have been defined within the IEEE 802.3 (Ethernet) 10Base5 and 10Base2 specifications. ThickNet or 10Base5 cabling is used for backbone cables, and although it has no official RG designation, RG-213 cable is usually used. ThinNet or 10Base2 cable is smaller in size and is designated RG-58.

Ethernet twisted pair cabling—IEEE 802.3, or 10BaseT as it is commonly called, is standard—is a bit trickier than LocalTalk twisted pair. One of the first things to notice is that 10BaseT Ethernet twisted pair uses two pairs of wires. There is a separate transmit pair and a separate receive pair.

The wiring used for Ethernet networks is 22 or 24 AWG data grade level 3, 4, or 5 (level 5 has four pairs). The difference in this wire, other than the extra pair, is the data grade of the wire. Regular telephone cable was not designed for data transmission; the signal strength for the cable was meant for voice transmission. LocalTalk transmission speeds do not tax the wire. However, the transmission speeds of Ethernet (10 Mbps) do tax flat wire. The transmission speeds of *Fast Ethernet* (100 Mbps) *really* tax the wire's capability to send data down its length. Only data grade 3 cable is certified for 10 Mbps data transmission, and only data grade 5 is certified for 100 Mbps data transmission. Notice in the two following photos that what makes the *most* difference in the cable's ability to carry the stronger, faster signal is the number of twists per foot of each cable. Try this some time: Crack open one of the connector cables that came with your Ethernet transceiver and see which of the two pictures looks most like what you find there.

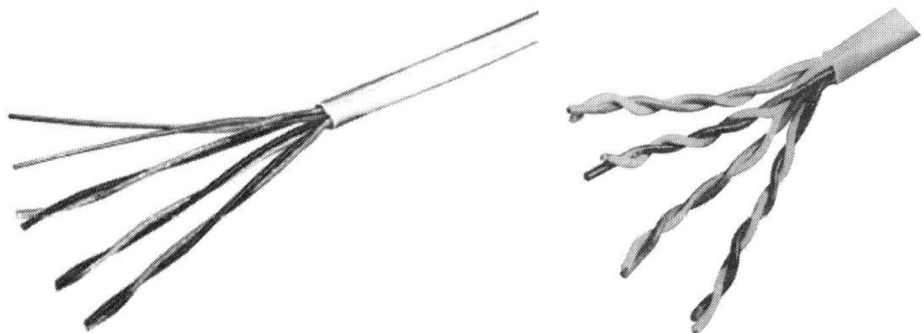

Category 3 Cable (left); Category 5 Cable (right)

Topologies

Ethernet can use daisy chain, trunk, and active star topologies as well as the free-form topology of radio frequency.

Number of Devices per Network

While the AppleTalk numbering scheme would theoretically allow gizillions of devices on an extended network, there are other practical limitations to consider, like the number of node entries per multiport bridge. There can be up to 30 nodes per ThinNet segment and 100 nodes per ThickNet flat wire segment. There can be up to 1024 nodes per 10BaseT segment, but realistically there should be no more than 300 computers on a single Ethernet segment. The network won't function as well with more than 300 devices.

Summary Information

The following table summarizes some of the information we just covered.

Medium	Topology	Max. # of Nodes	Cable Length
ThinNet or 10Base2	Daisy Chain Bus	30	606 ft.
ThickNet or 10Base5	Trunk	100	1640 ft.
UTP or 10BaseT	Star (active)	1024	328 ft. from hub to node

Common Ethernet Topologies and Their Wiring Distances

Chapter 2: Daisy Chain Systems

Now that you have refreshed your memory about how both LocalTalk and Ethernet deal with cabling issues, let's begin our investigation of some cabling topologies. The first of these topologies, the daisy chain, is the easiest to build and design into a network, and is usually how networks begin in an organization. In my humble opinion, a daisy-chained network should be used only when a temporary network is needed. Daisy chains are easy to break and cause too much havoc when they become overextended. But that's only my opinion.

PHONENET LOCALTALK DAISY CHAIN NETWORKS

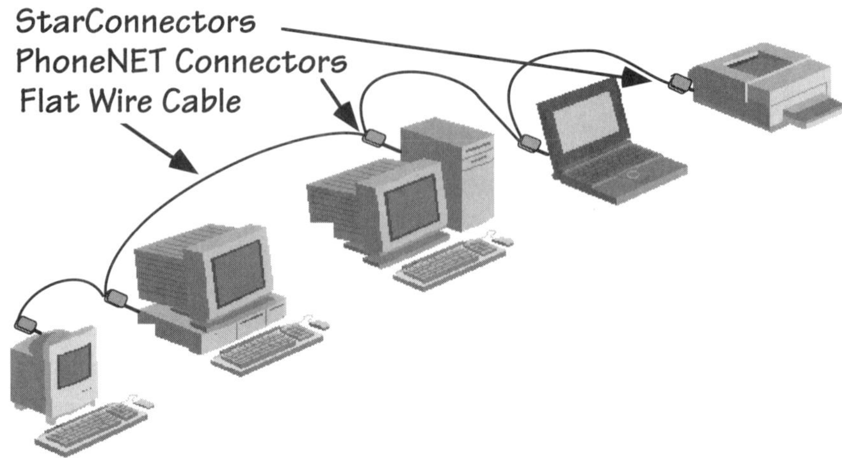

Small Daisy Chain Network

The preceding picture shows a small daisy chain network, the easiest of the networks to build. It's also the easiest of the networks to break—but hey, that's another book. The parts are simple: a PhoneNET connector or StarConnector to attach the computer to the network, and a small piece of flat wire, 24 AWG cable to connect them. POTS, or Plain Old Telephone System wire, is usually sufficient. You don't have to worry about whether you are plugging in the cables correctly, because it makes no difference to the PhoneNET system and LocalTalk. They autosense the signal as it reaches the computer.

Meet the PhoneNET Family

PhoneNET has been around for quite some time. PhoneNET is a derivative of the Apple LocalTalk connectors and wiring. While the Apple LocalTalk connector provided a modicum of grounding, the PhoneNET connector does not. While the Apple LocalTalk connector used shielded twisted pair and a special connector, the PhoneNET connector ships with flat wire with two RJ-11s at each end—

hence, the name "PhoneNET." The basic PhoneNET family is shown in the following picture. I'll describe each of the products by their respective letter.

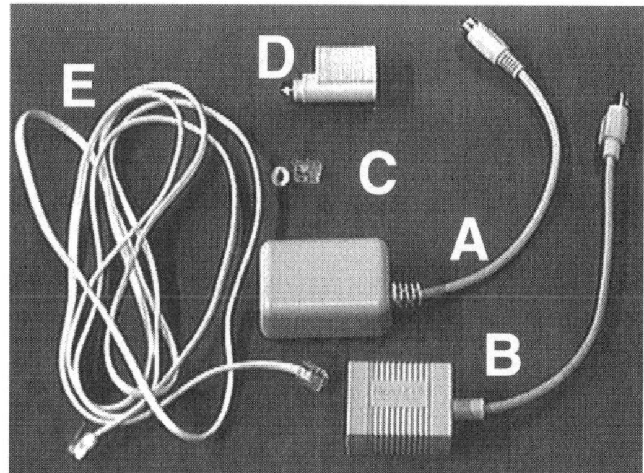

PhoneNET Family of Products

A. This is the original PhoneNET connector. It accepts two RJ-11 connectors for daisy-chaining. It has a mini-din8 connector that plugs into the computer.

B. This is the newer, slightly smaller version of product A. It comes with the same parts as A originally did.

C. This is the terminating resistor that you probably lost a long time ago. This 120-ohm resistor is used to terminate the signal at each end of the daisy chain.

D. This connector is a StarConnector. It is a single-jack version of the two-jack PhoneNET connector. As it's a single-jack version, there is no need for a terminating resistor.

E. This is the three-foot length of flat, silver satin cable that comes with all PhoneNET connectors. These cables come with RJ-11 jacks at both ends.

Building a PhoneNET Daisy Chain

There are two problems that I have with daisy chain networks. First, users tend to disconnect their computers, thus causing a break in the middle of the network. Second, daisy chain networks never stop growing! That's bad.

Here are the basics for building a PhoneNET daisy chain network:

- Daisy chain networks theoretically can reach 2000 feet from one end to the other. I have never seen one reach 2000 feet, but I have seen one at 1400 feet with one of the segments being 1010 feet in length. It worked just fine.

- Place 120-ohm terminators at both ends of the daisy chain. In place of the PhoneNET connector with the terminators at both ends, you can use a StarConnector. It will provide the same type of termination. This is depicted in the diagram to the right. One benefit of this type of design is that it prevents the users on the ends from adding more devices, as they simply don't have an open jack on their connectors.

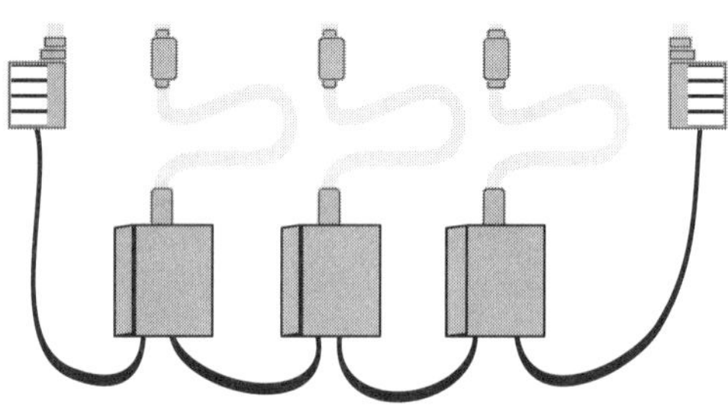

120-Ohm Terminators at Both Ends of the Daisy Chain

- If you are going to add more than four drops in close proximity, you might want to construct the cables out of a single spool of two-pair, twisted pair cabling. It can't hurt, and the twisting of the pairs provides better proximity shielding for the signal.

- Often, the end users pick up their computers to take them home or on the road. When they do, they sometimes pick up their PhoneNET connectors, too. Consider providing mobile users, or any users who are going to move their computers, with a telephone cable extender jack. These jacks, shown to the right, can be used to connect the two ends of the wire left by the users when they disconnected their PhoneNET connectors.

Telephone Cable Extender Jacks

- Don't add more than a dozen computers on a daisy-chained network. With more than twelve computers, connections tend to break frequently.

Make Your Own Resistors!

Does everyone say that you don't have a life? Well, do I have the nerd-envy hobby for you—120-ohm resistor making! But first, why do we even care? The LocalTalk daisy chain or bus that you have created must be terminated (but it was such a nice little network!) by a resistor. A resistor does just what its name implies; it resists a signal. Silver satin, used for LocalTalk networks, has a resistance of 100 ohms. To stop the signal spewing out the other side of the PhoneNET connector, you must offer more resistance than the nominal impedance of the wire the signal is traveling over (100 ohms). Otherwise, you have *reflection*. The network interface card (NIC) confuses the reflection with a real signal coming back through the open end. Thus, use 120-ohm resistors to counter the reflection.

Now, about that hobby . . . nobody sells 120-ohm resistors ready to place in RJ-11 jacks. You need to run down to your local GraybaR and pick up some handy how-to-make-friends tools: a crimper, a strip of 120-ohm resistors, and a bag of RJ-11s. You can identify the correct resistors by their design. They are banded or striped with color codes. The first and second bands indicate the value in ohms. For our resistors, brown equals one and red equals two, representing 12.

Color	Value	Multiplier
Black	0	1
Brown	1	10
Red	2	100
Orange	3	1,000
Yellow	4	10,000
Green	5	100,000
Blue	6	1,000,000
Violet	7	10,000,000
Gray	8	100,000,000
White	9	1,000,000,000

Resistor Color Codes

The third stripe is the multiplier. In our case, it is brown with a value of 10. Thus, our resistor is 120 ohms, or 12 multiplied by 10 ohms. The final band is the variation of resistor, as shown in the following table. Ours is gold, and thus the variation is ± 5%.

Color	Value
No Color	20%
Silver	10%
Gold	5%

Resistor Tolerance Color Codes

Put one end of the resistor in one outside slot and the other end in the other outside slot. Finally, pop the RJ-11 in the crimper and tah-dah, you're in business.

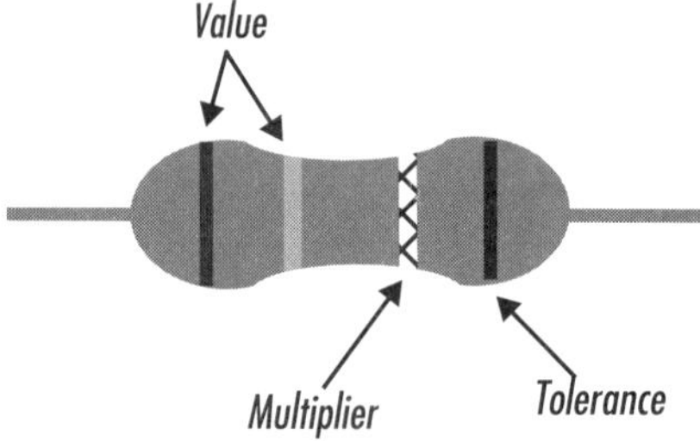

Resistor and Colored Bands

Cost Table

Here are some costs for this cabling design with seven devices—six computers and one printer. The printer could be added to the table as a "service," but we had to draw the line at costs for devices. Research and add those costs on your own.

	Qty.	Manuf.	Description	Part #	Cost/ea.	Total Cost
Connector	7	Farallon	PhoneNET Connector	NA	$11.50	$80.50
Terminators	2	Farallon	120-ohm RJ-11	NA	Included with transceiver	NA
Drop Cable	6	Farallon	10-foot Silver Satin	NA	Included with transceiver	NA
					Total Cost:	$80.50

Cabling Costs for LocalTalk over Two-Pair

LocalTalk Trunk Network with StarConnectors

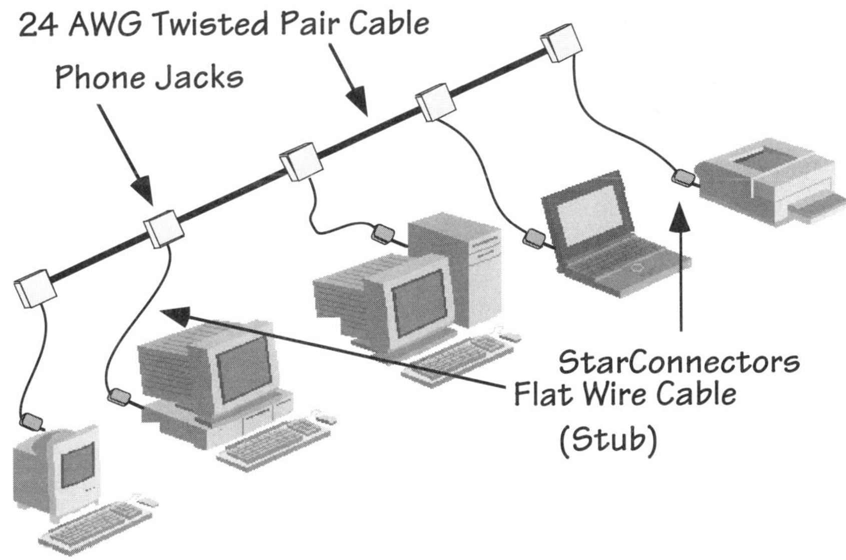

Trunk Network

A step up in "connectivity stability" from the daisy chain network is the trunk network. This network is usually preferred in small offices with users who won't be moving around much, in classrooms, or in labs where computers are lined up against a wall. While the connecting cables in a daisy chain network are small pieces of individual cable with jacks at each end, the trunk cable is one long, continuous cable connected to wall jacks and individual computer drops or stub cables. This type of network is more stable than the daisy chain in that if users disconnect from the network and take their PhoneNET connectors or StarConnectors with them, network service won't be disturbed as there won't be a break in the main trunk cable.

Due to the cable lengths involved in trunk networks, you should *never* use flat, untwisted wires for the trunk cable. Always use twisted pair wire, whether it is shielded or not. At the same time, ensure that you are using 24 AWG wire, which is heavier than 26 AWG wire (the smaller the number, the larger the core of the wire). Also, *think* before you run the trunk. Don't run a trunk 500 feet with one piece of wire and then add another piece of 250-foot wire. The best thing to do with a trunk is to run it all from one continuous piece of cable.

You don't want more than one computer per "stub" hanging off the trunk network. This is where a lot of networks quickly get into trouble. They start expanding beyond the basic trunk, and become a trunk with rampant daisy-chaining, such as is shown in the following diagram. The more stubs you have, the less length you can have in your trunk. Each of the stubs becomes less stable, because you run into all the problems you had with the basic daisy chain network.

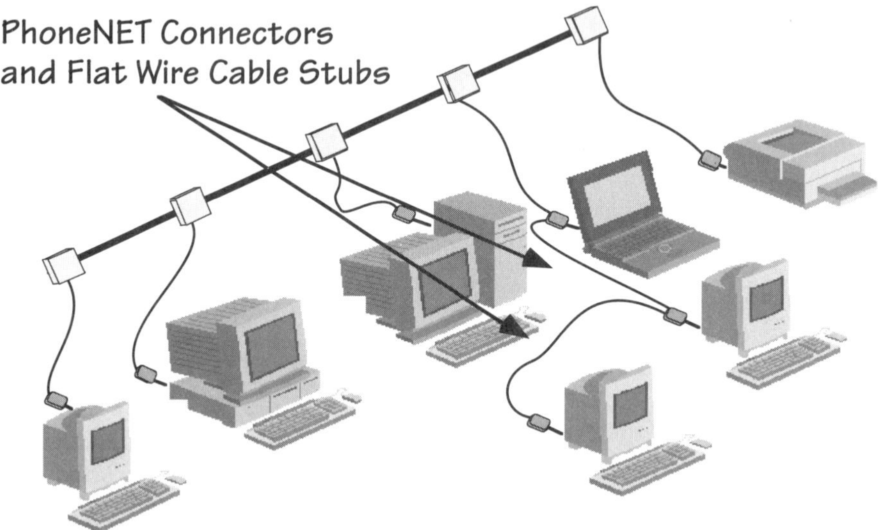

Trunk with an Extended Stub

Building a Trunk Network

Now it's time to look at building a trunk network. You are going to need the following parts to build the system:

- Trunk cable can be obtained from any GraybaR and comes in spools of 1000 feet. I would recommend at least Category 3 cabling, which is rated for 16 Mbits of data. You won't be running anything except LocalTalk through it (Ethernet doesn't use a trunk topology with this type of cable), but at least the Category 3 cable will give you solid service and no problems down the road.

- Wall jacks must be used for this type of networking. For screw-down jacks, first strip your cables back, which we show you how to do in a picture or two. Next, wrap the cable around the screw-downs in your wall jacks. You can use punchdown jacks instead, and I would recommend them over the screw-down jacks. If you buy four-pair punchdown jacks that meet Category 3 or Category 5 standards, you won't have to upgrade if you decide to switch to another type of networking system, such as 10BaseT or Fast Ethernet. If you *do* buy the punchdown wall jacks, you need a punchdown tool as well. Make sure that when you buy the punchdown tool, you also buy the 110 jack adapter for the cutter. They normally come only with the old PhoneNET punchdown block type, the 66 block cutters, and you need the 110 bit adapter.

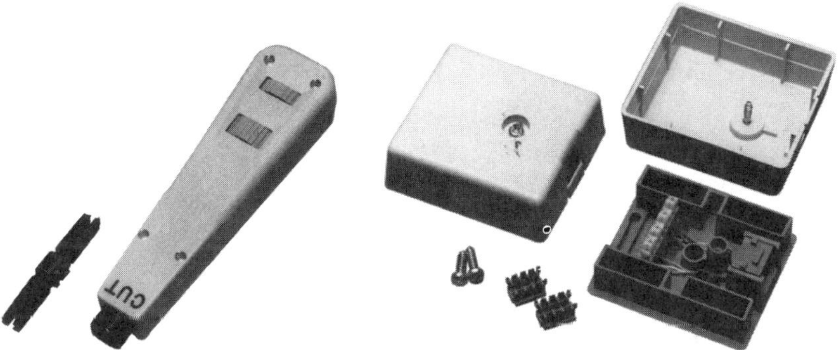

Punchdown Tool (left) and 110 Punchdown Jack (right)

- You will need something to trim the cable's protective sheathing back without cutting the cable. Most people would call this a stripper, but I have to be careful: My mother will read this book.

- You will need some StarConnectors.

Building the trunk network is a bit different than just plugging in the daisy chain cables and connectors. For one thing, trunk networks usually have their cables built into the walls of the office. That means that the trunk cable usually follows the ceiling of the office, goes around the walls, has cabling dropping down from the ceiling to the wall jacks, goes back up again, and then traverses the rest of the office. This will make more sense once we show an implementation of the trunk network in the physical designs we are going to run through. Anyway, a trunk looks something like the following diagram. It has cables running along the ceiling and then dropping down into the wall jacks.

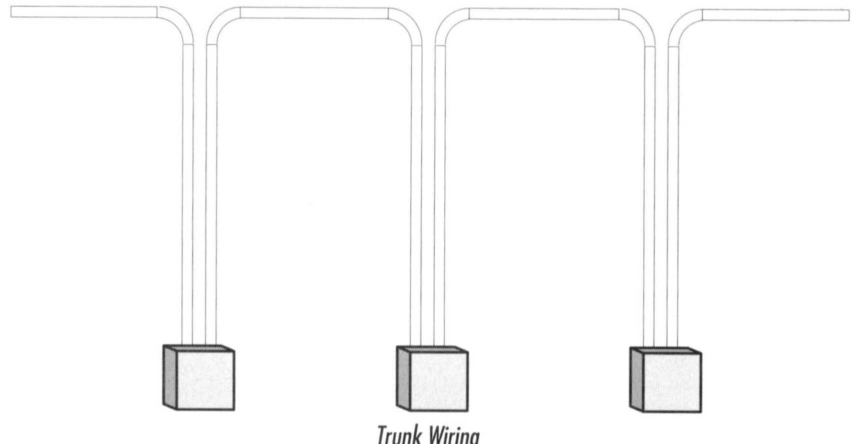

Trunk Wiring

Obviously, that isn't all there is to the system. The cable goes down and then comes back up again because the cable is actually looped inside the wall jack. On the right I show a wall jack with the cables stripped back and wires going to connector pin number 2 (black wire on jack) and then to connector pin number 5 (yellow wire on jack). If you use screw-down jacks, you won't break the cables when connecting them, unless you strip them incorrectly. However, if you are using a punchdown tool, make sure that the tool's impact is set to light instead of heavy. If you use heavy, you will probably break the wire *and* the 110 jack to which you are punching the wire down. For this reason, we suggest that you actually practice stripping wires and punching them down a few times before you launch

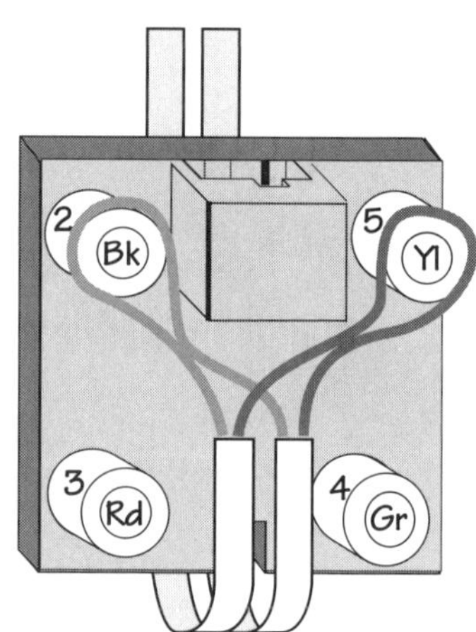

Cable Looped Inside the Wall Jack

into the real thing. It would be pretty darned awful if you cut the middle of a 1000-foot cable because you were careless and hadn't practiced.

Cost Table

Since we discuss trunk networks in depth in the section called "Networking the Cubicled Office," the cost table for cabling a trunk network is shown on page 126.

ETHERNET DAISY CHAIN NETWORKS

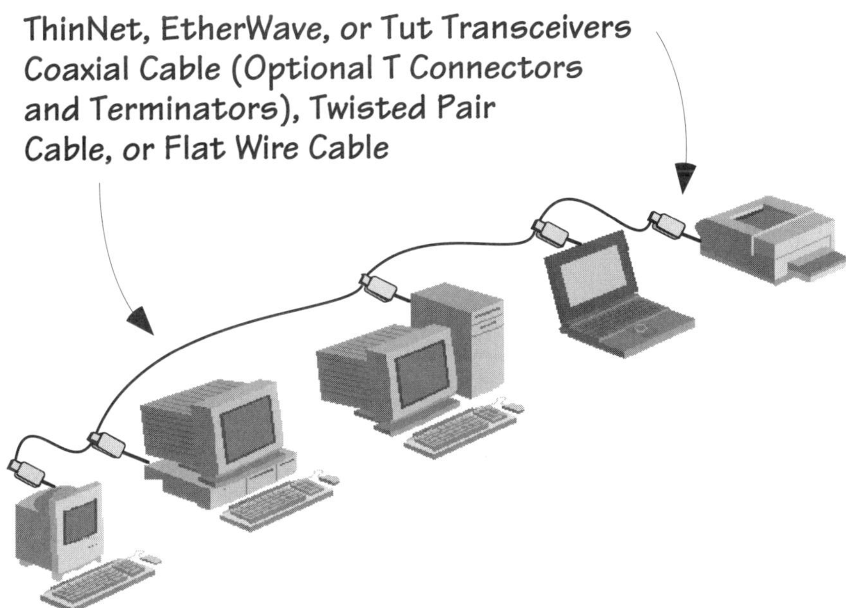

Ethernet Daisy Chain Network

As we mentioned earlier for LocalTalk networks, the easiest and least expensive of all the Ethernet topologies is a daisy chain network. There are really three options for an Ethernet daisy chain network. Option 1 is the tried and true coaxial daisy chain, option 2 is the EtherWave daisy chain, and option 3 is the Tut Silver Streak daisy chain. While you might know enough about the coax/ThinNet daisy chain, there are a few things to learn about the other two. Guess what? You can learn them here! Isn't that special?

In case you were wondering, in the preceding picture, ThinNet uses coax cable, EtherWaves use twisted pair cable, and Tut Silver Streak uses flat wire, PhoneNET-type cable.

Ethernet Daisy Chain with ThinNet (Coax)

The cable for ThinNet has a 50 ohm characteristic impedance and a stranded or solid copper conductor in the core. There are two cable types that meet these specifications: RG-58 A/U or RG-58 C/U. Each piece of cable segment can be no longer than 607 feet (185 meters) and no shorter than 1.5 feet (.46 meters). Each end of the ThinNet cable segment needs a male BNC connector, as shown in the following picture.

Segment of a ThinNet cable

If the Ethernet transceiver is *not* T equipped (and only the Apple product is T equipped, as far as we know), add a T-connector for computers in a series, and a T-connector with a 50-ohm terminator for devices at both ends of the daisy chain. Failure to terminate a ThinNet segment causes almost complete network failure. A completed ThinNet daisy chain is shown in the next picture.

Completed Coax Daisy Chain

The only time this rule can be broken is when you are using the Apple ThinNet transceiver. Not only is it T-connector equipped, it is also self-terminating.

Do not purchase RG-59 cable for ThinNet networks. RG-59 is what you use for your coax system at home when you plug into the neighbor's video box and steal their channels. Also, make sure that your terminators are 50 ohm instead of 75 ohm. You can buy them either way from places like GraybaR.

There can be a total of 30 devices hooked together on a single coax daisy chain segment. The limit on the number of connections supposedly helps reduce the direct current (DC) resistance caused by the T-connectors used in the system. If the DC resistance is too high, the Ethernet NICs won't be able to detect collisions and other network-related problems.

Cost Table

These are some sample costs for the cabling design we just covered for a small network of six computers and one printer.

	Qty.	Manuf.	Description	Part #	Cost/ea.	Total Cost
Connector	7	Generic; from MacWAREHOUSE	T-connector	DC01074	$5.29	$37.03
Terminators	2	Generic; from MacWAREHOUSE	75 ohm	DC01063	$2.89	$5.78
Drop Cable	6	Generic; from MacWAREHOUSE	10-foot ThinNet	NA	$9.95	$59.70
					Total Cost:	**$102.51**

Cabling Costs for Ethernet over 10Base2

Ethernet Daisy Chain with EtherWaves

EtherWaves are definitely different. The following picture shows the Macintosh family of EtherWave products. We won't cover them all; we cover the basic transceiver, and add more information as we touch on other areas.

EtherWave Family

EtherWaves can be defined as NICs for Macs and PCs, high-speed serial-to-Ethernet adapters, and transceivers for Macs and PCs. While these definitions are covered in our AppleTalk/Open Transport primer book, we will take a crack here at describing what these transceivers are, what they aren't, and how they affect a daisy chain network.

- EtherWaves are *not* small two-port repeaters. They do not function as repeaters, they do not isolate faults on a network cable segment, and they do not retime a signal. Because of this, they do *not* affect a 10BaseT network's four repeater hop count limitation and cabling distances. Cables can still be run no more than 328 feet from the hub to the farthest end-node.

- EtherWaves support power passage-through architecture. This means that if the device to which one of the computers is attached is turned off, the signal will still flow through. *However,* EtherWaves will automatically sense and convert the signal if one of the connected devices is using a cross-over cable. If the power is off on one of those devices, the network connection will be lost. Succinctly put, power passage works when using cables that go straight through, but does not work when using cross-over cables.

- EtherWaves have two RJ-45 jacks that are pinned for 1, 2, 3, and 6 only—the straight 10BaseT pinout. If for some reason you have a device downline of one of the EtherWaves that needs the full eight pins (four pairs), you are out of luck. It also means that you can't test for Category 5 cabling with the EtherWaves connected in a series.

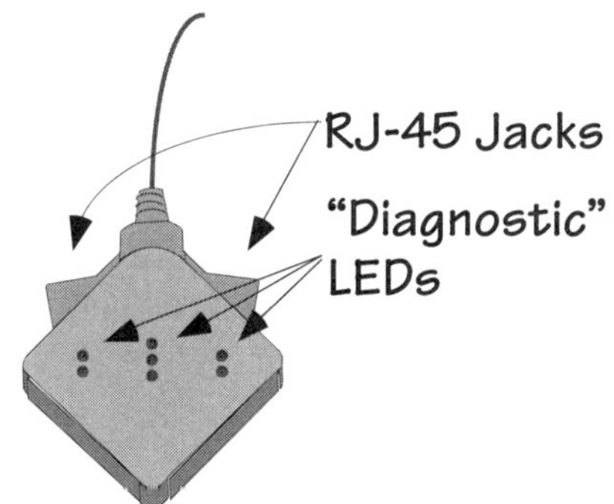

Farallon's EtherWave

- Farallon's marketing department states that adding nodes to the network doesn't mean "bringing it down." Yes and no. Remember, if the wire is broken in the middle of a series, the network temporarily comes down. You can add nodes to the *end* of the series without bringing the network down, but if you have to break the series to put a node in the middle, you will bring the network down, especially if you leave the two halves unjoined.

- You are allowed to connect up to eight devices in a daisy chain without a hub, and can connect up to seven devices off of a hub. Do you pay a penalty in performance quality when doing so? Yes, but it is small. We conducted a test by putting a hub in the middle and seven daisy-chained EtherWaves between two computers we were backing up. The time difference between having a pair of computers directly off the hub and the EtherWave solution was about 2.3% longer for the EtherWaves in series. That's not bad at all.

- EtherWaves are self-terminating. Thus, there is no need for a terminator at each end.

Cost Table

The following table shows some sample costs for this type of cabling design. Again, this is for seven devices—six computers and one printer.

	Qty.	Manuf.	Description	Part#	Cost/ea.	Total Cost
Transceiver/Connector	7	Farallon	EtherWave	PN802	$109.00	$763.00
Drop Cable	6	Allen-Tel	4-pair cable with RJ-45	NA	$3.32	$19.92
					Total Cost:	**$782.92**

Cabling Costs for Daisy-Chained Ethernet over Four-Pair with EtherWaves

Ethernet Daisy Chain with the Tut Silver Streak

If you thought that the EtherWave was different, wait until you get a load of this device. The Tut Silver Streak is also a two-port transceiver for Ethernet, but it doesn't require coax or 10BaseT. It can use the standard, flat wire, PhoneNET cabling that LocalTalk uses, and it *still* runs at Ethernet speeds. Now, *that's* amazing. The following picture shows the Silver Streak family. There is a transceiver, an NIC for Macs, an NIC for PCs, a PCMCIA connector, a parallel port connector, and a print connector. There is even a Silver Streak-to-10BaseT converter (shown in the middle of the following picture).

Tut Silver Streak Family

If you think that we might have been suspicious about the EtherWaves at first, when Cornelius from Tut first came over with a Silver Streak product, we really beat that thing into the ground. We pounded packets from all the computers over them, and when all was said and done, they performed incredibly well! Here is what's going on when working with the Silver Streak products from Tut (this was ripped off from their tech support department):

- Tut uses a proprietary balun with unsurpassed filtering techniques that are able to attenuate electronic noise (if you don't know what noise is, once again, refer to the primer) by a ratio of 10,000:1. That's 80 dB! Compare that to 10BaseT, which can only attenuate noise at a ratio of 100:1, or 40 dB.

- The reason that the Tut systems can use one pair of unshielded twisted pair (UTP) wire is also because of their special balun. On 10BaseT, the send and receive channels are separated by placing the send signal on one pair of wires and the receiving signal on another pair of wires. Tut's send and receive channels exist on the same pair. They do this by implementing a hybrid circuit technique that allows them to "see" packets while simultaneously transmitting packets.

- Very much like 10Base2, the Tut systems can accommodate up to 30 nodes on each segment and can handle cable runs of up to 500 feet. Their XC1500 UTP two-port repeaters can have cable runs of up to 1,500 feet.

Sample Costs

The following table shows costs associated with this type of cabling design for six computers and one printer.

	Qty.	Manuf.	Description	Part#	Cost/ea.	Total Cost
Transceiver/Connector	7	Tut	Silver Streak	NA	$99.00	$693.00
Terminators	2	Tut	120-ohm RJ-11	NA	Included with Transceiver	NA
Drop Cable	6	Tut	10-foot Silver Satin	NA	Included with Transceiver	NA
					Total Cost:	**$693.00**

Cabling Costs for Daisy-Chained Ethernet over Two-Pair with Silver Streaks

CHAPTER 3:
WIRELESS NETWORKS

Wireless networks are *really cool* and, for some odd reason, rarely used. I can't understand that, but hey, it's not my problem because I just build 'em, I don't sell the parts for 'em. We use an infrared system (IR) in our own office, to connect our conference table together with our LocalTalk and Ethernet network. I've used radio frequency (RF) in school systems for teachers who move from one classroom to another and don't want to be on the same network as their students. I use radio frequency and CDPD to connect from our company's boat to our office's network and then into the Internet where we receive weather feeds and port information. Each of the 5300 series of PowerBooks from Apple has IR built into them, as do some of Hewlett Packard's printers. In short, it's great stuff and should be considered seriously as a network connection option. Here is some information about wireless connectivity for your computers.

INFRARED NETWORKS

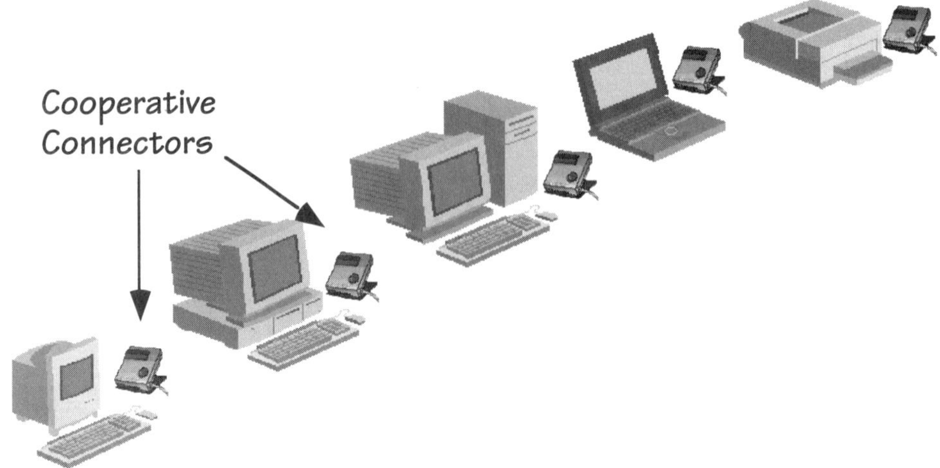

Small Infrared Network

With the advent of the new PowerBook models, there are two distinct types of infrared networking devices: those that work with the PowerBook 5000 series and those that work with the Photonics products. We like the Photonics networking products better than what Apple ships, as they work with both Macintoshes and PCs, have easily installed network bridge adapters, and are inexpensive and plentiful. Besides, you can obtain a pair of them in the GameNET pack along with two copies of Marathon. Now, *that's* a great way to build a network!

Basically, IR networking components use the same type of technology as your home television remote control device. IR network technology is a great one-room networking technology, but only "one room" because IR doesn't bounce around corners or go through walls or floors—line of sight is the rule here. Within the IR technology realm there are two basic types: direct and diffused. As the Photonics Cooperative Processor works within the diffused arena, that is the one we spend some time discussing in this section.

Because the signals of a diffused IR device don't need to be pointed directly at the other devices, networking them is somewhat simplified. The diffused IR lights bounce off walls, tables, and floors (except for my Aunt Mildred's ugly green shag carpet), and provide a basic coverage of around 25 × 25 feet. The speed is exactly the same as LocalTalk, a whopping 230.4 Kbps (roughly 0.48 megabytes per minute, point-to-point throughput).

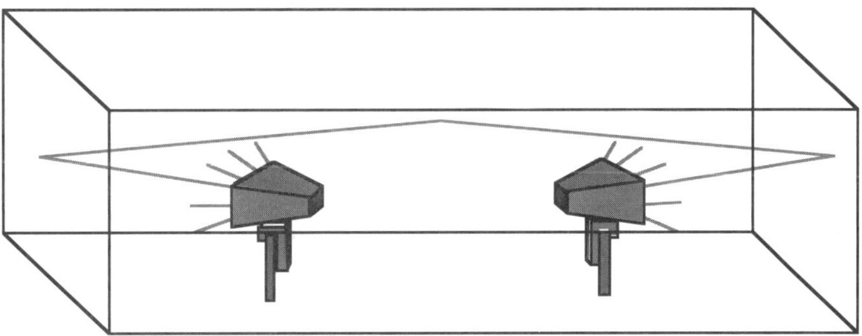

Diffused Infrared

Meet the Photonics Cooperative Family

In the following pictures, we show two basic options for the Photonics Cooperative adapters. There is a third product, for the Newton, but I haven't pictured it here because I don't have one. I don't plan on networking my Newton in the near future, either. The basic interface of the regular adapter is simple.

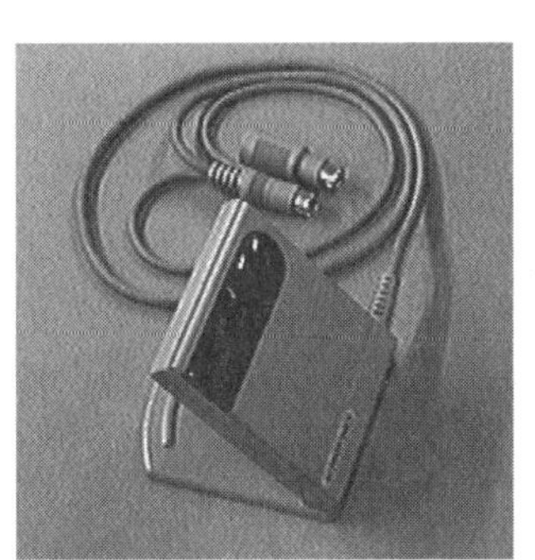
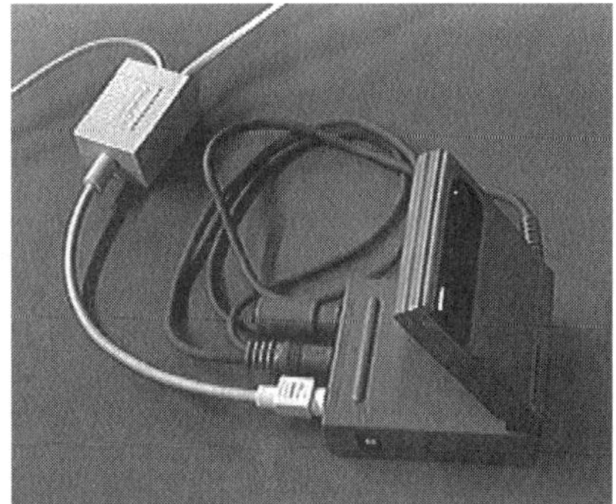

Photonics Cooperative Processor (left); Photonics Cooperative Processor Attached to Its
Network Access Point (right)

There are two cables coming out the back of the adapter. One plugs into the LocalTalk port of the computer and the other plugs into the ADB port of the computer to give the adapter power. If a computer doesn't have a free ADB port for power (like a printer), the access point can double as a power base through its power supply. They weigh in at all of about 4 ounces—that's 110g to you metric fans—and are completely versatile.

The network access point can also act as a sort of network bridge for the IR-based computers on your network, tying them into the cable-based computers. While it is not a bridge per se, it will transfer all traffic from the cabled side of the network through to the IR side of the network. I guess that's why they call it a network access point rather than a bridge. In our office, we have a Photonics Cooperative adapter attached to one of our computers that is also running a copy of Apple's LocalBridge software. It provides connectivity between our conference table and our Ethernet network!

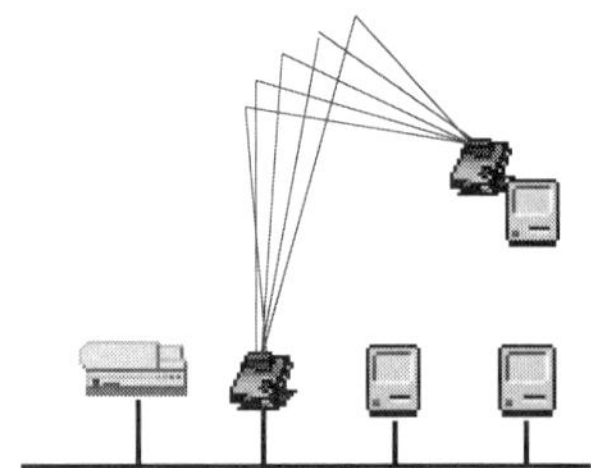

Cooperative Transceiver Connecting a Cabled Network to an IR-Based Computer

Building an IR Network

Here are the parts needed for building an IR network:

- You need an IR adapter for the computer and a LocalTalk connector.

- You need an IR adapter and access point base for devices that don't provide ADB power.

- Use an IR adapter and access point base as a cabled network-to-IR "bridge," although it doesn't perform the packet-segmenting functions of a bridge.

There isn't much to building an infrared network. Plug the devices into the backs of the computers, printers, and whatever other network devices you want to connect, aim the transceiver toward the center of the room, and that's it! If the transceiver can't sense the other computers, adjust the transceiver or move another one closer in to the rest. The biggest trick, really, is to make each adapter's cone of operation overlap with the other adapters' cones of operation. We highly recommend having the access point mounted high on the wall in a central location so that the other IR adapters can all see *it*. Then, even though they can't all see each other, they will be attached to the same network through the access point.

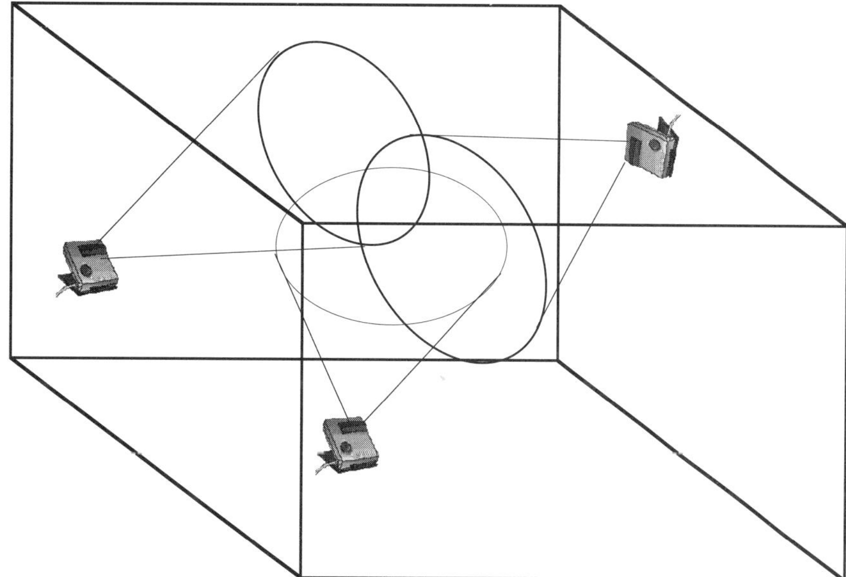

When networking IR devices, give them a central access point on which they can focus.

Radio Frequency Networks

While IR-based LANs are generally considered to fall within the LocalTalk LAN category, radio frequency-based LANs fall within the Ethernet LAN category— even without the benefit of true Ethernet speed. You can pretty much count on RF LANs running about 1.2–1.5 MB of throughput per minute.

While IR cannot transmit data around corners, RF LANs can transmit data *through walls, ceilings, and floors.* Thus, you can think of RF technology in terms of omnidirectional devices. Unlike IR devices, where you have to point the cone of transmission, RF goes everywhere. Okay, so it's easier to build a network with RF because it is omnidirectional and it penetrates solid mass—what are the drawbacks? One drawback is that RF signals use spread spectrum technology and are vulnerable to other signals in its ranges. RF uses the same types of signals as your garage-door opener and your cordless (not cellular) phone. You need to understand the frequency ranges for these devices, and what else is within them.

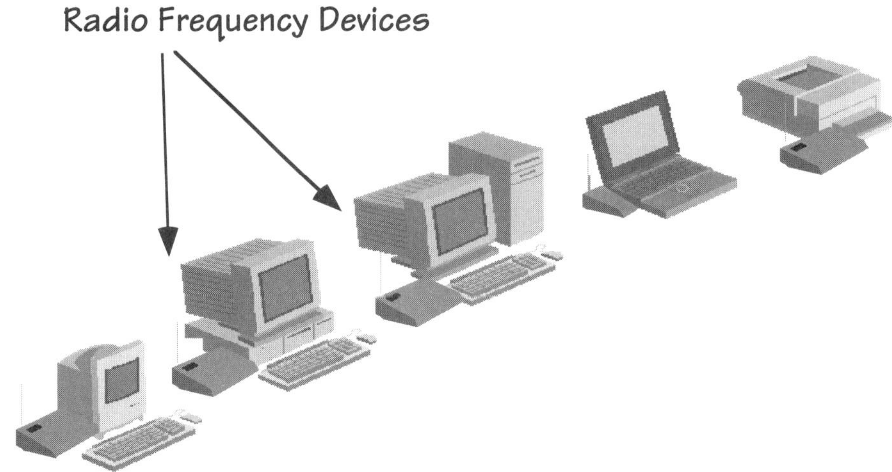

Radio Frequency Network

Radio Frequency Bands

This is basically a brief rehash of what we go into in the AppleTalk/Open Transport primer book. We like the Digital Ocean RF products the most. These products use the 902–908 MHz Direct Sequence Spread Spectrum (DSSS) radio frequency band. This is the lowest of the Industrial, Scientific, and Medical (ISM) bands in the ultra-high or microwave spectrum. The FCC considers these as unlicensed bands to be used for individuals' purposes. Because the DSSS band has been around for a while, it is heavily loaded with background noises. *However,* this rarely affects networking traffic or data rates. This is because the use of DSSS is limited to a power level of one watt in this frequency, and therefore the range of devices in this frequency is restrained to around 328 feet in a open office area, and about 150 feet within a close-walled office area. If you are wondering about security, Digital Ocean provides for that in their unique and easy-to-use software.

Meet the Digital Ocean Family

Digital Ocean products are built upon AT&T's WaveLAN 915 DSSS radio technology and Digital Ocean's patented protocol and software technology. They require no additional hardware or software to be loaded into the computers unless added security is required.

While we aren't covering them in this book, I do want to mention that Digital Ocean is shipping some pretty darned cool Newton products, including RF transceivers, a system that also includes a bar-code wand, and their new Tarpon product that supports receiving Global Positioning System (GPS) signals. These devices have 915 MHz or 2.4 GHz capabilities. Why mention them? How about this: Use your Newton as your GPS system for backpacking and for standard office memos and e-mail. I may be a geek, but that sounds great to me!

The main connector types for the Digital Ocean products are the Grouper, Manta, and Starfish. The Grouper is for a LocalTalk workstation with a din-8 connector, while the Manta is for an Ethernet workstation with an AAUI connector. These two RF workstation devices are designed to mount on the back of a PowerBook or Duo and provide for *Ethernet* connectivity to the network. That means that the Grouper, the LocalTalk connector-version, does connect to the LocalTalk port of the computer, but at the same times provides modified protocol support for Ethernet connectivity. If you need to know how a proxy device works, again, refer to the primer.

The other main device in the Digital Ocean family is the Starfish, the Ethernet Access Point. The Starfish provides wired LAN-to-RF connectivity. It simultaneously acts as a bridge, keeping RF-to-RF traffic off the wired network. It supports AppleTalk error detection, and even sports LEDs for radio on, transmit, and receive. The *really cool* part about the Digital Ocean Starfish is that users can install multiple Starfish on the network. This allows users to travel freely throughout the building, providing roving microcellular connectivity.

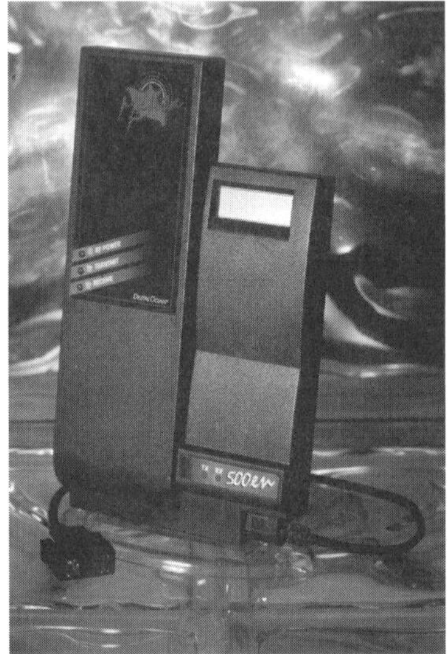

Digital Ocean Grouper (left) and Starfish (right)

Building an RF Network

There isn't much to it. Attach the devices and turn on the computer. If you need Ethernet access at the 10BaseT level, attach a Starfish to your network somewhere. Since you don't need to "point" the devices at anything, there is nothing special you need to know.

CHAPTER 4: STRUCTURED WIRING SYSTEMS

It has been said that a structured cabling system should become a building's fourth utility, along with gas, water, and electricity. With some buildings, the structured wiring system *is* that fourth utility. With other buildings, it is not, and therefore must be put in place before any

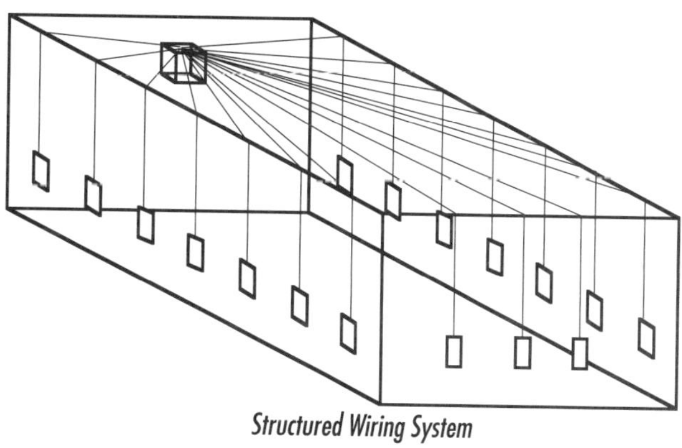

Structured Wiring System

other design factors can be examined. The basic infrastructure of a structured cabling system is shown on this page. It can be thought to begin at the central wiring closet or wiring location, and then it spreads out to each individual wall jack. Wall jacks should be located throughout the office and should have direct links back to the central location. In another chapter, we explain the concepts behind and configurations for connecting several floors together, but for now, you should simply grasp the basic idea.

Some of you might think I'm putting the cart before the horse—that you should know what types of services you want before you know what types of structured wiring you should have. Wrong. Design your wiring plant with the idea in mind that anything can be placed anywhere within the facility. By doing this, you ensure that your organization has maximum flexibility for its future needs. Therefore, this section on small office design is going to focus on what you need for a one-floor structured wiring system first, and then we will deal with the services that need LocalTalk and the services that need Ethernet. Once the wiring system is in place and run correctly, pick and choose your services and put the end users anywhere on the network that you want them to be. Basically, a structured wiring system provides you flexibility in the following ways:

- It provides a liberal number of connectivity locations throughout the building, whether or not you plan to use them as soon as the network is designed.

- Its cabling system lets you tie computing and service devices together with their hub, switch, or router components, irrespective of the speed or access methodology relevant to the networking device.

- With a centralized system, any computing device can be connected to any port on the network via patch cables, thus giving you the maximum design capabilities possible.

ELEMENTS INTRINSIC TO A STRUCTURED WIRING SYSTEM

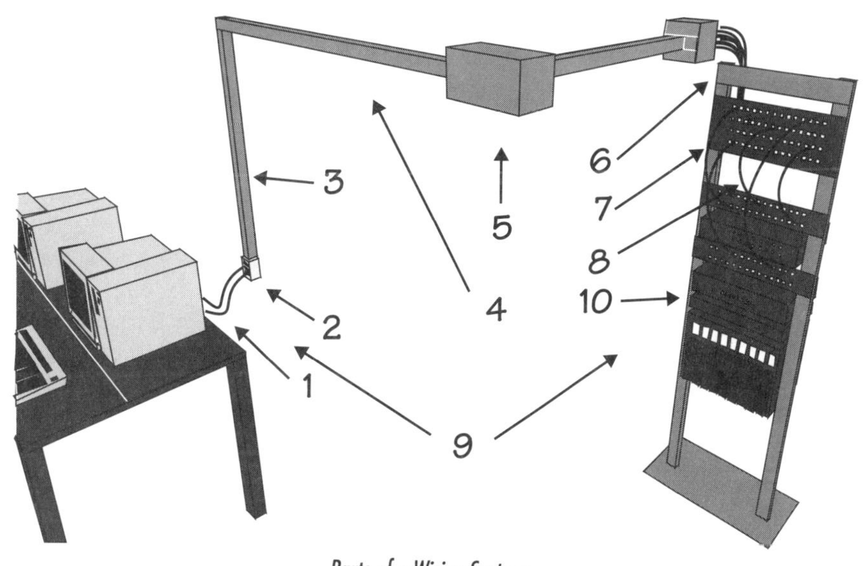

Parts of a Wiring System

Here is a listing of the basic elements that go into making a structured wiring system. We will cover planning for points 1–9 in this chapter.

1. Drop cables connecting the computer to the structured cabling.

2. Wall jack assemblies that hold single or multiple jacks.

3. Vertical runs—conduit, in this case—to protect the cabling in the walls.

4. Horizontal runs, which could be conduit, ladders, or "suspended" cabling.

5. Junction boxes for pulling cable. (This picture shows a bend—don't ever do that in real life. I just had to draw it that way. See the section on pull boxes beginning on page 60 for more information.)

6. Category 3 or 5 cabling that covers UTP and fiber as well.

7. Wiring rack and distribution panels, or *patch panels,* in the wiring closet.

8. Patch cables to connect the cables to the repeaters or switches.

9. Labeling for wall jacks, cables, and patch panels.

10. Devices that tie everything together, such as repeaters, bridges, and routers.

11. Elements that are not depicted, like testing, documentation, and certification.

We will help you understand the different elements that go into making a network what it is, and give you a feel for what is involved in managing the Physical layer of your network. We show you these parts in this order because this is the way your network was probably designed. We will cover the items in number ten later, because there is so much to it. We want you to focus on the Physical layer of the network design first, and then look at the connecting hardware.

Before we can start, though, there are some things you should know. You need to understand the certification ratings for certain equipment, and how those ratings affect the equipment's ability to conduct a signal. The goal is to build a Category 3 or Category 5 compliant network down to the "nth" degree. We stress Category 5 compliancy in this book, but for cost reasons you might want to build a Category 3 networking system. That means specifying, building, and testing the system appropriately.

Parts Ratings

Parts is parts—**not!** Parts are an important factor in determining whether your network meets Category 5 standards, or CAT5, as it is called in the industry. To meet the standard, your parts *must* be rated CAT5, and be installed and tested correctly. There are loads of manufacturers that make CAT5-compliant jacks, cables, patch panels, and horizontal cables, and boy, are they proud of it. Cables must be labeled by their category. They look like this:

*   "CAT3" or ③ for Category 3-compliant components.

    This is the minimum level of cable quality that you should ever allow when designing your networks. It uses 24 AWG, solid copper, unshielded twisted pair (UTP) cabling. This is tested at 16 MHz attenuation and near end crosstalk (NEXT). You can safely run 4 or 16 Mbps Token Ring, 230.4 Kbps LocalTalk, and 10 Mbps Ethernet on this type of cabling.

- "CAT4" or ④ for Category 4-compliant components.

  This uses 22 or 24 AWG, solid copper, UTP cabling. It is tested and rated at 20 MHz attenuation and NEXT. Because it is rated for 20 MHz, it should be able to run all networking types listed for Category 3.

- "CAT5" or ⑤ for Category 5-compliant components.

  This is what we recommend if you are installing cable today. The specification covers 22 or 24 AWG, solid copper, UTP, fiber, and even stranded copper patch and drop cables. It is rated and tested at 100 MHz attenuation and NEXT and can handle data transmissions of up to 155 Mbps.

Jacks and patch cables do not need to be labeled with their category rating, but you can bet your bottom dollar that if a jack or panel is CAT5, the manufacturer has a label on that product that says so. The object of the game is to make us think that something is CAT5 when it is below standard, not the other way around. It is always more costly to produce a product that meets CAT5 specifications than to produce an inferior component. Be on the lookout for cheap imitations.

Everything should be designed and managed with a single goal in mind: to make your network a fully functional Category 5 network, according to the Electrical Industries Association, Telecommunications Industries Association (EIA/TIA) 568 standard. This is commonly known as the "Category 5" standard. The standard also has implications and connections to TSB 36, 40, and 67, as well as to EIA/TIA 568-A, 569, 570, 606, and 607. Each of these standards is referenced at the appropriate time. Why do you need to manage this network as a fully functional Category 5 network? You want it to be as "state of the art" as possible when first built. You also want the network to be able to support as many different network services as possible. Therefore, knowing the network will be hit hard with network traffic from day one, you want to make sure the network "piping"–that is, the network cabling–is as solid as possible.

Cabling Basics

Choosing the right cabling for your computer network is a major economic decision. Initial purchase and installation costs should always be balanced against the capabilities of the selected media to meet your long-term requirements. When you are through with this section, you will be able to make a solid media choice for your organization. You will also understand a great many cabling problems and how to test for them and overcome them.

All about Unshielded Twisted Pair

Fortunately for us, the EIA/TIA and other watchdog organizations keep a close eye on cable manufacturers. They make sure that the cables in the marketplace meet CAT5 standards and are able to transmit up to 100 MHz. For fun, I have listed the requirements that UTP CAT5 cable must meet (I have a strange idea of what a good time is).

Quality	Standard
Gauge	22 or 24 AWG
Insulated Conductor	1.2 mm max.
Diameter	6.35 mm max.
Breaking Strength (not pull weight allowed)	90 lb/ft.
Bend Radius	1 inch minimum

Untwisted Pair Category 5 Specifications

In addition to meeting all these rules, there is a color scheme to follow. Unfortunately, the striping of the white member of the pair is not mandatory. It is helpful when you are pinning down the cable to know which white conductor matches with the solid conductor. Thus, we recommend cable with striped conductors.

Pair	Color
One	White Blue/Blue
Two	White Orange/Orange
Three	White Green/Green
Four	White Brown/Brown

Color Schemes for Cabling

How Does Copper Really Work?

Just how does that e-mail turn from a bunch of bits into something a copper cable can carry? After choosing a data link software—something like Ethernet or CDDI, and *not* LocalTalk, I hope—the network interface hardware turns your bits into an electronic signal that can be carried over anything having conductivity. Aside from silver, copper has the highest conductivity of any easily obtainable material. Based upon the table, you can see why copper is used for CAT5 cabling. I wouldn't hold my breath for the new sea water cable, unless you want to ransom grandma's silver tea set. Some conductivity rates are shown in the following chart:

Conductor	Conductivity (siemens per meter x 107)
Aluminum	3.54
Copper	5.80
Silver	6.15
Gold	4.50
Magnetic Iron	1.0
Sea Water	about 5 siemens per meter

Conductors and Their Conductivity

Still the nagging question lingers, how does that cable carry a signal? If you are willing to avoid questions like "Why is the earth round?" and "Why do conductors carry positive and negative charges?", it is easy to answer this question. A material that has conductivity can carry a positive or negative charge based on the particles flowing through it. The positive and negative charge is converted to binary numbers 1 and 0 by the network interface hardware on both the sending and the receiving ends. Bits (1 and 0) are deciphered using a self-clocking technique called *FM-0.* In a certain space of time (4.34 microseconds for LocalTalk; 9.8 microseconds for Ethernet), the signals traveling along the cable have the opportunity to represent a bit. If the zero voltage line is crossed once, a 1 is recognized. If the zero voltage line is crossed twice, from positive to negative and back to positive or vice versa, a 0 is recognized.

Fortunately for cable installers, the voltage required on data cable is low. It doesn't take a huge signal for the network interface hardware to recognize the crossing of the voltage line. For 10BaseT, a signal has to be only 2.2–2.8 volts for data sequences, but I still wouldn't put my tongue on a live data cable.

PATCH AND DROP CABLES

Station cables, drop cables, workstation cables, and patch cables are all relatively the same thing. The drop cables plug into the transceiver or the Ethernet port on the workstation and also into the jack on the wall or floor. The patch cables plug into the distribution panel and the hub, or the hub panel in the wiring room. Other than that, there are no differences. Therefore, we call them all patch cables. Patch cables are already outfitted with RJ-45, four-pair, eight-position plugs at each end. They should have CAT3 or CAT5 stamped on them, depending on the cabling type you are using to design the network.

Standard Patch Cable

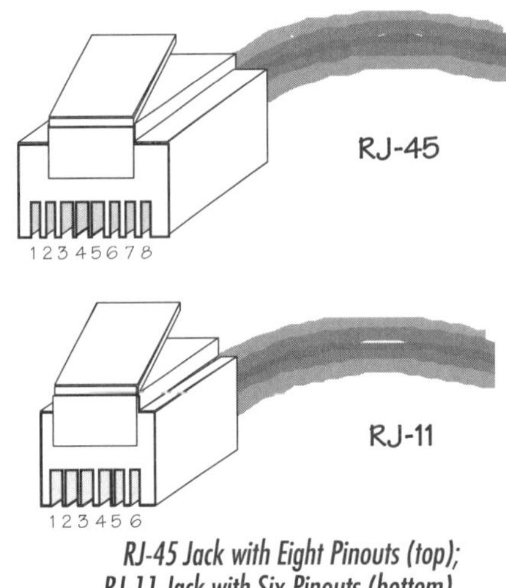

RJ-45 Jack with Eight Pinouts (top);
RJ-11 Jack with Six Pinouts (bottom)

Patch cables can be made from solid or stranded copper cable, both of which are covered in the Category 5 specifications. If you are wondering, you can run your cabling for Category 5 Ethernet throughout the rest of the network and then use RJ-11 connectors for plugging into LocalTalk. As LocalTalk uses only a single pair of wires, it will simply discard the rest of them. If you run the rest of the cabling and actual wire correctly, the LocalTalk pinouts will correspond correctly to a pair already existing in the cabling system. The only difference is the connector type at the end of the cables that plug into the patch panels and PhoneNET connectors. You can plug RJ-11 patch cables into RJ-45 wall jacks, but you can't plug RJ-45 connectors into RJ-11 wall jacks. This is because RJ-11 connectors are outfitted for four or six pins, while RJ-45s are outfitted for eight pins.

Rules for Drop and Patch Cables

- The use of flat, non-twisted cords is strictly prohibited. I don't care *what* some guy did that you read about on the Internet, they shouldn't be used.

- The cables need to have a RJ-45 connector at the end, as specified in IEEE 802.3. Cross-connect jumpers and patch cords need to meet or exceed the minimum performance requirements specified in EIA/TIA 568, sections 10.2.1.2.1–10.2.1.2.8.

- The total length of the drop cables cannot exceed 20 feet.

- The total length of the patch cables cannot exceed 10 feet.

- When testing for certification, drop cables and patch cables will be used in place of the cables supplied with the testing equipment. This is to ensure that you have impedance balances and total length requirements throughout your system. Using different cables for testing doesn't give you accurate results.

There should be some common-sense rules, as well. The following picture was taken at a site where the client had asked us to come troubleshoot their network. It seemed that their Internet connection was having problems. They felt that their WWW and Gopher searches were extremely slow. We found that the communication between the network gear was indeed slow, with multiple retries. When we tested packets on the other side of the router, the same side on which the Internet gateway was located, we found *numerous* bad packets flowing between the gateway and the rest of the network. The picture above shows why. The drop cable to the Internet gateway was being pinched *under a 200 pound free-standing camera rack!*

What about the Patch Cable that Came with My Computer?

Most of the patch cables that come with computers, printers, or Ethernet cards are *not* Category 5 rated cables. In fact, most of them are not rated at all, and I would recommend tearing them apart and using them for macramé or something else non-data related. If the cable jacket is silver, you know without a shadow of a doubt that the cable is a bad one. Here's another easy way to tell: Take both a Category 5 cable and the cable that came with your Ethernet card and hold them up side by side. Which looks more sturdy? If cut open, does the cable that came with the card have as many twists per foot as the Category 5 cable? Probably not. So, why do these companies ship crappy cables? Because they are cheapskates. They don't care whether your network meets high standards. They care about selling you Ethernet cards or devices. Go buy yourself some good patch cables.

DATA JACKS: A VERSUS B

Recently, I went to GraybaR, the electrical supply store, and a representative from AT&T introduced himself to me. We chatted about wiring and the A *vs.* B jack controversy. I told him that it didn't matter what I thought, but that the EIA/TIA preferred A over B. The rep turned taupe (he is African-American). AT&T owns the market in 568B jacks. They want the whole wide world to use B jacks. Sorry, guys—the standard says B jacks may be used only "optionally, if necessary." We specify A, the first configuration shown in the following diagram.

While 568A jacks put pair 3 in the first two positions, 568B jacks put pair 2 in the first two positions. While 568A jacks put pair 2 in positions 3 and 6, 568B jacks put pair 3 in positions 3 and 6. The difference may seem subtle, but if done incorrectly, it can mess up your data transmission in a big way. Remember, when buying jacks you probably won't be able to *see* the differences, and you'll have to trust the package labels to ensure that you have the right kind.

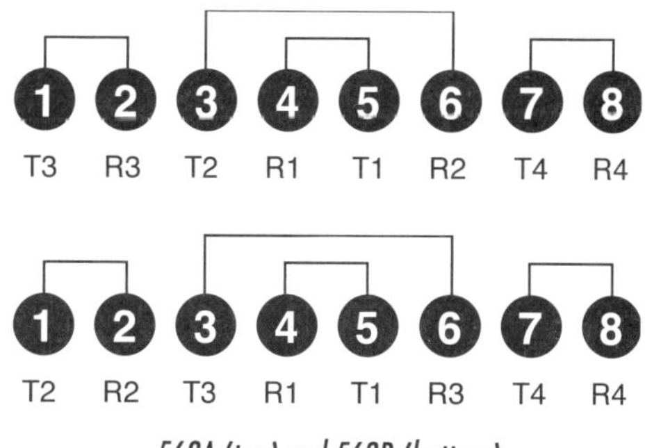

568A (top) and 568B (bottom)

Ethernet uses positions 1, 2, 3, and 6 to transmit signals. The other pinouts are for grounding, and the extra four conductors act as insulation. If you have the wrong conductors in the wrong positions you could end up with only half or no transmission of data.

What Goes Where

The nice thing about CAT5 jacks is that they come color coded. If you follow the color coding, you're home free. Well, almost—here are a few pointers to ensure proper jack installation.

Begin by carefully removing about three quarters of an inch of the outside jacket and then untwist the pairs so they lay flat. Untwisting should not take place under the jacket. Next, untwist and position the pairs for the positions 1&2, 3&6, 4&5, and 7&8 respectively (see preceding diagram). The only crossing taking place should be the orange wire over the green and green-white wires.

Trim the conductors so that they are not exposed more than half an inch. When inserting the plug over the prepared test leads, make sure the cable is pulled into the plug as far as possible up to the jacket. There should be no more than 1/16 of an inch of exposed conductors once the cable is jacked and the conductors have been trimmed.

The following picture is what you *don't* want the jack to look like when you are finished. Notice how far back the cable jacket is stripped. Also notice that *one* cable is servicing *two* jacks. *Never run one cable to more than one jack.* That's a big Bozo No-No, and when checking jack installation, always make sure that is not the case. It's happened more often than we care to think about.

Bad Jack Installation

Connector Specifications

- Each four-pair, 24 AWG, Category 5 cable needs to be terminated in an eight-pin modular jack at the work area. These connectors should be 100-ohm UTP outlets and should meet all criteria listed in section 6 of EIA/TIA 570 and sections 11–12 of EIA/TIA 568.

- The pin/pair assignments need to follow the 568A designation with applicable color code combinations. These pin/pair assignments are also in compliance with ISDN BRI (ISO 8877), Ref B1.24, so you should have no problem if you need to switch your connection type to ISDN.

- Each drop should have an appropriate face plate, either flush-mounted or box jack, installed for data. In office settings, the face plates may be fitted for RJ-11 jacks *for phone use* as well as RJ-45 jacks. In classroom settings, all jacks should contain RJ-45 jacks or blanks—otherwise, this is an excellent depository for chewing gum.

- Specify to your cabling contractor, if you have one, that only jacks, face plates, gang boxes, and blanks that are inventoried to be in your possession after inspection will be charged to you. Otherwise you will pay for parts that are sitting in your contractor's office or for parts that they broke during installation.

- When attaching the face plates or gang boxes to the wall, NEC Article 210-52 states that their center should be no less than 12 inches above the floor or working platform. However, many disabled accessibility regulations, such as California's Disabled Accessibility regulation section 3105 (f) 3, state that electrical and communication system receptacles on walls will be mounted no less than 15 inches above the floor. Where applicable, always try to follow the disability act information as the primary rule. Never mind the legal reasons for following the disability act, it just isn't cool to build something that other people can't access. That's a Bozo No-No.

CONDUIT AND CABLE BENDS

Network Frontiers has been working with a local contractor—and a good one, I might add—to develop a network for a high school that is being built. We are moving from the planning stage to the building stage and are having some problems with how the network cables have to be laid out for the new site. The biggest problem we are having is in determining how much conduit is enough. According to the state building code for schools, all data cable, and all other cable for that matter, must be encased inside conduit all the way through from the wiring room to the cable jack box at the computer location. That's a lot of conduit.

Naturally everyone is trying to squeeze by with the least amount of conduit possible, because conduit and its installation costs money. First, there are the members of the Network Frontiers staff who want to encase conduit in *huge* tubes, hoping to at least triple the size of the conduit we think we need now, so in a couple of years we won't have too little, as is often the case. Then there are the contractors and engineers who designed the high school several years ago and thought back then that a single daisy-chained cable would take care of everything. In between, there is the client and the onsite electrical contractor who are striving for a reasonable balance between costs and needs.

Finally, there's the *communication thing*. When I met with the onsite electrical contractor, I almost made a fatal mistake. Showing the contractor a bundle of wires (I'll never do *that* again), I said, "This is how many wires we are going to be running. What kind of conduit can you give me?" His response was to see how small a conduit piping he could *shove* the wires into. My thought was that he *knew* he had to have at least 30–50% free space left in the conduit. We had to rerun some conduit when we found out that he was putting six cables into a half-inch conduit; sort of like squeezing a 200-pound female gorilla into a bikini. Pretty darn ugly affair, and even if you could, *why would you want to?*

Even though Lynn gave them her conduit table, they persisted in questioning the conduit sizes. To set things straight, we decided to go directly to the source—the EIA/TIA-569 standards. We drew the information for this section directly from that standard. The following sections detail some of the more pertinent rules.

The Basics of Conduit

There are three types of conduit approved by the standard: metallic tubing, rigid metal conduit (tracking and ducting), and rigid PVC. There is one type that is *not* recommended, and that is the metal flex conduit with those ridges. It isn't recommended because the ridges can cause abrasion problems with the cables. The standard goes on to state that whichever type of conduit you use, the length of the conduit can't exceed 100 feet or contain more than two 90° bends between what they call *pull points* or *pull boxes*. Further, the conduit isn't allowed to feed more than three wall outlets. Given that each wall outlet can handle up to six cables per outlet, that means you can run a total of 18 cables per conduit home run.

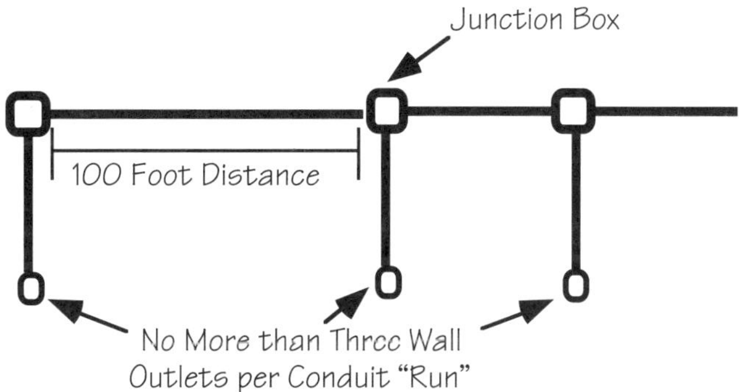

Conduit Runs for Junction Boxes

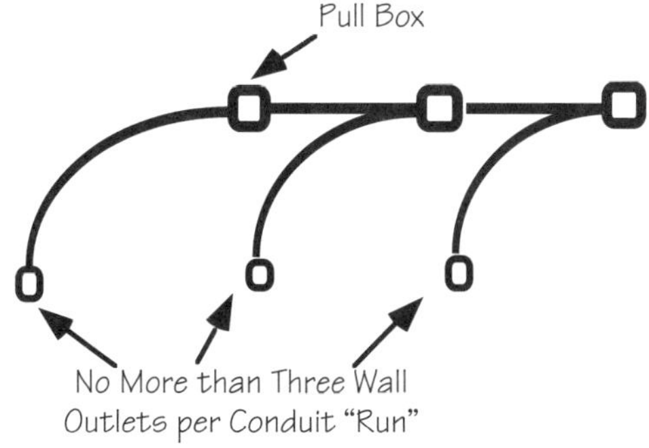

Conduit Runs for Pull Boxes

Conduit Sizes and Bends

Once you have the basics down, you are well on your way to understanding conduit. You only have one major hurdle left—math. The following basic, rule-of-thumb conduit table, as provided by the EIA/TIA, gives a fair range of conduit sizes, and we don't recommend putting many more cables in the conduit than what's shown in our table. The table, however, is simply a guideline, and shouldn't be considered the ultimate information source. The left-hand vertical column shows the trade sizes available for conduit that can be purchased any place selling conduit, like GraybaR or Anixter. The first horizontal column shows the outer diameter of the more common types of Category 5 cabling. The most common outer diameter is the 0.22 diameter, with 0.18 or 0.19 also available by special request, and at a higher cost. Below each diameter size, the column shows the number of cables that can fit into the conduit size for that row. Notice that only *one* 0.18 OD cable is recommended for a half-inch conduit, and that *nothing* is recommended for the 0.24 OD cable in a half-inch conduit. Although 0.22 OD cable is not shown in the EIA/TIA's table, you can arrive at the number of cables per conduit size by using the listing for the next largest cable OD. All conduit diameters must comply with the cable quantity limitations as shown in this table.

Conduit Diameter Trade Size	Wire OD (Outer Diameter of Cable)			
	0.18	0.24	0.31	0.37
0.5	1	0	0	0
0.75	5	3	2	1
1	8	6	3	2
1.25	14	10	4	3
1.5	18	15	6	4
2	26	20	12	7
2.5	40	30	13	12
3	60	40	20	17
3.5	-	-	-	22
4	-	-	-	30

Table Showing Number of Cables per Conduit Size

For wall-mount raceway, leave 50% of the raceway empty. Nobody has ever said, "What are we going to do with all this extra space in the conduit?" Nobody.

Finally, conduit has only a certain degree to which it can bend around corners. The bend radius for the conduit is based on a multiplier of six times the *actual*—as opposed to *trade size*—internal diameter of the conduit. Add to this that conduit fittings, such as T fittings and L fittings, cannot be used in place of a bend. However, pull boxes can be used in places where more than one conduit comes together in a bend, usually a T or a series of L fittings. All conduit bend radii of 90º must comply with the following table:

Scenario	Bend Radius
< 2 inches	6 × internal diameter of conduit
≥ 2 inches	10 × internal diameter of conduit
Fiber Pull	10 × internal diameter of conduit

Conduit Bend Radii

This means that if you had a two-inch conduit, the bend radius of your conduit would be 20 inches. In layman's terms, draw an imaginary circle with a 20-inch radius. If the conduit enters the circle and is bent too tightly, you need to adjust for the error. In the following picture, after we add the information for conduit sizing, notice the effect it has on our conduit plan.

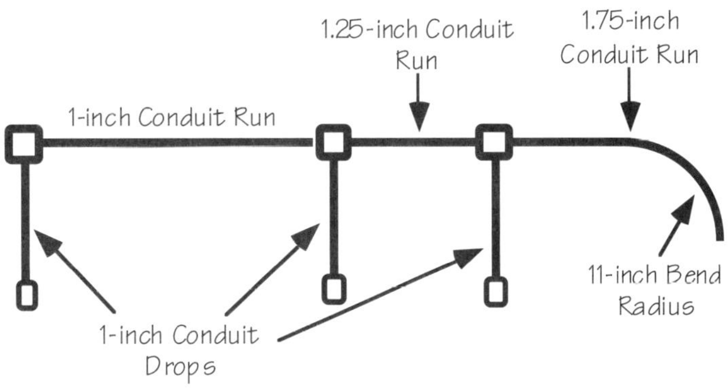

Conduit Run Measurements

Pull Boxes

Now, if you were paying attention to what we said earlier about bend radii (is that sort of like hippopotamii?), you are probably asking yourself this: If the bend radius has been specified by the committee, what about using pull boxes as bends to eliminate the need for bending the conduit? Well, they did indeed think of that. However, the following section of the EIA/TIA 569 standard for conduit is confusing. It states:

For angles and U pulls,

1. Have a distance between each raceway entry inside the box and the opposite wall of the box of at least six times the trade-size diameter of the largest raceway, this distance being increased by the sum of the trade-size diameters of the other raceways on the same wall of the box; and

2. Have a distance between the nearest edges of each raceway entry enclosing the same conductor of at least:

    a. six times the trade-size diameter of the raceway; or

    b. six times the trade-size diameter of the larger raceway if they are of different sizes.

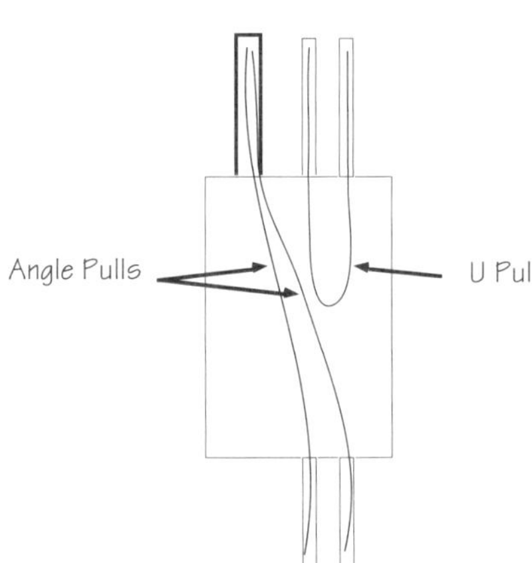

Junction Box Showing Angle and U Pulls

Remember that an *angle* does not mean a bend. An angle is when the cable goes from one side of the box to the opposite side of the box when a receiving conduit is not directly across from the original conduit. U pulls are just what they sound like: the cable has to make a U-shaped bend, as the receiving conduit is parallel to the original conduit.

If bends were allowed in pull boxes, cables would run the risk of being cut on the sharp edges of the conduit as they were being pulled. Also, cables could be stretched too tightly going from one conduit into another on a perpendicular wall, thus causing kinking of the wires.

Now that we are clear on that rule, let's go on to clarify the above passage. After persistently pestering Susan Hoyler at the Electronic Industry Association (EIA), she was able to put me in touch with Paul Kreager, a member of the standards board. Paul was able to make sense of the EIA/TIA-569 standard for me.

A pull box must be placed in conduit runs where the length of the run is over 100 feet, there are more than two 90° bends, or there is a reverse bend in the run. Added to that, the pull boxes can't be placed on the conduit *instead of a bend*. When sizing pull boxes, the length and *width* of the pull box must be at least eight times the size of the diameter of the raceway (trade sizes may be used here), and have a distance between each conduit entering the pull box of at least six times the diameter of the largest conduit attached. The distance the conduit can enter the pull box from each edge is six times the diameter of the incoming conduit.

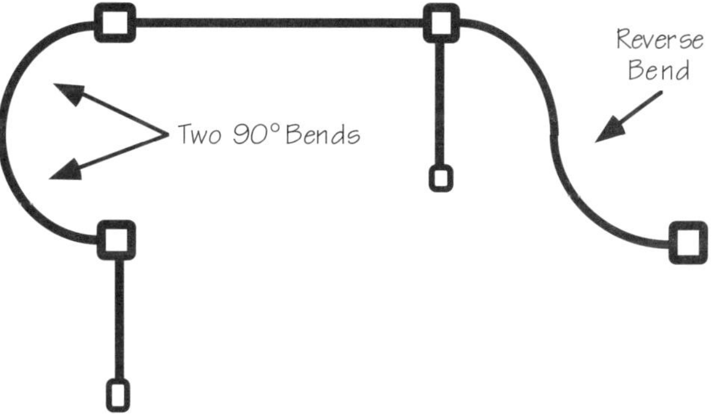

90° and Reverse Bend Radii

Notice that we italicized the word "width" in the previous paragraph. The width of a pull box is never actually discussed in the standard. A pull box could conceivably be too narrow. It would be difficult to find a box that is 14 inches long and two inches wide, but take a look at the following picture for a regular violation of the standard.

Conduit Entering a Junction Box That Is Too Narrow

Three two-inch conduits are entering a 10" × 10" box. A rule is being broken: The length of the pull box should be at least eight times the diameter of the largest conduit—16 inches (two inches multiplied by eight)—for a straight pull through.

For some real fun, take a look at the box in the following picture.

The Autobahn of Junction Boxes

On the side with the largest conduit, there are four 0.5" conduits and one 2" conduit. If we go by the rules for angle pulls, that side of the box should be the following size:

$$(6 \times 2") + 0.5" + 0.5" + 0.5" + 0.5" = 14"$$

Thus, the box is the right size—14" × 14". But hey, wait a minute! Look on the bottom left-hand side of the picture; there is another pull box. Someone has run a bend *inside* a pull box. As discussed before, you cannot go from one side of the box to a perpendicular side of the box; that is, you cannot use a pull box for a bend. To make a bend, you must first exit the pull box after the angle or U pull, and make the bend in the exiting conduit outside the box.

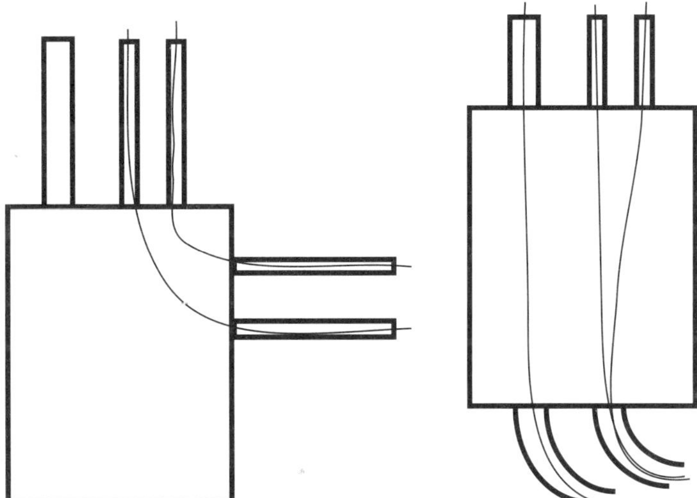

Wrong: Bends within a Pull Box (left) — Right: Bends outside the Pull Box (right)

The following pictures depict how contractors have created these bends in the real world. The first picture shows a pair of wiring gang boxes daisy-chained together inside of the wall. While we don't recommend daisy-chaining gang boxes like this, as it makes it difficult to run wires once the full walls are installed, this does show a good example of how bends are to be incorporated with pull boxes.

Two Gang Boxes Daisy-Chained Together

There are no set rules for the amount of space between conduits or between conduits and walls of the pull box when conduits are entering on the same side of a pull box. The only rules are ones that apply to the length of a pull box and to the sides into which cables may run on the opposite sides, not the perpendicular sides.

The confusion is caused by these standards being foreign to contractors and network administrators alike. One day we are running our coaxial cable hanging off the wall, sending so many million bits per second from the terminal to the mainframe, and the next day we are running 10BaseT and fiber in conduit, sending many more Mbps from the client to the server. In this ever-changing world, it's hard to know what wire to use to connect your network, let alone the standard by which to wire it.

Some More Real-World Examples

The following picture was taken in a feed-through wiring closet. Notice that the conduit coming through the floor isn't directly underneath the junction box on the left of the picture, and that the conduit has a reverse bend in it. There was no way the contractor could put another pull box there at the reverse end, so a pull box had to be placed on the wall before the cable could be fed up the wall and into the office above.

S-Curve Conduit

When running cable through the pull box, the cable installers ran it from the top floor to the lower floors, making it easier to pull the cables. As cables were being pulled to the lower floor, one contractor was below with a walkie-talkie and the other was at the pull box with a walkie-talkie. As the contractor pulled the cable from below, the other contractor gently fed the cable into the conduit at the pull box. In this way, no strain was put on the cable as it was being pulled through the conduit's reverse turn. The walkie-talkies were used for communication between the two contractors to let each other know when to push and pull in unison.

Part of the Cable-Pulling Team

Here's one for you: How do you know if the contractor actually followed the rules and ran solid, not flexible, conduit between junction boxes inside the wall? The answer is, you *don't*. Here is a picture we took from an installation that shows *both* kinds of conduit being used. Remember, flexible conduit shouldn't be used with data cabling, as the inside of the tubing scrapes and tugs at the cables as they are being pulled through it.

U Bends in Flexible Conduit

Finally, the next picture shows a *huge* junction box used to house all the data cables coming in from network feeds throughout the building. Use this type of junction box when you need to feed a large number of cables in from one direction and out the opposite direction, but need them to be dispersed as well. Below this junction box are several 16-port Ethernet hubs to which the data cables run. The "fingered" looking feeder trays between them house the cables and let the cables pass through the sides of the trays easily. Once finished, the junction box and feeder trays will be covered and the entire wiring system will be hidden from view.

Feeder Tubes, Cables, and Junction Box

Rules to Run By for Conduit

- No section of conduit can be longer than 100 feet or contain more than two 90° bends between pull points or pull boxes. When longer than 100 feet, the conduit tends to cause extra drag on the cables during installation. At every 100-foot interval there should be a pull box so that you can aid the pulling of the cables through the conduit.

- Any single conduit run extending from a hub or wiring closet should not serve more than three outlets. With more than three outlets, you will have too many bends and turns coming through the conduit.

- Cable trays or troughs with an extending conduit to the individual rooms are recommended between all wiring closets and hubs. This makes it much easier to run the cables. Also, you won't need as many pull boxes because you can lift the cables as you are pulling them.

- Areas above suspended ceilings should be considered "return air plenum." If you are running the cables "bare" on cable trays, specify that the cables be "plenum rated," meaning that they are coated with Teflon to prevent them from omitting noxious fumes during a fire.

- Neatness in cabling, ensuring that all cables are hidden from open view or run in wall-mounted raceway, is mandatory. Cables should not be stapled to walls, abutments, supports, or other objects. Concurrent data cable runs should be bundled together neatly and loosely. You should be able to feed a pencil into the wire clips easily. This prevents the wires from being crushed and flattened.

- If you have a cabling contractor doing the installation, specify that cable entrance paths, or conduit runs, be recorded electronically and that the information be provided to you in a tab-delimited spreadsheet. Otherwise, make your own spreadsheet and keep it in a safe place.

- Penetrations between walls should be fire-stopped according to all applicable codes. Remember, the job should specify neatness while fire-stopping.

Horizontal Wiring Runs

Home run cables go from the jack to the patch panel. They are fitted with a jack at one end and are punched down at the other end. They are never longer than 295 feet.

Measuring a Cable Run

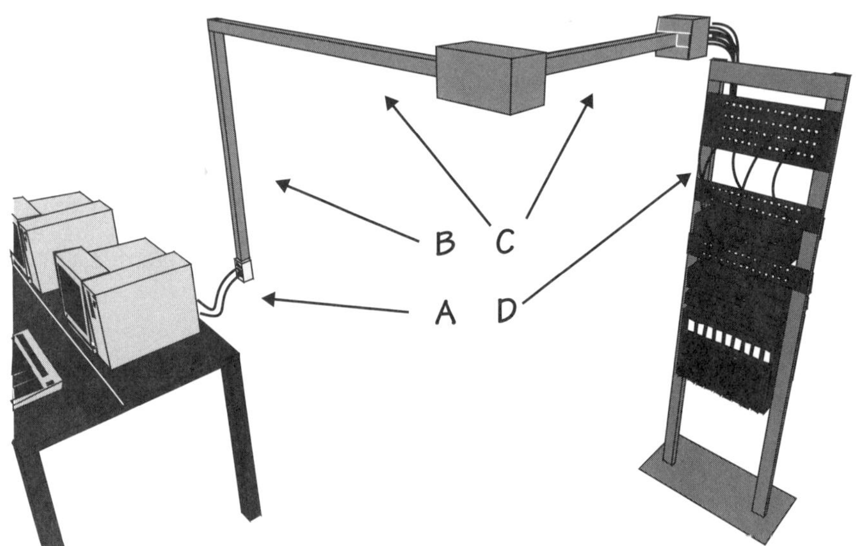

How to Measure a Cable Run

The previous picture shows a typical home run cable broken down by sections that make it easy to measure its length. (Once again, I had to draw it that way, but don't make a bend in the pull box.) We will now cover each of those sections.

A. Measure the cable length from the back of the device to the wall jack. This is usually a standard cable purchased for this purpose. We tend to buy 10- or 15-foot drop cables. It can not be *longer* than 20 feet.

B. Measure the vertical run through the wall-mount or surface-mount raceway into the ceiling.

C. Measure the horizontal run distance from the ceiling drop point at the jack to the ceiling drop point at the distribution panel.

D. Measure the distance from the ceiling drop at the distribution panel to the farthest point on the distribution rack, plus an additional 6–10 feet to account for patch cables.

Add together the measurements of A, B, C, and D, and then add the equivalent of 5% of the total length of the measurement so far for spare and rough-in needs. Make sure this length does not exceed 328 feet. If it does, redesign your wiring run and measure again. Repeat this process until the length is under the maximum distance recommended.

Making Sure You Have the Right Type of Cable

I know this might sound like I don't trust wiring contractors, *but* there are times you will need to inspect the wires and make sure the contractor purchased the type of wire you requested. Look for something written on the wire itself by the manufacturer stating what gauge the wire is, what its category rating is, and whether or not it is plenum rated. The cable will state whether it is 22 AWG, 24 AWG, or 26 AWG. The most common cable being used for Category 5 is 24 AWG, so ensure that it is rated that way.

Each cable has its National Electronic Code classification printed on the side of the cable, along with the rest of the information. Where the cable states **CMR**, the "CM" stands for low voltage rated data cable. If the cable states **CLR**, the "CL" would be an analog cable, to be used for phones only. The "R" in CMR is the cable's classification. There are generally one of two classifications printed on the sides of the cables: an "R" standing for *riser cable*, which must be enclosed in conduit when run through return-air plenum areas; or a "P" meaning that the cable is *plenum rated* with an outer coating that won't emit toxic fumes in a fire. Finally, the cable should be stamped that it has been verified for Category 5.

BERK-TEK 24 AWG CMR/MPR 75C (UL)   VERIFIED CATEGORY 5

Berk-Tek Category 5 Wire; Not Plenum Rated

Also ensure that the contractor used the same type of cable throughout the network installation. Different types of cable cause cabling mismatches, which in turn cause impedance problems.

Rules to Run By for Cable

In most instances, unless specifically referring to fiber cable, we are speaking of rules that apply to copper UTP.

- Cables with a run length of 295 feet or under should consist of 24 AWG thermoplastic insulated conductors formed into four twisted pairs and enclosed by a thermoplastic jacket covered with a Teflon fire retardant for plenum rating. Cables with a length of over 295 feet should be 62.5/125μm multimode optical fiber because of the length limitations of copper cabling. Cables must be rated by the manufacturer to be certified Category 5 compliant.

- The wire outer diameter (OD) of the cable can be no less than 0.18 and no more than 0.22 trade size. Trust us, 0.18 is better because you can fit more of them into a conduit run. Most cables ship with 0.22 OD, but you can order thinner ones. They don't cost any more than the thicker ones, either.

- The cable's pair assembly must meet the color code according to EIA/TIA 568, section 10.2.1.1.3. An easy way to ensure that the cables are truly Category 5 is to check for the correct colors. There is no such thing as a blue, red, green, yellow, and black Category 5 cable.

- All wires must not be bent tightly or kinked at the jack or elsewhere, or bent less than six times the OD of the cable. Check the table for how tightly the cable can bend. This is different than bend radius.

- Keep an eye on how tightly the cables are bundled. If you cannot fit a *dull* pencil into the bundle, it is too tight.

- No more than 25 pounds of pressure may be applied when pulling cables. Otherwise, you will stretch them and that's as bad as flattening them.

- If a cable installer is running your cable, have cables tested by a third party once they are installed. They should perform better than the minimum requirements outlined by the EIA/TIA 568, section 10.2.1.2.

- Any cable failing to meet third-party testing measurements should be completely rerun at the installer's expense. This includes equipment, parts, and time. This is very important. You will be wasting your own time by having someone rerun cable; don't tack the contractor's expenses on top of that.

- Record the lengths of cables using cable testing equipment. Only that cable, plus a standard, recorded deviation, should be paid for by you. All excess cable should be either turned over to you with recorded lengths, or returned to the installer at no charge to you. We have seen a lot of waste during installation, and usually that waste is being paid for by the client.

Electrical Considerations When Running Cabling

All wires must be run according to the following table:

Condition	<2 kVA	2–5 kVA	>5 kVA
Unshielded power lines or electrical equipment in proximity to open or nonmetal pathways	5 inches	12 inches	24 inches
Unshielded power lines or electrical equipment in proximity to a grounded metal conduit pathway	2.5 inches	6 inches	12 inches
Power lines enclosed in a grounded metal conduit (or equivalent shielding) in proximity to a grounded metal conduit pathway		3 inches	6 inches

Rules for Wire Runs

- All wires must be run at least seven feet from electromagnetic fields, such as those generated by electrical motors, converters, and inverters. By law, manufacturers must state the voltage output of their products—just look on the bottom or side of anything with a plug. Those volts ooze out from the plug to the piece of equipment. Don't let anyone tell you different.

- All wires must be run at least six inches from fluorescent lights. This is major mistake territory when you are running cable in a drop ceiling. Be aware.

- All wires must be run at least one foot from FAX machines, refrigerators, microwaves, and copiers.

- All concurrent wiring runs paired with electronic cabling must not exceed three feet in length.

WIRING CLOSETS AND RACKS

The wiring closets are a transition point between the horizontal distribution pathways and all or part of the backbone. They contain the termination for the horizontal cables, wiring racks, and hubs, bridges, switches, and routers. Some of them even contain file, mail, or other servers. These wiring closets are usually actual closets or small rooms. In other situations, such as cables running into a training room setting, the "wiring closet" is really the top of a teacher's closet or a small, ventilated area protected from intruders.

Main Closets

The main closet is the centralized space for telecommunications equipment that serves the entire network, including hubs. This room should house only equipment directly related to the telecommunications and data system and its environmental support system.

The closets themselves should be located as close to the center of the networked area as possible. By doing so, cables can be run in all directions without having to overextend some of the cables. While this is a perfect scenario, we don't often find that it is the case. Instead, we find that most building designers put utility closets in the building's design only after all the other rooms have been laid out. Even then, many of the architects don't build the room large enough to accommodate standard telecommunications gear, the gear necessary for computer communications, and space to separate the power systems from the data systems. Therefore, when designing the wiring closet, follow some strict rules concerning the placement of wiring racks and incoming wires.

Training Room Closets

If you are using hubs, as in the case of some organization's training rooms, the hubs should service each room as a transition point between the horizontal distribution pathways and the backbone or main wiring closet. The same rules for the wiring closets apply to these hubs, except, of course, for those rules concerning distances between the rack and the walls and lighting.

Rules to Run By for Wiring Closets

- They should contain one or more floor-, wall-, or ceiling-mounted racks. Each rack should be no taller than eight feet and should be exactly 19 inches wide. Each rack should have at least two shelving units. The only exceptions to this rule should be smaller "closets" built in training rooms on top of cabinets or in a corner. As these "closets" house only a hub or two, they can be swing-rack-mounted or have custom mountings created.

- EIA/TIA 569 states that wiring closets must have a 24-hour, thermostat-controlled, HVAC system to operate in a range of 64–75° F with 30–50% relative humidity measured at five feet above the floor. There are some perks to being a network administrator in August. Again, the training room closets won't be able to have their own thermostat, and because of that, should have some type of ventilation, such as louvered doors. In any case, positive air pressure should be maintained, with a minimum of one air change per hour.

- If using a UPS system, the batteries in the UPS require adequate ventilation. Refer to the manufacturer's specifications for this. Also, make sure that you can remove old batteries and install new batteries in your UPS system without the major hassle of moving other equipment.

- Drainage troughs need to be placed under the sprinkler pipes to prevent leakage onto equipment within the room.

- A separate circuit serving the wiring closets needs to be provided and terminated in its own electrical panel, per the EIA/TIA 607 standard. The closets should have as a minimum two 15A, 110-volt, AC duplex outlets. Lighting fixtures should not be powered from the same electrical distribution panel as the telecommunications equipment room.

- Multiple closets on a floor should be interconnected by a minimum of one conduit of trade size 3 or equivalent.

- Level, nonconductive flooring is preferred, such as linoleum or concrete. When using a UPS system with batteries, the sealing for the floors must meet NEC articles 480 and 503-14 standards.

- Penetrations between walls should always be fire-stopped according to all applicable codes. All sleeves and slots should be adjacent to doors to make the most effective use of wall or floor space.

Rules to Run By for Wiring Racks

- Each rack should be allocated no more than 200 wiring terminations. With more than 200, you won't have the slightest chance in the world of being able to manage those cables.

- Racks should have clearances of at least 30 inches to the rear, 36 inches to the front, and 14 inches to the side for access and cable dressing space.

- Per EIA/TIA 607, NEC 250–50, 250–74, 250–75, and 800-33 through 800-40, cross-connect hardware for cabling should be mounted on frames accommodating a grounding conductor that will provide a path of low DC resistance to ground. The grounding conductor should be bonded to the same grounding system employed by the power service for the same floor serving the cross-connect equipment. The grounding conductor must be no less than 6 AWG. Yes, you must install the grounding conductor.

- In accordance with EIA/TIA 607 and NEC applicable articles, all data cables with metallic shielding must be bonded correctly.

PATCH PANELS

The following pictures show wiring racks that we *don't* want to see. The wires are a mess and incorrectly labeled. Most of the wires aren't up to spec, meaning that they are flat cable. The rack is not grounded, and no one at the site could tell us where anything went.

Really Ugly Rack from the Side (left) and from the Front (right)

Distribution Panels

We do not recommend the usage of 66-block or 110-block cable panels. Rather, we recommend using AMP, Homaco, or any CAT5 jacked distribution panel. This is to ease moving from one computer system to the next. When a computer's cables have been wired to the 66-block or 110-block, they are hard-wired. If that computer needs to be logically moved around the network, a network specialist must come in, cut the original cable, and re-punch it to the new position on the 66-block or 110-block. When you use a patch panel, the cables can be moved from one position to the next with a simple "unplug-replug" move.

When punching down to your patch panel, the rules are the same as those for attaching a jack—with one exception. It is acceptable to have up to half an inch of exposed conductors when punching down to a patch panel. If you do invest in a punchdown tool, always set the impact to the lowest setting. If you don't, the clips on the punchdown block over-separate and are unable to form a solid connection with the conductors.

Concentrator Panels

There is no concentrator on the market today that is CAT5. AT&T was threatening to have a CAT5 amphenol cable out on the market in 1995 sometime, although there is still no word. Some hubs come with their own concentrator panel. Thus, we will describe this setup as well. With a Farallon concentrator, the patch cables go directly from the front of the distribution panel to the concentrator. With a concentrator panel, you need patch cables that go from the distribution panel to the concentrator panel, and then an amphenol cable runs from the back of the concentrator panel to the hub.

Rules to Run By for Patch Panels

- The transmission properties of internally wired connecting devices should meet or exceed the transmission performance requirements specified in EIA/ TIA 568, section 12.2.6.2, interfaces included. In other words, make sure that your patch panels and connectors are all Category 5.

- Standard telecommunications interface jacks and plugs must meet the requirements of EIA/TIA-TSB-31, Ref B1.37. This is the same as above, but for your jacks.

- Telecommunications interface jacks should be eight-pin jacks with pin/pair assignments according to the 568A or 568B designation with applicable color code combinations. These pin/pair assignments are compatible with ISDN BRI (ISO 8877), Ref B1.24.

LABELING

Labeling is needed throughout the cabling process Your cables should be labeled at the jack, the closet, and on the home run cable, preferably at both ends inside the conduit or raceway near the jack and the patch panel. The following information is needed on every label: wiring closet termination point, room, drop, position, type, length, and jack label. A sample is shown in the following table:

Closet	Room	Drop	Position	Type	Length	Jack ID
B121	B122	1	2	ENA	56	B122.1.2

Example of Cable Labeling

The following is a description of each category of information:

- **Closet:** Where the home run cable originates—not necessarily the main closet.

- **Room:** The actual room number. If the room number is different from the one on the blueprint, use the one on the blueprint. The secretary is not going to be doing your wiring. Whoever looks at your blueprints will be using the numbers as a reference.

- **Drop:** The gang box holding from one to eight jacks.

- **Position:** The jack.

- **Type:** The network connection, such as LocalTalk, Ethernet, cross-connect, or the like—the more detailed, the better.

- **Length:** The physical, not the tested length—otherwise, only your contractor knows for sure.

- **Jack ID:** Room, drop, position.

How to Read a Floor Plan

Now that you know what needs to be labeled, you are probably wondering what those labels mean, and how you can relate that information to something you can use, like a floor plan. First of all, get a floor plan in your hot little hands. If you don't have a floor plan, don't even *think* of continuing with cable management. If you don't know the rooms, and where those rooms are in your building, then how in the world can you manage the cable locations or have any idea of what their lengths mean? So, where do you find one of these floor plans? Property management should have one. A copy *must* be filed with the state and local government commissioner's office. They are called "as-built" plans. You can't receive a license to build unless you file the floor plans with somebody. Therefore, I *know* you can obtain a copy. Once you have the copy in hand, look for the following types of markings for cable drops:

 This is a normal telecommunications drop. What *should* be located at these jacks are phone cables. Many of these jacks have an extra space that you can probably use for data cables. These jacks should be found on the walls.

 This is a data drop. These drops *should* contain only data communications wires. Like the telecommunications jacks, these jacks should be found on the walls.

 This is a data drop that is *floor-mounted*. It should be just like the wall-mounted jack, except that it's on the floor.

 This is a *power outlet*. You don't want to run your data *or* telecommunications drops to the power outlet. This is because of *electromagnetic interference*. It will definitely ruin your day.

The following picture shows a blueprint for a typical administrative office. Each of the previous markings are depicted.

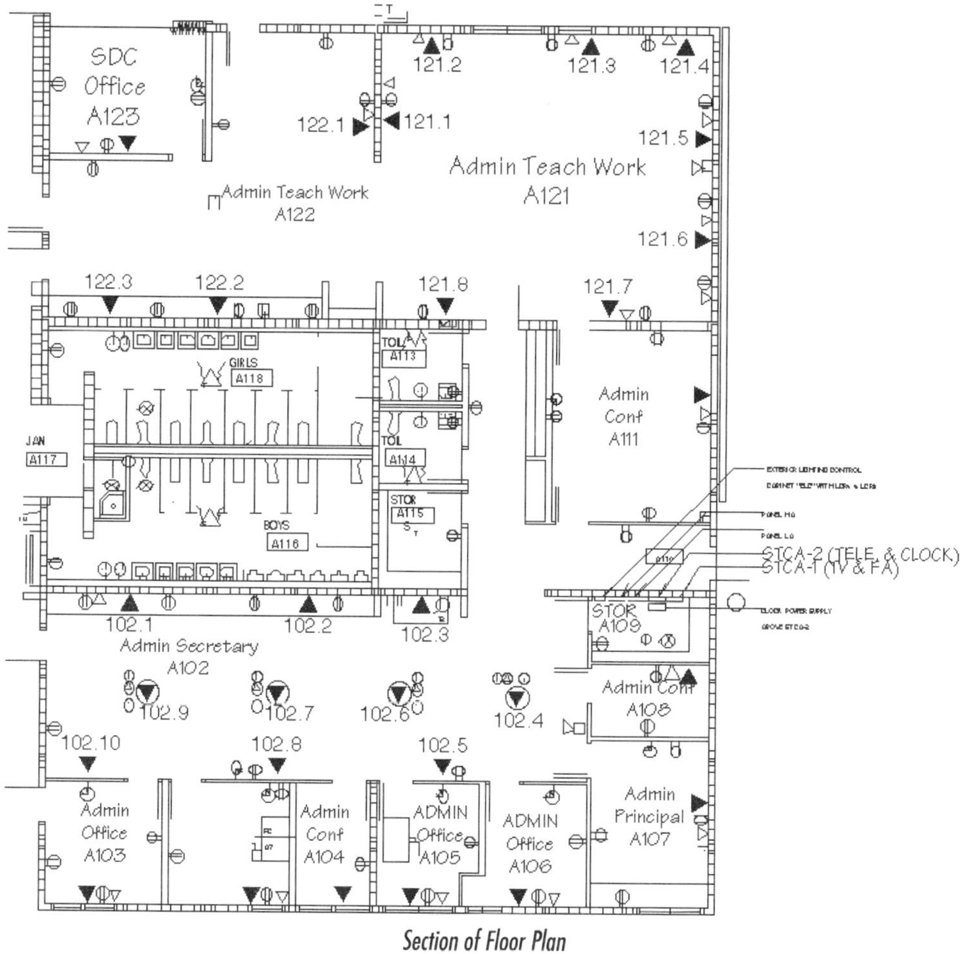

Section of Floor Plan

Rules to Run By for Labeling

- Ensure that the horizontal run cable is correctly labeled, as are the corresponding patch panels and wall jacks. When checking the labeling, see if the cable is marked with its run location, and make sure the cable's length is noted. This will help when troubleshooting the cable.

Marked Cable Showing Room Number and Length

- Labeling all wall jacks, cables, patch cables, and patch panel jacks is mandatory. If a contractor is doing the cabling, leave the method for applying labels to the discretion of each bidder, but have them supply a sample for approval.

- The labels themselves should be according to the descriptions given in a Request for Proposal, or RFP, to the contractor. For a sample RFP, see Chapter 5, "Writing Your Cabling RFP," starting on page 85.

- Cable conduit entrance paths should be marked on the floor plans, and, following completion of the work, a blueprint should be provided depicting all locations and label IDs of each jack and patch panel.

TESTING

I was working with a client who just put in a "CAT5" network. Now, knowing me, why would you think that I put CAT5 in quotation marks? Because the network hadn't been tested. The "installer" (a mindless moron with a loud mouth) told the client that AT&T would come by, test the cables, and certify them for installation. To make a long story short (leaving out the part about me having to take the installer outside and beat some sense into him), the AT&T sales guy, who still wore loafers because he couldn't tie his shoes, walked over to one of the 100 jacks, opened it up, looked at it, and pronounced the *entire* network CAT5. Once I pulled myself off the ceiling, I tested some cables with my trusty MicroTest Pair Scanner and found four out of five cables faulty. One of them had only three of the wires installed correctly. As the client hadn't written testing into the contract, the installer got away with it. Ooo, I hate that. Take it from me: Test your cabling system. Here are the things you are looking for when testing cable:

Wire Mapping Wire mapping is the first test performed, as the goal of the test is to ensure that there are a total of eight cables and that the cables are pinned straight through. This means that if a cable starts out at pin 1, it also ends up at pin 1. Wire mapping tests also check the cable length, ensuring that the cable is no longer than 328 feet and no shorter than 10 feet.

NEXT Near end crosstalk (NEXT) is the measure of interference that the signal on adjacent cables causes during communication. It should be measured from both the workstation and the hub to be determined correctly.

Attenuation This is simply the measure of signal loss as the signal travels the length of the cable.

ACR Attenuation-to-crosstalk ratio (ACR) shows the value of the received signal after the effects of attenuation and NEXT.

Impedance This test cannot be conducted if the cable is shorter than 40 feet. It is a measure of the characteristic impedance of the cable.

Loop Resistance This is a measurement of the DC resistance of the conductors in the cabling pairs.

Capacitance This is the measure of the mutual capacitance between the conductors in a pair.

Rules to Run By for Testing

- All cable testing should be performed once by the installation vendor, and a second time by a third party using a certified, calibrated MicroTest PentaScanner, according to an accepted and approved Category 5 test procedure. Save all tests in the PentaScanner's memory until they can be downloaded to a tab-delimited test file by a member of your staff. Accept no test measurements that are not downloaded directly from the PentaScanner by a staff member of your company. Match tests performed by the installation vendor against tests performed by the third-party testing authority.

- Any tests in question should be run a third time, in the presence of a staff member of your company, the installation vendor, and the third-party testing authority. This should be considered a final test and the results will need to be treated and recorded accordingly.

- All cable runs that fail to meet the specifications in the RFP given to the installation vendor and fail the PentaScanner test will need to be completely rerun at the full expense of the installation vendor. They will hassle you about this, but if you wrote it into your contract, and they agreed to it, there's nothing they can do.

- Further testing expenses should be paid for by *your* company to the testing authority. Test all rerun cables for compliance, as if they were the first run of the cable. Deal with the test results in the same manner as the first run.

All cables, after being tested, should be recorded in a database. Know the cable identification information, where it is run *from* and *to,* and other pertinent information. We have scoured the Category 5 listings to provide you with the exact information the standards require of cable management. You can create a cable management system easily in an application like ClarisWorks or FileMaker Pro. The sample shown in the following diagram was created in FileMaker Pro. Most of the information in this example is provided by the test results obtained from a PentaScanner. That means that once cables are tested, you can directly print that information from the PentaScanner to your computer through anything that accepts text file transfers, such as ZTerm or ClarisWorks. You can then enter the information into your database automatically, keeping a journal of all the cable's statistics and changes.

Cable Identifier C25.1   **Cable Type** 4-Pr. UTP, EIA-568 spec.

	STC	Jack ID	Hub	Hub Port
Term. pos. record	C129	C25.1.1	60652-a	6
Entrance Conduit	C10			

Test	Expected Result	Actual Test Results				Pass/Fail PASS
Wire Map	**12345678**	Near Map 12345678	Far Map 12345678			

Test	Expected Result	Pr 12	Pr 36	Pr 45	Pr 78
Length (ft)	**10 - 328**	76	76	72	72
Impedance (ohms)	**80 - 125**	104	102	111	110
Resistance (ohms)	**0.0 - 18.8**	4.4	4.1	4.1	4.1
Capacitance (pF)	**50 - 5600**	1114	1143	1038	1013
Attenuation (dB)		4.2	4.1	3.9	3.6
@ Freq (MHz)		100	100	100	100
Limit (dB)		23.6	23.6	23.6	23.6

NeXT Pair Combinations	12/36	12/45	12/78	36/45	36/78	36/78
NeXT Loss (dB)	42.8	40.2	45.2	39	39.3	45.5
Freq (0.7 - 100.0) (MHz)	47.9	96.5	98.3	98.1	99.7	35.1
NeXT Limit Cat 5 formula (dB)	32.6	27.3	27.2	27.2	34.9	27.1
Active ACR (5) (dB)	41	38	44	37	35	44

EIA/TIA 606 Approved Database

CHAPTER 5:
WRITING YOUR CABLING RFP

There are two ways to ensure that you come out on top of the wiring installation; meaning, you end up with the wiring system that you want, within the budget you set. One way is the Overbearing Mother approach. This means you follow the contractors around your office, monitoring their every move, making sure the work is performed correctly. The contractors will do the job right, and fast—even if all that means is that they get away from you as quickly as possible.

The other approach is to write a rock-solid Request for Proposal (RFP). Spend the time before the installation checking out past work performed by the bidders, and then confirm that the bid winner follows the RFP to your specifications. An RFP should be generated for each episode of wiring. You do not want to leave yourself open for the old "I thought the other guy was going to do that."

So, now comes the question I know is looming in your mind: "How do I write an RFP?" Funny you should ask—it just so happens that we have a dandy RFP template you can have. We include it here. Anywhere you see brackets, insert the information specific to your organization.

RFP FOR [YOUR COMPANY]

1. Invitation for Proposal

(Here you are simply defining the bid. This is a sort of preamble to the rest of the RFP and shouldn't be much more than what we have here.)

[Your company] has defined its needs and requirements for the installation of data wiring for [whatever building or buildings]. You are invited to submit a proposal and bid that will meet the general criteria outlined in this request. The information and specifications presented in this document are intended to be used as a guide by vendors in developing their proposals.

We are asking you to create an initial bid to install a Category 5 data network from the cable locations in Appendix A. The lengths are approximated in that table. We have included sample part numbers for parts we find acceptable. You may quote using those part numbers or suggest and justify changes for parts of equal or greater quality and performance.

Prior to proposal submission, a site walk-through will be scheduled so that bidders may familiarize themselves with the layout of [your company]. Bidders must attend the scheduled walk-through. A $250.00 refundable deposit will be required for a copy of building plans. All bids will be reviewed based upon the submitted proposals.

[Your company] reserves the right to terminate any contract if Category 5 specifications are not adhered to upon final inspection. If at any point within the contracted installation the Category 5 standard cannot be upheld, written notice must be submitted to a representative from [your company] for signature approval. If an agreeable solution cannot be reached between the installing party and [your company], the contract will no longer be valid.

2. Proposal Preparation and Submission

a. Point of Contact

The point of contact for vendors regarding questions, correspondence, or submission of proposals will be:

[Your name]

[Your company]

[Your address]

[Your phone]

[Your fax]

(Make sure that vendors can contact only a single person. This avoids having the vendors play favorites within your company.)

b. Contract Timetable

(This speaks for itself. You are setting milestones in this section. Set a different walk-through date and time for each vendor. Be advised here—if the vendor can't keep a bid date, how in the world can the vendor be expected to finish the job on time?)

1. Site walk-through/vendor meeting

2. Bid due date and time

Note: If a vendor can't keep to the due date for the bid, this will automatically exclude that vendor from the award process. For the site walk-through, meet at [your destination] at described time.

3. Award date and time

4. Completion of wiring installation

5. The contract will be awarded according to the phase schedule in which this RFP is written. Proposals must include the following phases with coordinating costs:

   Phase One: Complete fiber installation

   Phase Two: Wiring closet A and all serviced hubs, jacks, and surface-mount raceway.

(Include a separate "phase" for each wiring closet you will have and all hubs, jacks, and surface-mount raceway that the wiring closet will service.)

6. Upon successful completion of the first run job, additional run jobs will be awarded and a purchase order will be submitted. Purchase orders will be paid 30 days after the completion of each phase.

3. Site Location

(Decide what locations, both by building and room number, you want to wire.)

4. Construction Company

(The construction company contact is vital to the proper installation of your cabling. Because construction companies are vitally important to the sizing and placing of conduit, the construction company will need to provide detailed drawings, showing both drop locations and conduit sizes, to all parties bidding on your RFP.)

a. Contractor/Subcontractor Qualifications

1. Contractor/subcontractor must have three years experience in the installation of Category 5, fiber optic cabling, and LAN equipment.

2. Contractor/subcontractor must have successfully completed five similar projects.

3. Contractor/subcontractor must provide satisfactory evidence of financial stability.

4. Contractor/subcontractor must be capable of providing bonds as required in the Contract Provisions—Division 1, General Conditions, Supplementary Conditions, and Section 16050 *(This provision is only an example. Find out what kind of bonds are appropriate for your company in your state).*

5. Contractor/subcontractor must have certification by the manufacturer of the proposed equipment. A company certification must exist with each manufacturer used in this section that the contractor/subcontractor is a certified installer.

6. Contractor/subcontractor must provide a list of five references in which similar materials and labor were required.

7. All bidders are required to carry $[xxx] of liability insurance per incident and agree to hold [your company] safe and harmless in the event of any incidents.

b. Submittals from the Contractor/Subcontractor

1. Alternates or alternatives: Alternatives or alternates to the specified materials and installation must be approved in writing during and not after the submittal phase.

2. All equipment provided in this contract section must be UL listed, verified, and classified to meet or exceed the performance specifications.

3. Any costs associated with preparing bids in response to this specification are the sole responsibility of the bidder.

4. A representative from [your company] will provide illustrated documents and specifications to the party awarded the cabling contract. Both conduit paths and diameters for raceways intended for data will be noted on the illustrated documents and specifications.

c. Installation

1. The contractor shall maintain a clean work place. Storage of any equipment shall be approved by the client prior to storage. The location of any

stored equipment shall be coordinated with the client. The client is not responsible for any loss or damage to contractors' equipment on its premises. The client must be notified of any shipments of equipment prior to delivery. The client is not responsible for any material deliveries that were not signed for by an authorized client representative.

2. Damage caused by the contractor during installation and testing must be replaced or repaired by the contractor at no cost and to the satisfaction of the client.

3. After the contract has been awarded, but before the contractor orders the cables and equipment components, the contractor shall submit to the client samples and part numbers of the cables for approval before they are ordered. For composite cables, samples of each section of the composite cable are adequate.

   As of this writing, we are specifying ST as opposed to SC fiber connectors. If the contractor can supply SC connectors far more quickly than ST connectors, we will accept SC connectors.

4. The contractor shall obtain all manufacturer's instructions, including current bulletins, for the installation of the cable and cabling system components provided by the contractor. Copies of these documents and all manufacturer's warranty documents shall be sent by the general contractor to the client when the installation of the cabling system begins.

5. The contractor shall provide the necessary protection to safeguard its own work, as well as the work of other trades, from damage. The contractor must take care not to damage ceiling tiles.

6. The contractor shall provide all necessary tools, hardware, and test equipment needed by its laborers to install, label, test, and document the cabling system.

7. The installation of the voice and data communications system by the contractor will not be considered complete until all cables and components described in this specification are installed, labeled, and tested, and until documentation is delivered according to the specifications. Furthermore, the cabling system will not be considered to be complete until there has been a successful inspection by the client without any corrections required of the contractor.

8. All bidders are fully responsible for coordinating their work with the general contractor during construction. No claims will be entertained for failure to coordinate with the general contractor.

9. All bidders will be fully responsible for hoisting and transporting all their materials into the building.

5. Scope of Work

(In this section, you are telling the vendor briefly what you want wired. You are telling them that you want wiring run according to how you marked your blueprints.)

a. Install, label, and test (plenum rated for ceiling tray locations) data Category 5, twisted pair, 24 AWG wire in locations specified on the attached blueprints and added as Appendix A to this RFP. This is for a home run network from each workstation location or hub marked on the floor plan and the attachment to a patch panel on the [wall-mounted, cabinet-mounted or free standing] cable rack in the appropriate wiring closet as stated in Appendix A.

b. Install, label, and test fiber cables through conduit running from runs marked XX to the appropriate termination point.

c. Wiring closets and room hubs are located in various rooms as marked on the floor plans. In Appendix A, room hubs are designated as runs of type CR. In Appendix A, wiring rooms are the rooms in the first column.

d. Each run in Appendix A is designated as follows: wiring closet termination point, room, drop, position, type, suggested length, and jack label. A sample is shown here:

Closet	Room	Drop	Position	Type	Length	Jack ID
B121	B122	1	2	ENA	56	B122.1.2

e. All work will be according to Category 5 specifications as published in EIA/TIA standards 568, 568-A, 569, 570, 606, and 607. Additions are listed in TSB 31, 36, and 40. In addition, all installation will be compliant with ISDN BRI (ISO 8877). Cable connectors shall meet the IEEE 802.3 (100BaseX and 10BaseF) and IEEE 802.3i (10BaseT) specifications. Where there is gray area concerning this RFP, these guidelines will be the principal deciding factors. The only exception to this will be in the case of ST vs. SC connectors and Section 13.a of this RFP, which allow more wiring drops per rack (200) than 568 section 12.3.1 allows (96).

6. Conduit and Cable Bends as Currently Installed

a. In the case that wall-mount raceway is used, leave 50% of the raceway empty. It is to be expected that some conduits will be filled up to 75% capacity due to the limited diameters of certain pathways. Otherwise, all conduit diameters must comply with the cable quantity limitations as per the following table.

Conduit Diameter Trade Size	Wire OD (Outer Diameter of Cable)			
	0.18	0.24	0.31	0.37
0.5	1	0	0	0
0.75	5	3	2	1
1	8	6	3	2
1.25	14	10	4	3
1.5	18	15	6	4
2	26	20	12	7
2.5	40	30	13	12
3	60	40	20	17
3.5	-	-	-	22
4	-	-	-	30

b. All conduit bend radii must comply with the following table:

Scenario	Bend Radius
< 2 inches	6 × internal diameter of conduit
≥ 2 inches	10 × internal diameter of conduit
Fiber Pull	10 × internal diameter of conduit

c.   No section of conduit shall be longer than 100 feet or contain more than two 90° bends between pull points or pull boxes.

d.   Any single conduit run extending from the wiring closet shall not serve more than three outlets.

e.   Areas above suspended ceilings will be considered "return air plenum".

(If you are running the cables "bare" on cable trays, specify that the cables be "plenum rated," meaning that they are coated with Teflon to prevent the emission of noxious fumes during a fire.)

f.   Neatness in cabling, ensuring that all cables are hidden from open view or run in wall-mounted raceway, is mandatory. Cables will not be stapled to walls, abutments, supports, or any other objects. Concurrent data cable runs will be bundled together neatly and loosely.

g.   Cable entrance paths, or conduit runs, will be recorded electronically and that information will be provided to the client in a tab-delimited spreadsheet.

h   Where wall-mount raceway runs horizontally, it will be fastened mechanically as per the manufacturer's specification and the connection joints will be centered between the vertical standard brackets.

i.   All wall-mount raceway will be run parallel to the floor and will be mounted at the minimum acceptable distance from the floor.

7. Telecommunications Outlets and Connectors

a. Drop Cable Specifications

1.   All drop and patch cables should not exceed 20 feet.

2.   The total length of the drop and patch cables shall be no more than 25 feet. All patch and drop cables will be Category 5 rated, as explained in Section 8 of this RFP.

3.   When testing for certification, drop cables and patch cables will be used in place of the cables supplied with the testing equipment.

4. Only drop cables that are inventoried to be in the client's possession after inspection shall be charged to the client.

b. Connector Specifications

1. Each four-pair, 24 AWG, Category 5 cable will be terminated in an eight-pin, modular jack at the work area. These connectors shall be 100-ohm, UTP outlets that meet all criteria listed in EIA/TIA 570 (B1.2), and EIA/TIA-TSB-31 (B1.37), and EIA/TIA 568, sections 12.2.5 and 12.2.6.

2. The pin/pair assignments shall be according to the 568A designation with applicable color code combinations. These pin/pair assignments are compatible with ISDN BRI (ISO 8877), Ref B1.24.

3. We are requesting that each drop have a MOD-TAP flush-mounted or box jack face plate installed for data. In most instances, jacks will contain RJ-45 jacks or blanks. Where appropriate, the MOD-TAP face plates may be fitted for phone jacks (RJ-11) for phone use as well as RJ-45 jacks, as long as all open sockets are fitted for blanks. Although SC connectors for fiber cables are specified in the 568A standard, ST connectors will be implemented in this installation.

4. Only jacks, face plates, gang boxes, and blanks inventoried to be in the client's possession after inspection shall be charged to the client.

8. Wiring Description for CAT5 Horizontal Cabling

a. All cables with a run length of 295 feet or less shall consist of 24 AWG thermoplastic insulated conductors formed into four twisted pairs and enclosed by a thermoplastic jacket. If the cable is to be plenum rated, it must be covered with a Teflon fire retardant for plenum (CMP) rating. All cables over 295 feet will be 62.5/125µm six-stranded optical fiber. All cables shall be rated by the manufacturer to be certified Category 5 compliant.

Note: It is our expectation that fiber will not need to be run from the STC to the wall jack. It is our expectation that the contractor will be able to install cable under this limit by finding alternate pathways. If any length is to exceed 295 feet, written notice must be submitted to [your company] for signature approval.

b. The wire OD of the UTP copper cable shall be no more than 0.21. The wire OD of the six-stranded fiber cable shall be no more than 0.50 trade size.

c. The pair assembly shall mcct thc color code according to EIA/TIA 568, section 10.2.1.1.3.

d. All wires must not be bent tightly or kinked at the jack or elsewhere, or bent more than 6% OD of the cable.

e. Cables will be tested by a third party once installed, and shall pcrform bcttcr than the minimum requirements outlined in EIA/TIA 568A—section 10 for UTP copper and section 12 for fiber. A serial download of the test files will be provided to [your company].

f. After the serial download has been provided, spot checks in each building will be performed by a qualified technician hired by [your company].

g   If any cable fails to meet the specified requirements during testing measurements by the third party or conflicts with the contractor's test results, the cable will be completely rerun at the installer's expense, including equipment, parts, and time.

h. The lengths of cables will be recorded using cable test equipment. Only cable (plus a standard deviation) that has been recorded will be paid for by [your company]. All excess cable shall be returned to the installer at no charge to [your company].

9. Electrical Considerations

a. All wires must be run as per the following table:

Condition	<2 kVA	2–5 kVA	>5 kVA
Unshielded power lines or electrical equipment in proximity to open or nonmetal pathways	5 inches	12 inches	24 inches
Unshielded power lines or electrical equipment in proximity to a grounded metal conduit pathway	2.5 inches	6 inches	12 inches
Power lines enclosed in a grounded metal conduit (or equivalent shielding) in proximity to a grounded metal conduit pathway		3 inches	6 inches

    b.   All wires must be run at least 6.6 feet from electromagnetic fields such as those generated by electrical motors, converters, and inverters.

    c.   All wires must be run at least six inches from fluorescent lights.

    d.   All wires must be run at least one foot from FAX machines, refrigerators, microwaves, and copiers.

    e.   All concurrent wiring runs paired with electronic cabling must not exceed three feet in length.

10. Wiring Closets

    a.   The wiring closets are a transition point between the horizontal distribution pathways and all or part of the backbone.

    b.   The wiring closets are to contain one or more floor-, wall-, or ceiling-mounted racks. Each rack will be no taller than eight feet and be exactly 19 inches wide. Each rack will have at least four shelving units. For more information, see Section 13.

(If you live near a fault line of any significance, specify that earthquake bracing be installed for a seismic rating of 4.)

    c.   Multiple closets on a floor shall be interconnected by a minimum of one conduit of trade size 3 or equivalent.

    d.   The wiring closets will have a 24-hour, thermostat-controlled, HVAC system or will operate in a range of 64–75° F with 30–50% relative humidity.

    e.   Drainage troughs shall be placed under the sprinkler pipes to prevent leakage onto equipment within the room.

    f.   A separate circuit serving the wiring closets shall be provided and terminated in its own electrical panel.

(Although rule "F" is not common practice, it should be. Don't power lighting fixtures from the electrical distribution panel in the telecommunications equipment room.)

11. Training Room Teacher's Closet or Classroom Hubs

(If you have a classroom or training room hub, add this section to your RFP.)

a. The classroom hubs are to service each classroom as a transition point between the horizontal distribution pathways and the backbone.

b. A hub set is up to three repeating hubs, 36 patch cables, and 36 ports of patch panel (in the case of Homaco, one 24-port and one 12-port).

c. Each hub set will be fitted into the teacher's closet.

d. The patch panels will be fitted on the back wall of the louvered box or on the back wall behind the box.

e. A separate circuit serving the classroom hubs shall be provided.

12. Main Closet

(If multiples, give the main closet location.)

a. The main closet is the centralized space for telecommunications equipment that serves all of [your company].

b. This room shall house only equipment directly related to the telecommunications system and its environmental support system.

c. The main closet is to contain two floor-, wall-, or ceiling-mounted racks. Each rack will be no taller than eight feet and be exactly 19 inches wide. Each rack will have at least four shelving units. Additional shelving may be built at this time for all servers. In the case of fiber, one patch panel will be bonded in the same area of the wiring closet and extra space will be allotted for an additional panel at a later date.

d. This room will have a 24-hour, thermostat-controlled, HVAC system or will operate in a range of 64–75° F with 30–50% relative humidity.

e. Drainage troughs shall be placed under the sprinkler pipes to prevent leakage onto equipment within the room.

f. A separate circuit serving the main closet shall be provided and terminated in its own electrical panel. Do not power lighting fixtures from the same electrical distribution panel as the one that services the telecommunications equipment room.

13. Distribution Rack Specifications

a. Equipment Racks

1. Each rack shall be allocated with no more than 200 wiring terminations.

2. Racks should have clearances of at least 30 inches to the rear, 36 inches in front, and 14 inches on the sides for access and cable dressing space.

b. Grounding and Bonding

1. Cross-connect hardware for cabling should be mounted on frames that will accommodate a grounding conductor that will provide a path of low DC resistance to ground. The grounding conductor should be bonded to the same grounding system that is employed by the power service for the floor serving the same floor as the cross-connect equipment.

2. The grounding conductor shall be no less than 6 AWG.

c. Patch Panels (Connecting Hardware)

1. The transmission properties of internally wired connecting devices shall meet or exceed the transmission performance requirements specified in EIA/TIA 568, section 12.2.6.2, interfaces included.

2. Standard telecommunications interface jacks and plugs shall meet the requirements of EIA/TIA-TSB-31, Ref B1.37.

3. Telecommunications interface jacks shall be eight-pin jacks with pin/pair assignments according to the 568A designation with applicable color code combinations. These pin/pair assignments are compatible with ISDN BRI (ISO 8877), Ref B1.24.

d. Jumper Cables

1. Cross-connect jumpers and patch cords shall meet or exceed the minimum performance requirements specified in EIA/TIA 568, sections 10.2.1.2.2 through 10.2.1.2.8 as well as section 10.2.1.2.1.

2. The use of flat, non-twisted cords is strictly prohibited.

3. The cables shall consist of a cable with a male connector at each end: RJ-45 connectors as specified in IEEE 802.3 (10Base2), Ref B1.4.

4. Each jumper cable shall not exceed 10 feet in length.

14. Wiring Labels and Wire Management

a. Labeling all wall jacks, cables, patch cables, and patch panel jacks is mandatory. The method for applying labels will be left to the discretion of each bidder but each bidder will supply [your company] with a sample for approval.

b. The labels themselves shall be according to the Jack ID descriptions given in Appendix A of this RFP.

c. Cable conduit entrance paths will be marked on the floor plans, and, following completion of the work, a blueprint will be provided to [your company] depicting all locations and label IDs of each jack and patch panel.

15. Testing

a. All cable testing shall be performed once by the installation vendor, and then a second time by a qualified technician (a third-party firm) hired by [your company].

b. All copper cables shall be tested by a certified, calibrated Phase II MicroTest PentaScanner or a Fotec ST310 in the case of multi-mode fiber cable, according to an acccptcd and approved Category 5 test procedure.

c. All tests shall be saved in memory within the tester until they can be downloaded to a tab-delimited test file by a member of [your company's] staff. No test measurements shall be accepted that are not downloaded directly from the PentaScanner by a staff member from [your company]. Tests performed by the installation vendor shall be matched against tests performed by the third-party testing authority.

d. Any tests in question shall be run a third time, in the presence of a staff member from [your company], the installation vendor, and the third-party testing authority. This will be considered a final test and the results will be recorded by the installation vendor accordingly.

e. Any cable runs that fail to meet specifications in this RFP and fail the PentaScanner test shall be completely rerun at the full expense of the installation vendor.

f. Further testing expenses shall be paid by [your company] to the testing authority.

g. All cables that are rerun will be tested for compliance as if they were initial runs. The results of these tests will be dealt with in the same manner as initial cable runs.

16. General Considerations

(This section gives generalized instructions for working with a contractor.)

a. Rules, Codes, and Regulations

1. All work and materials shall be in full accordance with the latest rules, codes, and regulations as follows: [Your State's] Building Code [include the acronym, if commonly used]; NFPA Bulletins; [Your State's] Electrical Code [include the acronym, if commonly used]; utility rules and regulations; and all other applicable regulatory documents.

2. Nothing on the drawings or in the specifications shall be construed to allow work not in conformance with these rules, codes, and regulations.

3. The drawings and specifications shall take precedence where work and material described therein exceeds that required by rules, codes, or regulations.

b. Authority of [Your Company]

1. The authority of [your company] shall be absolute with respect to all performance under this specification. In case of dispute, the decision of [your company] shall be final.

2. Where optional materials, methods, or installation techniques are allowed under the provisions of this specification, they may be used at the discretion of [your company]. [Your company] may require specific materials, methods, or techniques be used in specific situations where use of other materials, methods, or techniques might in [your company's] judgment result in accidental damage, life safety hazard, loss of aesthetics, or loss of utility over the system design's lifetime.

3. No additional charges will be allowed for work or material required to be supplied under the conditions of this paragraph unless the need for such material or work could not have been anticipated by thorough study of the site, drawings, and specifications and through knowledge of all applicable codes, laws, and ordinances.

c. Permits, Fees, and Inspections

1. The contractor shall obtain all permits and licenses required and pay all fees incidental to construction.

2. Inspections shall be arranged by [your company] and the contractor. The contractor shall provide [your company] with a schedule of inspections, where applicable, and submit all certificates of inspection to [your company].

d. Guarantee

All electrical work, material, and equipment shall be guaranteed to be free from defects in workmanship or material for a period of five years from the date of final acceptance. The contractor shall repair or replace all such defects in a timely manner and any damage to the owner's property resulting from such defects or the repair thereof. All equipment and material provided and all work accomplished under the requirements of this section shall be at no expense to [your company].

e. As-Built Drawing

1. The contractor shall keep a separate set of electrical drawings at the job site to be used as "as-built drawings." These drawings are to be kept current and in a neat and clean condition at all times. They are to be available for inspection by [your company] or engineer at any time during site visitations. These drawings shall be "red-lined" to indicate all changes in equipment, devices, and outlet locations, and to indicate the true locations of all concealed or underground work where different from that shown on the drawings. Each sheet of this set shall be clearly and permanently marked "AS-BUILT."

2. Upon completion of the project and prior to final payment, the contractor shall purchase a fresh set of prints from [your company] and transfer all as-built information to it. All information shall be clearly drawn with ink. The contractor shall deliver the original and final as-built sets to the architect and [your company] for approval.

f. Pathways

1. In the instance where additional pathways must be installed, [your company] or the contractor will be notified. Parties installing data cable will not be held responsible for installation of data pathways, such as conduits and ladders.

2. Where conduits and ladders for data pathways are a distance of one foot or more from each other, a trapeze or suspension hook will be put in place to assist the pathway from the ladder to the conduit.

17. Products

a. Materials

1. Unless specifically indicated otherwise, all material shall be new and free from defects, it shall be listed by Underwriters' Laboratories where applicable, and it shall have been manufactured in the United States. Like

items shall be of the same manufacturer, except lighting fixtures, which should be as specified.

(Parts manufactured in the USA must adhere to strict standards. If you allow parts to be used that have been manufactured in other parts of the world, you run the risk of having parts with different chemical make-ups or substandard parts.)

2. Except as noted otherwise, where material of a particular manufacturer is specified, the intent is to describe the quality and function of the item. The term ". . . or approved equal" is implied. A substitution of any of these items will require that the item be presented in a submittal whether or not it is specifically listed in the "Submittals" paragraph below.

b. Submittals

1. Material submittals shall be complete and submitted all at the same time. The individual groups of submittal types, meaning such things as lighting fixtures, writing devices, and distribution equipment, MUST be prefaced with a list of contents identifying each item by its project name or symbol, manufacturer, and complete catalog number. Each copy of each submittal group shall have the list of contents attached. These lists will be used to report submittal comments. The contractor is responsible for submitting this information in a timely manner so that material may be ordered early enough to meet the construction schedule. If material is not ordered in time for whatever reason, pay such premium prices and special handling charges as are required to meet the construction schedule. No substitution of an "accepted" item will be allowed due to failure to plan for adequate material procurement lead time.

2. Submittals are required for at least the following items for both the fiber backbone and the copper runs: patch cables, patch panels, cable, jacks, wall plates, and drop cables.

3. Substitutions: Only one substitution will be considered for any item. Substitute materials must be equal in quality and function to that specified. Allowance of a substitution does not permit any reduction of system performance or utility, and the contractor is responsible for additional costs incurred due to use of a substituted item. If the proposed substitute item is "rejected," the specified item shall be provided. Note that resubmittal is required.

c. Sealing Penetrations

The contractor shall flash and counterflash roof and wall penetrations with equipment manufactured for the purpose and as described in other divisions of these specifications or as directed by [your company]. The contractor shall apply mastic as required to seal absolutely watertight.

d. Cutting and Patching

The contractor shall obtain [your company's] approval prior to cutting existing surfaces or surfaces under construction. All such surfaces must be repaired or patched to the satisfaction of the architect.

e. Protection, Cleaning, and Repairs

1. Protect all electrical equipment from damage or degradation during construction. Electrical equipment stored or installed shall be protected from dust, water, or damage from other sources.

2. After all other work has been accomplished and prior to final review by [your company], all electrical equipment, especially equipment enclosures, panel boards, switchboard, and communications system equipment, shall be thoroughly cleaned (inside and out) of all dirt, water, grease, plaster, paint, or other construction debris. All surfaces shall be clean and in "new" condition. All such defacements as scratches, dents, marks, and cracks shall be repaired to the satisfaction of [your company] or the equipment shall be replaced at no additional cost.

18. Acceptance of Bids

All bids must be sent to:

[Contact name in your company]

[Your company]

[Your company's contact's address]

[Your company's contact's phone]

[Your company's contact's FAX]

(Often this will be an unbiased third party who is charged with simply collecting the responses to the RFP.)

[Your company] reserves the right to reject any bids.

Appendix A: Cable Planning Information

For the last pages of your RFP, give the bidding vendors a listing of cable runs, lengths, ID numbers, and a sense of what you think the part numbers and associated costs should be. Listing the part numbers you want used ensures that you are comparing apples to apples and oranges to oranges when looking at the RFPs. You don't want Vendor Number One specifying one kind of wire, while Vendor Number Two specs another kind. Start them off as closely as possible and see what happens from there. You'll be able to tell if one or more of them are wildly off the mark if you have the parts and lengths listed within the RFP. Also, include blueprints showing the drops, like the one we showed on page 79.

The following portion of a page, from a simple database created in FileMaker Pro, can hold a listing of 45 drops. The spreadsheets tables can expand indefinitely for as many drops as are needed.

STC	Room	Drop	Position	Type	Length	
B118	B116	1	1	EN	30	B116.1.1
B118	B116	1	2	EN	30	B116.1.2
B118	B116	2	1	EN	39	B116.2.1
B118	B116	2	2	EN	39	B116.2.2
B118	B117	1	1	EN	32	B117.1.1
B118	B117	1	2	EN	32	B117.1.2
B118	B117	1	3	EN	32	B117.1.3
B118	B117	1	4	EN	32	B117.1.4
B118	B115	1	1	EN	75	B115.1.1
B118	B115	1	2	EN	75	B115.1.2
B118	B114	1	1	EN	53	B114.1.1
B118	B114	1	2	EN	53	B114.1.2
B118	B114	1	3	EN	53	B114.1.3
B118	B114	1	4	EN	53	B114.1.4
B118	B114	2	1	EN	69	B114.2.1

Cable Drop Information

The next page of the RFP should have your standard parts list built directly from your drop information. The page should have a table that derives all its information directly from the cabling list preceding it.

Qty	Manuf.	Model	Part #	
11	Allen Tel	For EN	AT1510-8C	RJ45/10 feet (24 AWG/Cat.5/plenum)
0	Allen Tel	For LT	AT1510-8C	RJ11/10 feet (24 AWG/Cat.5/plenum)
7	MOD-TAP	US 1	15-101-2	Surface, single-gang base, 2.75"W x4.5"L x1.85"H, W
7	MOD-TAP	N/A	17-0121-2	Single-gang bezel, 2.75"Wx4.5"Lx1.85"H
11	MOD-TAP	System 100	17.1B.017. B012 Cat. 5/568A	RJ45 Category 5, 568A 8 Position Data Jacks
	MOD-TAP	N/A	17-0433-2	Blanks, white
0.398	Belden		1585A	Cat.5, 24 AWG, plenum, 1,000 feet
1	Harris/ Dracon		46353-501	72"Hx19"W
1	Harris/ Dracon		10250-006	9'11.5" length, 6" width, 1.5" bar width, gray
2	MOD-TAP	Two position	25.B011G	Equipment shelf 17.3"Wx3.5"Hx8"D
1	Perma Power		J126A0-11	6', 12-outlets
1	APC	Smart-up 250 VA		175 WATTS, 2 outlets, 2.25"Hx11.9"Wx15.5"D
1	AMP	(32-port)	555501-1	rack-mount, 32-port
1	Panduit	2 Side Wire Mgmt	WMP1	rack-mount, front & rear management panel
1	Panduit	Bracket	WMBV1	2" Wire Mgmt bracket
11	Allen Tel	N/A	AT1503-8C	RJ45/3 feet (24 AWG/Cat.5/plenum)
0	Allen Tel	N/A	AT1503-8C	RJ11/3 feet (24 AWG/Cat.5/plenum)
17.5	Hours Labor			

Last Page of the RFP

Once you have created your RFP and sent it out to the different vendors, be ready to do your follow-up. Be ready to walk through the site with each vendor. Be ready to answer a slew of questions. Write down the questions from each of the vendors. Keep a tally of which vendors asked good questions, bad questions, and no questions. This will tell you a bit about the vendor's attitude toward this job.

As you walk the site with the vendor, ask how the vendor plans on bringing cable from the cross-connect to the jack. Ask the vendor about other jobs on which their company has worked, and ask if you can visit or see photos of some of the more recent ones. Follow up and talk to the clients. Go and see the work for yourself.

CHAPTER 6:
TOOLS YOU NEED

You are going to need a few tools to build your network, unless you are building a network using all infrared or all radio frequency devices. If you are building a completely IR- or RF-based network, just plug in the devices, make sure that they are aimed correctly for IR, and you are finished. Every other kind of network, however, takes some building materials. That's what we cover in this chapter. Here is what you *don't* really need:

- Extra cable: If you are building a hubbed network, buy cables that fit the length of the system you are building, especially if you are building an Ethernet network that won't require any punchdown jacks.

- An expensive pair scanner: You won't need this right away to tell you if the cabling is run correctly for 10BaseT. You can rent one, or hire someone to run your cabling who will also test it for you. Review the chapter entitled "Structured Wiring Systems," beginning on page 43, if you want more information on this topic.

- Electrical tape, 13-penny nails, 50-mile-an-hour packing tape, and spray paint: My father thinks you can build the Empire State Building with this stuff. He also thinks they can fix the rust on your car or hang a picture. Well, keep this stuff away from your network. It won't help you here.

Wall Jacks and Raceway

If you want to make your wiring neat and tidy as it comes down the walls, invest in some of the Panduit raceway system pieces. They look nice, install easily, and give your network a professional touch. The best thing they do is keep sloppy installers from stapling the cabling to the wall. That's fine if you do it well, but we have seen some *bad* stuff out there, right Barb, Cello, and Russ? The next picture shows an example of the Panduit system. There is the straight run section, the T-connector, the jack housing, and their own version of a Category 5 wiring jack.

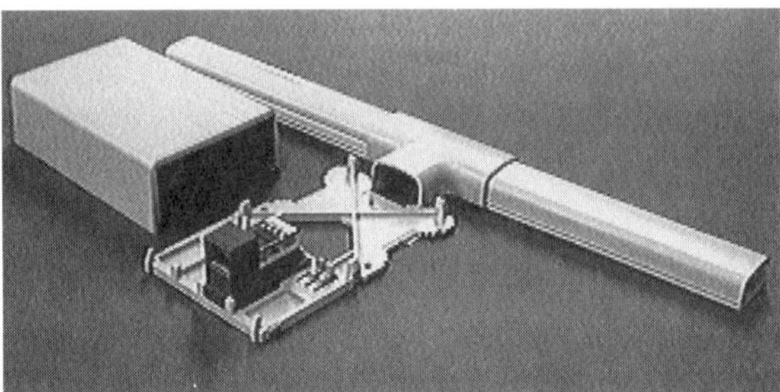

Panduit Raceway, Jack Housing, and Category 5 Jack

When building your network, you will quickly realize that there are many different jack types and jack housings out there, and that most of them don't fit with each other. Of course, all AT&T products fit with all AT&T products, and all Panduit products fit with all Panduit products, but you won't find a Panduit jack that fits in an AT&T wall mount, and vice versa. Good ol' competition strikes again! I love being a capitalist, but I hate it

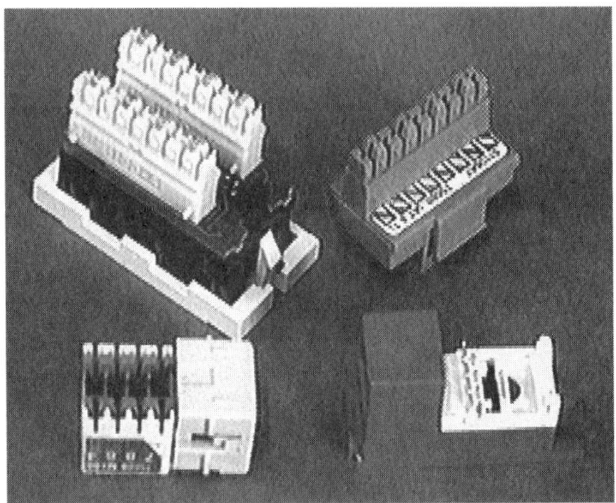

Different Jack Types

when others act like capitalists. In the preceding picture, we show some of the jack types. These jack types are *all* Category 5, and, except for the Panduit brand, they all utilize the 110 punchdown pinouts for Category 5. Some of them are jacked for 568B and some are jacked for 568A. On the top left is a jack from Mod-TAP. I don't know if you can tell from the picture, but it is on a printed circuit board! On the bottom left is the AT&T jack. It is different from the Mod-TAP and the AMP (top right) jacks in that the 110 connectors are side by side. This allows the installer to make the jack's connections nice and tidy. That doesn't *ensure* that they will be nice and tidy, but it makes it more feasible.

Also shown in the preceding picture is the Panduit connector, on the bottom right. Its connectors are *not* 110; they are proprietary to Panduit. On the one hand, we like the Panduit products because they are easy to use and look nice when implemented correctly. Also, we like that their jack housings have enough room in them for the wires to be bent within the Category 5 specifications. On the other hand, notice how Panduit jacks are built. The jacks are in two parts—the body and the labeled top. Look at the two in the next picture. Notice the difference? Some of them are straight through and the others are cross over. If you have both types, make sure to keep the tops matched with the bottoms, or all hell will break loose.

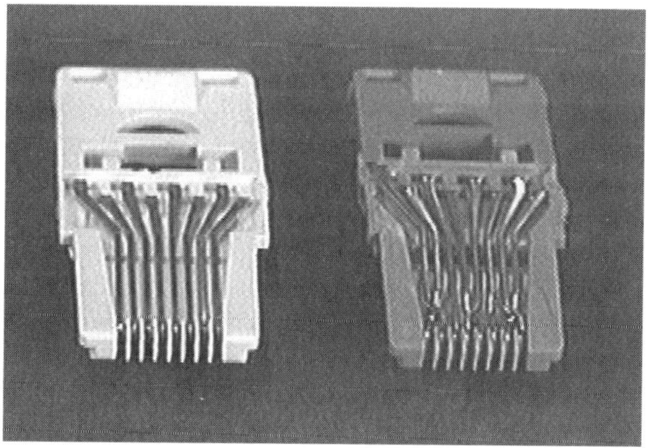

Disassembled Panduit Jacks Showing Straight Through (left) and Cross Connected (right)

Cable Cutters and Markers for Jacks and Cables

When creating a LocalTalk trunk, you need something to trim the PVC coating off the wires, and then to trim the wires without cutting them. A simple cable cutter will do, like the one shown on the right in the following set of picture. Once you get the hang of working with them, you shouldn't have any problems, especially as they are spring-loaded to stay open. You also need a screwdriver—you can use the one next to your hammer and 13-penny nails—and something with which to mark the cables and jacks.

When putting together the trunk cable, you don't want to cut it. You want to trim it to fit within the jack. On the left in the following set of pictures, I show what it looks like when you have the cables trimmed back and the pairs ready to be moved out of the way. Don't cut them. Use the green pair in a four-pair cable, or the black and yellow in a two-pair cable. Keep them twisted. Usually the twists show which wires can be used the easiest. Next, label them as to which wire leads to which wall jack in the series. As far as labelers go, I like the pre-numbered peel-off kind from Panduit.

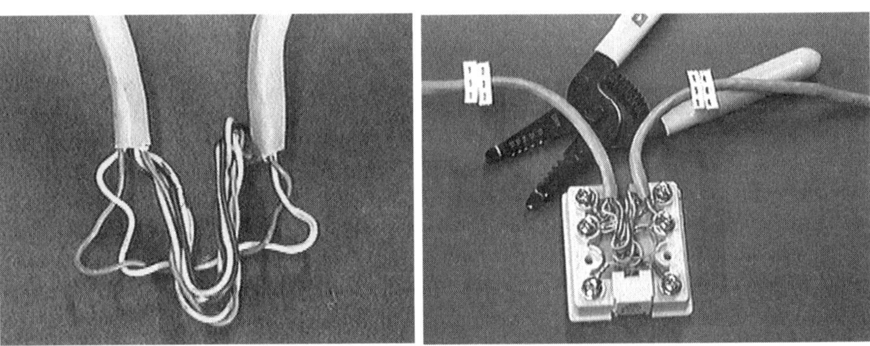

Trunk Cable Ready-to-Go (left) and In Place in the Jack (right)

120-Ohm or 50-Ohm (Coax) Resistors

Whatever you do, don't forget your resistors. If you are using daisy chain coax, you will want resistors labeled 50 ohm. If you are using LocalTalk, you will want to have 120-ohm resistors. Either way, make sure that you have more of them on hand than you think you will need. Trust me, you will need more of them before you know it. I don't know why, but resistors seem to disappear. In our office, Lynn seems to think that they go and hang out with that extra sock you can't find from the laundry. I think they end up in user's desk drawers. Everyone has a theory. Anyway, the following snappy picture is what your LocalTalk resistors should look like. You have my permission to use this picture to create an APB and hang it on the wall at the Post Office.

120-Ohm Resistor

Unmounted and Mounted
LocalTalk Resistor

Spare Transceivers, NICs, and Cables

Network cards don't often break, unless you plug the wrong thing into them, which reminds me of a guy I knew who kept plugging his monitor into his Ethernet port and wondered why it didn't work. I also have personally witnessed some clod-footed bozo trip over his own transceiver drop cable *several* times during a class lecture. Of course I didn't bring an extra one on that trip. I hate that. The point here is that you should always have an extra transceiver and an extra cable to go with it. You never know when you will need it.

Latest and Greatest AppleTalk Network Installer

While building a network at a school, I began to wonder why the Ethernet routers were acting up after I put them in and why the computers on the network were now having a hard time. Then I noticed it: System 6 on a bunch of computers. Like the good little packet head that I am, I whipped out my trusty packet analyzer and, *voila*, Phase1 EtherTalk. That's bad news for Phase2 networks. Phase1 hasn't been around for, oh, I don't know, I'd guess at least five years. But there it was, right in front of me, and there I was without any upgrade disks. The point, kiddies, is to ensure that you have the most current, appropriate network driver, and that you install it on the computers of the Ethernet users on your network. You can usually find these drivers on all the major bulletin boards and the WWW. Of course, if you can't find it there, you can always call us. We have it here.

Tie-Downs, Rollerpads, and the Like

I fully believe in tie-downs and roller pads. There is a company around the corner from us that I want to mention here—Rip-Tie. This is a great company, and the owner is really nice to boot. They make velcro add-ons. When I spec a network, I usually have to argue with the client about putting Rip-Tie velcro ties on their computer cables until they see them in action. Once shown the difference, I don't get an argument.

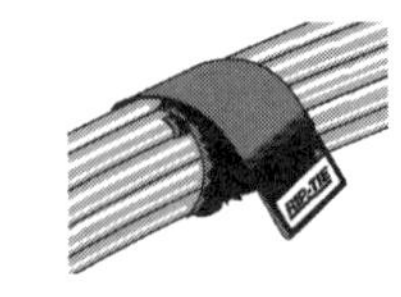

There are two types of Rip-Tie product. One is for wrapping around bundles of cables, and the other has a sticky side for mounting on walls and using as a cable run support. I like using the kind with the sticky stuff as the cable run support on long desks. In this way, the cables are kept off the ground. I use the cable wrap product to keep all the cables coming off the back of my computer tied together into a simple system. It makes these cables easier to manage, and keeps them from becoming cluttered.

Regular Rip-Tie Cable Wrap (top); and Wall-Mount Cable Wrap (bottom)

MicroTest PentaScanner

How do you know whether your cabling is installed correctly? The only real answer to the question is to test the cabling with a piece of equipment capable of doing the job. The one we think is the best is the PentaScanner from MicroTest.

The PentaScanner is actually a two-piece unit. The piece shown on the right is what we call the "master" unit because it has all the buttons for the commands, as well as the device screen that shows the results. There is another piece that comes with this, which is more or less the slave unit. This second piece is placed on one side of the cable being tested and the master unit is placed on the other side. The tests are run from the master unit first, and then the master unit sends a command down the wire and the tests are run from the opposite end. A cable scanner must run its tests from both ends, or it's not worth it. If tests aren't run from both ends, how do you know if the cabling is any good? Not only does this device test for Category 5, but also for 10BaseT, coax, and even LocalTalk. It's a great device.

MicroTest PentaScanner

Chapter 7: Sample Cable Plant Implementations

In this implementation chapter, I want to cover the different networking options, and help you see what we do when we are creating a network for a client. I want to weigh the pros and cons for each of the different types of cabling schemes so that you can see why we make some of our decisions. We will break down this chapter into the following:

- Networking the conference room

- Networking the small lab

- Networking the cubicled office

- Networking the training room

- Small office structured wiring systems

NETWORKING THE CONFERENCE ROOM

Most companies have conference rooms, and sometimes they are networked. Take, for example, a conference room with two hardware services in it. One of the services is the familiar PostScript printer. The other is a service that *should be* familiar, a SoftBoard. This thing is great. You write on it with standard dry-erase markers, and everything you write is sent to computers connected to it on the LAN, or even on the WAN with special software and a hookup.

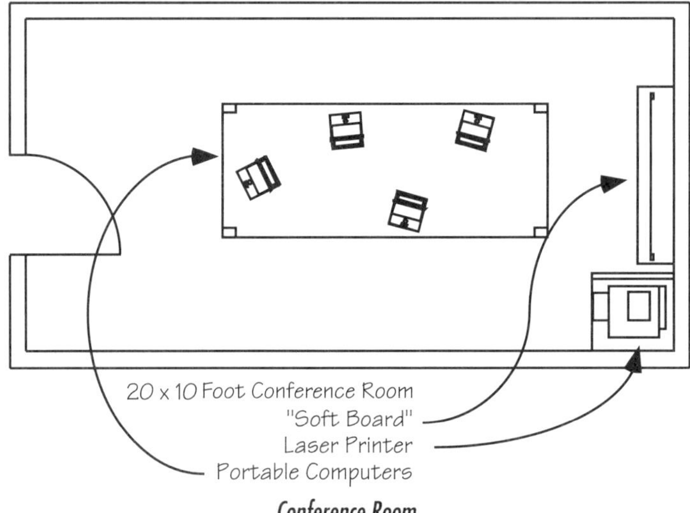

Conference Room

When networking conference rooms, the problem is usually that most of the devices in the conference room, such as the computers themselves, aren't there when the room is not in use. People bring in their portable computers, set up a network, work for a while, and then leave. Well, this is one of the best reasons I can think of for IR or RF networking! You can equip the permanent devices with standard network gear, and then equip the room itself with a cable-to-IR or RF bridge. If you have multiple conference rooms in the same vicinity, your best bet is RF. With RF, you can attach a single wire-to-RF bridge in, say, the central room, and then have the peripheral rooms use that device as a connecting point to the rest of the network. Remember, RF goes through walls and can travel about 120 feet when you have many walls, like you would with distributed meeting rooms. If you have a single meeting room, a cable-to-IR or RF "bridge" will work.

I don't like daisy-chaining everything, or other types of "wired" solutions, because the biggest part of the network isn't there at all times. When it *is* there, if you ran a "wired" network, you would have to run a wire or a set of wires from the wall to the desk, and someone—usually me—is bound to trip on the wire. The following picture is a bird's-eye view of the conference room with IR connectors, mostly because IR is all I could draw. I'll explain each numbered piece in the picture.

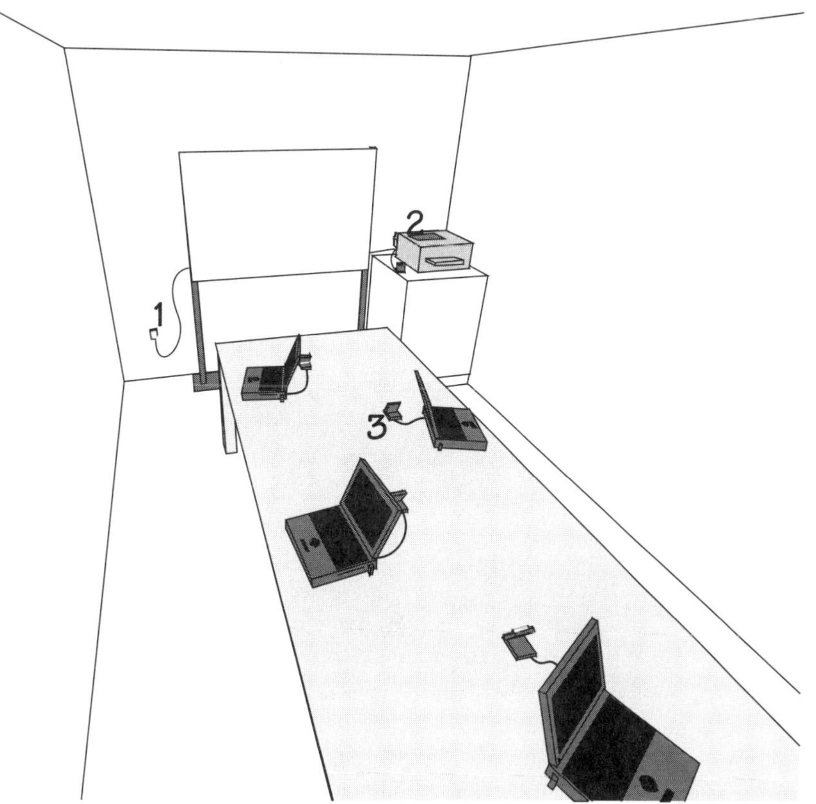

Bird's-Eye View of the Conference Room

1. This is the regular LAN connection. It's a wall jack with a single LAN cable coming out of it. You would use this as your base back to the rest of the network. Usually, there is only one LAN connection into the room. You *could*

always skip the daisy chain part and have the SoftBoard, printer, and RF or IR connection have their own drop cable, but nobody ever seems to want to do that. Since this connection ties back to the rest of the network, and since the RF bridge doesn't support a coax connection, stick with twisted pair wiring for the cable portion of this network design.

2. If this is a LocalTalk network, you can easily daisy-chain the SoftBoard device, the printer, and the LocalTalk-to-IR adapter for the Photonics Cooperative processor. If this is an Ethernet network, you could use the Farallon Ether-Wave or the Tut Silver Streak to create a three-port daisy chain. Instead of using the LAN-to-IR connector with the Photonics device, you would have to use the Starfish RF bridge. Don't put this on the shelf with the printer. If using the RF Bridge, you could easily daisy-chain it off an EtherWave or Silver Streak, but either way, you would want to mount it higher on the wall. The RF bridge includes a wall-mounting kit.

3. Finally, these could be the Photonics Cooperative processors for IR or the Digital Ocean transceivers. Both products have Mac and PC equivalents. Both products can take their power from the computers to which they are attached or they could work off batteries long enough to finish a meeting. If they don't hold out, what a great reason for cutting the meeting short!

Cabling Plant

The cabling plant for this network is simple. If you are linking back to a regular LAN, all you need is a single drop to the room. From there, use daisy chain connectors and IR or RF transceivers. Because IR and RF transceivers tend to "walk" in larger companies, make them "checkout" items available only when using the room. Some companies have these transceivers in a box at the secretary's desk. When a user wants to use the room and bring in computers, he or she "checks out" the room and the networking equipment. It is then checked back in when the users are finished with the room.

Cost Table

The following tables should help you budget for the small networks just discussed. These are for six computers and one printer. Again, we do not include the printer in the "services" section, although we do price the SoftBoard for you.

	Qty.	Manuf.	Model	Part #	Description	Cost/ea.	Total Cost
Cables	5	Allen Tel	NA	AT1210-6C	RJ-11, 10-foot, 24 AWG	$3.60	$18.00
	1	Dar-Tek	Serial Cable	NA	DB8-to-DB8 cable from workstation to board	$11.50	$11.50
Jacks	1	Mod-Tap	USO Multimedia Components	17-0121-2	Single gang bezel, white, 2.75" W × 4.5" L × 1.85" H	$1.23	$1.23
	1	Mod-Tap	System 100	17-51-60-62	RJ-11, double modules, white	$11.50	$11.50
	2	Mod-Tap	USO Multimedia Components	17-0433-2	Blanks, white	$0.38	$0.76
Transceivers	6	Photonics	Cooperative Adapter	21861	Infrared transceiver	$109.95	$659.20
	2	Farallon	PhoneNET Connector	NA	2-port LocalTalk transceiver	$11.95	$23.90
Hubs	1	Photonics	Cooperative Access	21950	LocalTalk-to-IR hub	$159.90	$159.90
Services	1	Microfield	SoftBoard	Model 201	Stationary white board	$3,295.00	$3,295.00
						Total Cost:	**$4,169.99**

Cabling Costs for Infrared Conference Room

	Qty.	Manuf.	Model	Part #	Description	Cost/ea.	Total Cost
Cables	2	Allen Tel	NA	AT1210-8C	RJ-45, 10 feet, 24 AWG, CAT5	$3.32	$6.64
	1	Dar-Tek	Serial Cable	NA	DB8-to-DB8 cable from workstation to board	$11.50	$11.50
Jacks	1	Mod-Tap	USO Multimedia Components	17-0121-2	Single gang bezel, white, 2.75" W × 4.5" L × 1.85" H	$1.23	$1.23
	1	Mod-Tap	System 100	17-1B-027.B012	CAT5, 568A, double modules, white	$10.35	$10.35
	2	Mod-Tap	USO Multimedia Components	17-0433-2	Blanks, white	$0.38	$0.76
Transceivers	6	Digital Ocean	Manta	500EN	Radio frequency transceiver, Ethernet remote station	$799.00	$4,794.00
	2	Farallon	EtherWave	DET1061	2-port Ethernet transceiver	$109.00	$218.00
Hubs	1	Digital Ocean	Starfish	1000TA	Ethernet radio frequency hub, Ethernet access point	$1,800.50	$1,800.50
Services	1	Microfield	SoftBoard	Model 201	Stationary white board	$3,295.00	$3,295.00
						Total Cost:	**$10,137.98**

Cabling Costs for Radio Frequency Conference Room

NETWORKING THE SMALL LAB

Okay, every office has one. When I worked at Price Waterhouse, even though we had computers on every desk, we still had that one office with a couple of computers and some printers forming the "Mac Design Center." Hee, hee, hee . . . I loved that room. The designers sat there and worked on all sorts of great graphic designs and presentations and then gave them to the partners. The partners would in turn take the designs, add their own fonts and graphics (you know the rule: Use as many fonts on a page as you have loaded in your computer), and proceed to make a professional project look like something "Mikey" put together while eating cereal. So, why give others access to this material? Why let the partners mess up what has been refined in the lab? Because this is the real world, and while planning the rest of the company network, you will probably have to deal with that single lab issue again and again. When the office starts to branch out, the first thing to be networked is that lab. So, here's a floor plan for a small lab within a small office. We focus only on networking the lab here.

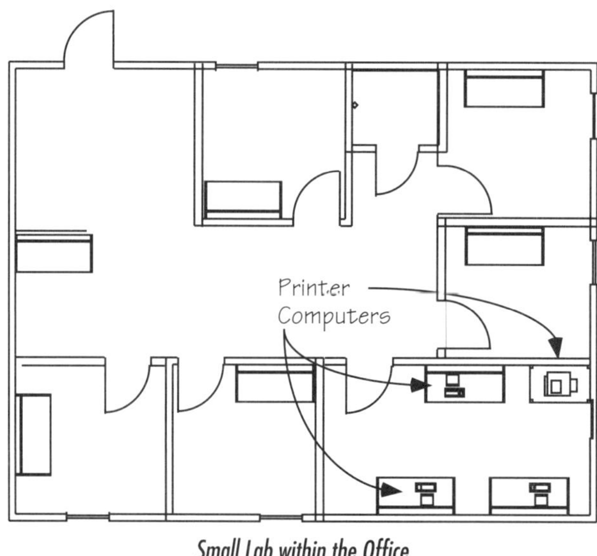

Small Lab within the Office

If the lab is being networked *first* in an office, and the rest of the office will be planned and installed later, you probably won't have to worry about anything like drops or feeds. If you design the lab correctly, all the desks for the various computers and printers will be facing the wall. This will facilitate creating a perimeter daisy chain within the room. By using something like the Rip-Tie product (see page 112), you can fasten the daisy-chained cables of the network to the outside walls so that nobody trips on them. That is the design we show you here. The following picture shows a small lab with computers and a printer being connected with a daisy chain network. All the computers look like a MacPlus because at the time I drew the network, that was all I could draw. You will have to use your imagination for Ethernet, too. If you want something different, come draw it for me; e-mail me and I'll give you the format.

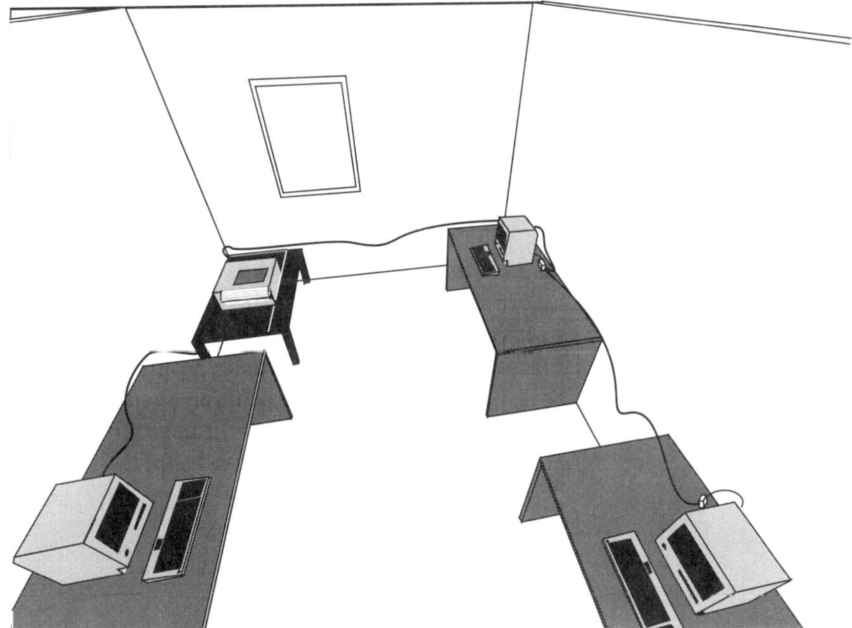

Bird's-Eye View of Computer Lab

This one is so simple that it doesn't even need to have numbered items in it. There is only the daisy-chained network. If that is LocalTalk, ThinNet, or twisted pair, the only parts are the cables, connectors, and terminators, if necessary. Pretty simple, huh? You betcha.

Cabling Plant

If the computers aren't using LocalTalk, they will need a transceiver. Even if the computer has a 10BaseT connection port on the CPU, you will need an Ether-Wave, a Tut Silver Streak, or a plain old ThinNet transceiver, as you are using a daisy chain topology. Some of the computers that don't have Ethernet cards might already have a ThinNet port on the back. This is a consideration when deciding which type of network you want to install. Here is the breakdown:

- For LocalTalk, you need a LocalTalk connector for each computer, the appropriate length of cable, and a terminator at *both ends* of the network. Don't ever loop the cable back in on the first and last computers, thus forming a circle. That will break the network. For costs, see the table on page 22.

- For ThinNet, you need a BNC-type transceiver, or a card with one. You also need a T-connector for each device and a 50-ohm terminator at each end, unless you use the Apple AAUI ThinNet transceivers. Again, no looping. For costs, see the table on page 29.

- If you are going with EtherWaves, you need an EtherWave transceiver for each device, and the appropriate length of cable. Printers use a special Ether-Wave, so make sure that you have one equipped for the printers. Yes, Tom, I know you guys make LocalTalk-to-Ethernet EtherWaves, but we aren't going to discuss them right now. We are dealing with either Ethernet or LocalTalk. For costs, see the table on page 31.

- If you are going to use Tut Silver Streak, you need a Silver Streak connector for each computer, the appropriate length of cable, and a terminator at *both ends* of the network. Don't form a circle by looping the cable back in on the first and last computers. That will break the network. (Heard this before?) Again, for costs, see the table on page 33.

So, what about IR or RF in this situation? Usually, if you have a bunch of computers stacked together in a room, it means that they are doing some intense work. Therefore, you will want the fastest network possible, like Ethernet. If speed isn't an issue, then the IR and RF configurations work well. I'm not showing them here because I want to show daisy chain solutions. That's all.

NETWORKING THE CUBICLED OFFICE

In this section, I want to show you a trunk network and cover the implementation and costs of such a network. The cubed office in the following picture is a perfect example for a LocalTalk trunk network. The office is a "shotgun" office and one wall of the office can be utilized easily for trunk cabling. Notice that most of the walls are half-walls, and that the computers share a common bottom wall, or are lined up with the half-walls. This is an advantage when networking. If, for some reason, you decide to completely cheap-out on your network, you could theoretically build a daisy chain for LocalTalk or Ethernet in this office. The biggest hurdle, though, would be those half-walls. Tossing a cable over them is both ugly and inefficient design—inefficient in the sense that cables going over walls could cause them to break or kink easily. What you need here is a cable system inside Panduit conduit that runs down the walls, looking good. That's what we are going to show you here.

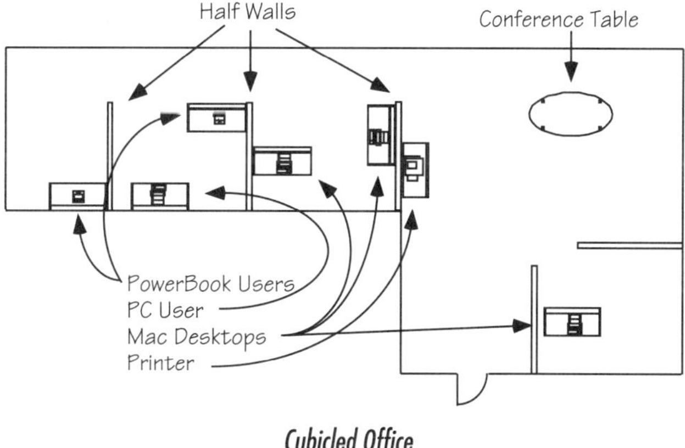

Cubicled Office

Cabling Plant

The cabling plant, as mentioned earlier, will be for LocalTalk, and we aren't talking flat wire cable here, either. We are talking gen-u-ine unshielded twisted pair (UTP) wire, preferably Category 3 for stability and good signal strength.

Measurement

When measuring this wire, remember to start at one end and measure from 18 inches off the ground up to the point where you want to begin running it horizontally. Next, measure along the walls until the next drop-down point. When you reach that next drop-down point, measure it twice, going down and then back up again, and add about two inches for stripped-back wire. The easiest way to do this is to measure all the horizontal runs, and then add the standard length for each drop. Remember, both end drops need to measured only once; they go down and don't need to come back up again. This should give you the measurement for the number of feet of Panduit surface-mount raceway that you will need. Don't forget to include all the Panduit T-connectors for drops and elbow joints at the corners. A one-inch wide piece of Panduit should do just fine.

Dual Jacks, if Necessary

If you have drops that require dual jacks, save yourself some cabling and Panduit costs and buy a jack housing and jack that can hold two receptacles. All you have to do is run the cable down, loop one jack, loop the other jack, and then run the cable back up. Make sure that you give yourself an extra four inches of cable when running a second jack.

Labeling

When installing the cable in the jack, label the jack, and then label the cable itself with the number of the jack to which it is run. Otherwise, there will be no easy way to figure out which of the two cables coming down the drop goes left or right.

Drop Cables

If you are smart, you will take your leftover wire and have RJ-11 jacks placed on both ends to make drop cables. Having UTP drop cables made from the same wire as your trunk is a great way to ensure that the characteristic impedance of the cables stays the same. I suppose you could use the flat wire patch cables that came with your StarConnectors or PhoneNET cables for your telephones. Like somebody near and dear to my heart once suggested, another option is to paste them all over yourself for Halloween and go as a wiring geek. The point is that I don't care what you do with them as long as you remove them from your network.

Termination

Finally, terminate the two ends of the trunk network. The easiest way to do that is to put a 120-ohm terminator in the final wall jack. If you do it that way, place the terminator across the two pins used for your LocalTalk cabling. Otherwise, use a PhoneNET connector at both ends with a terminator in it. You will have to make sure that no one takes it off the network. The last option is to make sure that both ends have StarConnectors, which is what we prefer.

When finished, your network cabling plant should look something akin to the one shown in the following picture. For you purists out there, you will have to bear with my drawing capabilities. I know this drawing shows a cable that looks like it is just lying on the floor. If you design the system right, you will have the cable tied up with a Rip-Tie or covered. I will describe the numbered items next.

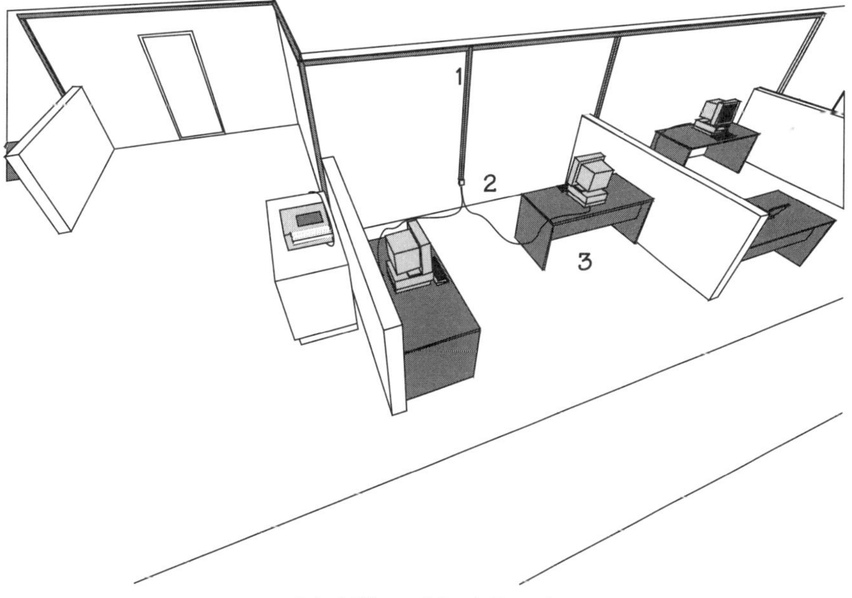

Cubed Office with Trunk Network

1. This is trunk cabling within Panduit raceway. Notice how it follows the contours of the office wall and is run high enough so that it clears the door.

2. This is the wall jack at the bottom of the conduit raceway. The one shown has two jacks inside of it.

3. This is the drop cable going to the computer. The drop cable should be hooked to the computer with the same type of cable used to create the trunk network. The PhoneNET connector type we prefer is the StarConnector, as it has only one connection and won't allow any further daisy-chaining.

Cost Table

Here are some costs associated with the trunk network we just discussed. This is for seven computers and one printer.

	Qty.	Manuf.	Model	Part #	Description	Cost/ea.	Total Cost
Patch Cords	8	Allen Tel	NA	AT1510-8C	RJ-45, 10-foot, 24 AWG, CAT5	$3.32	$26.56
Jacks	8	Allen Tel	Simplex	AT468-8	Surface, single outlet for RJ-45	$1.84	$14.72
Surface-Mount Raceway	20	Panduit	PAN-WAY	T3B4.5X1WH6A	Adhesive or mounted base raceway, 4.5" W × 6' L	$3.61	$433.20
	20	Panduit	PAN-WAY	T3B4.5X1WH6A	Snap-on cover, white, 1" H × 4.5" W × 6' L	$2.00	$240.00
	1	Panduit	PAN-WAY	CDC10-L	Mounting clips, 50-pack, 0.25" screw holes	$55.12	$55.12
	18	Panduit	PAN-WAY	T3CF4.5X1WH	Coupling, white	$2.40	$43.20
	2	Panduit	PAN-WAY	T3ECF4.5X1WH	End cap, white	$3.30	$6.60
	1	Panduit	PAN-WAY	T3OCF4.5X1WH	Outside corner, white	$5.20	$5.20
	3	Panduit	PAN-WAY	T3ICF4.5X1WH	Inside corner, white	$5.00	$15.00
	8	Panduit	PAN-WAY	T3TRF4.5X1WH	Junction box, white	$6.45	$51.60
	8	Panduit	PAN-WAY	LD10WH6A	1.5" W × 6' L base, white	$1.45	$69.60
	8	Panduit	PAN-WAY	CD10WH6	1.5" W × 6' L cover, white	$1.24	$59.52
Horizontal Cabling	240	Berk-Tek	NA	5NP4P24GYPBERPV	4-pair, 24 AWG, non-plenum, price per foot	$0.74	$177.60
						Total Cost:	**$1,197.92**

Costs for Trunk Network

NETWORKING THE TRAINING ROOM

Now we move on to the training room or regular classroom—the layout could be used for either. We won't be finished with this training room network design after this section. We will revisit it again after we have looked at standard network designs for regular rooms. In this section, we are going to design a LocalTalk network. With Ethernet there are *many* different options, and we will want to tackle them separately. The following picture shows the training room floor plan as we have designed it, and next I will go over each numbered item.

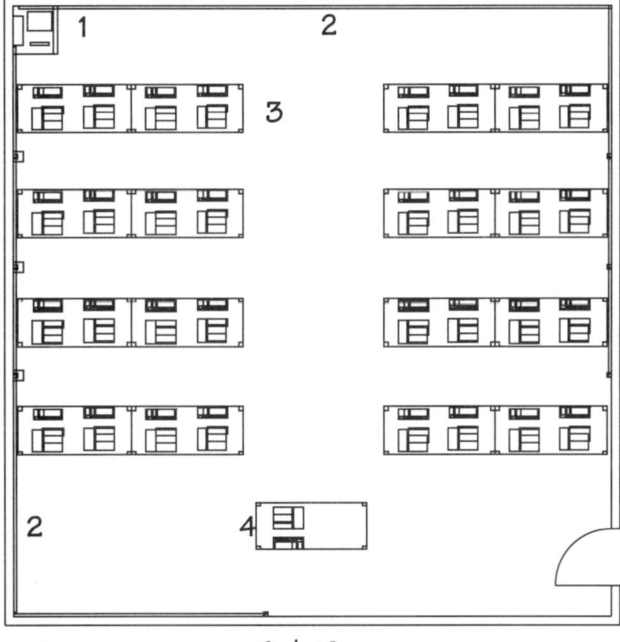

Student Room

1. This is the teacher's closet with a hub or switch on top, along with the appropriate patch panels. All cables are home run down the conduit to the wall jacks. There are four cables per row, or one for each computer in the row.

2. This is the horizontal conduit with drop conduit going between the rows. Conduit is connected at each junction by a junction box large enough to accommodate the appropriate bend radii for cables. The conduit is also wide enough to support whatever multiple runs need to go through it.

3. These are the computers on regular desks. The desks should be outfitted with velcro fasteners on the backs of the tables so that the drop cables can be run from the wall jacks to the tables without being dropped on the floor. The Rip-Tie brand of fasteners gives you the flexibility to remove cables, if necessary.

4. This is the teacher's desk. This is where you bring the apple only so that you can get out of staying after school to clean the chalkboard. Unless, of course, the teacher is *my* second-grade teacher, Miss Kelley, whom I adored—then you bring the apple because you love your teacher. God bless you, Miss Kelley, wherever you are.

Hub System

We are going to break the hub system down into hub, patch panels and patch cables, home run cables, drop cables, and StarConnector jacks.

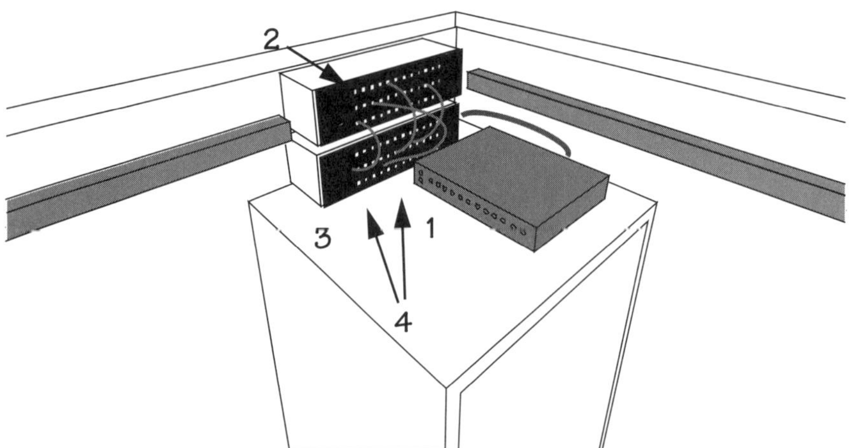

Hub System for the Classroom Located on Top of a Teacher's Closet

1. This is the hub or switch. If you have 1–24 computers in your classroom, you could probably use a standard LocalTalk hub. I've found that 12 computers

at work at once in a classroom is a bit tricky. Thus, I'd recommend looking at switch solutions, namely the TribeStar, when you have more than 17 computers. Our network design, shown in the preceding picture, is for 32 student computers. With more than 24 computers, the TribeStar is a must. Whichever hub you decide to use, put it in one corner of the room, preferably on top of some sort of cabinet or closet. The drawing shows our hub mounted on top of one such teacher's cabinet along with the two prerequisite patch panels. One of our network designs for a local high school and two junior high schools went as far as having custom louvered panels built on top of the closet, along with a locked door. This is to keep the little monsters, uh, I mean the darling children, off the hub and its associated patch panels. You can bet that they are going to get their hands on anything they can find.

2. This is the cross-connect panel or the patch panel. Wires running out to the walls jacks are terminated on one end in this type of panel. The wires come in the back, and have RJ-11 or RJ-45 jacks on the front. Different patch panels available on the market today are able to accommodate from 12–120 devices. Choose one that can hold at least 36 devices. Yes, I know you only have 32 students, but there are also such devices as the printer, and the teacher's computer. If this isn't the kind of patch panel that bolts to the wall, you will need a wall-mount swing-out rack to bolt it down, and some bolts.

3. This patch panel is the one that connects via amphenol cable to your Star-Controller or your LocalSwitch. In the picture, that's the amphenol cable coming out the back of the hub on top of the teacher's cabinet.

4. These are patch cables. To connect the cross-connect panel to the patch panel you need patch cables. They don't normally come with your hub or switch, so you will have to make a trip to your local GraybaR. If you are smart, you will have had them made from the cable left over after the room's cabling plant has been run. You know the drill by now: You want your cables' characteristic impedances to match as closely as possible.

Cabling Plant

Just like we broke the hub system down into a few constituent parts, we are going to break down the cabling plant into its constituent parts. We will divide it into horizontal and drop cable raceway, junction boxes, wall jacks, home run cables, and then drop cables and StarConnectors. The following picture shows what the network might look like if run this way.

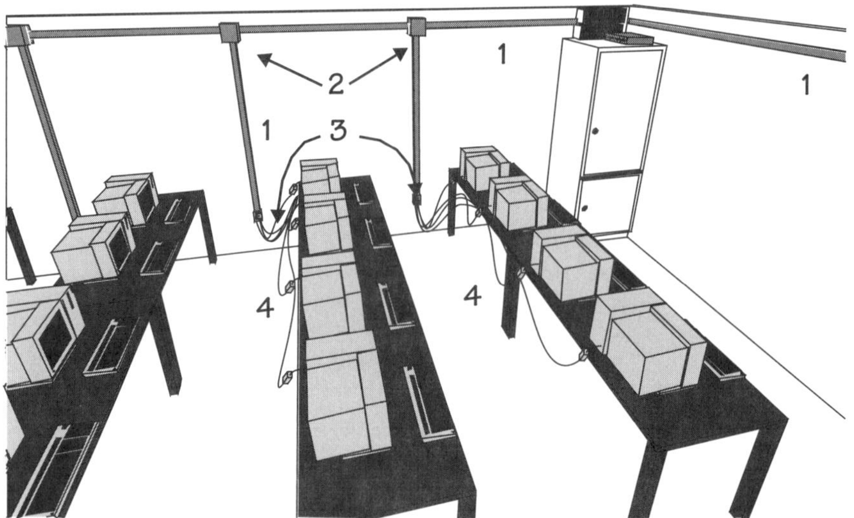

Student Room Side View

1. This is the horizontal and vertical Panduit raceway with cabling inside. This is the same type of raceway we used for the trunk network. This time, however, obtain wide enough raceway for the number of cables you will be running. A trunk network only runs one cable horizontally and the same cable twice vertically. This time, if you have a network with 32 computers, and you are running cabling up one side of the room for up to 18 of them, that section of Panduit nearest the hub has to be able to accommodate all 18 cables. After the first horizontal drop, you will lose four cables. After the next drop, you will lose another four and so on until you reach the end of the run. Greasing them and forcing them into the conduit isn't the appropriate plan here, either. For Category 5 networks, there is a whole table of information about the number of cables that can fit into any given trade-size conduit, but we already covered that back in the section called "Conduit Sizes and Bends" starting on page 58. If you are going to wire one of these networks, you might as well wire it for Category 5 today, even if you are simply using LocalTalk. You will probably change the network at a later date, and you will be the hero because you saved your organization the cost of rewiring for the move to Fast Ethernet.

2. Because four cables at a time are making a 90° bend from the horizontal run to the vertical drop, you need some bending room. The easiest way to do this is to attach what is known as a *junction box* at each bend. Putting a simple T-connector on the raceway won't cut it, or as a matter of fact, just might cut into your cables as they bend. A good rule of thumb is to have the diameter of the junction box be four times the diameter of the surface-mount raceway.

3. These are the wall jacks with data jacks within them. Hey, all you cheapskates, don't skimp here. If you are going to use this type of network, use CAT5 jacks. Remember that thing I said a while back about LocalTalk? You never know when you might just move this classroom to Fast Ethernet and you will need the Category 5 wiring system to do it. Also, use wall jacks that are modular or support up to six connections a piece. Even though you will only be putting four in them at this time, you might want that extra device in each of the rows at a later date. Don't forget to label these wall jacks, too. Whatever label is on the wall jack should correspond to a label on the cross-connect panel. Put a label on the wires themselves, just in case the wires separate from the wall jacks. Trust me, it happens.

4. These are the drop cables and StarConnectors. Want to take two guesses about what I'm going to say the drop cables should be made of? Your first guess doesn't count if it wasn't "the same stuff as the horizontal cable and patch cables." Drop cables should never be longer than 20 feet. It says so right in the Category 5 standard, which you should be following when building your network. You will need StarConnectors on each of your computers. If you don't plan on moving your computers any time soon, and don't plan on taking the StarConnectors off them, you can forgo putting 120-ohm resistors on each of the data jacks in the wall. If you are using 110 style punchdown jacks for possible Category 5 usage later, you can't put resistors on them anyway, as the resistors ruin the jacks.

Finally, to make everything tidy, tie down drop cables with Rip-Tie velcro fasteners on the desks.

Standard Classroom with Ethernet or LocalTalk

Now we will take the same standard school classroom or training room and network it for Ethernet. I won't go into the System Folder stuff you need, even though you didn't need any for a LocalTalk network. Instead, I will explore different methods for networking this same room with a few Ethernet products mixed together. I will also give you some cost-related reasons for why you might not want one method over another. Knowing that we can put 32 students, one teacher, and a printer in the room, we came up with a plan to network the room so that each classroom can become its own LAN. First, we will use EtherWaves and then we will use Apple minihubs. Afterwards, we explain how to wire the network, and we'll examine the costs for each option, comparing apples to apples and noting the changes each plan would introduce—in other words, the oranges. We hope that doing this will show you how to justify using one plan over the other.

Notice a miniature wiring center with three Ethernet hubs on top of the standard teacher's closet in the top right of the following diagram. The room has a total of 33 computers: four rows of four computers each, plus a teacher's computer at the front of the room. If we were to design the room using a standard Ethernet or CAT5 network design, this would mean that each computer in the room would have a cable running to the computer. That is what we have shown here.

The same classroom could be designed using LocalTalk instead of Ethernet by switching out the Ethernet hubs with the Tribe LocalSwitches or TribeStars, and switching out the Ethernet transceivers for LocalTalk StarConnectors. With plain LocalTalk hubs in the classroom, the concentration of computers and the likelihood of collisions on LocalTalk increases. Therefore, it is best to put classrooms on LocalTalk into a LocalTalk switched environment.

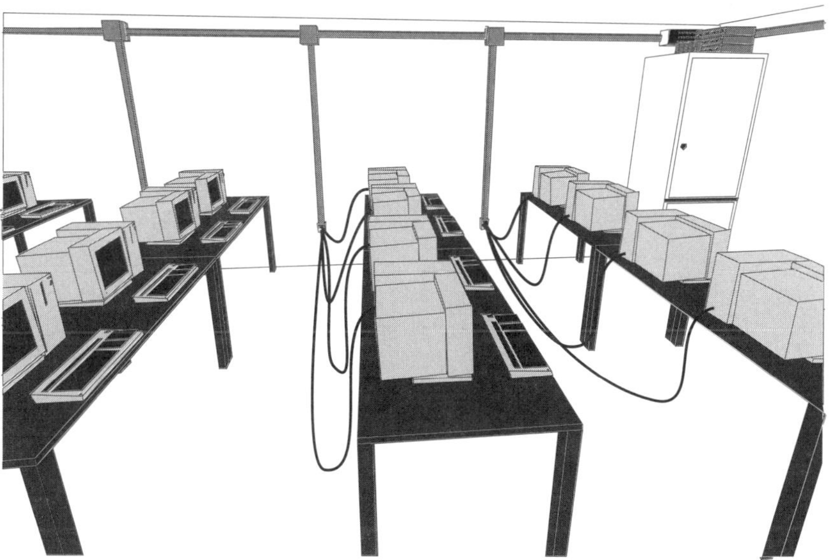

Standard Network Design

Cost Tables

Okay, the basic design is presented, and we have gone over it a few times already, so let's take a look at what it would cost to network this room. In the listings of the different wiring cables that run from the classroom hub to the computers, remember that there are two sides of the room, although you are only looking at one in the previous picture. Thus, there are four rows with eight computers each separated by about eight feet each. Remember, this is for 34 devices—32 student computers, one teacher's computer, and a printer. The first table is for LocalTalk and the second is for Ethernet.

	Qty.	Manuf.	Model	Part #	Description	Cost/ea.	Total Cost
Drop Cords	16	Allen Tel	NA	AT1210-6C	RJ-11, 10 feet	$3.60	$57.60
	14	Allen Tel	NA	AT1220-6C	RJ-11, 20 feet	$6.93	$97.02
	30	Farallon	PhoneNET Connector		2-port LocalTalk transceiver	$11.95	$358.50
Jacks	8	Panduit	PAN-WAY	MFPW4WH	4-port face plate	$2.02	$16.16
	30	Panduit	PAN-JACK	MUJC588WH	CAT5, 568B, white jack	$3.41	$102.30
	8	Panduit	PAN-WAY	JBX3510WH-A	Junction box base and cover	$3.22	$25.76
	2	Panduit	PAN-JACK	MBWH-X	Blanks, white	$0.47	$0.97
Surface-Mount Raceway	16	Panduit	PAN-WAY	T3B4.5X1WH6A	Adhesive or mounted base raceway, 4.5" W × 6' L	$3.61	$57.76
	16	Panduit	PAN-WAY	T3B4.5X1WH6A	Snap-on cover, white, 1" H × 4.5" W × 6' L	$2.00	$32.00
	1	Panduit	PAN-WAY	CDC10-L	Mounting clips, 50-pack, 0.25" screw holes	$55.12	$55.12
	12	Panduit	PAN-WAY	T3CF4.5X1WH	Coupling, white	$2.40	$28.80
	2	Panduit	PAN-WAY	T3ECF4.5X1WH	End cap, white	$3.30	$6.60
	2	Panduit	PAN-WAY	T3ICF4.5X1WH	Inside corner, white	$5.00	$10.00
	8	Panduit	PAN-WAY	T3TRF4.5X1WH	Junction box, white	$6.45	$51.60
	8	Panduit	PAN-WAY	LD10WH6A	1.5" W × 6' L base, white	$1.45	$11.60
	8	Panduit	PAN-WAY	CD10WH6	1.5" W × 6' L cover, white	$1.24	$9.92
Cabling	2	General Cabling	NA	2133200	CAT5, 24 AWG, non-plenum, 1,000 feet	$70.91	$141.82
Horizontal Wiring Rack	1	Panduit	Style E Duct	E2X2.5WH6	2" W × 2.5" H × 6' L, white	$3.69	$3.69
	1	Panduit	Style E Duct	C2wh6	2" W × 6' L duct cover	$0.88	$0.88
	1	Homaco	Optima	MGWC5-8-37TB	Covered, wall- or rack-mount, 24-port, CAT5, 568B	$192.00	$192.00
	1	Homaco	Optima	MGWC5-8-37TB	Covered, wall- or rack-mount, 12-port, CAT5, 568B	$110.00	$110.00
	30	Allen Tel	NA	AT1503-6C	RJ-11, 3 feet	$2.28	$68.40
Hubs	1	Tribe	NA	T02032LT	32-port patch panel	$345.00	$345.00
	1	Tribe	TribeStar	T04009LE	8-port switch, LocalTalk hub with Ethernet uplink/bridge	$1,795.00	$1,795.00
						Total Cost:	**$3,578.47**

Cabling Costs for LocalTalk TribeStar Training Room/Classroom

	Qty.	Manuf.	Model	Part #	Description	Cost/ea.	Total Cost
Drop Cords	18	Allen Tel	NA	AT1210-8C	RJ-45, 10 feet	$3.32	$59.76
	16	Allen Tel	NA	AT1220-8C	RJ-45, 20 feet	$5.86	$93.76
	34	Asanté	FriendlyNet Adapter for 10BaseT		1-port Ethernet transceiver	$39.99	$1359.66
Jacks	9	Panduit	PAN-WAY	MFPW4WH	4-port face plate	$2.02	$18.18
	34	Panduit	PAN-JACK	MUJC588WH	CAT5, 568B, white jack	$3.41	$115.94
	9	Panduit	PAN-WAY	JBX3510WH-A	Junction box base and cover	$3.22	$28.98
	2	Panduit	PAN-JACK	MBWH-X	Blanks, white	$0.47	$0.94
Surface-Mount Raceway	16	Panduit	PAN-WAY	T3B4.5X1WH6A	Adhesive or mounted base raceway, 4.5" W × 6' L	$3.61	$57.76
	16	Panduit	PAN-WAY	T3B4.5X1WH6A	Snap-on cover, white, 1" H × 4.5" W × 6' L	$2.00	$32.00
	1	Panduit	PAN-WAY	CDC10-L	Mounting clips, 50-pack, 0.25" screw holes	$55.12	$55.12
	12	Panduit	PAN-WAY	T3CF4.5X1WH	Coupling, white	$2.40	$28.80
	2	Panduit	PAN-WAY	T3ECF4.5X1WH	End cap, white	$3.30	$6.60
	2	Panduit	PAN-WAY	T3ICF4.5X1WH	Inside corner, white	$5.00	$10.00
	9	Panduit	PAN-WAY	T3TRF4.5X1WH	Junction box, white	$6.45	$58.05
	9	Panduit	PAN-WAY	LD10WH6A	1.5" W × 6' L base, white	$1.45	$13.05
	9	Panduit	PAN-WAY	CD10WH6	1.5" W × 6' L cover, white	$1.24	$11.16
Cabling	2	General Cabling	NA	2133200	CAT5, 24 AWG, non-plenum, 1,000 feet	$70.91	$141.82
Horizontal Wiring Rack	1	Panduit	Style E Duct	E2X2.5WH6	2" W × 2.5" H × 6' L, white	$3.69	$3.69
	1	Panduit	Style E Duct	C2WH6	2" W × 6' L duct cover	$0.88	$0.88
	1	Homaco	Optima	MGWC5-8-37TB	Covered, wall- or rack-mount, 24-port, CAT5, 568B	$192.00	$192.00
	1	Homaco	Optima	MGWC5-8-37TB	Covered, wall- or rack-mount, 12-port, CAT5, 568B	$110.00	$110.00
	34	Allen Tel	NA	AT1503-6C	RJ-11, 3 feet	$2.28	$78.20
Hubs	1	Asanté	10BaseT Hub	99-00280-01	12-port repeater	$329.00	$329.00
	1	Asanté	10BaseT Hub	99-00281-01	24-port repeater	$499.00	$499.00
						Total Cost:	**$3,304.35**

Cabling Costs for Ethernet Training Room/Classroom

EtherWave Classroom

The idea behind an "EtherWave Classroom" design is to eliminate the need to run individual cables to individual computers. What we would do instead is run one cable to the row, and then daisy-chain the EtherWaves throughout the row. Supposedly this will save in cabling and other costs. I've shown this situation in the following picture.

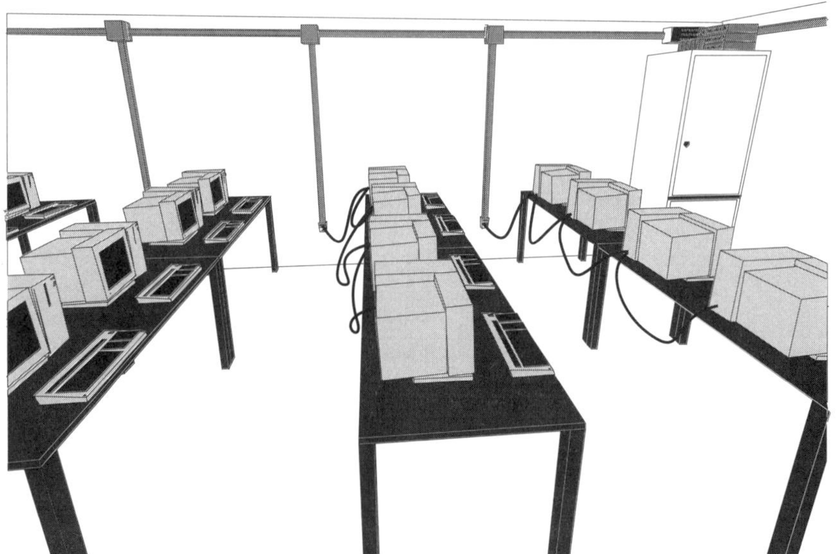

Classroom with Macintoshes Daisy-Chaining Off of EtherWave

Cost Table

Now that you know what it looks like, let's talk about what it would cost to run this scenario. Instead of running four sets of eight cables to each row, we'd only have to run one set of cables to each row, with the other three cables being daisy-chained together via the EtherWaves. We'd also need fewer jacks, but the same number of jack boxes, since we'd still be running a single cable to each computer. We'll also need a smaller patch panel and fewer patch cables. We will need those extra 19 EtherWave connectors, but that also means we'll need fewer Ethernet transceivers and a smaller hub. You might wonder why we don't just buy an eight-port hub instead of a 12-port hub. That's because of the teacher's computer, which makes it nine computing devices, one over the eight-port limit.

	Qty.	Manuf.	Model	Part #	Description	Cost/ea	Total Cost
Drop Cords	34	Allen Tel	NA	AT1210-8C	RJ-45, 10 feet	$3.32	$112.88
	19	Farallon	EtherWaves	PN802	2-port Ethernet transceiver	$109.00	$2,071.00
	9	Asanté	FriendlyNet Adapter for 10BaseT		1-port Ethernet transceiver	$39.99	$359.91
Jacks	9	Panduit	PAN-WAY	MFPW4WH	4-port face plate	$2.02	$18.18
	9	Panduit	PAN-JACK	MUJC588WH	CAT5, 568B, white jack	$3.41	$30.69
	9	Panduit	PAN-WAY	JBX3510WH-A	Junction box base and cover	$3.22	$28.98
	27	Panduit	PAN-JACK	MBWH-X	Blanks, white	$0.47	$12.69
Surface-Mount Raceway	16	Panduit	PAN-WAY	T3B4.5X1WH6A	Adhesive or mounted base raceway, 4.5" W × 6' L	$3.61	$57.76
	16	Panduit	PAN-WAY	T3B4.5X1WH6A	Snap-on cover, white, 1" H × 4.5" W × 6' L	$2.00	$32.00
	1	Panduit	PAN-WAY	CDC10-L	Mounting clips, 50-pack, 0.25" screw holes	$55.12	$55.12
	12	Panduit	PAN-WAY	T3CF4.5X1WH	Coupling, white	$2.40	$28.80
	2	Panduit	PAN-WAY	T3ECF4.5X1WH	End cap, white	$3.30	$6.60
	2	Panduit	PAN-WAY	T3ICF4.5X1WH	Inside corner, white	$5.00	$10.00
	9	Panduit	PAN-WAY	T3TRF4.5X1WH	Junction box, white	$6.45	$58.05
	9	Panduit	PAN-WAY	LD10WH6A	1.5" W × 6' L base, white	$1.45	$13.05
	9	Panduit	PAN-WAY	CD10WH6	1.5" W × 6' L cover, white	$1.24	$11.16
Cabling	1	General Cabling	NA	2133200	CAT5, 24 AWG, non-plenum, 1,000 feet	$70.91	$70.91
Horizontal Wiring Rack	1	Panduit	Style E Duct	E2X2.5WH6	2" W × 2.5" H × 6' L, white	$3.69	$3.69
	1	Panduit	Style E Duct	C2WH6	2" W × 6' L duct cover	$0.88	$0.88
	1	Homaco	Optima	MGWC5-8-37TB	Covered, wall- or rack-mount, 12-port, CAT5, 568B	$110.00	$110.00
	9	Allen Tel	NA	AT1503-8C	RJ-45, 3 feet	$2.30	$20.70
Hubs	1	Asanté	10BaseT Hub	99-00280-01	12-port repeater	$329.00	$329.00
						Total Cost:	**$3,442.05**

Cabling Costs for EtherWave Training Room/Classroom

Looking at the numbers, the EtherWave option in a setting like this costs a bit more than a standard network design. That's due to the difference in cost between

Dayna's connector ($57.00), and the EtherWave device ($109). Needing 19 of them brings up the price *just a little bit more* than we'd want.

Apple's Solution

Now it's time for Apple Computer's version of a "minihub." Each of the "hub-transceivers" has four ports, so you don't have to daisy-chain the computers together as with the EtherWaves. You can connect three computers directly to the minihub. Even though the minihub has four ports there needs to be one port left open for what I call an "uplink" connection to the rest of the network. The next picture shows what the classroom would look like with the minihubs connected to the first computer in the row, and then the rest of the computers in the row connected via that computer. Unlike the EtherWave design, each of the computers connecting through the minihub has fewer "breaks" in the cabling on the cable's path to the main hub—meaning that it doesn't go through as many different sets of RJ-45 connections.

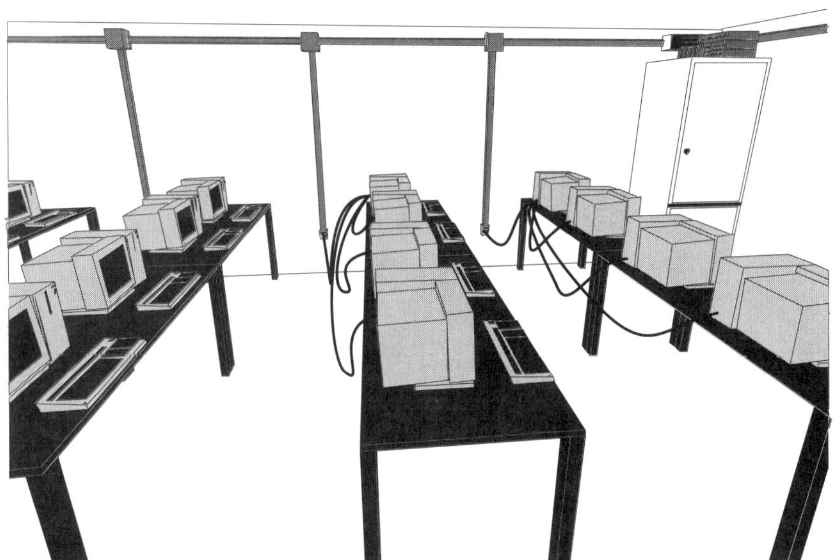

Classroom Setup with Apple Hubs

Cost Table

Finally, we come to the cost table.

	Qty.	Manuf.	Model	Part #	Description	Cost/ea.	Total Cost
Drop Cords	17	Allen Tel	NA	AT1210-8C	RJ-45, 10 feet, CAT5 cables	$3.32	$56.44
	8	Allen Tel	NA	AT1220-8C	RJ-45, 10 feet, CAT5 cables	$5.86	$46.88
	9	GraybaR	NA	NA	Cross connect cable, RJ-45, CAT5, 10 feet	$5.60	$50.40
	25	Apple	10BaseT Transceiver		Ethernet transceiver	$67.99	$1,699.75
	9	Apple	10T/5 Ethernet Workgroup Hub		4-port Ethernet hublet with AUI connector	$144.99	$1,304.91
Jacks	9	Panduit	PAN-WAY	MFPW4WH	4-port face plate	$2.02	$18.18
	9	Panduit	PAN-JACK	MUJC588WH	CAT5, 568B, white jack	$3.41	$30.69
	9	Panduit	PAN-WAY	JBX3510WH-A	Junction box base and cover	$3.22	$28.98
	27	Panduit	PAN-JACK	MBWH-X	Blanks, white	$0.47	$12.69
Surface-Mount Raceway	16	Panduit	PAN-WAY	T3B4.5X1WH6A	Adhesive or mounted base raceway, 4.5" W × 6' L	$3.61	$57.76
	16	Panduit	PAN-WAY	T3B4.5X1WH6A	Snap-on cover, white, 1" H × 4.5" W × 6' L	$2.00	$32.00
	1	Panduit	PAN-WAY	CDC10-L	Mounting clips, 50-pack, 0.25" screw holes	$55.12	$55.12
	12	Panduit	PAN-WAY	T3CF4.5X1WH	Coupling, white	$2.40	$28.80
	2	Panduit	PAN-WAY	T3ECF4.5X1WH	End cap, white	$3.30	$6.60
	2	Panduit	PAN-WAY	T3ICF4.5X1WH	Inside corner, white	$5.00	$10.00
	9	Panduit	PAN-WAY	T3TRF4.5X1WH	Junction box, white	$6.45	$58.05
	9	Panduit	PAN-WAY	LD10WH6A	1.5" W × 6' L base, white	$1.45	$13.05
	9	Panduit	PAN-WAY	CD10WH6	1.5" W × 6' L cover, white	$1.24	$11.16
Cabling	1	General Cabling	NA	2133200	CAT5, 24 AWG, non-plenum, 1,000 feet	$70.91	$70.91
Horizontal Wiring Rack	1	Panduit	Style E Duct	E2X2.5WH6	2" W × 2.5" H × 6' L, white	$3.69	$3.69
	1	Panduit	Style E Duct	C2WH6	2" W × 6' L duct cover	$0.88	$0.88
	1	Homaco	Optima	MGWC5-8-37TB	Covered, wall- or rack-mount, 12-port, CAT5, 568B	$110.00	$110.00
	9	Allen Tel	NA	AT1503-8C	RJ-45, 3 feet	$2.30	$20.70
Hubs	1	Asanté	10BaseT Hub	99-00280-01	12-port repeater	$329.00	$329.00
						Total Cost:	**$4,056.64**

Costs for Apple Minihub Training Room/Classroom Network

SMALL OFFICE STRUCTURED WIRING SYSTEM

Okay, now that you have the "load" of information we have been trying to pipe into your head, it's time to look at a sample office and determine how to use this knowledge. The diagram on this page shows a small office. We will plan the physical aspects of the wiring for this office.

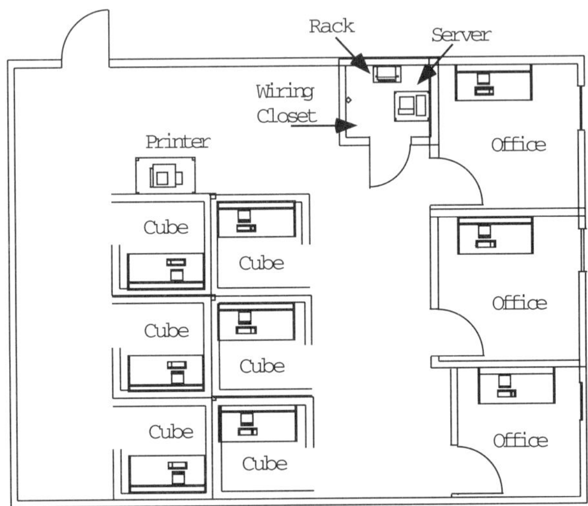

Small Company Office

Office Tour

Okay, I'll admit that this is a pretty small office, but don't worry about that. There's plenty to think about in the first network design without worrying about scaling it to something much larger. The company's facility is comprised of three offices on the right-hand side of the floor plan. There are also six cubicles more or less in the center of the floor plan. Each cube and each office holds a single user and a single computer. There is also one printer, located next to the cubes in the general office area. The company's file server is located inside the wiring closet, next to the wiring rack. All in all, this gives us a whopping total of eleven network devices—one shy of a dozen, just like a few consultants I know.

Now that we have seen the floor plan, let's look at a few different views of the office. The first view, shown in the following picture, is a sort of bird's-eye view of the office. The walls are clear so you can see the computers within the office itself. While you might be working on a floor plan to create a wiring schematic, you would miss a some crucial elements if you didn't think in three dimensions.

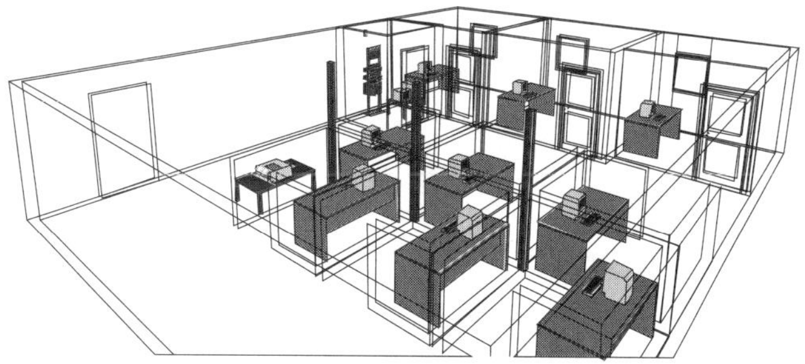

Bird's-Eye View

Planning Runs for the Office

This is a short description of how to plan *new* cabling for your office. Remember that the cabling system we are planning will be for a Category 5 certified system. I know and you know that many of the offices already have some cabling installed. Let's forget about that right now, however, and concentrate on planning a new system, as if the only thing you have worth using is your conduit. We'll cover the rest of the design process later.

Step 1: Labeling Drop Locations

The first thing to visualize when you create your plan is the location of your wiring closet and the end-points at the computers you need to connect. To do this effectively, standardize a way of marking your data cable runs. If you have an office with office numbers, use that. If you don't, here is the way we have accomplished this many times and each time I'm more convinced it's the best way to do it.

We always begin with the top right-hand corner of the office and mark that room number one. We then move through the office clockwise and mark the rooms accordingly. We show a suite in the diagram to the right, which we called Suite A440. From there we numbered the offices A441–A443, marking the last room, the wiring closet, room A444. We always mark open areas as the last office in the suite. In this case, A445.

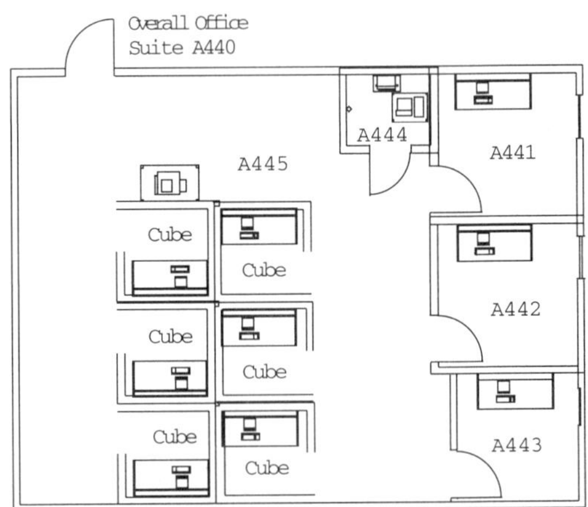

Overview of Office with Numbering System

One potential problem is when there is more than one drop in a single room, as is the case with the cubicled area. When that happens, the best thing to do is to number the drops sequentially. Because we are numbering them that way, we have numbered all the drops with the room number, followed by a decimal, followed by the drop number for that room. Thus, we have numbered the drops in the cube area A445.1–A445.3. The next picture shows the labeling sequence for each of the major drops. We have put the label by the drop's conduit. In reality, this conduit would be running through the wall or running through the power pole in the case of computers in cubes.

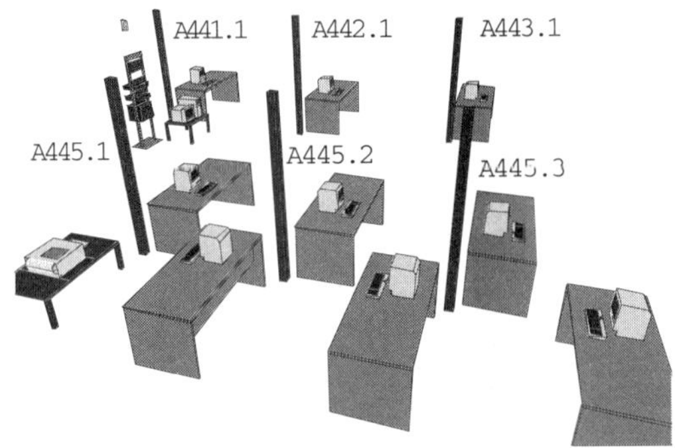

Room without Walls or Wires

Each gang box can handle a total of six jacks, data or otherwise, and thus each of these drops serves up to six computers. Rooms A441–A443 won't need additional runs, as there is only one computer per room. However, the cube areas have more computers than there are power poles. Therefore, some of the gang boxes will have two data jacks, and thus two computer runs. Jack A445.1 will serve the printer (A445.1.1) and the far left computer (A445.1.2). Jack A445.2 will serve the two computers closest to it (A445.2.1 and A445.2.2). Jack A445.3 will serve the three far right-hand computers (A445.3.1–A445.3.3).

Step 2: Estimating Horizontal Lengths

Now it's time to estimate the drop lengths for the cables. Remember, for Category 5 cabling, the horizontal length can only be 295 feet. When measuring your run, start with the STC, or wiring room. STC stands for Signal Termination Can and is used by contractors when describing where the wires come out of the wall to go into the wiring rack. Write all wiring plans around each individual STC and organize them that way.

The following table, which you may remember from the RFP (p. 106), shows a sample of the information I usually gather when creating a drop plan. Start by entering the STC room number and then enter each drop's room number, drop number, and position number. Next, enter the estimated length of cable for that run. The software we used to create this table, FileMaker Pro, automatically generates a Run ID number. Finally, enter yes or no to the question of whether or not the run is Ethernet.

STC	Room	Drop	Position	Type	Length	
B118	B116	1	1	EN	30	B116.1.1
B118	B116	1	2	EN	30	B116.1.2
B118	B116	2	1	EN	39	B116.2.1
B118	B116	2	2	EN	39	B116.2.2
B118	B117	1	1	EN	32	B117.1.1
B118	B117	1	2	EN	32	D117.1.2
B118	B117	1	3	EN	32	B117.1.3
B118	B117	1	4	EN	32	B117.1.4
B118	B115	1	1	EN	75	B115.1.1
B118	B115	1	2	EN	75	B115.1.2
B118	B114	1	1	EN	53	B114.1.1
B118	B114	1	2	EN	53	B114.1.2
B118	B114	1	3	EN	53	B114.1.3
B118	B114	1	4	EN	53	B114.1.4
B118	B114	2	1	EN	69	B114.2.1

Drop Length Planning Table

The next picture shows what the runs could look like. The gray wires show horizontal runs emanating from the wiring closet to the individual drop locations.

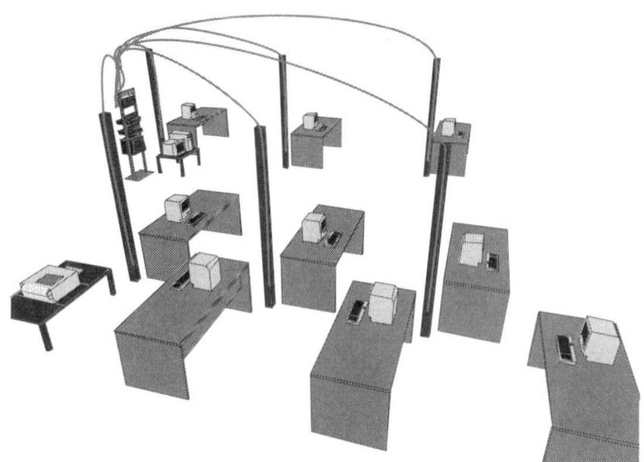

Horizontal Runs for the Office

Step 3: Adding Jack and Drop Cable Information

Next, plan the jack and drop cable information. Start with individual gang boxes for each horizontal drop location, a gang box being the box to which the face plate and jack are attached in the wall. Gang boxes can be flush-mount so they go into the wall or surface-mount. They can also be single or double gang. Single gang boxes are what most people use. They can hold a total of six jacks each. Double gang boxes can hold a total of 12 jacks each. We'll plan for single gang boxes.

Each drop location needs a gang box and a face plate. Each computing device needs its own data jack and drop cable. The drop cable is the cable going from the data jack in the wall to the back of the computer, to either the LocalTalk connector or the Ethernet transceiver. The data jacks should be Category 5, eight-position jacks, whether you use LocalTalk with two wires or Ethernet with four wires for 10BaseT. The only difference should be whether the drop cable itself is a 10BaseT cable (RJ-45) or a LocalTalk cable (RJ-11).

I've shown the individual cable drops in the next picture to help you visualize what we have been talking about.

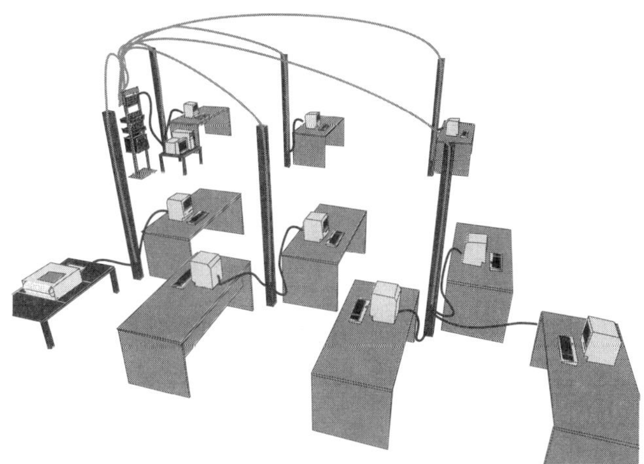

Individual Cable Runs in the Office

Cost Table

Once you know where you want to put your runs, begin the cost estimation process. Estimate your costs as closely as possible so that you can enter the information in your RFP. You want to enter parts, amounts, and potential costs into your RFP for two reasons. First of all, you want to know what an estimate should be before you go through the RFP bidding process. The second reason is that you want to send a message to the bidders that shows you know what you are talking about. I've worked with companies that have paid two to three times as much as they should have for parts because they were too lazy to do their homework. First I will show you the actual table, and then I will explain some of the sections shown in the table. This table is for 13 devices.

	Qty.	Manuf.	Model	Part #	Description	Cost/ea.	Total Cost
Drop Cords	11	Allen Tel	NA	AT1210-6C	RJ-45, 10 feet	$3.32	$36.52
	11	Asanté	FriendlyNet Adapter for 10BaseT		1-port Ethernet transceiver	$39.99	$439.89
Jacks	7	Mod-Tap	USO Multimedia Components	17-0121-0	6-port faceplate	$1.78	$12.46
	5	Mod-Tap	USO Multimedia Components	17.1B.021.B001	2-port, CAT5, 568B, white jack	$9.24	$46.20
	3	Mod-Tap	USO Multimedia Components	17.1B.011.B001	1-port, CAT5, 568B, white jack	$4.78	$14.34
	13	Mod-Tap	USO Multimedia Components	1-0433-0	Blanks, white	$0.43	$5.59
Patch Panels	1	Panduit	PANDUCT	WMP1	Front and rear management panel	$36.12	$36.12
	1	Panduit	PANDUCT	WMBV1	2-inch wire management bracket	$8.08	$8.08
	11	Allen Tel	NA	AT1503-8C	RJ-45, 3 feet	$2.30	$25.30
	1	AMP	CAT5 Patch Panel	555501-1	Rack-mounted, 32-port patch panel	$119.72	$119.72
Cabling	.398	Belden	NA	1585A	CAR5, 24 AWG, plenum-rated, 1,000 feet	$191.00	$76.02
Horizontal Wiring Rack	1	Harris/Dracon	NA	46353-501	72" H × 19" W ladder	$173.00	$173.00
	1	Harris/Dracon	NA	10250-006	Wiring Rack, 9'11.5" L × 6" W × 1.5" D	$57.00	$57.00
	2	Mod-Tap	Two Position	25.B011G	Equipment Shelf, 17.3" W × 3.5" H × 8" D	$58.00	$58.00
	1	Perma Power	NA	J126A0-11	6 foot, 12 outlets	$46.00	$46.00
	1	APC	Smart-UPS	NA	250 VA, 175 Watts, 2 outlets, 2.25" H × 11.9" W × 15.5" D	$250.00	$250.00
Hubs	1	Asanté	10BaseT Hub	99-00280-01	12-port repeater	$329.00	$329.00
Labor	17.5			Labor Hours		$60.00	$1,050.00
						Total Cost:	**$2,841.24**

Costs for a Small Office Network

Horizontal Cable Costs

The spreadsheet we use has the part number for a rather standard wire type made by Belden. This is good wire, and the price is from GraybaR (December 1995).

The number entered for length is multiplied by the cost per thousand foot roll. I don't know if you can buy parts of a roll, but this is one thing in this spreadsheet that would have thrown everything off if it wasn't calculated this way.

Jacks

The number of gang boxes and face plates is determined by the number of drops alone, not the number of jacks in a drop. If you had two drops in a room, and one drop had five jacks while the other drop had one jack, you would only need two gang boxes and two face plates—one for each drop. The number of jacks is determined by the total number of cables being run. The jacks, face plates, and gang boxes we chose, as you have probably noticed from the preceding cost tables, are all MOD-TAP. I love those guys. Their stuff is great. Again, the part numbers and prices came from GraybaR Electronics around December of 1995.

Patch Cables

Patch cables are determined by whether you answered "yes" or left the column blank for Ethernet. If you entered anything at all, the table would count that as a "yes." These are the cables that plug into the jack at the wall and into the back of the computer or into the LocalTalk connector. The patch cables are all Allen Tel. They make great stuff, too. You should know by now where we found our part numbers and prices.

Building the Rack

Now, plan for the wiring rack and patch panel system. When we spec wiring racks, we normally spec a single wiring rack per STC. When we state that only 220 computers should be put in a wiring room, it's because that's how many will fit onto a single wiring rack. We have found over time that unless you are putting the wiring rack out in the open in some person's office (like yours, "Bob"), you won't have room for more than one of them.

The numbers in the table aren't drawn from the number of runs you have. The quantity of wiring racks was typed in and everything else in this table is taken from that number. The rows in the table, then, from top to bottom are the 72-inch tall, 19-inch wide wiring rack itself, and a ladder rack that is bolted horizontally to the top of the wiring rack and then onto the wall. This ladder rack gives stability to the wiring rack.

Next, we always specify that each wiring rack should have two shelves on it. You may wonder why until you build a rack yourself. If you build a rack, you will discover what we did; if the shelves are there, you'll use them. If they are not there, you will be propping stuff up everywhere. You will also need the world's longest power strip, included in our table. This baby is six feet long and fits on the side of the wiring rack. You plug your hubs and routers and stuff into it. Finally, we have allocated a row for a small APC UPS. This is just about enough UPS to run a few hubs and maybe a router for a while if the power goes out. Make absolutely sure your rack has its own UPS.

Once the rack is in place, move on to the patch panels. I've attempted to draw, in the following two diagrams, how a 72-inch wiring rack might look with a single patch panel. The left diagram shows the front of the rack. The right diagram shows the back of the rack where cables that go directly to the computer jacks are "punched down" to the back of the patch panel. This should suffice until you get your hands on a real one. The real ones, of course, look a bit different. There are some things in our table of information that I didn't draw—I'm not an artist.

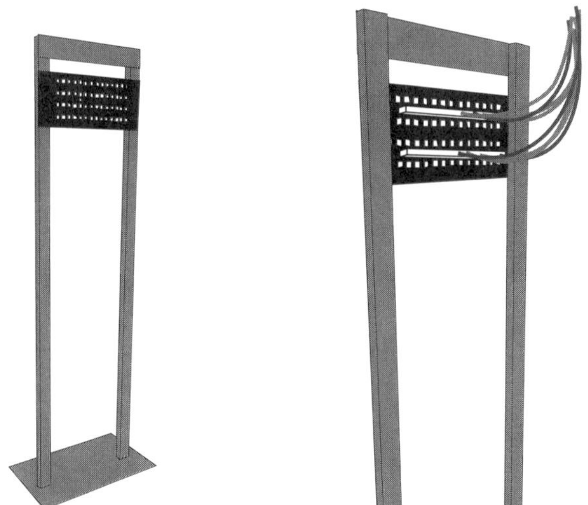

Front View of 72-Inch Rack with Patch Panel (left); Same Rack with Cables to 110-Blocks in Back (right)

We haven't listed just the 32-port patch panel, but the wire management system and the patch cables as well. The numbers are derived from the total number of Ethernet and LocalTalk runs.

Planning Labor Costs

Finally, figure your labor costs. Our estimation of labor costs are based upon *the number of drops,* and not the total number of runs. Wiring contractors don't pull cable by the single piece. They pull cable by the drop, which means they can pull several cables at a time. The smart ones know how to pull small bundles of 6–18 cables at once. Therefore, we have given the contractors a total of 2.5 hours per drop location to run the wires. This should account for running the wire, terminating it at the patch panel *and* at the jack, labeling the cables correctly, and testing the cables for Category 5 compliance.

CHAPTER 8:
FIBER OPTIC CABLING—A PRIMER
FOR YOUR NETWORK

Special thanks to Richard Willis of AT&T

A high-fiber network is very much like a high-fiber diet. A bran muffin here and there is good for you, especially if you need to "go the distance." However, unless you are competing in a triathlon, it is not recommended to run fiber everywhere. Okay, you don't *have* to laugh at my jokes, but even if you don't get it now, laugh anyway. You'll get my joke later.

HOW FIBER WORKS: THE SIGNAL SOURCE

Personally, I think this is way cool, but then again, I'm a geek.

Copper cable expresses its signal by changing the voltage that travels over the wire. As the electronic signal crosses a positive or negative voltage threshold, either a 1 or a 0 is registered by the network interface card. The number of times a threshold is crossed within a certain time frame results in either a 1 or 0 being detected. The same principal of 1's and 0's applies in the world of fiber, but rather than voltage change, it is a change in the presence of light being transmitted. Within a particular frame of time, the network interface card is waiting to detect pulses of light. In turn, those pulses of light are detected as 1's and 0's.

For single-mode fiber, the light source is a laser (this gives us another good reason why single-mode is not an option—you could burn your eye out). The light source for multi-mode cable is an LED and no one ever went blind looking at their clock radio. The light source generates a signal that is detected on the receiving network interface card. A single signal is sent down single-mode fiber.

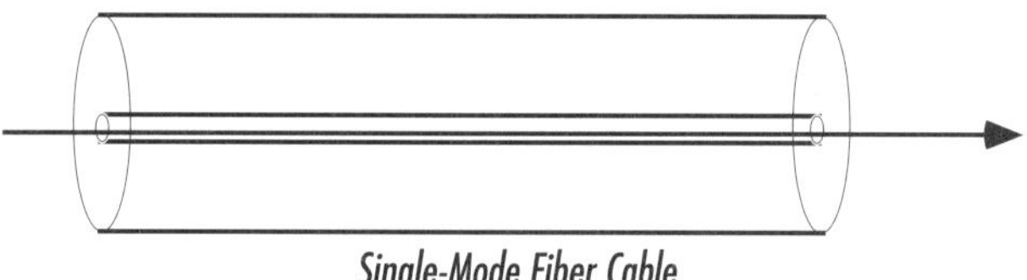

Single-Mode Fiber Cable

Multi-mode fiber cable uses multiple signals, thus the name. In wider core areas—62.5μ as compared to 9μ—different rays of light bounce along the fiber at different angles as the signal travels down the fiber cable. Thus, the total distance that the light signal travels is different for each originating signal, but that isn't a result of the speed at which it travels or the overall length of the cable.

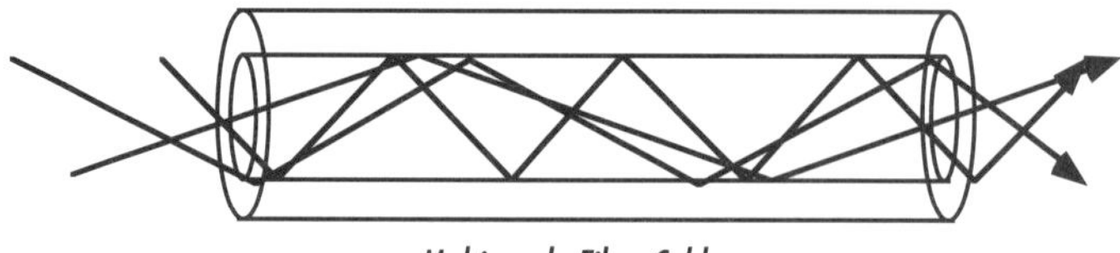

Multi-mode Fiber Cable

All this bouncing around results in dispersion of the light signal. The signal traveling over multi-mode fiber is not as robust as the signal traveling on single-mode fiber. Thus, multi-mode should not be longer than 2 kilometers, while a single-mode fiber cable can be run over 50 km between repeaters. This is not as complicated as you thought it would be, eh?

FACT VS. FICTION

Even though fiber cable has been in use for over a decade, the technology that allows a signal to be transmitted over fiber is still treated like science fiction. In defense of our lack of knowledge, the concept of light traveling over a strand of glass has not been around as long as the polarization of ions in a conductive medium—or, data on copper for us English-speaking folk. That has been implemented since the time of Alexander Graham Bell. Before I get all wrapped up in this whiz-bang technology, let's clear up a few misconceptions.

Fiber will make your network faster.

The speed of the signal going over your copper cable is equal to about 0.82 times the speed of light. The optical signal used by fiber also travels a little slower than the speed of light. Aside from the internal speed of the processors, the thing that has the most bearing on the transmission speed between two nodes is the algorithm used to process the optical or data signal. If you are implementing Ethernet using 10BaseT, you have a theoretical throughput of 10 Mpbs. If you are implementing Ethernet using 10BaseF, or Ethernet over fiber, you have a theoretical throughput of 10 Mpbs. If you are implementing FDDI, or fiber distributed data interface, your theoretical throughput is 100 Mbps. You can also obtain that same 100 Mbps with copper by implementing CDDI, or copper distributed data interface. So, why don't we recommend CDDI? The biggest reason is because you can't find any parts. The difference between using CDDI versus FDDI is like choosing between BetaMax versus VHS. While the BetaMax format might have been technically superior to VHS, VHS was internationally adopted and the BetaMax format was not. This isn't saying that CDDI is better than FDDI; it is just that if you try to find CDDI products and can't, you aren't the Lone Ranger.

Fiber is ten times more expensive than copper.

Every day the cost of multi-mode 62.5/125μ fiber cable nears the cost of unshielded twisted pair. When doing your math, remember that you need eight copper conductors or two strands of fiber for every CAT5 Ethernet termination. The going rate for 1000 feet of AT&T six-stranded fiber cable is $1,168.60. The going rate for AT&T CAT5 four-pair UTP is around $191.00 per 1000 feet. However, don't let the straight numbers fool you. For every run from the patch panel to a jack using the six-stranded multi-mode fiber, you may attach up to three devices. With CAT5 copper cabling, you can attach one device per cable run. Therefore, *if* you run fiber from one point to another *and* you hook up all three devices, the cost of fiber versus the cost of copper is about two to one.

Conductor Type	Length	Number of Jacks at Drop	Cost per Conductor Set
Multi-mode Fiber	100 Feet	3	$38.90
CAT5 Copper	100 Feet	3	$19.10

Comparison of Three-Drop Fiber Run vs. Three-Drop Copper Run

Fiber costs the same as copper.

Of course, this is absolutely untrue, as we have just seen. There is a wide variety of ratios between fiber and copper components. Previously, we saw that multi-mode indoor fiber cable was about twice as expensive as its copper equivalent. What about the rest of the parts? The following tables demonstrate that the final cost for fiber to the desktop—not including the cost difference in network interface cards—is around three times higher than the final cost of copper.

	Qty.	Manuf.	Model	Part #	Description	Cost/ea.	Total Cost
Patch Cords	12	AT&T	ST ST Patch Cords	FL1E-E-08	Multi-mode fiber interconnect, 8'	$52.00	$624.00
Horizontal Cable	8.98	AT&T	Multi-mode Fiber	LGBC 006D LPX	General purpose 6-stranded, interior cable, plenum-rated	$116.86	$1,049.40
Patch Panels	1	AT&T	Lightguide Interconnect	100A3 LIU	LG front access termination shelf, 12 terminations	$39.20	$39.20
	12	AT&T	ST II Connector	P2020C-C-125	Multi-mode connector	$6.18	$74.16
	12	AT&T	Coupling	C2000A-2	Threaded coupling	$6.64	$79.68
	2	AT&T	LIU Panel	104 141 858	10A LIU ST coupling panel, 6-position	$6.48	$12.96
Jacks	12	Mod-Tap	Wall Jack	11.B0280	Dual ST module for multi-mode	$10.70	$128.40
	4	Mod-Tap	Face Plate	17-0121-0	Single gang bezel	$1.53	$6.12
Hubs	2	Asanté	6-Port Fiber Repeater	AH2072H6-FST	10BaseF host multiport repeater module, 6 ST connections, single slot	$1,499.00	$2,998.00
Labor	12				Labor Hours	$85.00	$1,530.00
						Total Cost:	**$6,541.92**

Cost of Fiber to the Desktop for 12 Nodes

The cost of fiber is around $6,500—far more than the $2,200 for UTP:

	Qty.	Manuf.	Model	Part #	Description	Cost/ea.	Total Cost
Drop Cords	12	Allen Tel	NA	AT1210-8C	RJ-45, 10-foot patch cables	$3.32	$36.52
Jacks	12	Mod-Tap	Passport	17-0121-0	Single gang bezel face plate	$1.53	$18.36
	12	Mod-Tap	Passport	11.B023	Blanks	$0.48	$5.76
	4	Mod-Tap	Passport	11.1B.017.B001	CAT5, 568B jack	$3.75	$15.00
Cabling	893	General Cabling	NA	NA	CAT5, 24 AWG, non-plenum, 1000 ft.	$0.43	$5.59
Horizontal Cable Wiring Rack	1	Panduit	Style E Duct	E2x2.5WH6	2" W × 2.5" H × 6" L, white	$3.69	$3.69
	1	Panduit	Style E Duct	C2WH6	2" W × 6" L duct cover	$0.88	$0.88
	1	Homaco	Optima	MGWC5-8-37TB	Covered, wall- or rack-mount, 12-port, CAT5, 568B	$110.00	$110.00
Hubs	1	Asanté	10BaseT Hub	AH2072H12	RJ-45, 12-port repeater	$819.00	$819.00
Labor	12			Labor Hours		$60.00	$1,080.00
						Total Cost:	**$2,155.85**

Cost of UTP to the Desktop for 12 Nodes

Don't worry if all the line items in the fiber spreadsheet don't make sense. We will explain them to you—that's why you are reading this chapter.

Fiber is more secure than copper.

This is my favorite myth. Trust me, if someone is willing to take an EMI oscilloscope-to-data converter to the data signal traveling along your copper cable, they are just as willing to splice into your fiber cable and read the optical signals traveling down it. If you are worried about security, breaches happen due to carelessness such as poor designation of passwords—as in, letmein, admin, server, or Apple—not because you choose copper over fiber for a data transmission media.

THE PARTS

It is lucky for all of us who are familiar with copper twisted pair cabling that fiber optic cabling has the same basic components: the cable, the jack, the punchdown block, and the jumper cables. There are certain variations on a theme, but for the most part the parts look the same.

Fiber Cables

The following table shows some of the variety available for fiber cable:

Manufacturer	Model	Part Number	Description
CommScope General Instrument	Multi-mode Fiber Cable	P-006-BO-xy-25	6-stranded, interior cable, plenum-rated, OD 0.34
AT&T	Multi-mode Fiber Cable	DSX-006-HXM or 106346489	General purpose OSP cable lightpack core, LXE metallic sheath, outdoor-rated, OD 0.49
AT&T	Single-Mode Fiber Cable	4DRX-006-BXC-FB6 or 105934491	General purpose OSP cable lightpack core, LXE rodent lightening sheath, outdoor-rated, OD 0.49

Variety of Fiber Cables

Multi-mode vs. Single-Mode

There are many reasons why LAN technology uses multi-mode and not single-mode fiber. Single-mode is more expensive to make than multi-mode. Single-mode uses laser light to transmit information and multi-mode uses light-emitting diodes, or LEDs. Signal generation systems for lasers are not only more expensive but also more dangerous than LED generation systems. Nobody ever went blind looking at their digital alarm clock. I know; I have stared at many an LED clock in hotel rooms all night long.

Distance is the primary reason for any kind of fiber being used for LAN technology. Where 22-gauge twisted four-pair can only transmit an acceptable signal for roughly 300 feet, multi-mode fiber can transmit a signal up to 1.5 miles and single-mode can transmit up to 10 miles. In almost all buildings and campus systems, it is safe to say that no one room is more than one and a half miles from any other room. How would you make it to your next class before the bell rang? Therefore, although the EIA/TIA has chosen to include both types of fiber in the 568A spec, we will limit our discussion to multi-mode fiber, and will mention single-mode cable only where necessary. Since single-mode is required for distances beyond 1.5 miles, it is more than likely that major money is being spent. I do not feel comfortable discussing the implementation of such a costly cable run in this book. Before you dig an eight-foot deep trench across town, you might want to talk to your phone company, the streets and sanitation commission, and anyone else on the mayoral payroll. Currently, WAN connections are leased by North American phone companies to anyone with the bucks. As you can see in the table below, the phone company can achieve speeds comparable to Ethernet and Fast Ethernet with a dedicated line.

T Carrier	Speed
T1	1.544 Mbps
T2	3.152 Mbps
T3	44.736 Mbps
T4	274.176 Mbps

T Carriers and Their Transmission Speeds

Just a little heads up here: In California, the rates for a T1 line are about $1,300 for installation and $700 per month to lease. This is much cheaper than a 1.5 or 10 mile trench.

So, What Does This Stuff Look Like?

The CAT5 standard specifies that only 62.5/125μ multi-mode fiber or 8.3/125μ single-mode fiber can be used. The following illustration shows what a cross-section of fiber cable looks like. We will explain the ratios and how each type of cable transmits a signal later in this chapter.

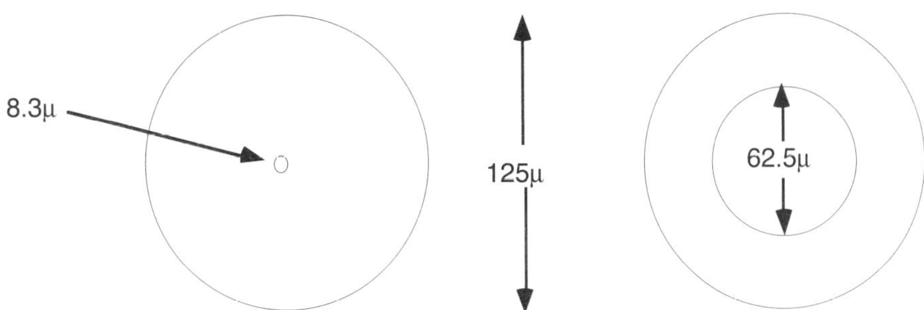

Single-Mode Fiber Cable (left) and Multi-mode Fiber Cable (right)

Aside from the fiber used for the actual transmission, there are bizillions of variations on what can encase the fiber cable: fiber coating and cladding, steel armor (really), water-blocking tape, steel wire for strength, ripcord, packing gel, packing foam, my cousin Eddy's duct tape, and finally, the outside coating. The jacketing all depends on the purpose of the cable. If it is riser cable going between floors and you can place 200–600 pounds of pulling pressure on the cable, you want a casing that uses a nonmetallic strengthening system and a standard PVC coating. If it is outdoor cable, the cable must be rated for up to 600 pounds of pulling pressure. Therefore, you need the water-blocking tape and HDPE coating. While all these coatings and layers of protection assist in the strength and durability of the fiber cable, the single most significant consideration when choosing coatings is whether the cable is going indoors or outdoors.

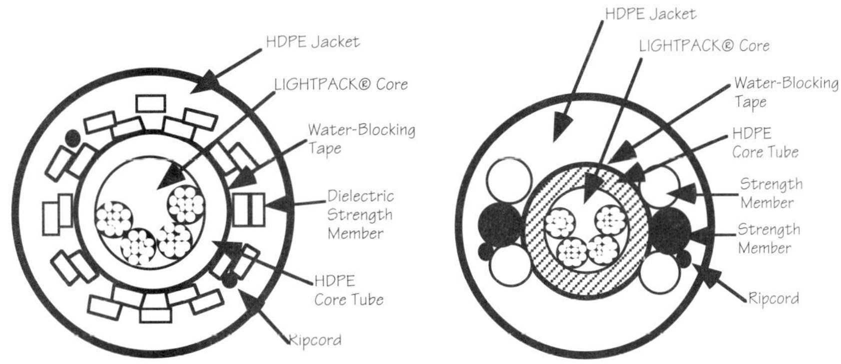

Two Types of Nonmetallic Exterior Fiber Cable

Indoor vs. Outdoor—Bend Radius and Space Determinations

While most fiber cable is at least one half inch in diameter—larger than 125μ—there can be some variation for indoor-rated cable. So, in addition to allowing ten times the cable diameter for the bending radius, the conduit needs to have enough room to accommodate a cable that is over twice the diameter of your average UTP. For example, the bend radius of your conduit must be at least $0.5 \times 10 = 5$ inches. If your main wiring closet is on the 10th floor and you need to service 14 closets, one on each floor, the conduit containing 14 half-inch fiber cables would need to be four inches in diameter.

Since indoor and outdoor fiber cable cannot be interchanged, this creates a less than perfect world. I was recently at a client site where we needed a rodent-proof indoor cable, and since all cable manufacturers seem to believe rodents are only found outside, only outside cable is rated to be rodent-proof. We had no choice but to risk violation by Ratso. Another interesting point about outdoor fiber is that the casing contains a metallic element. Can you say grounding? Yes, buckaroos, you must ground *any* cable that has a metallic compound, regardless of whether it is the sheathing or the conductor that is made of the conductive metal.

Connectors and Couplings

Even though with fiber the patch panel houses the couplings, we discuss the couplings here, instead of in the patch panel section.

Manufacturer	Model	Part Number	Description
AT&T	Buffer Tubing	D-181755 or 105342463	Kit of parts for buffer tubing and end prep
AT&T	ST II Connector	P2020C-C-125 or 105143911	Multi-mode connector
AT&T	Coupling	C2000A-2 or 104148028	Threaded coupling

Connectors and Couplings for Fiber

A long time ago, everyone had a different type of phone system and the parts were incompatible with one another. People had to have adapters so that they could connect the different systems. Eventually, everyone used systems similar enough to allow us to interchange parts, and thus a de facto standard evolved. However, even to this day, our system is not easily interchangeable with Europe's telephone system. We depend on our service providers to bridge the gap in our communication link. In an attempt to make all parts the same for fiber on an international level, the EIA/TIA decided to select the fiber connectors preferred in Europe, called SC connectors. Even though the United States had been using and manufacturing hubs with the fiber ST connector ever since fiber was implemented, the EIA/TIA thought they could slide this one by. This decision split the market between those who had selected American ST connectors and others who had adapted to the European SC connectors. You may be asking yourself, "What's the difference?" The only real difference is that the ST connector is made of metal and has a "ramped-latching" mechanism to attach to the coupling

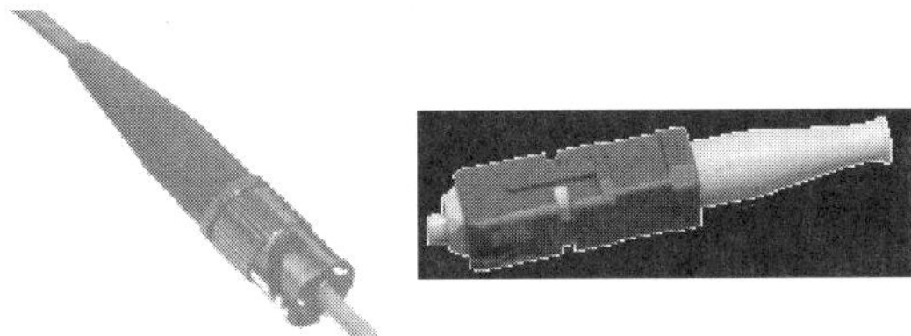

The Culprits: ST Connectors (left) and SC Connectors (right)

So, what's a network designer to do? Manufacturers that have SC connections on their hubs are just starting to crop up. Asanté has a fiber SC uplink on their new NetStacker repeater, and Xyplex seems to be using only SC connectors on all their hubs. However, PlainTree, Asanté, and Cisco are building their newest hubs, such as the Cisco Catalyst 5000, with ST connectors. When deciding which connector to use, here are some rules of thumb:

- If you know what types of hubs or other devices you are buying, check to see what type of connections they have. That is the type you must install.

- If you already have a large installation of fiber, stick with the same type of connector that you are currently using. The exception is if the building or campus can be logically divided into sections, with no risk of confusion.

- If you have never installed fiber at your site, see if SC parts are readily available in your area. If the SC connectors, couplings, and coupling panels are available, installing SC is a safe bet. If they are not available, do not hold up your fiber installation for SC parts. The worse that can happen is that you will need to buy some relatively inexpensive ST-to-SC convertors.

Finally, the EIA/TIA is accepting and including the ST type connectors in their latest version of the 568A standard. Thus, you have a couple of years before you need to jump on the SC bandwagon.

The parts listed in the beginning of this section are needed to terminate outdoor rated multi-mode fiber cables with ST connectors. In addition, we have listed the couplings needed to fit into the couple panels of the boxes where your fiber terminates. Now that you have decided what type of connectors you are using, it is time to finish the rest of your parts list.

Patch Panels, Patch Cables, and Other Stuff

	Manuf.	Model	Part #	Description
Patch Cords	AT&T	ST-ST Patch Cords	FL1E-E-02 OR105351795	Multi-mode fiber interconnect, 4'
	AT&T	ST-ST Patch Cords	FL1E-E-08 or 105351829	Multi-mode fiber interconnect, 8'
Patch Panels	AT&T	Lighthouse Interconnect	100A3 LIU or 106896947	LG front access termination shelf, 12 terminations
	AT&T	LIU Panel	105 276 570	10A LIU ST coupling panel, blank
	AT&T	LIU Panel	104 141 858	10A LIU ST coupling panel, 6-position
Main Patch Panel	AT&T	LIU Panel	LST1F-072/7	LF front access termination shelf, 72 terminations
	AT&T	1000ST	105 392 005	ST coupling panel, 6-port
Other	AT&T	Clamp	12A1 or 104384490	Grounding clamp
	AT&T	6-Unit Splitter	D-181781 or 105342463	Cable organizer

The Rest of the Parts for Running Fiber

Patch Cables

Fiber patch cables are always two-stranded—one strand to send data and one to receive it. That is why you always see two fiber ports for every fiber connection on a hub. The conductors within fiber patch cables are always coated and buffered with a thickness of 1150μ to allow for more flexibility of the cable. The bend radius of a fiber patch cable is generally around 1.25 inches. Where the two fiber strands lie side by side, the cable is usually around 0.1 by 0.21 inches.

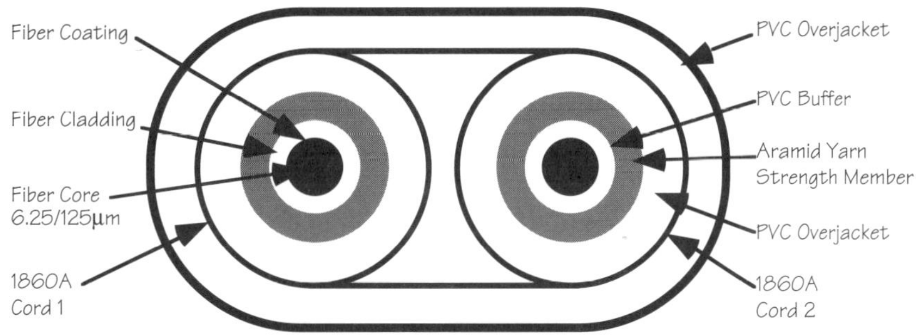

Cross Section of a Fiber Patch Cable

Fiber Patch Panels

Fiber patch panels are basically wall- or rack-mounted boxes with little plates that hold the couplings. The fiber cable enters the box and the terminations are protected within the box.

12-Port Patch Panel (left) and Same Patch Panel Disassembled (right)

The only tricky thing about fiber patch panels or LIUs (lightguide interface units) is trying to configure them in a cost-effective manner. In the preceding spreadsheet I have one LIU that can hold up to 12 terminations (100A3) and one that can hold up to 72 terminations (LST1F-072/7). Common sense dictates that the LST1F-072/7 would be less expensive than six 100A3s. Guess again. The cost per 100A3 is $39.94, while one LST1F-072/7 costs $464.64. Although it doesn't look too pretty to have six little boxes, you would save over $100 in parts. Go figure.

Other Pieces and Parts

You know what I find incredibly annoying? There are a bizillion different ways to organize UTP and GraybaR stocks half of them, but try to obtain the parts for fiber and it takes a month to receive a simple little piece of plastic. Anyway, don't forget a grounding clamp if there is metal in your sheathing. Also, remember to bulk up on cable organizers, as you never know when you can get your hands on more fiber cable organizers when you need them.

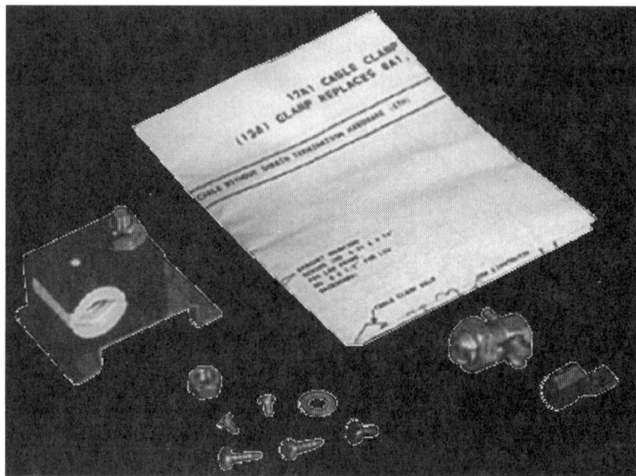

One of the Little Extras—A Grounding Clamp

Now that we have defined the parts, let's learn about fiber as a transmission media for the Physical layer.

Fiber Installation

The installation rules for multi-mode fiber cable are similar to those for twisted four-pair copper cable. The subtle differences in how one installs the two types have to do with the style of transmission (light versus an electronic signal), what makes up the cables (glass versus copper), and what encloses the transmission media (as in, the sheathing).

Horizontal Cabling

Just in case you bought this book to design your network of desktop Cray computers, remember that for fiber optic cable, the inside radius of a bend must be at least 10 times the internal diameter of the conduit.

Backbone Pathways

Before we get started, let's refresh our memory on the definition of backbone cabling from the 569 standard:

> Backbone pathways consist of intra- and inter-building pathways. The term *backbone* replaces riser, house and building-tie cable terminology. Backbone pathways may be vertical or horizontal. Interbuilding backbone pathways extend between buildings. Intrabuilding backbone pathways are contained within a building.

Ahh, now we are finally there—putting the fiber where it belongs.

Intrabuilding Pathways

The rules for running fiber cable within buildings are exactly the same as for running copper, with a few exceptions. The first exception is that the bend radius for conduit that contains fiber is 10 times the diameter of the conduit. Thus, if your conduit is two inches in diameter, your bend radius should be 20 inches.

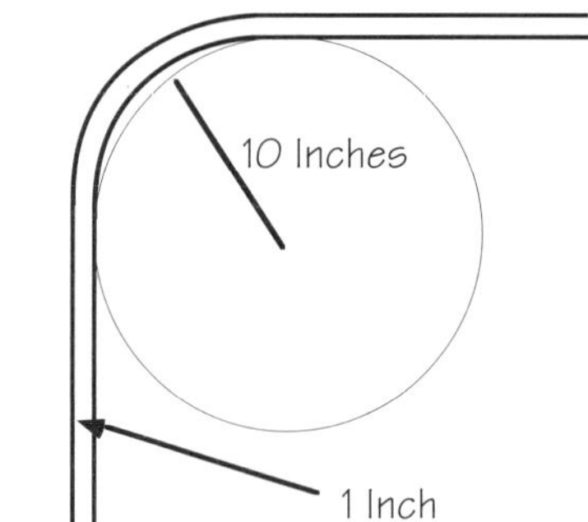

10-Inch Bend Radius for a Conduit One Inch in Diameter

It is also important to note that fiber cables are usually thicker than UTP. First, they have at least six strands per cable. More important, there is all that strengthening around the fiber conductors. Thus, riser cable with six strands can have an outside diameter, or OD, of 0.5. Distribution cables are usually closer to 0.25. This excess in diameter is also important due to the weight of the cable. Not only does the raceway containing the fiber cable need extra support, but the fiber cable itself must also be supported, especially when running between floors. Fiber cables should be lashed to a support structure on each floor before going on to the next floor, even if there is no termination taking place on that floor. This prevents placing excessive weight on the cable.

Interbuilding Pathways

This section is specific to fiber, since distances between buildings are usually greater than 300 feet. As I stated before, you cannot run copper cable over distances greater than 300 feet.

Interbuilding pathways can be aboveground, aerial, or underground—direct burial or tunneled. Tunneled pathways usually refer to the housings of all building services, such as telephone, power, gas, and water. Tunnels are accessible (but rather creepy) and easily entered by an administrator. There are many rules for tunneling, and here are a few of the most important ones:

- Use corrosion-resistant pathways and associated hardware.

- Metal pathways must be bonded to ground as per applicable code.

- Separation from electrical facilities must be per applicable code.

Most underground pathways are composed of raceway, such as conduit. The requirements are the same here as for intrabuilding pathways—rigid conduits that are smooth inside and not rodent friendly. The strength of the conduit should be impervious to moisture and breakage. Some acceptable types are PVC Type C, multiple plastic duct, and steel and fiberglass, of an acceptable thickness.

It may be necessary for your contractor to take a soil sample to insure that your underground raceway will not break down, especially if you are on a landfill site. A bit of prevention is worth a Gig of cure. Did that translate? Sorry, I had to throw in a geek joke to keep you awake.

In addition to running your underground-rated cables (not direct burial) directly in conduit, they can be run in lighter weight PVC Type B. This is helpful if you are running multiple cables in a single concrete encasement where the concrete will not hold out the moisture, but the PVC will.

Remember when you are running interbuilding conduits that it is possible you will need to cross over someone else's—like Uncle Sam's—property. Make sure you are a good neighbor and obtain any special permits you may need to cross their property. In addition, if you are running aerial conduit, care must be taken not to interfere with any antenna fields or line-of-sight areas. The train supervisor still needs to see her "comin' round the mountain…"

Costs

Without including the costs of digging the trench or laying the conduit, this is a general idea of what a fiber backbone costs. We've priced it with 12 runs of six-stranded fiber cable.

	Qty.	Manuf.	Model	Part #	Description	Cost/ea.	Total Cost
Patch Cords	12	AT&T	ST-ST Patch Cords	FL1E-E-02 or 105351795	Multi-mode fiber interconnect, 4'	$65.41	$784.92
	12	AT&T	ST-ST Patch Cords	FL1E-E-08 or 105351829	Multi-mode fiber interconnect, 8'	$66.95	$803.40
Horizontal Cable	4,800	AT&T	Multi-mode Fiber Cable	DSX-006-HXM or 106346489	General purpose OSP cable lightpack core, LXE metallic sheath	$110.11/ 100 feet	$5,285.28
	2	AT&T	Buffer Tubing	D-181755 or 105342463	Kit of parts for buffer tubing and end prep	$118.20	$236.40
Patch Panels	12	AT&T	Lightguide Interconnect	100A3 LIU	LG front access termination shelf, 12 terminations	$39.94	$479.28
	12	AT&T	6-Unit Splitter	D-181755 or 105342463	Cable organizer	$11.10	$133.20
	12	AT&T	Clamp	12A1 or 104384490	Grounding clamp	$40.17	$482.04
	72	AT&T	ST II Connector	P2020C-C-125 or 105143911	Multi-mode connector	$6.43	$462.96
	72	AT&T	Coupling	C2000A-2 or 104148028	Threaded coupling	$6.05	$435.60
	12	AT&T	LIU Panel	105 276 570	10A LIU ST coupling panel, blank	$7.62	$91.44
	12	AT&T	LIU Panel	104 141 858	10A LIU ST coupling panel, 6-position	$6.61	$79.32
Main Patch Panel	1	AT&T	LIU Panel	LST1F-072/7	LG front access termination shelf, 72 terminations	$464.64	$464.64
	12	AT&T	6-Unit Splitter	D-181781	Cable organizer	$11.10	$133.20
	12	AT&T	1000 ST	105 392 005	ST coupling panel, 6-port	$16.06	$192.72
	1	AT&T	Clamp	12A1	Grounding clamp	$40.17	$401.7
	72	AT&T	ST II Connector	P2020C-C-125	Multi-mode connector	$6.18	$444.96
	72	AT&T	Coupling	C2000A-2	Threaded coupling	$6.64	$478.08
Hubs	12	Lantronix	Transceiver	LTX-FL	Fiber-to-10BaseT converter	$249.00	$2,988.00
	1	PlainTree	WaveSwitch	3030-01-HW	12-port, 10 Mbps, Ethernet switch	$9,596.00	$9,596.00
Labor	72				Labor Hours	$80.00	$5760.00
						Total Costs:	**$29,238.41**

Total Cost Table

I have found these prices to be close to the national average. For copper installations, California prices are low to middle, the South's are low, and the East Coast's prices are absurd. What costs $150.00 in the rest of the country costs $300.00 in Manhattan. I'd just like to know who is pocketing the extra $150.00. It sure isn't the IS staff or the guy really pulling the cable.

Testing

Fiber testing is rocket science. Oops, another myth to dispel! Way back when, fiber was tested with an OTDR, or an optical time domain reflectometer. The OTDR could not only read overall attenuation and length, but could check for attenuation at splice junctures. OTDR testing equipment and the amount of time it took to do the actual testing was expensive.

Today this is accomplished with OLT, or optical loss testing equipment. OLT testing for multi-mode fiber cables is much like copper testing. There is an optical light source that sends a signal at wave lengths of 850 nm and 1300 nm, and a fiber optic power meter that records the characteristics of the signal that is output. The characteristics measured are attenuation or signal loss, connector quality, and continuity. Prior to testing, the testing equipment must be calibrated with a patch cable similar in tolerable attenuation loss and connector type as the run cables being used. Fiber testing is the result of what is expected versus the real outcome. To do these comparisons, you need the following information:

- Length of fiber strand calculated manually
- Attenuation reading from the scanner
- Maximum fiber loss from the cable manufacturer's specifications
- Loss of the connector from the cable manufacturer's specifications

The following table gives you the usual loss to expect with each part:

Part	Loss
SC Connector	0.3 dB
ST Connector	0.3 dB
Multi-mode at 850 nm	3.4 dB/km
Multi-mode at 1300 nm	1.0 dB/km

Expected Losses When Testing Fiber

As with all parts, this is just an average. Some manufacturers of multi-mode cable have attenuation loss as high as 3.75 dB for 850 nm and 1.5 dB for 1300 nm. This is also the maximum currently allowed by the EIA/TIA—funny how that works. The reading you obtain from your handy-dandy scanner is the following:

(max. specified attenuation loss $\times$ length of run) + (2 $\times$ connector loss)

For example, if your run was 0.5 km long, your loss at 850 nm would be calculated as $(0.5 \times 3.4) + (2 \times 0.3) = 2.3$. Also, add 0.1 dB because field testing is accurate only to ± 0.2 dB. Thus, your test result should be no more than 2.5 dB at 850 nm. Test results should never be higher than 0.9 dB at 850 nm or 0.7 dB at 1300 nm and should be performed from both ends. If test results are higher than that, the installer needs to repolish the ends or replace the faulty connector. Tests are not just a matter of PASS or FAIL, but of how well the cable performs.

There are many scanners on the market. Both Fotec and MicroTest make dependable fiber testers.

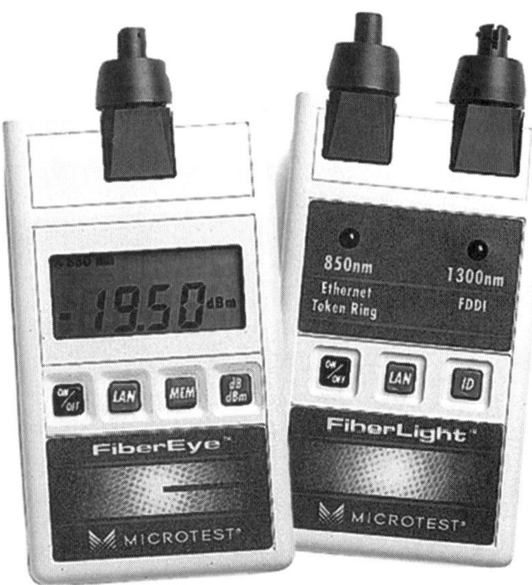

MicroTest Fiber Eye

IMPLEMENTATION

By now, I hope you have realized that fiber is just the Physical layer. It is no "faster" than copper. Both signals travel at the speed of light until they reach your network interface card. From that point, the speed of the signal is dependent on what you have chosen for your Data Link layer. Currently, there are three popular choices: 10BaseF, FDDI, and 100BaseFX.

FDDI is often used as the Physical layer implementation for the backbone. Since many backbones must be made of fiber due to length, there are a multitude of hubs that not only support 100 Mbps on the fiber backbone, but also serve as a bridge to Ethernet. Thus, the less expensive UTP is used on each floor or building where Ethernet is implemented and the FDDI is used over the fiber backbone. FDDI is effective for well-managed networks that need additional bandwidth over the backbone. Unfortunately, FDDI hubs are expensive. The average per port cost of an FDDI hub is over $1,000.

Fiber Repeaters and Switches

Hey manufacturers, are you listening? This is the perfect backbone hub:

- A switch that bridges between regular and Fast Ethernet
- Up to 36 ST fiber ports running 100BaseFX
- Up to 24 RJ-45 ports that can be configured on the fly for regular Ethernet or Fast Ethernet.

Is this too much to ask for? Apparently it is. The best thing for your busy backbone is a switch or a really fast processor in a repeater. I have focused my discussion on Fast Ethernet and fiber. Unfortunately, there is neither a Fast Ethernet switch nor a repeater on the market that supports fiber and copper—except for one (count it, *one)* fiber switch running Fast Ethernet made by Bay Networks. The current price is around $1,000 per port. Although that seems high, regular Ethernet is not much less. The new version of switches by Bay Networks are called the BayStacks and are indeed stackable (going head-to-head with Cisco), but there are no fiber modules for Fast Ethernet.

BayStack Stackable Switches

Here is what is on the market, or promised for the first quarter of 1996.

Cisco Switches (formerly Kalpana)

They have a regular Ethernet chassis that can take up to three cards with a total of 15 ports. Each card has five ports and can be ST fiber or RJ-45. They also have the best product on the market for cost and flexibility, the Cisco 3000. It is stackable to 10 hubs if you implement the ProStack module on the bottom. It comes with 16 RJ-45 ports and two slots, giving you many options. Since I am on the fiber bandwagon, let me mention that each slot can hold up to three fiber ports, thus yielding six fiber ports per switch.

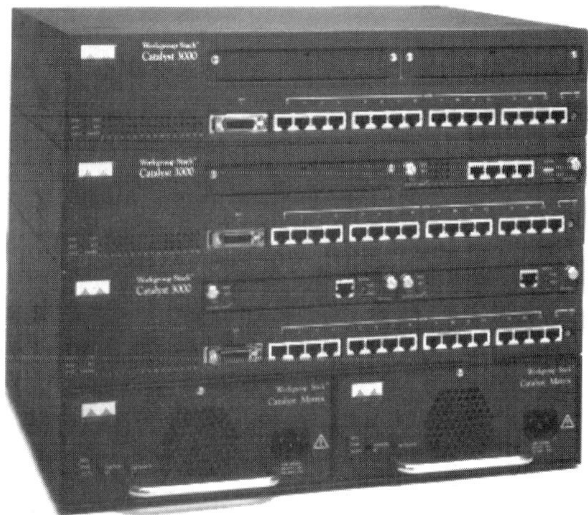

Cisco Catalyst 3000

Recently, being the clever girl that I am, this is what I came up with on a large installation—use three Cisco switches and one Matrix. Use the 18 fiber ports (6 fiber ports × 3 hubs) and 16 of the RJ-45 ports for the backbone. Connected to the backbone is a router from each building of the campus and the main servers used by the entire campus. That was one domain. With the remaining 32 ports, I created two domains by connecting a router to a port of each of the domains, as well as the backbone. Each set of 15 ports was its own domain and serviced the hubs and servers of the building that housed the backbone, as well as a major administration area and up to 12 classrooms (four classroom hubs are shown).

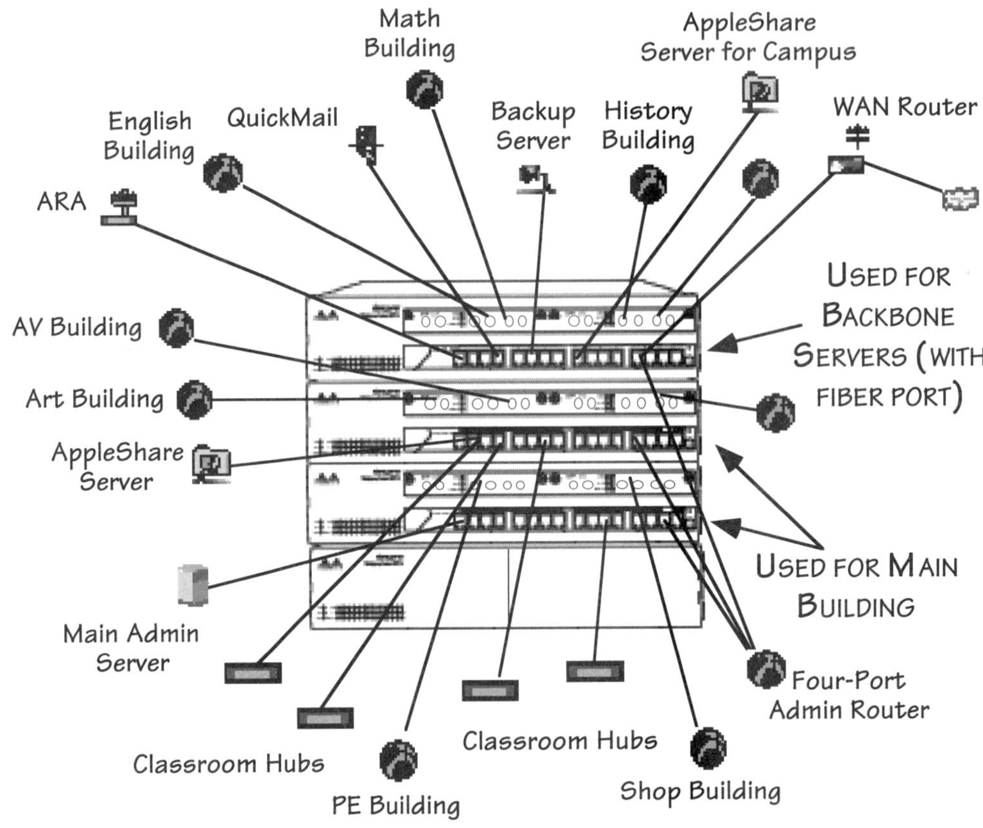

Cisco 3000 Used for Backbone and Local Switch

PlainTree Switches

These are OEMed by everyone and their sister. They are nonstackable, with eight or 16 RJ-45 ports or 12 10BaseF ports. In addition, they have two slots on each switch that can support a card with one Fast Ethernet port in fiber or copper. This is a good switch if your network is busy, but you don't have many general servers that need to be on the backbone.

LANart Managed Hubs

One of the most cost-efficient fiber repeaters is the LANart Managed Hub. The 8-port 10BaseFL hub costs $2,795 and the 16-port one costs $4,195. Granted, you don't receive Fast Ethernet performance or switched technology, but you will save $700 per port. Let's just say you better know a lot about switched technology and its increased performance if you are going to spend the money.

LANart Managed Fiber Hubs

This brings me to how many strands you need. The first rule is never to have less than four. If one set of strands goes down, you always want a backup. The second rule is to take every hub run directly to your backbone from any floor or building and multiply that number by two. Personally, I prefer at least six strands.

For example, let's say you are networking a large floor where the distances between closets are greater than 100 meters. There is a main closet in the center and two satellite closets. In the main closet, there would be a fiber switch servicing the rest of the floor and its area. The fiber pull to closet C needs six strands, but I would budget for at least 10. The fiber pull to closet A needs eight, but I would budget for 12. Ah, but there is a fly in the ointment: you cannot say to a contractor, "I'd like four strands here, 20 strands there, and…" You must settle on one strand count and run additional pulls. In this instance, I would do the 12 strands to cover for the maximum amount needed. Although you will pay for the additional parts and termination, you will not need to buy the hubs until you are ready.

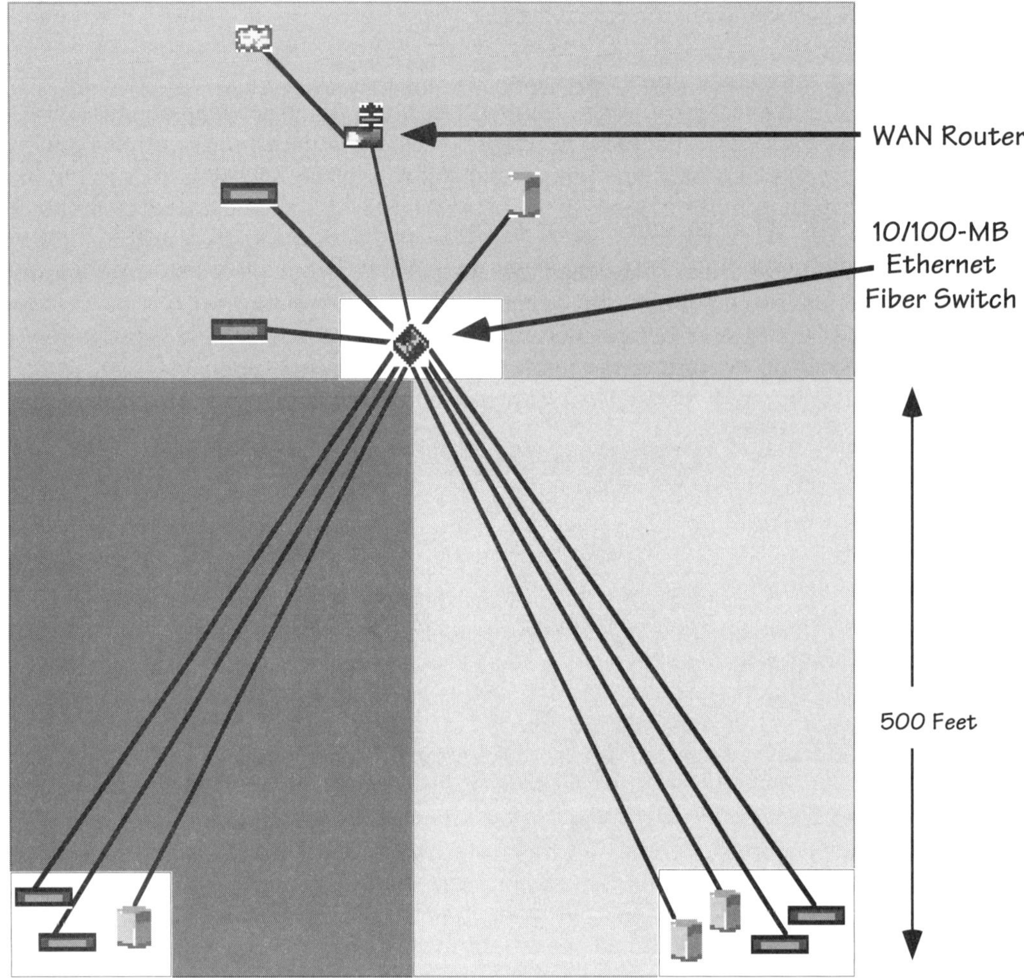

Fiber Switch Serving Different Floors

Finally, connect each repeater connected to the fiber switch with the fiber uplink port on the switch. Now you know whether to spec AUI or fiber for your uplink port. How do you connect your 10BaseT servers to the fiber switch? Read on.

FOIRL

Ever wonder how they convert fiber to copper, or how an optical signal is turned into an electronic signal? Well, guess what? I don't know, and I'm just going to believe that my trusty FOIRL, fiber optic inter-repeater link, is working like a champ. Underrated and often overpriced, this little device is about the same size as an AUI-to-RJ-45 or an AUI-to-BNC converter. They are available from such folks as Lantronix and Asanté for about $250. If you are trying to waste money, Black Box has them available for about $500. Since most affordable routers do not have a fiber port and the first thing you usually encounter after coming from the main fiber backbone is a router, budget in these little guys anywhere you are going from copper to fiber—most likely from 10BaseF to 10BaseT.

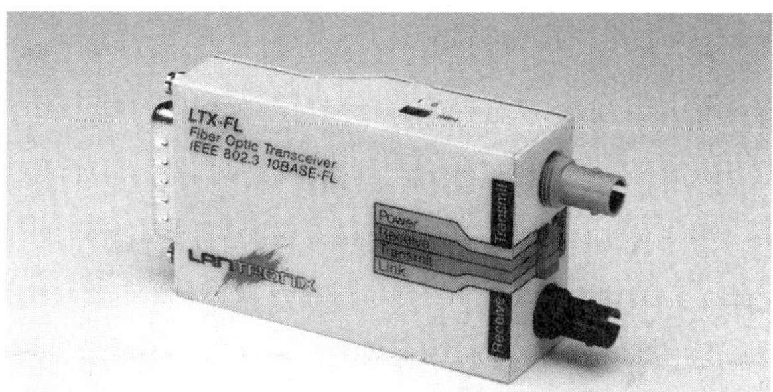

Lantronix FOIRL

The Future

If I could predict the future, I wouldn't be writing this chapter. Still, I know a lot about what is real and what is still vapor. This I know for sure—fiber is not going away. As we have more temperamental algorithms that require smaller and smaller frame rates, the ability of the media to support a dependable signal becomes much more crucial. Because fiber is immune to the outside forces of magnetism and electronic noise, the cost of providing a vacuum-like environment for UTP to maintain a healthy signal has begun to exceed the costs for the actual fiber installation. This has two implications: one that pushes us into using more fiber and one that encourages planners to provide secure pathways for data so we can use the much less costly UTP.

The moral of the story is that in all new building structures, there is absolutely no excuse to put in less than EIA/TIA 569 standards so that UTP can be used. But if the ceilings and the floors are stuffed with scary things and walls, floors, and ceilings must be torn out to put in conduits that are safe from electrical noise, fiber might just be a cheaper alternative. You have the spreadsheets—just do some number crunching and the answer will be as simple as 2 + 2, or better yet 2 + $20,000.

PART 2:
INTERCONNECTIVITY HARDWARE AND SOFTWARE

This section covers hubs, switches, bridges, routers, and gateways. It deals with what you are putting in your wiring rack. This covers more than what these devices *do*—it also covers how to implement them correctly. It focuses not only on how to correctly design *an* interconnectivity center for your network, but also on how to correctly design *several* interconnectivity centers to tie a diverse network together.

How to Use This Section

This section is about the equipment that goes on the equipment rack in your wiring closet.

Automatically assume that any piece of networking hardware examined in this section has at least *two* ports—an *in port* and an *out port*.

It would hardly be internetworking hardware if it had a single port, but hey, some folks get some strange ideas sometimes, and we don't want to lose anybody before we've even begun.

This section is about repeaters, multiport repeaters, switches, and routers. These are interconnectivity or *interlinking* devices. Due to the layered nature of the OSI model, networks can be interlinked at any of the levels of the layers. Most commonly, though, repeaters are used to interlink the Physical layer of the OSI model, bridges are used to interlink at the Data Link layer, routers are used to interlink at the Network layer, and gateways are used all the way up on the Application layer.

You should be able to use this section to help you define your needs, whether they are for a repeater or maybe a gateway. You should also use this section to help you identify what it is you need to know to implement these devices. We immediately go into the details of each type of device, hopefully shedding some light on how they work in the real world.

CHAPTER 9: REPEATERS

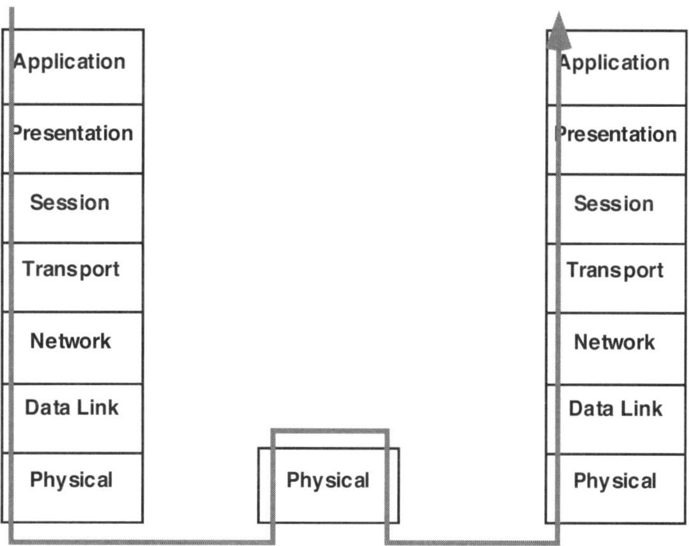

Model of a Repeater

Repeaters are fairly simple and are used to link networks *of the same type* at the Physical layer only. Basically, repeaters are used to overcome the wiring distance limitations caused by the limits of cable lengths. **Repeaters cannot be used to segment network traffic**, as they only "understand" 1's and 0's on the network. They don't understand the differences between AppleTalk or TCP/IP. They also don't care where the packets are coming from or going to. Mainly, they retransmit data signals. Therefore, cable segments connected together through a repeater are all members of the same network.

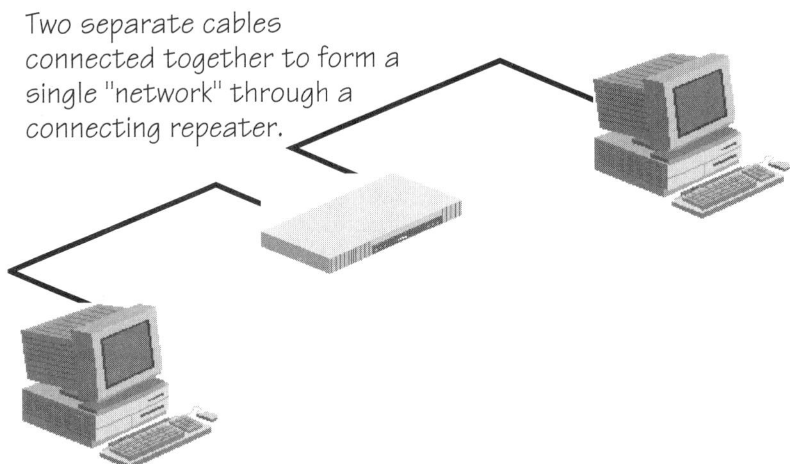

They can, however, be used to connect LANs of the same type (Ethernet to Ethernet) that use different media. For example, they can link a coax (10Base5) LAN together with a twisted pair (10BaseT) or a fiber (10BaseF) network. This doesn't mean that the mixed media cables form different networks; it only means that the repeaters can regenerate the same type of signal (Ethernet or LocalTalk) while moving it over the different types of media that the signal supports.

What all of this amounts to is that the repeater is used to extend the general designs of the networks beyond their initial specifications. Because of this, the connected cabling systems can often go awry and will need more management capabilities as they become more complex. Therefore, most repeaters also offer fault management capabilities. We will now summarize these basic functions.

Signal Regeneration

Attenuation is a measurement of power loss as the signal travels the length of a network cable. Signals attenuate as they travel down the wire, and if they don't have enough signal strength when they reach their destination, the receiving computer won't even know a message is coming in. Attenuation and mutual capacitance combined have the most effect on signal quality. Attenuation in unshielded twisted pair (UTP) media is greater than on coaxial cable.

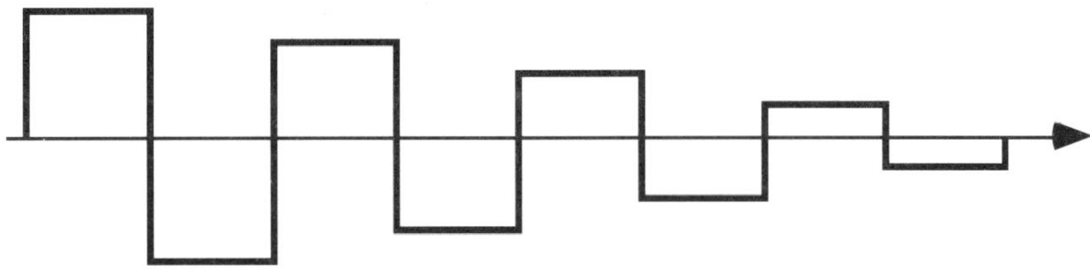

Simplified Example of Signal Attenuation

Attenuation isn't the only enemy of a network signal. Capacitance is just as detrimental to a data signal. Capacitance is a measure of the electrical energy the dielectric between the cables picks up and stores as a result of network signals flowing through the cables. In other words, capacitance is a measure of how much energy is absorbed by the cable as the signal passes through it. A cable's capacitance is determined by its dielectrical constant, distance between the cable conductors, and the total cable length as specified in picofarads per foot or meter. Capacitance causes signal distortion, resulting in the node no longer being able to distinguish the network signal from common network "noise." The effects of capacitance are more or less to "round out" the signal's wave from that of a squared data signal to that of a native sine wave.

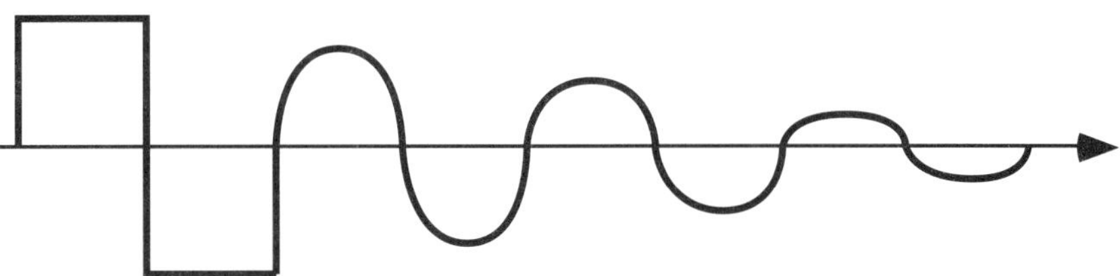

Effects of Capacitance on a Data Signal

Because repeaters are specifically built to combat these problems, the primary objective of a repeater is the regeneration of a network signal to its original form and structure. A repeater, therefore, is not merely responsible for reamplifying the signal; it literally recreates the signal according to the patterns of 1's and 0's. So, what's the difference? Think of signal *strengthening* as taking the same signal and making it stronger. Think of signal *regeneration* as *interpreting* the original signal and creating an identical *new* signal when forwarding to the other port(s).

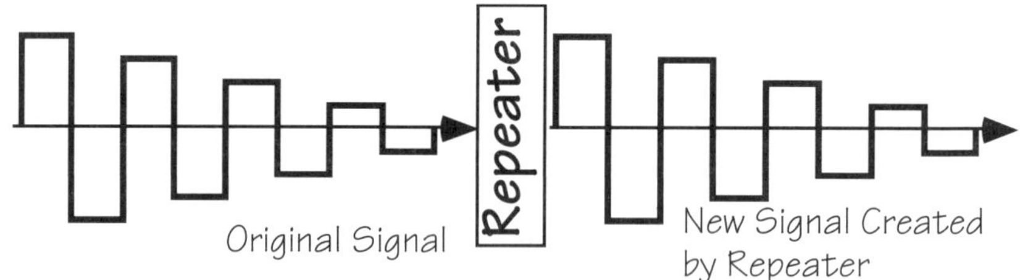

Effects of a Repeater on a Signal

Every 1 and 0 that makes it to a repeater is faithfully regenerated, meaning that repeaters cannot be used to segregate traffic. This also means that if a network device is sending out "bad" packets, such as runts or CRC errors, the repeater will just as faithfully regenerate those. Further, if electronic noise reaches a point at which it could be mistaken for 1's or 0's, the noise will be regenerated as well.

If you are thinking about the problem in the right way, you also realize that each of the repeaters causes small delays in the signaling process each time a signal passes through one of them. Keep this in mind, because after we look at some other things a repeater can do, we'll cover the rules of repeater usage and design.

Fault Isolation

As repeaters are used to connect many segments together and are therefore placed on the same network (often many hundreds at a time), the repeating device has to be capable of isolating problems occurring on one port and preventing them from entering all the other ports. To accomplish this, most repeaters monitor each port in order to detect and then isolate—hopefully automatically—any faulty segments. The jabbering of one network device could lead to the downfall of an entire networking segment if the device's jabbering were transmitted to every part of the network.

Before a repeater can isolate a faulty area it has to detect the faulty area. When monitoring a port for contention problems, the repeater will count the number of consecutive contentions. At some predetermined point, it will then segment that port from the rest of the network. Theoretically, repeaters should then be able to automatically reconnect the port once the contentions are no longer present—the specifications call for looking for 512 bits of valid data. Theoretically.

Mixed Media Support

Very few repeaters offer mixed media support on a port-by-port basis. However, most repeaters at least offer mixed media support between their node-end ports and their "backplane" ports. Most offer it in the form of AUI (to which most anything can be attached), ThinNet, and 10BaseT.

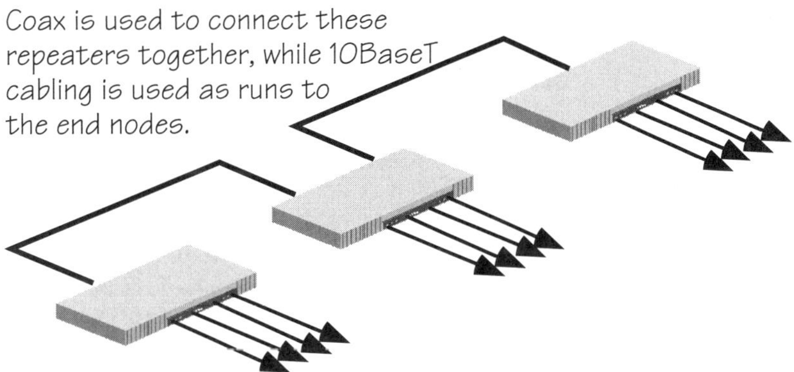

REMOTE ETHERNET REPEATERS

Right now in the AppleTalk world there is only one remote repeater pair, and that is the Tut Systems' two-port remote repeater system. This system uses two two-port repeaters to extend a cable length well over 1000 feet. One port of the repeater connects to the "normal" network and the other port is used to connect the two repeaters together and can be connected to *any* twisted pair cabling segment. When I say *any* segment, that means that I've even tapped into a Bell 50-pair cable to run a network cable from a school building out to the football field (the Bell cable ran under the field up to the press box). This device has an RJ-11 jack for the twisted pair connection and an AUI or a self-terminating coax connection to the "main" network.

This repeater is used on both ends to connect the segments together into a single network.

Remote repeaters are deployed in pairs and are sometimes called "half repeaters."

Tut 10Base2 to Twisted Pair Remote Repeater Design

A two-port repeater works by connecting two network segments with a repeater on each segment. You can then run—with the Tut repeater—up to 1,000 feet of Category 3 twisted pair cable between them. Once connected with the repeaters, the network acts as a single segment. This is the same as if you were using a single, shorter cable.

You need remote repeaters at each end so the repeater can send the signal to the other side. Putting a single repeater at one end would only allow one of the segments to have enough power to send the signal down to the other end. Signals coming from the end without the repeater wouldn't have the strength to make it to the other side.

IMPLEMENTATIONS OF HUB REPEATERS

Hub repeaters—also called hubs, whether for LocalTalk or Ethernet—use the same principles as any other repeater. The number of ports on each repeater is normally up to the individual manufacturer, but is usually 8, 12, 16 or 24. Multiport hubs for LocalTalk use either shielded or unshielded twisted pair cabling for the cables that run from the hub to the wall. Many systems administrators or designers will then use the flat wire cables that come with their PhoneNET or StarConnectors to connect to the wall jacks. While that is common practice and doesn't greatly impede the network's functionality, it's not the best design.

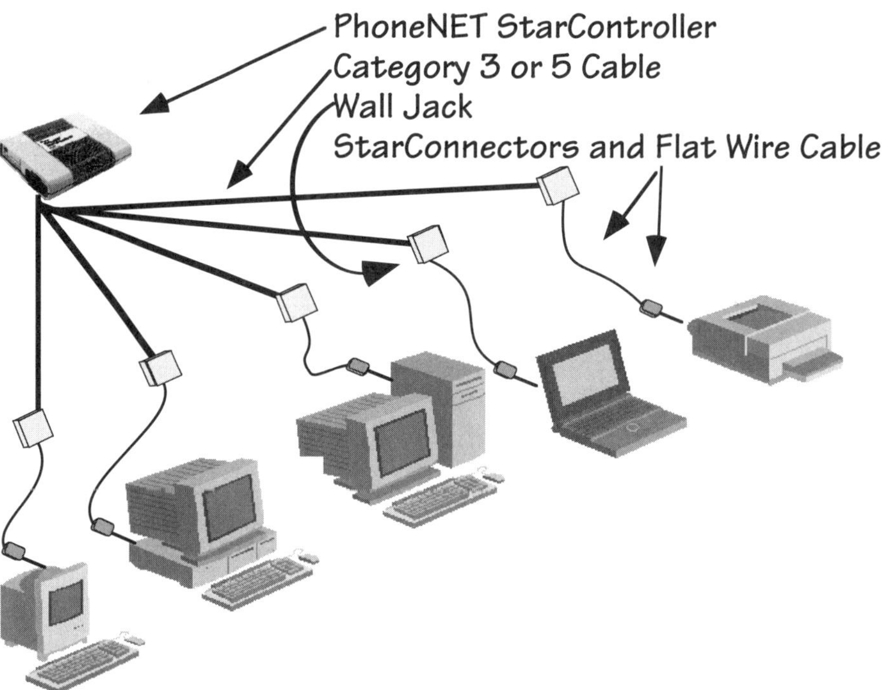

Basic LocalTalk Hub Network

Farallon LocalTalk Hub

For LocalTalk, there is but one contender: the trusty Farallon LocalTalk hub, commonly known as the PhoneNET StarController. There are two versions of this hub: a 12- and a 24-port version. Both versions fit into the Farallon Concentrator (covered further on) or can be used as stand-alone devices. These are managed hubs in that they can be managed with Farallon's StarCommand software—which we cover extensively in our book *Managing AppleTalk Networks*—but can't be managed through SNMP. Some ludicrous wiring distances are recommended coming out of each port, and I'll explain to you why you don't want to use them, besides the fact that it doesn't really work. While we are on the subject, I personally don't ever recommend the 12-port hub. The 12-port hub comes with a 48-port patch panel (four devices per port). I don't recommend more than 24 devices on a LocalTalk network without a switch. But hey, that's just me. People say that I build battleship networks. Okay, so I build battleship networks, but at least they don't break. Anyway, I prefer the 24-port hub because it fits the 24-port patch panel kit, and that means one device per port. I like that. By the way, that equals the maximum number of devices I believe you should be putting on a LocalTalk network segment without a switch.

Farallon PhoneNET StarController Hub

Characteristics

- StarController hubs have 12 or 24 ports with an RJ-21 amphenol connector to support 66-block or patch panel wiring connectivity. We like the 24-port model, as it has a matching 24-port patch panel. This helps ensure a one-device-to-one-port ratio.

- There is no backplane for uplink connectivity. To connect these devices you must "steal" the twelfth port for interconnectivity, thus reducing the number of devices per hub to 11.

Mini-Multiport Ethernet Repeaters

Ethernet has so much more "bandwidth" or "utilization" that we don't believe that you need an Ethernet switch in a one-room environment. (We prefer the term *utilization* to *bandwidth;* it is more accurate in a baseband environment.) Therefore, the smaller four-port or eight-port Ethernet hubs we discuss here are for use in designing *temporary* Ethernet networks and are not for use in conventional network design. When you decide to move up to a structured wiring system, replace these hubs with regular hubs and a regular wiring design. You can use these same hubs later for more temporary work, if necessary. The following picture shows the Apple 10T/5 hub sitting atop the TechWorks "hublet." Notice that there isn't much difference in size between the two. However, there is a difference in characteristics between the two.

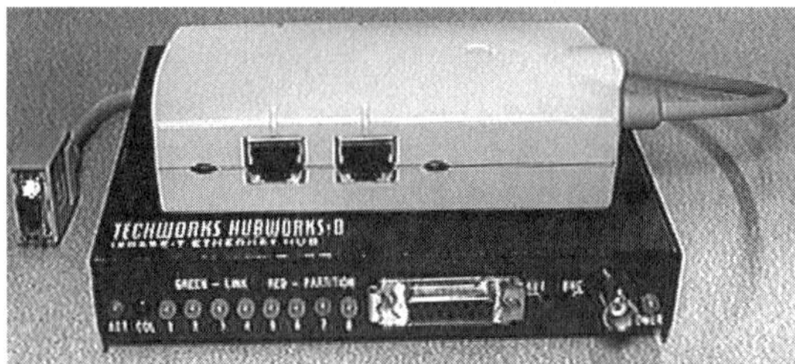

Apple Hub (top) and TechWorks Eight-Port Hublet (bottom)

The Apple 10T/5 has five ports: one AAUI that can be attached to a computer's port to act as the computer's transceiver, and four RJ-45 ports to connect to other computers. That's it. The minihub, like most other minihubs, has eight RJ-45 jacks to connect to eight devices, as well as an "uplink" port in the form of AUI, BNC (shown in the previous picture), and an "uplink/node" port capability on port 8 of the hub (not shown). The Apple minihubs can be used for dropping in to a group of 4–5 computers. I wouldn't connect to more devices than that, as the hub is a *retiming* hub and there can be a *total* of four retiming hubs in serial. When you expand later, there is a good possibility that you will forget about these types of hubs (like none of you ever "forgot" something was on the net) and you might quickly and easily overextend your network — but more about that later.

Apple 10T/5 Workgroup Hub

Apple's Ethernet 10T/5 hub is a standard 802.3i compliant multiport repeater. It has five ports: four 10BaseT ports and one AAUI port. The hub draws its power from the AAUI port itself or an external power supply, such as the same power supply for the QuickTake camera. The external power supply *must* be purchased separately.

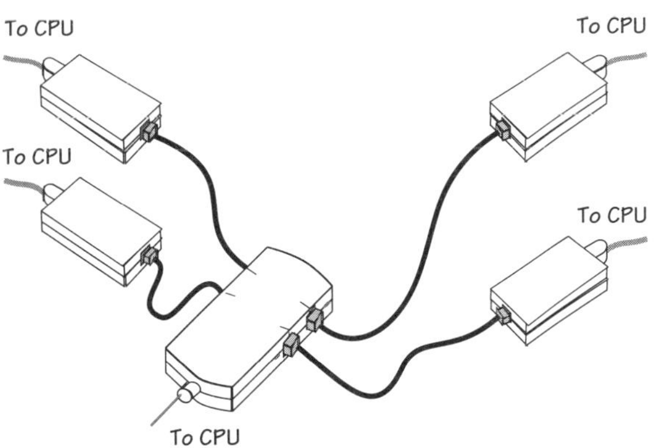

Apple's Ethernet 10T/5 Hub Connecting to CPUs

An important note here: If you accidentally hook the power supply from your original StyleWriter into the hub, you will burn out the hub. Make sure that you label the power supply, "Use Only for StyleWriter."

Also remember that if you aren't using an external power supply you'll need to turn on the computer that is directly connected to the hub *first*, before turning on computers that use the hub for connectivity. Without the hub "on" via the host computer before other computers start up, they won't be able to activate Ethernet simply because there will be no power to the hub.

Characteristics

- There are four ports for "other connectivity" and one port of "direct connectivity," for a total of five ports.

- There are *no* specific uplink ports or a backplane for connectivity to other hubs. This means that one of the ports has to be used for uplink connectivity.

- This hub doesn't support power pass-through. If there isn't any power, there isn't any connectivity.

- Apple ships a small "cross-over" connector with the hubs. If you want to plug your hub into an existing port on another hub, or if you want to connect hubs together, you can plug a drop cable into the hub on one end, into the cross-connect on the other, and come up with an "inverted pair." This is an inverted pair because hubs cannot be connected together via a straight-through cable. If you lose the cross-over connector, you will have to make or purchase a cross-over cable. Apple calls it an *expansion adapter,* but you can buy it as a cross-over connector at any GraybaR.

Standard Rack-Mountable Hubs

Asanté Hubs Stacked One on the Other

Standard Ethernet hubs can be classified in two ways: dumb hubs and smart hubs. Both can be mounted onto 19-inch racks in the wiring closet. The only type of Ethernet hub that can't be mounted onto one of these racks is the Farallon 12- or 24-port Ethernet "smart" hub. For that reason alone, I hate the device. It promotes bad network design by making the administrator bolt it to the wall or lay it on top of something on the wiring rack—not a good idea.

Dumb Hubs

Another device that is connectable to a portable Ethernet hub is the standard mass market hub, also known as a "dumb hub." They are called dumb hubs because most of them have neither management software nor SNMP reporting capabilities. Basically, either they work or they don't.

At the same time, they come with RJ-45 ports built-in for each of the computers to which they can connect and communicate, as well as AUI or BNC "uplink" ports to attach them to the rest of your network. The question becomes: Would we suggest that you attach them to the rest of your network? Not really. If I were designing the network—this is Dorian talking here, and this probably isn't the opinion of every consultant at Network Frontiers—I wouldn't use a hub that doesn't support RFC 1243, the AppleTalk implementation for SNMP. The more management I can have on a network, the better I feel. I'd rather have an application monitoring my network 24 hours a day, telling me when something goes wrong, than have *my butt* down on each segment doing packet testing and capturing traces to see what's happening. But hey, that's just me.

Smart Hubs

One of the differences between a smart hub and a dumb hub is that all smart hubs are able to identify cables that are "backward" or are cross-connect cables, meaning that pairs 1 and 3 are switched. The other *real* difference between a smart and dumb hub is that a smart hub usually refers to a hub that has some management capabilities, usually SNMP. Therefore, smart hubs should register their services as an NVE on your network.

Ethernet Concentrators and Stackable Hubs

One of the problems with standard Ethernet hubs is that you quickly run out of ports and therefore need to interconnect your hubs. When doing this, you create "hub hops" and extend your network's design, potentially *overextending* it. Hub manufacturers found two solutions to this problem of keeping the number of hub hops to a minimum. One solution is the Ethernet concentrator, and the other is the stackable hub. Both the concentrator and the stackable hub solution have one similar feature: a *common backplane* that connects the many hubs in the concentrator or stacked hubs together into a single unit.

Concentrators

Concentrators are basically boxes into which you slide hubs. The concentrator allows the hubs to share a common Ethernet backplane as well as a single power source. Most of the concentrators also offer additional features, such as SNMP or out-of-band management features in case in-band management is impossible. They also allow different types of hubs—such as Fiber, 10Base2, and 10BaseT—to be intermixed.

The Farallon Concentrator not only has a standard Ethernet backbone, it has *two* Ethernet backbones and several LocalTalk backbones as well. You can put Local-Talk and Ethernet hubs, router/hubs, and multiport routers into the Farallon Concentrator. Most hubs that fit into concentrators have individual RJ-45 jacks for direct connectivity.

Stackable Hubs

Stackable hubs, which are becoming more common than concentrator-based hubs, allow the designer to accomplish the same goal of a shared backbone, but *without* the concentrator's enclosing box and the additional cost. Most stackable hubs come with a smart hub as the base device and several dumb hubs as the slave, or stacked, devices. Most hubs that are stackable have RJ-45 jacks for direct connectivity. Some of them, as one in the stack shown in the following picture, have RJ-21 jacks for amphenol cables as well.

Hub Concentrator (left) and Stackable Ethernet Hub (right) from Asanté

Fast Ethernet and 100-Mbps Ethernet Repeaters

So, what in the world is Fast Ethernet, and what do I need to know about it before I integrate it into my networking scheme? Fast Ethernet is also called 100BaseT and 100BaseFX Ethernet for Fast Ethernet running over twisted pair cabling or fiber cabling, respectively. Its official title from the IEEE is 802.3u, just like 10BaseT is 802.3i.

Fast Ethernet uses the same CSMA/CD (Carrier Sense Multiple Access/Collision Detection) algorithms as 10BaseT Ethernet networks. They are sped up appropriately for the higher speed ratios of Fast Ethernet. This makes Fast Ethernet networks 100% compatible with regular 10-Mbps Ethernet networks. This means that migrating to Fast Ethernet is as easy as incorporating it into the cards, computers, hubs, and appropriate 10/100-Mbps bridges or routers on your network.

802.3u Standard Specifics

The 802.3u standard not only specifies the same CSMA/CD standard, but also the new bit rate that is 10 times faster than standard Ethernet. It further specifies what is being called "auto-negotiation" on the Network Interface Card (NIC) and bridge/switch ports. Auto-negotiation allows an NIC with 10/100 capabilities to match the capability of the hub or bridge to which it is connected. When a bridge or switch is capable of both 10/100 capabilities, it will then detect the capabilities of the NIC and set its port rate at 10 or 100 Mbps, whichever is appropriate for the card, or in the case of a 10/100 card, it will automatically set to 100 Mbps.

The rules for 100BaseT as defined by 802.3u also state that the number of hub hops—the 5-4-3 rule discussed in a moment—for 10BaseT doesn't apply in 100-Mbps situations. The number of hub hops available in a 100BaseT environment is one or two, depending upon the class of the 100-Mbps hub that is being used. The two classes are, simply put, Class I and Class II hubs. We'll discuss the differences of the two classes of hubs, and their design rules, as a part of this chapter.

100-Mbps Ethernet Hubs

As the 100-Mbps hubs aren't a year old yet, all these hubs come in the smart format. The rack-mountable hubs with which we have worked and that we've tested are all stackable as well. Each of them has RJ-45 jacks mounted on the front because there isn't a Category 5 RJ-21 amphenol connector available. Other than that, there are no differences between the 100-Mbps hubs and the 10-Mbps hubs.

The only 100-Mbps hub we know of that *isn't* rack-mountable is the Farallon 100 Mbps hub. Because it isn't rack-mountable, I call it a "boutique" hub and don't recommend it for large network designs. You will probably find them in smaller, artsy-fartsy networks.

Most 100-Mbps stackable hubs allow up to six devices to be linked to act as a single unit, supporting a total of 144 unmanaged or 132 managed ports.

Asanté FAST 100BaseTX Stackable Hub Family

I want to give special mention to the Asanté FAST 100BaseTX stackable hub family. This family provides 100BaseTX connectivity to 100BaseTX Ethernet devices. Up to 15 hubs can be stacked for a maximum of 180 100BaseTX ports. A single network management module provides port-level SNMP management over the entire stack. A 100BaseFX-equipped module can be added to the stack to provide fiber connectivity to a 100BaseFX backbone. Since the Asanté FAST 100BaseTX stackable hubs are Class II 100BaseTX repeaters, they can be connected to a second 100BaseTX Class II repeater.

CABLING DESIGN ISSUES FOR HUBS

Most repeaters are designed to support either shielded or unshielded *twisted pair* wiring from the hub to the wall jack. Definitely avoid using two-pair or four-pair flat wire to connect the wall jack to the hub. It is recommended that you use twisted pair cabling from the wall jack to the computer, and from the hub's patch panel to the wiring closet patch panel. However, I know many of you won't do that with LocalTalk segments, so just be careful when using flat wire from the jack to the computer.

 When designing with hubs, there is a basic rule that you should follow: Avoid extended stub lengths. I know you will violate the Dorian Rule of Design that says one computer per home run cable, so I won't say don't *ever* add additional devices. Still, I do want to emphasize the fact that you shouldn't be allowing rampant stub extensions.

Cabling Termination

Every LocalTalk cable must be terminated at each end, which means that you can't have looped networks, either. This also means that each cable should be terminated properly with a 120-ohm resistor.

True Story   I was once redesigning a network in Chicago. While conducting the walk-through, I counted 57 networked devices in one office. Then I walked into the wiring closet. There were two 24-port Farallon PhoneNET StarController hubs, each with 5–6 ports full and about as many open. The math, even though I really stink at math, didn't add up: 48 ports for hubs, 57 devices, and almost 12 ports left open. I decided that I would go out and trace the cabling to see where the devices were connected. You aren't going to believe this one, unless you are a designer yourself or in tech support. One of the hub ports had 12 computers on it. Another port had six. Many of the hub ports that had wires connected in the closet had no computers connected to the cables in the office. Unbelievable. Once the wires were redistributed properly and some of the computers moved up to Ethernet, their problems magically went away and their network seemed to run so much smoother. Who'd-a-thought?

10-MBPS HUB ARCHITECTURE DESIGN ISSUES

You need to know whether your repeaters are retiming devices (all Ethernet 10BaseT hubs *are* retiming), and their propagation of delay. Retiming devices incur delays when they resynchronize packets to their "incoming time clock." This could incur up to 35μs (one byte time) of delay per packet. Because Apple-Talk uses key timers (the interframe gap is < 200μs and the interdialog gap is ≥ 400ms), extended cable lengths and other factors could cause propagation delays close to 1000μs, thus making it extremely difficult for the computers to distinguish collisions. This in turn causes network problems. The easiest way to avoid this is to keep the cabling down to Ethernet specifications of around 100 meters when designing with hubs. It also makes it important to *not* daisy-chain multiple hubs together. No more than four should ever be allowed.

So, now that you know what a hub is and how delays in the signal can cause a problem, you must learn the network design rule for implementing these hubs. This is where most people go wrong. They start stringing these things together willy-nilly and pretty soon their network isn't functioning the way it should. So, here it is, plain and simple:

Do not place more than four repeaters between any two nodes!

Hub Hops

Did you get that? Let me pound it into your heads for a few more minutes. The following diagram shows two multiport repeaters connected together. The computer on the left is sending a packet onto the wire. Remember, the packet is sensed by everybody on the wire. As it traverses the network, it crosses the hub on the left, goes through the interconnection wire between the hubs, goes through the hub on the right, and then travels down to the receiving computer's cable. In this case, these two nodes are two hub hops away from each other. Basically, any time a repeater forwards a packet through one of its ports, the repeater causes enough delay to fall within this hub hop category. The only hubs that don't incur these delays are hubs designed to be stacked on top of each other. These are usually called *stackable hubs*. Once stacked together, they only retime outside of their normal grouping. We have covered these earlier, and will go over them again in a couple of pages.

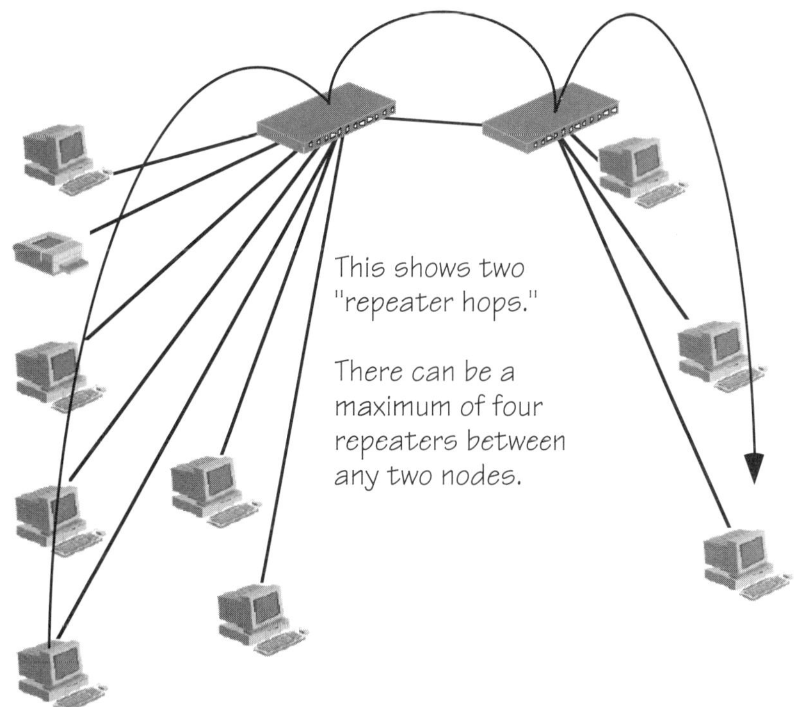

Physical Implementations of Hub Hops

So, why in the world would you want to interconnect your hubs? Well, for one thing, each hub can handle a maximum of 16 or 24 direct connections. Therefore, if you have 26 computers, you need two hubs. That's one reason. Another reason is that regardless of whether you could fill each hub with users, there are some times when a user is going to be farther than 295 feet from the hub, such as when a user is on the fifth floor and your hub is on the fourth floor. Your choice at that point will be to run your individual device cables from one floor to another using fiber for greater lengths —which could be pretty costly—or to put a hub on the upper and the lower floors and then run a single cable between them. The following diagram shows four computers (printers count, too, you know) on the fourth floor hub and three computers on the fifth floor hub. The problem to solve will be how to best connect the hubs.

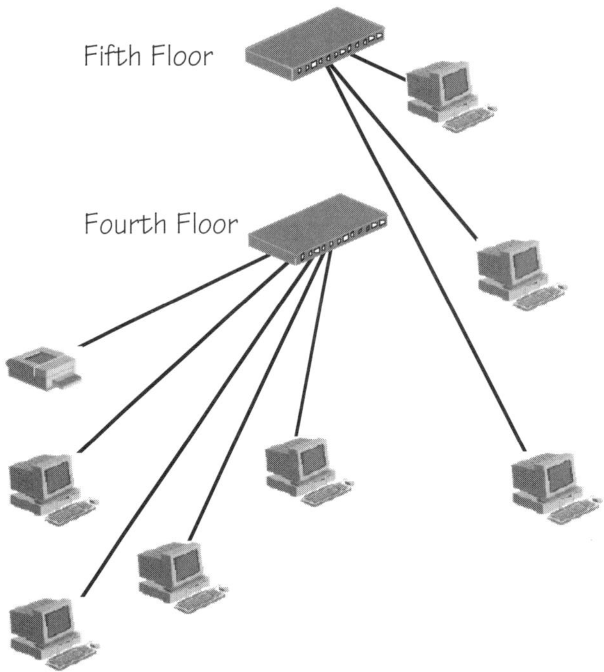

Hubs on Two Floors

The following are some options involved in connecting these two hubs.

Interconnect Port

Most hubs are built so that the "12th" or "16th" or "24th" port of the hub can be enabled as an interconnect port. This means that when set for interconnection, the port is actually looking for another multiport repeater instead of a computer or printer. For LocalTalk hubs, all you need to do is run a cable with RJ-11 jacks at both ends from one of the hub's 12th port to the other hub's 12th port. For Ethernet hubs that have that special node/interconnect switching port (MDI/MDI-X), you simply use a standard 10BaseT cable with dual RJ-45 plugs to connect the two. For those hubs that don't have the special port, such as the Apple minihub, you need to use what is called a cross-connect cable. A cross-connect cable crosses pin 1 to 3, 2 to 6, 3 to 1, and 6 to 2. Again, this works as long as the two hubs are no farther apart than 295 feet. The only problem with using one of the hub's end-node ports as a cross connect is that each of the hubs loses a single port, meaning the hubs are now down to 11 or 15 ports each. If you do the math, this drives up the price-per-port of the hub.

So, is there a better mousetrap? You betcha. While many of the hubs have interconnect ports, even more of the hubs have what I call, for lack of a better term, an Ethernet backplane. (LocalTalk hubs do not have this backplane and *must* be connected using one of their ports as an interconnect port.) Basically, this is another port on the hub that is set up as a ThinNet connection, an AUI connection, or, in the case of some Asanté hubs, whatever connection you want. On the bottom right of the next picture, two hubs are shown connected via ThinNet on the Ethernet backplane. While this connection still puts both hubs between nodes on opposite sides, it does at least allow full port usage for the hub itself. This is also a better way to connect, because the length of the coaxial cable can be extended 185 meters instead of 100 meters.

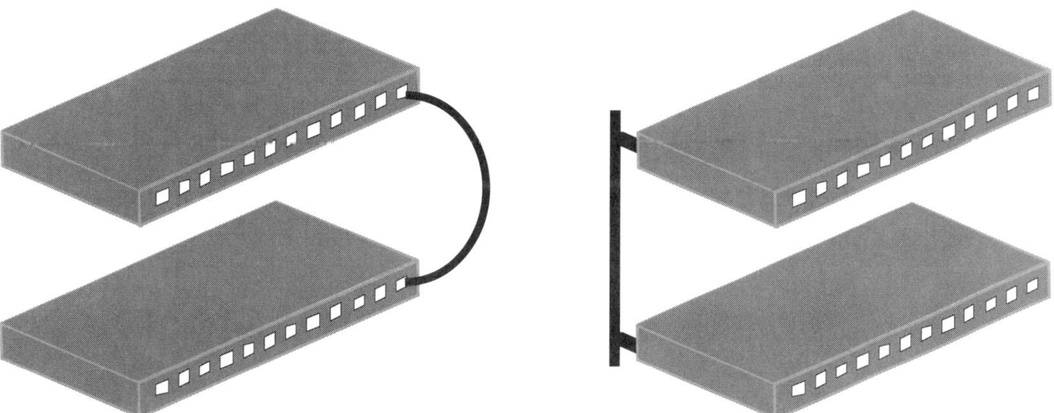

Interconnect Port with Twisted Pair (left) and Hubs Connected via Ethernet Backplane (right)

Distributed Backbone

What happens when you have more than two hubs on the network? First of all, don't cascade one hub off another ad infinitum. There are three main ways of setting up multiple hubs. We are going to cover two of them immediately, and cover the third in a few minutes (unless you fall asleep reading this, in which case we'll be covering it some time tomorrow).

One way is to use the Ethernet backplane. By using that backplane, you can more or less stack hubs one on top of the other—remember, some of these hubs might be on different floors—sharing a single ThinNet cable. This is called a *distributed backbone*. This might look like the following diagram.

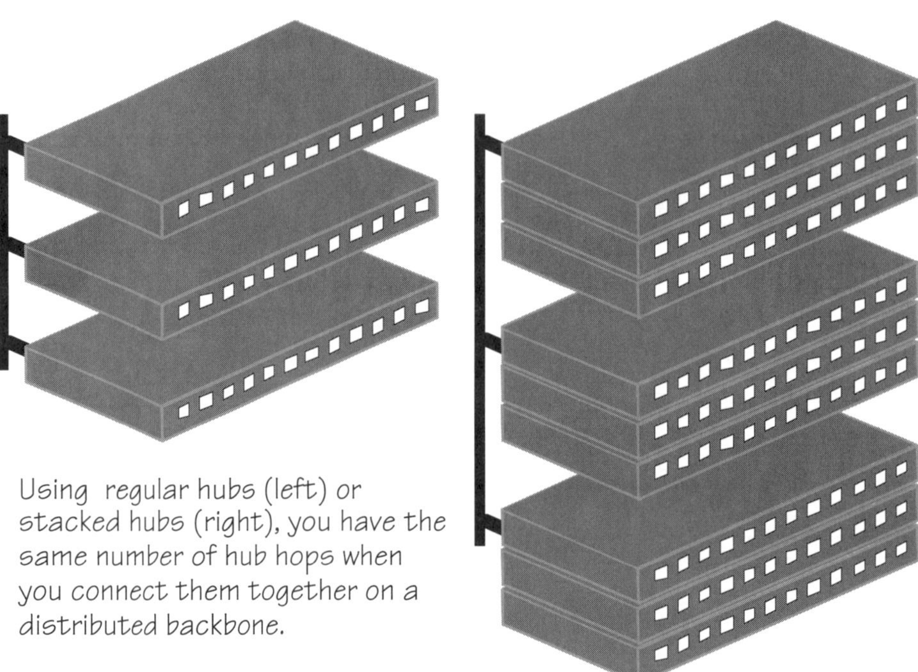

Using regular hubs (left) or stacked hubs (right), you have the same number of hub hops when you connect them together on a distributed backbone.

Remember what we said earlier about stackable hubs: If they are truly stackable hubs, then once stacked—usually up to five per stack—they can be thought of as a single hub. Therefore, the two pictures above really represent the same thing— a distributed backbone. Because the three hubs in the diagram share a common ThinNet cable, and the cable doesn't have to pass through any of the hubs, a packet sent from a computer connected to the bottom hub doesn't have to pass through the middle hub before it reaches the top hub. Thus, any computer attached to these hubs is two hub hops away from any other computer on the network. That's why it's called a distributed backbone—each of the hubs is distributed evenly across the backbone.

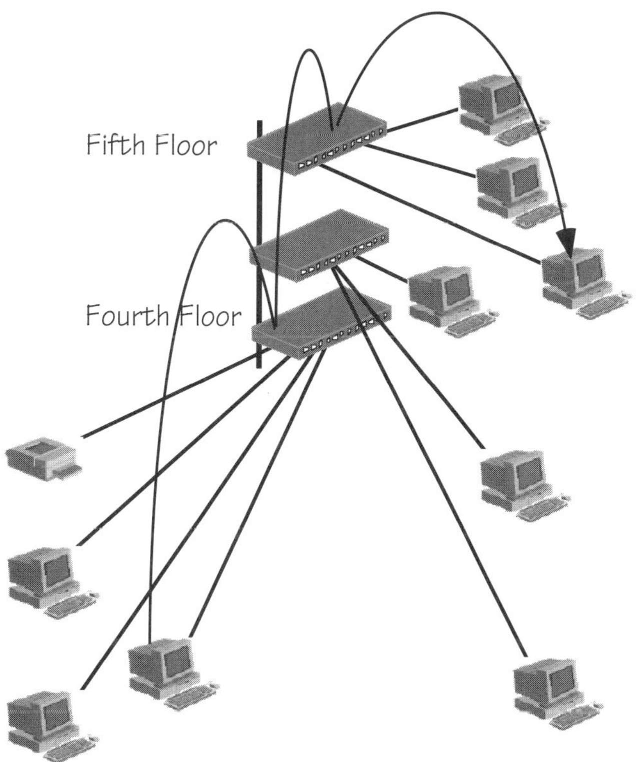

Packet Hopping Across a Distributed Backbone

Hierarchical Backbone

Distributed backbones are easy to set up and fairly common in the industry. From there, as far as management is concerned, we move to another design principal called the *hierarchical backbone*. If you have ever read one of the Farallon manuals, you have seen it. This type of backbone has one "master" hub serving "slave" hubs below it. The idea behind this type of network design is that the slave hubs can be dumb hubs and the master hub should be a smart hub. The smart hub should be able to discern when one of the ports is having a problem, shut down the port, and then tell you what it did, either through a notification dialog box or an idiot light. If it can't discern problem ports and shut them down automatically with notification, there's no use having a hierarchical backbone. Why put the See-No-Evil monkey in charge of the Hear-No-Evil and Speak-No-Evil monkeys?

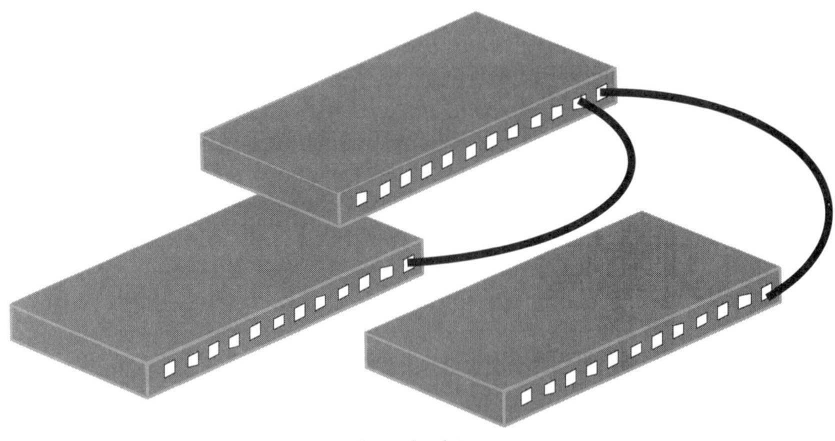

Hierarchical Setup

One thing you need to remember about the hierarchical setup is that it adds another hub hop to packets as they travel from one computer to another, and it wastes a port. There are going to be some times, though, when you really can't help using a hierarchical backbone. Usually that will be when you have decided to incorporate some of the smaller hubs—such as the minihubs—into your network designs. Apple minihubs, remember, don't have a backplane *at all,* and *any* time that you incorporate one of them into your network design, you add one of these hub hops into the equation.

The 5-4-3 Rule Applied to Hub Architectures

The 5-4-3 rule is fairly simple and applies to Ethernet hub topologies, whether they are 10BaseT, coax, or fiber. The rule is:

Between any two devices there can't be more than **5 segments and 4 hubs, and only 3 segments** may be **populated** with other devices.

We have drawn a diagram showing what we mean. In the following diagram there are a total of five segments. The (1) symbol represents the node segments, meaning that those segments are one drop, one device. From there the nodes are connected to the hubs. There are a total of four of them between the two devices. The (2) symbol indicates *populated* segments between the hubs. The reason that the (2) segments are considered populated is because each of the runs includes a device hooking up multiple devices instead of a single device.

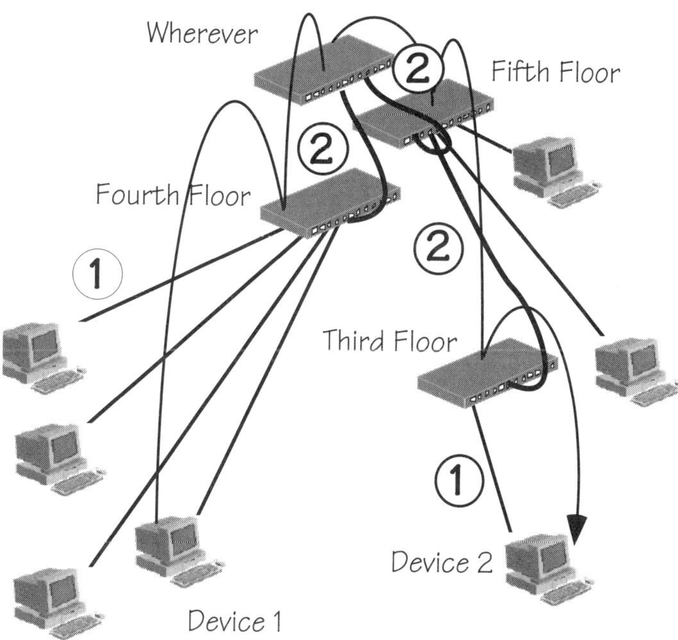

The 5-4-3 Rule of Hub Design

When designing your network, one of the rules to follow as religiously as possible is this one. The 5-4-3 rule not only applies to hubs, but to bridges and switches as well. This is because at the upper layers of the network protocols, the bridges and switches are invisible. This brings us to the point where we can begin teaching you about bridges and switches and their implementation.

100-MBPS HUB ARCHITECTURE DESIGN ISSUES

There are two basic categories of 100-Mbps hubs: Class I and Class II. In other words, another BetaMax versus VHS war is ensuing. The Class I hubs can support 100BaseTX, 100BaseT4 (not covered in this book), and 100BaseFX wiring standards. Class II hubs can support only 100BaseTX and 100BaseFX wiring standards. Currently, the makers of Class I 100-Mbps hubs are Bay Networks and 3Com, while the makers of Class II hubs are Asanté and Cisco/Kalpana/Grand Junction. (I wonder why they don't just call the company CisKal Junction, or Grand Cispana? How about Grand Cispana Junction? Boy, have I had *way* too many lattes this morning.) Anyway, getting back to the hubs, the Class I hubs are more limited in design scope than the Class II hubs. Here's how it works.

Class I 100-Mbps Hubs

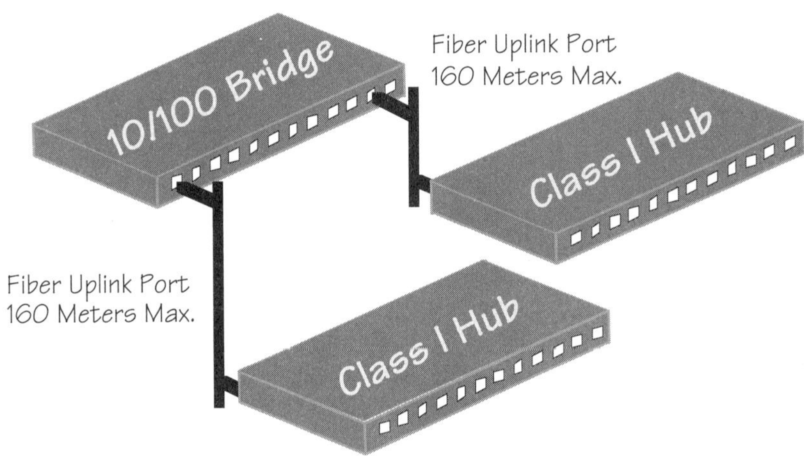

Class I 100-Mbps Hubs

There can be only a single Class I 100-Mbps hub per collision domain (we discuss collision domains in the next chapter, "Bridges and Switches," beginning on page 209). The maximum distance that the hub can be run from the bridge or router using fiber is 160 meters.

Class II 100-Mbps Hubs

With Class II hubs, there can be a total of two 100-Mbps hubs per collision domain. The maximum distance that the hub can be run from the bridge or router using fiber is 208 meters, and the maximum distance that the hubs can be interconnected is a total of 5 meters. This basically means that if you are structuring your hub hops for 100-Mbps repeaters, they better be on the same wiring rack.

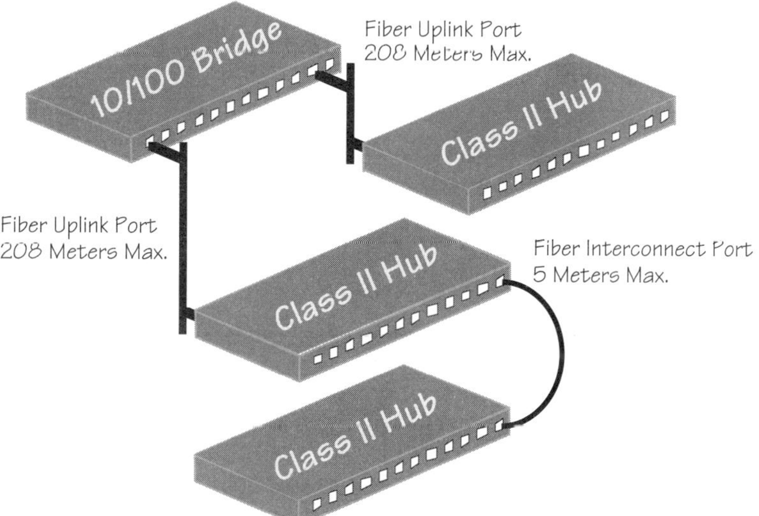

100-Mbps Class II Hub Hop Rules

CHAPTER 10:
BRIDGES AND SWITCHES

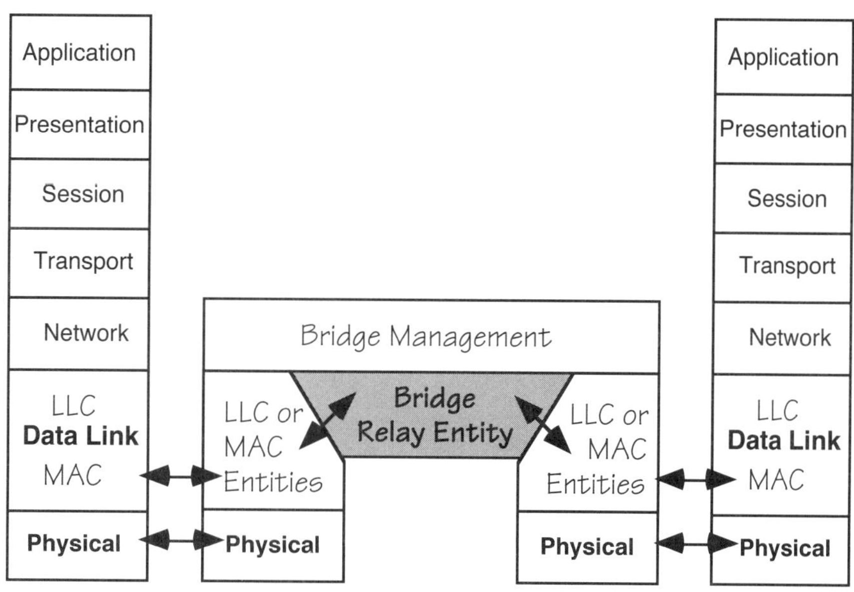

Model of a Bridge or Switch

While repeaters interpret signals at the bit level, bridges interpret signals at the packet level. However, bridges don't read addresses of packets up through the protocol layer, or Network layer. They only read the destination address. *Bridges offer the same signal regeneration capabilities of a repeater plus the added value of filtering data packets before sending them out a port.* Therefore, to a certain extent, bridges can be thought of as relay devices that offer the added service of limited traffic isolation. A bridge provides this traffic isolation by inspecting each packet's destination address and then deciding where the packet should be forwarded. In the case of a two-port bridge, the packet would be forwarded to the other side; or, in the case of a multiport switch, the bridge decides to which port the packet should be forwarded. Therefore, the bridges are dependent on both the Physical and the Data Link layer of the OSI model to function properly.

Because of their dependence upon the Data Link layer for destination addressing, bridges *automatically pass all broadcast and multicast traffic to all ports.* Therefore, the fundamental usage of a bridge is to isolate local, or port-based, point-to-point traffic and thus improve the network's performance *capabilities.* This *does not mean* that a bridge speeds up network traffic. It merely reduces the number of devices accessing each port of the bridge and thereby gives each computer a greater percentage of access to the overall network. At the same time, bridges, by their very nature, decrease the number of collisions.

Differences Between a Bridge and a Switch

The original differences between a bridge and a switch lay in the fact that a bridge would read the *full length* of a data packet and then forward only "good" packets to its other ports, while a switch only read enough of the header to ascertain the destination address.

When a packet hits a port on the multiport bridge, the bridge first stores it, then examines it to determine whether to forward it to a different port. Part of this process is the examination of the FCS (Frame Check Sequence) field at the end of each packet using a CRC (Cyclic Redundancy Check) calculation. This must first be checked by the multiport bridge to determine whether the packet is a good one or a runt or jabber packet. If a packet is determined by the bridge to be a good one, it is forwarded to the appropriate port.

Multiport switches do not use *full packet* store-and-forward technology when passing network traffic from one port to another. Multiport switches use on-the-fly connections and only check the first part of the packet to determine the destination before opening a circuit to the destination port. Multiport switches, very much like telecommunications gear, use what is called a *cross-point matrix* when establishing point-to-point virtual circuits between ports. What this means is that each time a port wants to connect to another point, a circuit is opened between them and the ports are temporarily connected so that the packets can be forwarded through. If the switch determines that the packet is going to be a runt or jabber, the switch will "kill" the packet as it is moving *through* the device to ensure that the errant packets aren't propagated across the network.

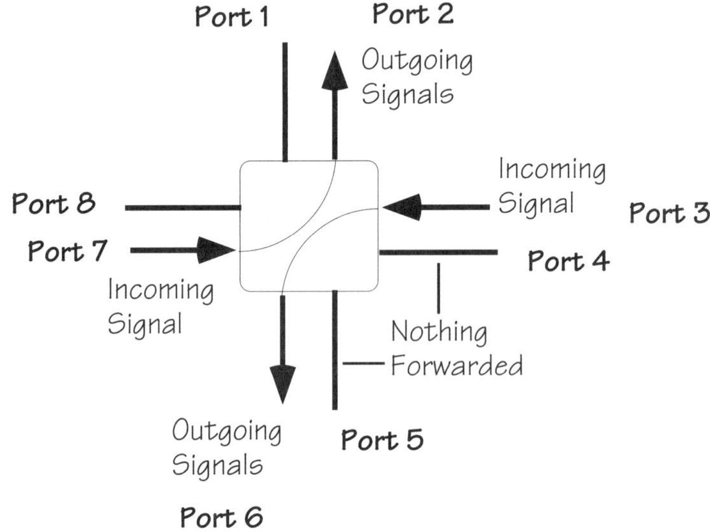

Overview of a Switch's Architecture

However, with the higher speeds in multiprocessors, the differences between a bridge and a switch are almost nil. It seems, though, that marketing folks in the companies that make these devices have decided that they are going to call devices "switches" when all they offer are bridging or switching capabilities. The hardware manufacturers seem to call devices "bridges" when they also offer routing capabilities. The Compatible Systems 3000E and 4000s RiscRouter are devices that offers to "bridge" or route AppleTalk, TCP/IP, IPX, and other protocols on a per-port basis (there are four ports to these devices).

DEFINITION OF A CATANET AND FUNCTIONS OF A BRIDGE OR SWITCH

I didn't make this up—really, I didn't. According to the *Design and Planning of AppleTalk Networks,* published in 1993 by the AppleTalk Networking Forum, a "collection of LANs interconnected using bridges [or switches] forms a bridged LAN, or catanet." While the networked devices appear to the upper layers as being on the same network segment, the bridge does offer a modicum of network traffic management by relaying signals between entities at the second (Data Link) layer instead of the first (Physical) layer. In reality, there are two types of bridges: MAC bridges that are used to connect similar LANs (EtherTalk to EtherTalk), and link or translational bridges that are capable of connecting dissimilar LANs (such as EtherTalk to LocalTalk). Therefore, while a bridge also regenerates a signal like a repeater does, the general functions required of a bridge are as follows.

Self Learning

First and foremost, today's bridges and routers are pretty smart. It used to be that in order for a bridge or router to function properly, somebody had to enter into each bridge's ports all of the devices' addresses that "lived" off that particular port. Once the bridge had knowledge of a device's address, it would forward all packets destined for that device to the appropriate port. It doesn't have to work that way anymore. Today's bridges and switches have the capability to add addresses to their ports *dynamically.* Bridges promiscuously *listen* to data traffic on each of their ports. As a bridge observes a device sending packets on a given port, the bridge will then cull the device's source address and assign that device's address to the given port.

This means that, as a device is moved from one port to another, the bridge has the capability of dynamically readjusting its address table, effectively relocating the device within its table of addresses. This adjustment process has certain limits, though, because bridges can usually hold from 1000–8000 devices per port on Ethernet (it's much lower for LocalTalk devices) before they run out of "address spaces" for that port. This means, then, that there has to be some sort of address *aging* process whereby the bridge can delete old addresses that no longer "live" on the given port. Many of the bridges have set this time-out factor somewhere around 300 seconds.

What happens if a device starts up on the network, the bridge culls the device's address, and the device doesn't transmit any packets for the next few hundred seconds and is thus aged out of the bridge's address tables? Does the device become invisible to the network? No, thank goodness, it doesn't. When a bridge doesn't have an entry for a device, the bridge simply forwards the packet to *all* of its ports, *ensuring* that the packet will reach its destination. Once the destination node sends a new packet, the bridge then adds the node to its table of addresses on the port from which it culled the address and is therefore able to correctly filter packets to that destination again.

A sample table for a bridge is shown in the following picture:

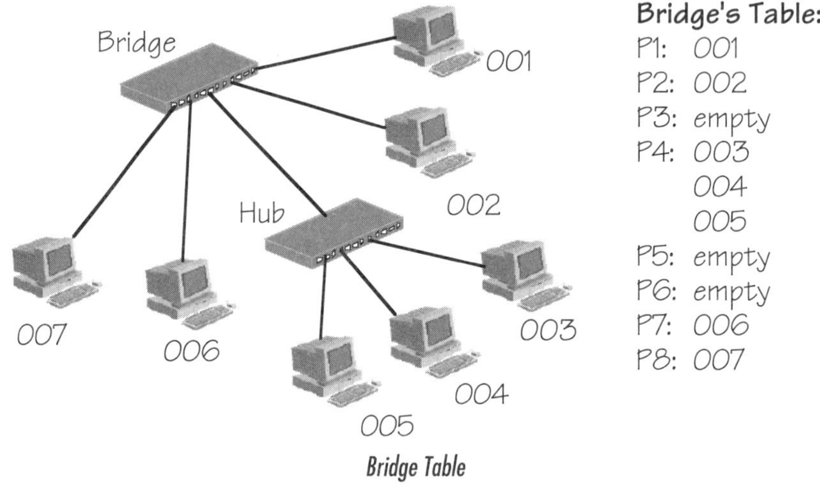

Bridge Table

Implications of Self Learning

If you have been paying attention to what you have been reading, you might be asking yourself what a bridge does with broadcast or multicast traffic. Well, since there isn't a specific port to which the bridge can assign a multicast or broadcast address, the bridge forwards those types of packets to *all* its ports *all* the time.

This, then, brings us to the definition of the type of traffic a bridge can filter: *directed traffic.* Given that a bridge doesn't have the capability to filter out broadcast or multicast traffic, it stands to reason that a bridge can be used only when attempting to filter out directed node-to-node traffic.

Frame Filtering and Forwarding at Near Wire Speed

We now know what types of packets, or frames, a bridge can filter. Now let's examine another of the functions of a bridge: forwarding those packets at near wire speed. The function of frame filtering must always be examined in lieu of how fast the frame filtering takes place. Since you can read, you have already discovered that the important part of frame filtering is that it happens at near wire speed. Wire speed is the speed of a packet moving across the wire without interruption. From reading the chapter about repeaters, we know that every time a signal passes *through* a given networking relay device, there is a small amount of latency. Well, if a repeater imposes a certain amount of latency, how much latency must a device impose that actually filters packets before sending them on to their relative ports?

Bridges operate in promiscuous mode. They actively listen to each and every frame on every port of the device. This means that they must receive each frame, buffer it, and then examine it as quickly as possible. The ability of the bridge to receive, buffer, and inspect a packet is called its *filtering rate*. The filtering rate for each port of a bridge on an Ethernet-to-Ethernet segment should be at least 14,881 frames per second, as defined in *The Design and Planning of Enterprise-Wide AppleTalk Internetworks* (ANF, 1993).

Since bridges must forward packets between their ports, the bridge's *forwarding rate* defines the maximum number of packets per second that a bridge can move from one port to the other. Taken together, a bridge's filtering and forwarding rate should be as fast as possible. It is *absolutely impossible* to filter and forward packets without some delay, and thus there are no networks in the world running at full tilt, or 100% utilization. Hence, in the best bridges, check out the *near wire speed*. Typical bridge delays are anywhere from 25μs all the way up to 100μs.

Some recent tests we conducted on standard Ethernet bridges have shown that many of them are only capable of supporting between 30–50% utilization on the networks to which they are attached. After that, their ability to forward packets at near wire speed is greatly diminished.

Loop Isolation Using Spanning Tree Protocol

Bridges also provide for loop isolation. Earlier we discussed the effects of loops in the network, and how a loop in the network causes many problems. The basic rule that we proposed is that there should never be a loop created in the system. This leads to a problem: Every cable running on the network can become a single point of failure. To overcome this obstacle, bridges offer a service through the *Spanning Tree Protocol* that is used to eliminate loops in redundant wiring systems. The Spanning Tree Protocol is implemented in all Ethernet bridges. Bridges implementing the Spanning Tree Protocol regularly communicate with each other and dynamically exchange information about which bridge ports should be forwarding traffic on to the other bridges and which bridge ports should be ignored because they have the potential loop cable.

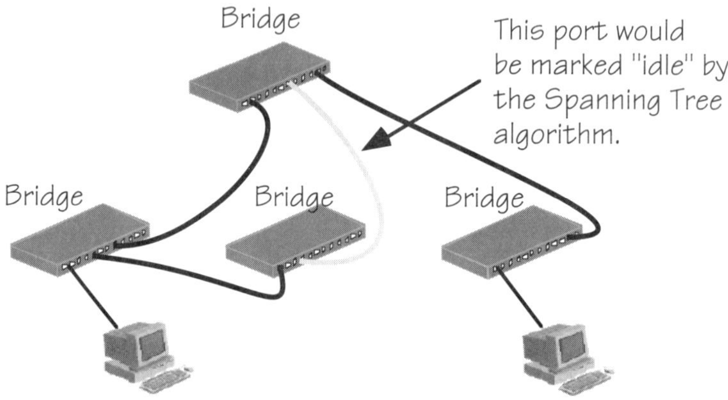

Example of the Spanning Tree Algorithm

How Spanning Tree Works

When a bridge is started, it automatically assumes that it is a *root* bridge, which is the base from which a connectivity tree is then introduced. Because a bridge "learns" the locations of devices on the network by culling their addresses from packets as they are being sent, the bridge has to have the ability to

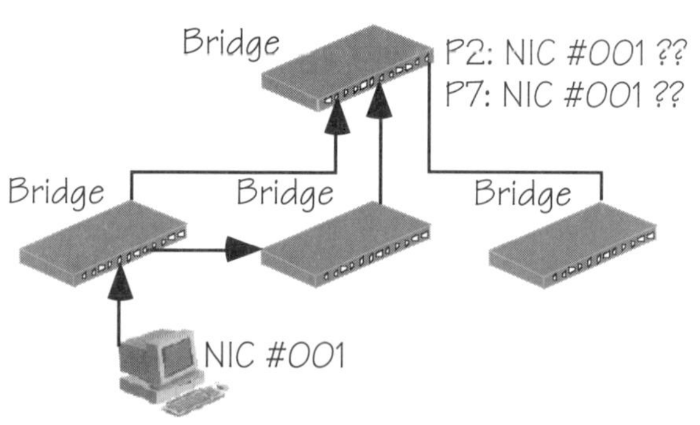

A device can't have two locations.

decide which port to assign a device to if it "hears" from that device on multiple ports simultaneously. In the previous diagram, the bridge is sensing **Network Interface Card 001** on two different ports. Since this would cause a loop in the network, a root bridge must be determined and a single route propagated while "turning off" the other path to the same location. Of all the bridges that are starting up and assuming they are the root bridge, a methodology must be in place for them to resolve which single bridge will become *the* root bridge from which all packets will ultimately be forwarded:

- If the bridges are "manageable" bridges, the bridge with the lowest "bridge identifier" assigned by the administrator becomes the root bridge.

- If there isn't a "bridge identifier," the bridge with the greatest number of ports becomes the root bridge.

- If there isn't a "bridge identifier" and all bridges have the same number of ports, the bridges must thumb wrestle. Just kidding. If all things are the same, the bridge with the lowest address is declared the root.

Once the root bridge has been identified, a designated bridge for each network is identified as well. The root bridge chooses the designated bridge to any given path through a "path cost" algorithm. Again, the path cost is usually something the network administrator enters into a setup field for the bridge. The following screen shot shows a sample configuration of a multiport bridge port, showing where the administrator needs to set the bridge's priority—for root bridge assignment—and the bridge's path cost. Again, this is usually per port instead of per bridge.

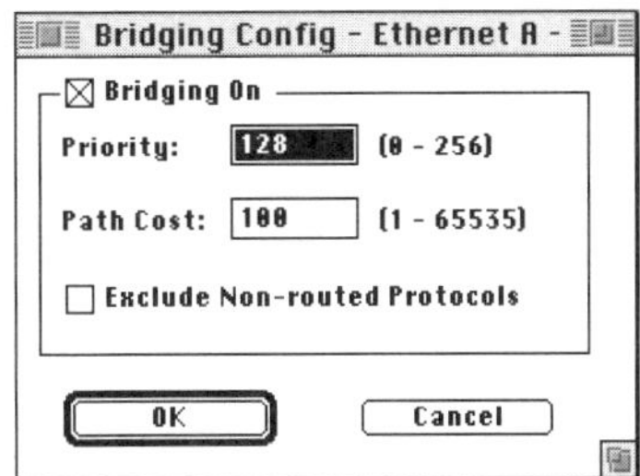

Bridge Config Window from a Compatible System's Bridge/Router

What to Use This for

Basically, this type of design allows dual cabling architectures to be run to the same bridges, thus overcoming the single point of failure of one cable. That's all.

A Major Problem to Watch Out for . . .

Don't think that if a bridge or switch using Spanning Tree algorithms is connected to hubs *looped back into the bridge* that Spanning Tree automatically creates a single path, as if the looped system were created with multiple bridges. It doesn't work that way. In other words, as shown in the following diagram, Spanning Tree can create only a single path from a redundant system if multiple bridges are connected, but does not work if multiple hubs are connected.

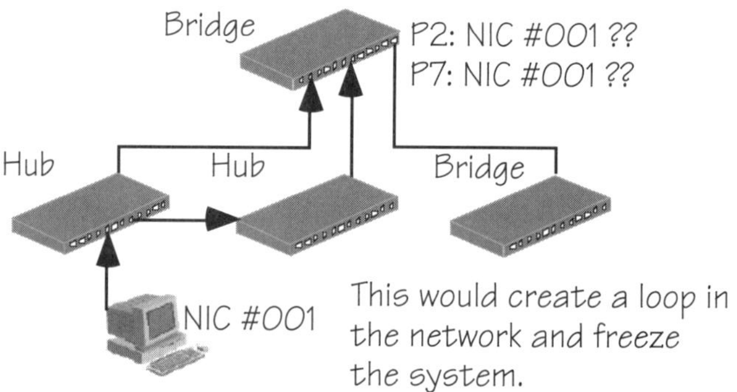

This creates a loop in the system and creates havoc on the network.

Translational Bridging

Another type of bridging function is the translational bridge function. A translational or link bridge is a device that supports mixed LAN (Ethernet and Local-Talk) interconnectivity by changing the packet structures from one format (Ethernet) to the other (LocalTalk). Tribe Computer Works' TribeStar and Compatible System's 3000E in bridge mode can do this. Although we cover the Tribe-Star and 3000E in depth in our section on routers, I wanted to mention here that it can be set up for routing or bridging. Farallon's EtherWave Serial, EtherWave Printer Adapter, and their EtherMac Printer Adapter are translational bridges, even though Farallon likes to call them "forwarding devices." The Dayna and

Compatible Systems Ethernet-to-LocalTalk printer boxes are also translational bridges. Finally, there are two software translational bridges from Apple: the Laser-Writer bridge, which is really a one-device translational bridge, and the LocalTalk bridge that supports up to 32 devices. Translational bridges are great additions for networks in which you don't want many routers, but you do have mixed media. Apple ships their translational bridge for the LaserWriters with each LaserWriter Select printer that they sell.

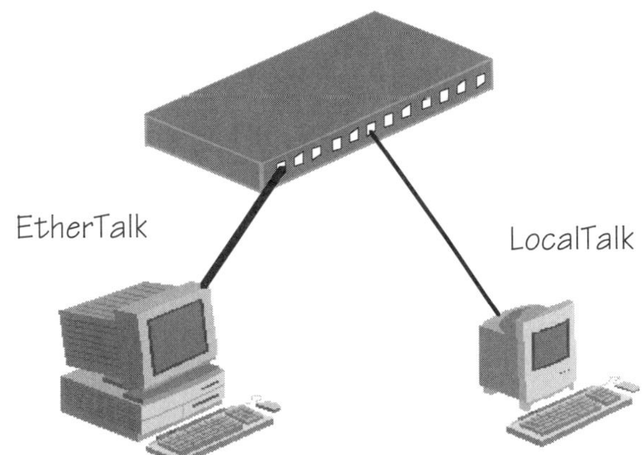

A translational bridge can support both EtherTalk and LocalTalk devices.

I won't explain how the translational bridge changes packets from one format to the other at this point. I do need to point out, however, that there are certain inherent limitations to a translational bridge:

- The device acting as the translational bridge *must* act as a multinode device. Thus, if multiple users are starting up on the LocalTalk side, each user is automatically assigned the bridge's Ethernet NIC MAC Physical address.

- Since the bridging device itself is registering each user's address on the Ethernet network, the devices on the LocalTalk side are all placed into a single zone, even in a multizone Ethernet segment. Furthermore, that zone is usually the network's default zone or the zone in which the bridge device is located.

- Finally, since LocalTalk doesn't support TCP/IP, all IP packets are encapsulated inside of LocalTalk on that portion of the bridge, and the IP address *must* be assigned by the bridge itself on the Ethernet forwarding port or through an IP gateway server, like the Apple IP gateway.

Virtual LAN Technology

Many of today's switches—and even some of today's multiport repeaters—have what is called "virtual LAN" technology embedded into the system. This is a fancy way of saying that the switches and bridges have a way of partitioning their ports *logically* so that they do not connect to each other on the same network. The next picture shows a 12-port switch. This switch was segregated into four separate virtual domains, each with a total of three ports.

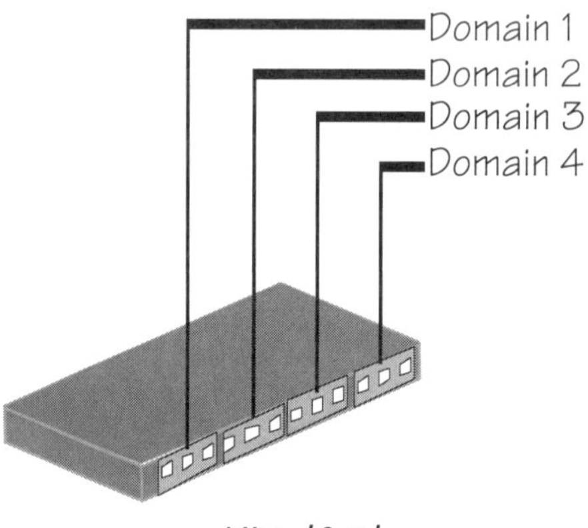

A Virtual Switch

As far as the network is concerned, devices connected to Domain 1 have no way of accessing devices on Domain 2 unless the domains are connected by another device, such as a router or another switch, as shown in the next picture.

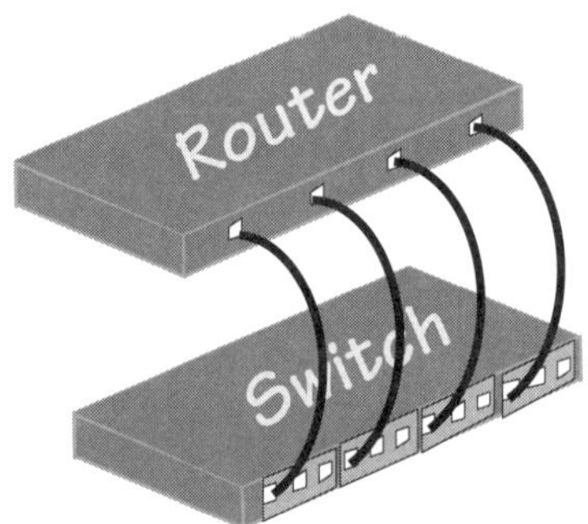

Router Connecting a Virtual Switch

Virtual LANs are great if you want to divide an area into multiple collision domains, but don't have enough of such zones to warrant purchasing multiple switches. Let's say that you have a four-port router and a 16-port switch. You might want four ports of the switch attached to one port of the router, another six ports attached to a second port of the router, and six ports attached to the third port of the router. At any given time you could quickly and easily rearrange the port configurations without any additional hardware!

IMPLEMENTATIONS OF BRIDGES AND SWITCHES WITH APPLETALK

Tribe LocalSwitch LocalTalk Switch

You know, when these first came out, I really hated them (although *now I love them*). I did not hate them because of their performance, which is excellent. I hated them because of Tribe's marketing. Whether intentional or not, the marketing was misleading to end users and administrators, leading them to believe that by installing one of these switches, they would be speeding up their network. Switches don't speed up networks. LocalTalk gives a maximum throughput performance of about 0.85 megabytes per minute, whether you use a daisy chain, trunk, hub, switch, or IR device.

So, what *does* the LocalSwitch do for you? It segments the network into 16 different *collision domains*. What is meant by a collision domain is that each of the ports of the switch acts like a mini-network, segregating the other ports' traffic. Thus, while Joe Bob is talking to Mary Jane on one port, Sam the Banana Man could be conversing with Luis Lollipop on another port *and the point-to-point traffic between the two pairs is not seen outside of their respective ports.* That, folks, is what the LocalSwitch does. It segregates point-to-point traffic. It does not, however, segregate broadcast or multicast traffic. By nature, those two types of traffic *must* be passed to all ports simultaneously. The LocalSwitch allows each port greater access to the network as it segregates the traffic from the other ports.

Tribe's LocalSwitch

Though the LocalSwitch isn't a *true* switching/bridging device, since true bridging and switching is an Ethernet or Token Ring implementation, it does carry the full characteristics of any of the bridges, and should be implemented for the same reasons that an Ethernet multiport bridge is implemented.

Characteristics

- The LocalSwitch has 16 ports, but a patch panel allows up to four devices per port for a total of 64 devices.

- The LocalSwitch is *not* a translational bridge, and is LocalTalk only. This means that there isn't an Ethernet or any other type of backplane for an uplink port. Therefore, connectivity to the rest of the network has to take place by utilizing one of the ports—usually the highest numbered port.

- When connecting the LocalSwitch to the rest of the network, we have found that it is best to *put only one connection point into the "uplink" port* of the LocalSwitch. Don't attempt to add other devices to that port. This effectively takes the number of total devices supported by the switch down to 60, which is more than enough, if you ask us. There are no virtual LAN capabilities.

Farallon's EtherWave and EtherMac Serial-to-Ethernet Translational Bridges

Farallon has two types of translational bridge adapters: the standard Ethernet transceiver type and the serial-to-Ethernet type. These devices allow the end node on LocalTalk to access the Ethernet network. Although Farallon does ship special software to allow the user to change zones on a multizone Ethernet network, the end-user device doesn't need any special software to connect to Ethernet through the printer port.

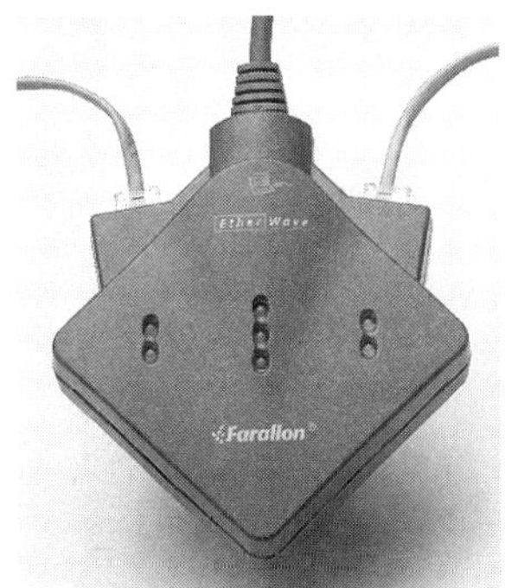

Characteristics

- The single-port device has two Ethernet ports for daisy-chaining into a 10BaseT topology, and a Mini-Din8 connector for connecting into the device's printer, or LocalTalk, port. The end node sends standard LocalTalk packets, and the device translates them into Ethernet.

- Because this device "speeds up" the serial port, it offers about 1.25 MB per minute throughput, whereas standard LocalTalk offers around 0.85 MB per minute throughput.

- Even though the four-port devices are labeled as "printer" connectivity devices, they don't filter out any packets and therefore can act as a translational bridge for *any* type of LocalTalk-based end node. These devices don't have the serial "tail" like the single-node version. In place of that tail is a single RJ-11 jack to which any PhoneNET-style cable can be attached.

- If more than four devices are connected to the four-port EtherWave or Ether-Mac bridge, only the first four devices will have Ethernet access. This is on a first-come, first-serve basis as that is the total number of devices for which the bridge will translate and gain addresses.

- Unlike the EtherWave transceivers for Ethernet-based devices, both the single and multiport EtherWave bridges need an independent power supply before they can operate. They also don't support "power pass-through," meaning that if the device doesn't have power, there is no connectivity.

Tribe's TribeSwitch EN

This product is actually the Kalpana five-port 10-Mbps switch with an extra feature that gives it a nicer touch than the model Kalpana ships. The TribeSwitch EN has 5–10 Mbps Ethernet ports that are manageable via IP-based SNMP. It comes with a set of compatible IP-based SNMP modules on diskette. There isn't a backplane. Therefore, one of the ports *must* be used as an uplink port. Unlike the Kalpana version of the same product, the TribeSwitch EN version has the addition of an AUI port adapter for the fifth port, as well as the normal RJ-45 jack.

TribeSwitch EN

Characteristics

- The TribeSwitch EN has five RJ-45 jacks, with the fifth jack also having an AUI connector that can be used to attach ThinNet or FOIRL adapters.

- It has SNMP MIBII management capabilities with compatible MIBs.

- There are no virtual LAN capabilities.

- There is no Ethernet backplane. One port must be used as an uplink port.

Apple's LaserWriter and LocalTalk Bridge Translational Bridge Software

The LaserWriter bridge software is installed during the installation of AppleTalk version 58.1.5 and later. It is used to connect a *single* LocalTalk device to an Ethernet network. The LocalBridge software can support up to 32 total LocalTalk devices, although I wouldn't suggest attempting that many. Basically, these two pieces of software turn the host computer into a translational bridge that AARPs for and gains an Ethernet address for each of the LocalTalk devices. Devices on the LocalTalk side of the bridge are placed in the bridge's zone.

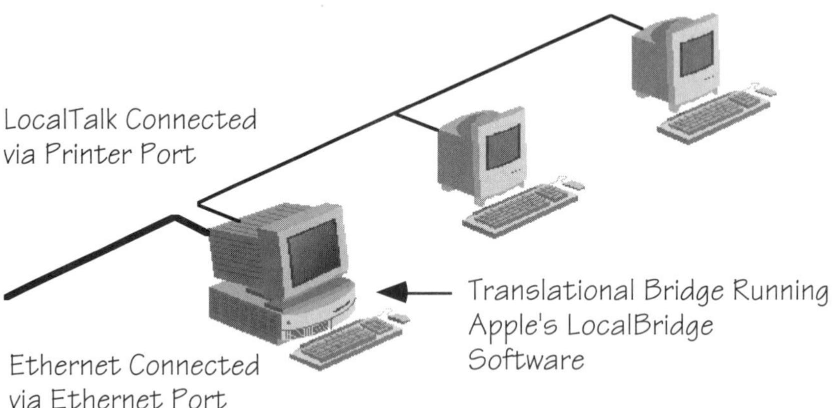

Apple's LocalBridge Software Implementation

Used in conjunction with the Apple Ethernet 10T/5 Hub and the appropriate media adapters, network cards, or connectors, the Apple LocalTalk Bridge can provide a complete upgrade to an integrated Ethernet or Token Ring and Local-Talk network without the high degree of cost and complexity normally associated with bridging or routing different networks.

The LaserWriter Bridge software allows users on an Ethernet network to have access to a LocalTalk printer connected to a Macintosh. The LaserWriter Bridge 1.0.1–2.0 is intended to be used with the LaserWriter Select 360 only. However, testing indicates that the LaserWriter Bridge 1.0 functions as a full LocalTalk bridge, except that bridging occurs for only the first device the bridge recognizes.

Characteristics

- The software only bridges for the LaserWriter Bridge and LocalBridge.

- It can only utilize two ports: the host device's Ethernet port and its printer, or LocalTalk, port.

- The LaserWriter Bridge supports a single device, while the LocalBridge supports up to 32 devices.

- The device can use any support media for LocalTalk or Ethernet, meaning that it can be connected to a cabling system on either port, or infrared on the

LocalTalk port and radio frequency on the Ethernet port, or a combination of cabling and cable-less physical access media.

- The LocalTalk and LaserWriter Bridge features dynamic, user-selectable access modes. When access is set to Private, the LocalTalk devices and services—such as LaserWriter printers and shared Macintosh volumes—are hidden from users on Ethernet or Token Ring, while LocalTalk-only devices retain full access to the services on both sides of the network. In contrast, when access is set to Public, all devices are visible from both sides of the network.

Asanté's 10/100 Media "FAT PIPE" Bridge

This bridge has four 10BaseT ports and one 100Base-TX port and is designed to be a 10/100-Mbps bridge. It is especially designed to work with Asanté's 100-Mbps Fast Ethernet hub. It has a 10/100-Mbps backplane that will support each of the four 10-Mbps channels to alleviate any possibilities of contention when forwarding packets to the 100-Mbps port. The Asanté FAST 10/100 Bridge bridges between 100BaseTX and 10-Mbps Ethernet. The 10-Mbps port has both 10BaseT and AUI ports, allowing connectivity to 10BaseT, 10Base5, 10Base2, or FOIRL.

Asanté's ReadySwitch 5104

The ReadySwitch 5104 is a four-port 10BaseT segment switch with an integrated 100BaseTX port. It provides segmentation and connectivity between all ports. With support for 1024 MAC addresses, the switch can be used to connect small or large 10-Mbps Ethernet collision domains. The 100BaseTX port can be used for an entire 100BaseTX network or a single 100BaseTX server. The 10BaseT ports can also be used to connect 10Base2, 10Base5, and 10BaseFL/FOIRL segments using additional repeaters. Integrated SNMP management and support for spanning tree make this switch very versatile. The ReadySwitch is most appropriate for connecting multiple 10-Mbps segments to a 100BaseTX network.

Bay Networks' Ethernet Workgroup Switch

This is a multiport 10BaseT segmenting switch that also has an optional 100-Mbps Fast Ethernet "uplink" port. A step up in power and configurability from the five-port switches, this is one of my favorite smaller workgroup switches. Two versions of the Fast Ethernet interface adapter are available. The 100BaseTX adapter features an RJ-45 modular receptacle for Category 5 cabling, or the 100BaseFX adapter offers an integrated SC-type connector for supporting Fast Ethernet over 62.5/125-micron multimode fiber optic cabling. This switch offers equal switching between both the 10-Mbps port *and* the single 100-Mbps port.

Ethernet Workgroup Switch

Characteristics

- This switch has six 10BaseT ports and one 100-Mbps port that can be configured for UTP copper wiring or SC-type multimode fiber cabling.

- It has a backplane fast enough to support full near wire speed access for all ports when linking "up" to the single 100-Mbps port.

- Each port can be virtually segmented from the other ports.

Bay Networks' EtherCell Ethernet-to-ATM switch

The Bay Networks EtherCell is the only Ethernet-to-ATM switch we know of. It is primarily designed to be an ATM-to-Ethernet backbone switch. It features 12 10BascT ports onto a single, 155 megabit-per-second (Mbps) SONET/ 

EtherCell Ethernet-to-ATM Switch

SDH ATM compatible port. While also offering standard switching capabilities, the EtherCell switch's main purpose is to convert Ethernet-style variable length packets—up to the full packet sizes allowable by Ethernet—to the fixed-length ATM-cell-based frames. EtherCell's Ethernet packet-to-ATM mapping is compatible with the ATM Forum's LAN emulation specification, as well as the IETF RFC 1483 Multi-Protocol Encapsulation over ATM Adaptation Layer 5 (AAL5) standard. This compatibility allows EtherCell to work with any networking devices that are equipped with ATM Networking Interface Cards conforming to these specifications.

Characteristics

- This device is a 12-port, virtually configured 10BaseT Ethernet switch.

- Each of the 12 Ethernet ports has an integrated RJ-45 jack.

- The ATM uplink port is configured for SC-type 6.25μ multimode fiber as specified by the Category 4 committee.

Centillion 100 EtherSpeed Ethernet-to-ATM Switch

This switch, which should be deployed as a backbone switch, comes in an 8- or a 16-port version. It has the highest frame rate at full-traffic utilization of any switch we have seen, ATM or not. Designed to combine multi-LAN switching and ATM on a single platform, the Centillion 100 supports any combination of Ethernet, Token Ring, and ATM modules. Port-level virtual LAN capability allows network microsegmentation without changing the physical network topology.

Centillion 100 Switch

Characteristics

- This switch is a 3.2 gigabit-per-second (Gbps) ATM backplane that allows full Ethernet-to-ATM switching without any port contention.

- It allows distributed parallel LAN and ATM switching.

- Each port of the Centillion can be configured into a virtual LAN.

- Up to six switch modules, each equipped with an autonomous local switch, can be plugged into the Centillion 100.

Digital Ocean's Radio Frequency Starfish

Digital Ocean, the same folks who make the Manta and other Ethernet-based radio frequency products, make a 10BaseT-to-RF bridging product called the Starfish. This is a great product. While simple to set up and use—if you aren't concerned about security, it is plug and play—it can be configured so that multiple Starfish are deployed throughout the network to provide cellular roaming for RF-based users. Each Starfish gives RF users anywhere from 120–400 radial feet of access to the LAN through this ingenious bridge. When deployed throughout a building, the entire area can be covered with a few of the Starfish in key locations. Because it is a true bridge, RF-to-RF communications are segregated from the LAN-based traffic.

Digital Ocean's Starfish

Characteristics

- The Starfish has up to 120–400 feet of radial access, allowing for structural interference.

- This device provides true Ethernet-to-Ethernet bridging, with an access rate of around 1.5 or so MB per minute throughput, the limiting factor being the RF throughput itself.

- You can have either plug-and-play connectivity or, through Digital Ocean's Grouper Admin software, device-by-device security.

- It has a single 10BaseT RJ-45 jack for LAN connectivity. Unfortunately, there is no AUI adapter for FOIRL.

BRIDGE AND SWITCH ARCHITECTURE DESIGN ISSUES

For switches, I will offer just a few suggestions here. I tackle the greater issues of incorporating switches and hubs and routers in one fell swoop in the next chapter about routers. What I do want to do here, however, is to quickly review what a repeater provides in a network design and the difference between what a multiport bridge or switch provides. Next, I will cover one of the major errors in switch design that often goes unnoticed until it is too late: port contention.

Repeated versus Switched Connections

The following diagram shows a multiport repeater, such as a Farallon StarController or Asanté hub. This repeater has three computers and a file server attached to it. When computer A talks to the file server, both B and C hear the conversation. If there is enough overall traffic, since a repeater regenerates the signal on each port, network traffic "slows down" access to the network. This is due to rules that affect CSMA/CD access.

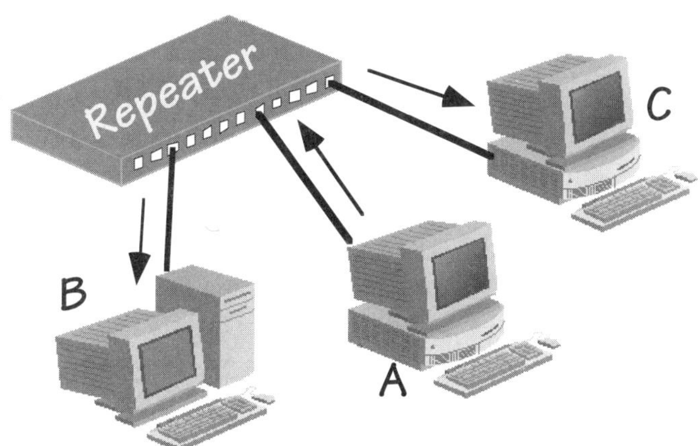

Repeated Connections

By inserting a multiport bridge or switch in place of the multiport repeater, the bridge or switch can act as a traffic cop for packets that don't need to be heard by other devices on the network. Because the bridging device doesn't forward *directed* packets to ports that aren't part of the conversation, those ports don't "hear" irrelevant conversations. Thus, device C isn't privy to the packets between A and B.

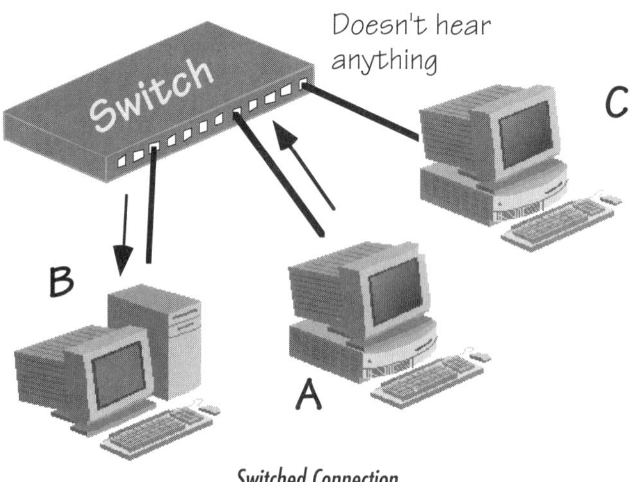

Switched Connection

Contention

There's one major drawback in using a switch instead of a repeater. Any time two or more devices are attempting to forward a packet to the same third port, one of the two devices will suffer contention for the port. The definition of *contention* is "the state of those who disagree and lack harmony," or so says my Thunder thesaurus. When contention for a port happens, the packets heading for that port must be placed within a "buffer" inside of the bridge or switch device before they can be delivered. This causes extra latency between when the packet was sent and was expected to be received, and the time when the packet is forwarded through the bridge or switch and is *really* received. The protocols state that packets have a certain amount of time to travel from sender to receiver before they are considered lost and must be resent. Luckily, the overall latency for switches is much faster than for other devices, like routers. Where an Ethernet-to-Ethernet router's latency might be something like 800 milliseconds, most bridge's or switch's latency is 40 milliseconds. Thus, even when switching devices are in moderately heavy usage, the latency factor is within acceptable limits. However, when the devices are in very heavy use, or are strung together in a row, as in bridges linked in serial to other bridges, the latency can become out of hand and can cause some major network problems.

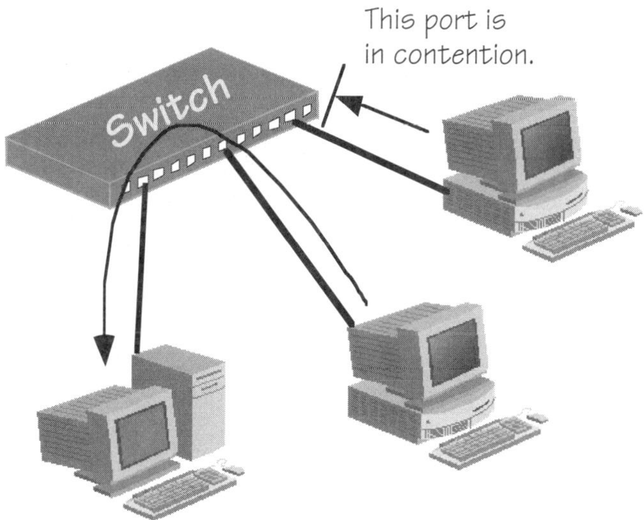

Contention on a Switched Network

As long as you understand the nature of contention and remember to limit it as much as possible, you will be fine. The following are some basic design rules for working with switches that should help you in your efforts.

Switched Backbone

One of the most common network designs for a switched or bridged network is the switched backbone design. This design has at its center a multiport bridge or switch. Attached to the center bridge or switch are groupings of devices attached to multiport hubs. The general workstations and printers are attached to the hubs, which create multiple collision domains. The faster workgroup servers, such as file and database servers that are normally accessed by many members of the network simultaneously, are placed on their own ports of the bridge or switch.

This does cause some contention when the bridging device is a 10-Mbps device. However, many of today's multiport bridges are configurable 10–100-Mbps devices on a *per port* basis. This means that access to the 100-Mbps ports on the bridge can be accomplished at a much higher rate, and therefore the contention for the 100-Mbps ports almost completely goes away.

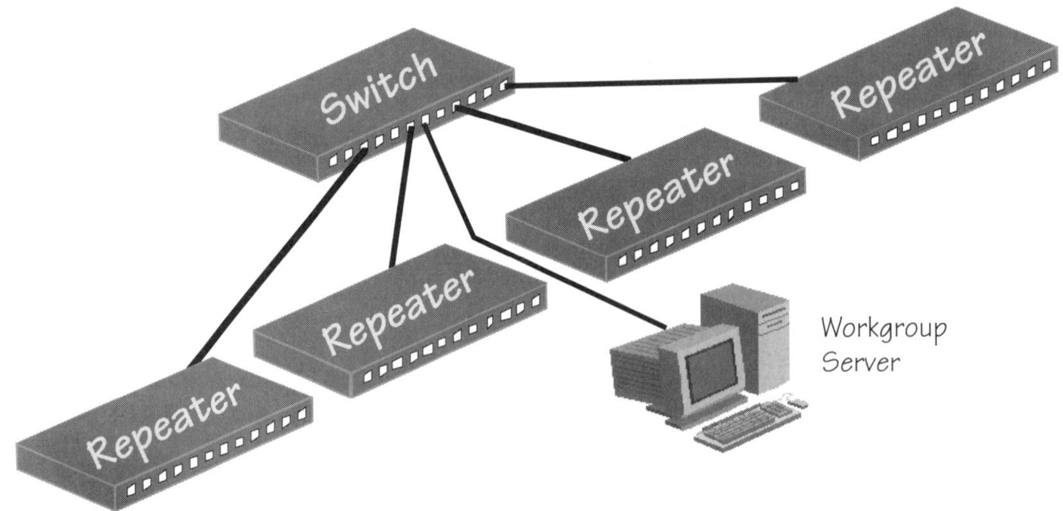

Sample Switched Backbone Ethernet Network

Distributed Switched Backbone

A distributed switched backbone is a step up in the network design hierarchy from a standard switched backbone. The goal of a standard switched backbone is to create multiple collision domains and give uncontended access to multi-user workgroup devices, such as servers. The goal of a distributed switched backbone is to add high-speed, less "traveled" links between bridging or switching devices.

This basically means that you need a standard repeated segment as the "center" of the network running Fast Ethernet to give the design high-speed connectivity at the core and 10 times more utilization than standard Ethernet. From the center, the configurable 10–100-Mbps bridges or switches are attached to give 100-Mbps connectivity to the "backbone" and 10-Mbps connectivity to the hubbed collision domains where the regular workstations and printers reside. As in the switched backbone, you probably still want to have workgroup servers and other highly accessed networking devices on their own 100-Mbps port to provide contention-less access and a single device collision domain. In the following diagram, we show a small drawing of what one of these designs could potentially look like.

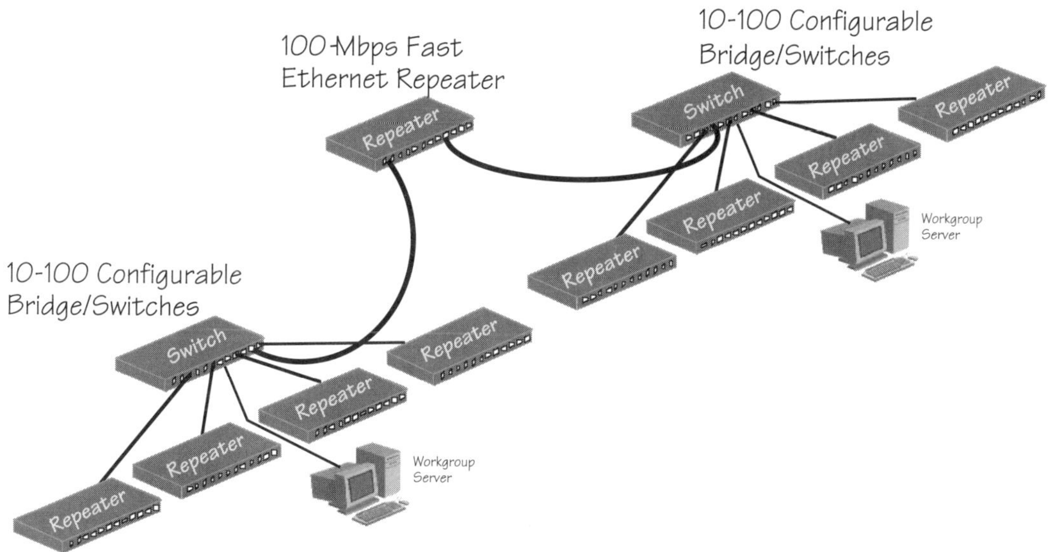

Sample Distributed Switched Backbone

A Bridge Too Far

There is one lesson that the Allied paratroopers learned in World War II: A bridge too far can put you into an area in which you don't want to be and can cause heavy casualties. So what does that have to do with network design? Just this: the *rules* say that you can have up to seven bridges in serial before you have surpassed the Ethernet design rules. However, common practice has led us at Network Frontiers to believe that you never want to have more than *two* sets of bridges per network. Don't go freaking out at that statement. Remember, a network is defined as a shared cable segment between routers. If you have two bridges in serial and a router in between two more bridges in serial, that doesn't count as four total bridges. That counts as two bridges in serial in our design book.

PART 3:
IN-DEPTH REVIEW OF ROUTERS AND BASIC ROUTING FUNCTIONS

		Routing Table Maintenance Protocol (RTMP)	AppleTalk Echo Protocol (AEP)	Name Binding Protocol (NBP)	Zone Information Protocol (ZIP)	AppleTalk Update Routing Protocol (AURP)	
Transport & Session							
Network		Datagram Delivery Protocol (DDP)					
		AppleTalk Address Resolution Protocol (AARP)					
Data Link		SNAP LLC Type 1	SNAP LLC Type 1	SNAP LLC Type 1	LLAP	X.25, Frame Relay, SMDS, HDLC LAPB	
Physical		802.3 EN	802.5 TR	FDDI	LocalTalk	V.35, RS232, RS422, X/21 HSSI	

Model of a Router

Routers operate at the Network layer of the OSI model. Thus, it can be said that routers *route* the upper layer (Transport and up) protocols *from one point to the next.* This does not mean, though, that they perform any protocol conversion operations, such as from AppleTalk to TCP/IP—that is the function of a gateway.

A router, therefore, is a device used to connect different subnetworks that support the same protocol.

Now that we have that formal definition out of the way, let's focus on the statement that routers move data from one point to the next. To make it a little clearer, a router depends on tables of information that hold specific *routes* to specific *networks.* Therefore, routers, unlike bridges, do not forward data based upon individual end node MAC- or LLC-based addresses. So, where does the route and network information come from? That information is protocol specific. While there are *multiprotocol routers* that support AppleTalk, TCP/IP, IPX, and DECNet all in the same box, each of these router devices must route those protocols *independently.* Let me try to explain this differently.

What in the World Is a Router Used for?

Let's start with some basics. Let's say that you have a small LocalTalk network like the one shown in the next picture. Everyone is fairly happy, your computers are all on the same floor of your building, the cabling is pretty good, and because there aren't too many of you, the network isn't too busy and the world seems fine. When someone sends a message from one computer to the other, the message is placed onto the cabling and then picked up by the receiving device.

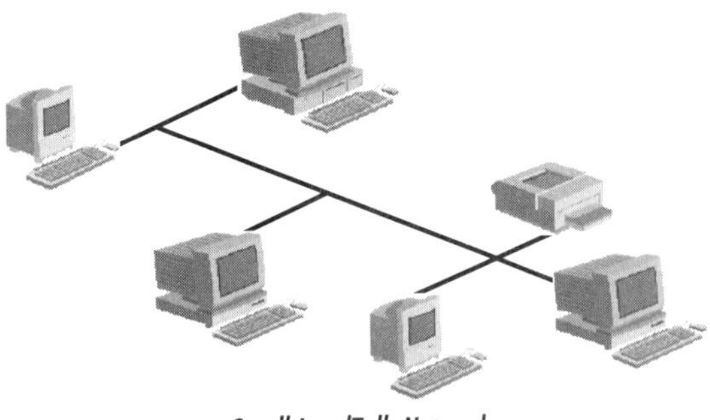

Small LocalTalk Network

Then other people, like the beancounters, want to get in the picture. They have decided that they want to add a VAX or some other heavy iron to the network, as well as faster machines that require more bandwidth than the ones you are currently using. Because your beancounters' department traditionally has more money than the Catholic church, they decide that *everything* they implement is going to be Ethernet. So, they use different cabling than you do, and they use Ethernet Network Interface Cards on their computers, thus making their network completely different from your little LocalTalk network.

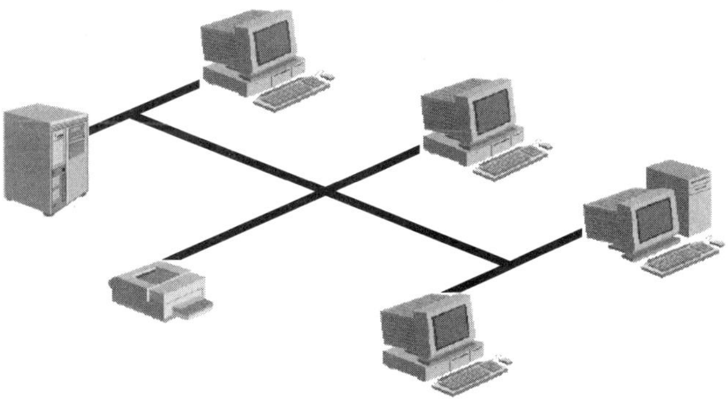

Small Ethernet Network

You are left with two dissimilar networks. One network is the original small LocalTalk network and the other network is an Ethernet network. How do you enable them to talk to each other? With Camp David peace agreements completely out of the question, you have to come up with a different solution. The solu-

This picture designates a router.

tion, of course, or I wouldn't be writing this book, is to use a product called a *router* to tie them together. Think of it this way: a *route* is the path a packet takes when moving from the sending computer or device (source) to the receiving computer or device (destination). When the source's networking schemata (cool word, huh?) is different from the destination's networking schemata, the packet has no way of reaching its destination. Therefore, in the simplest of terms, a router is a device that facilitates moving the packet from the source to the destination when the source's networking methodology is different from the destination's networking methodology. Whereas bridges pass any packets that aren't destined for the single segment from which they came, routers are able to make tighter distinctions when passing packets back and forth. Along with using a router to move packets in between dissimilar networks, they can also be used as traffic cops to direct traffic and aid in traffic management. Thus, to round out our network, we place a router between the Ethernet network and the LocalTalk network, and the router will be the device taking packets from one network and passing them on to the next network. This allows both networks to communicate within their own network and with each other as well.

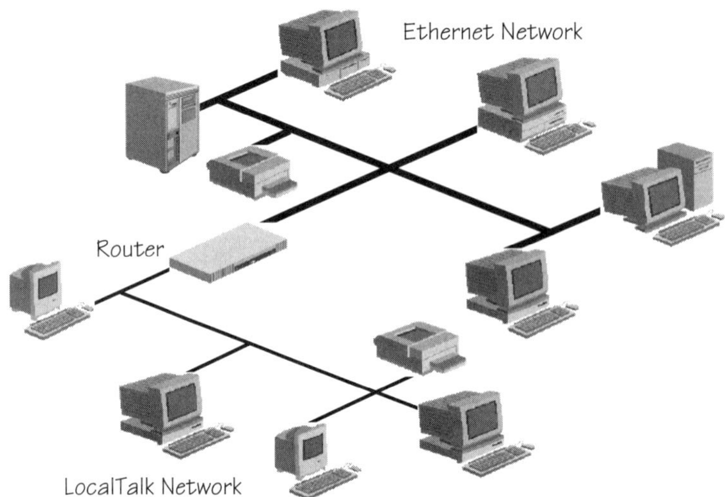

Networks Connected via a Router

So, What's the Big Whoop?

Now there is a device between the two networks. So what? It doesn't *look* like it's doing anything. However, what is going on here is a *connectionless* data transfer service between one Physical layer architecture (LocalTalk) and another architecture (EtherTalk) within the same protocol. That, my friends, is pretty important. Let's take a look at how a computer would communicate with a printer on the LocalTalk network without a router, and then with one:

Step 1 The initiating computer user issues the command to print. Before the page is spooled, the computer sends out an NBP Lookup Request onto the network in broadcast form, looking for the printer that had been selected previously in the Chooser. This ensures that all computers running LocalTalk inspect the packet for its contents and react appropriately. When sending an NBP Lookup, there are always three parts to the object's identity: the name, type, and zone. The type is what we select in the Chooser—such as, AppleShare servers or printers. The name is returned in the right-hand side of the Chooser. The zone is something added with a router or the default zone of "*" when there are no routers.

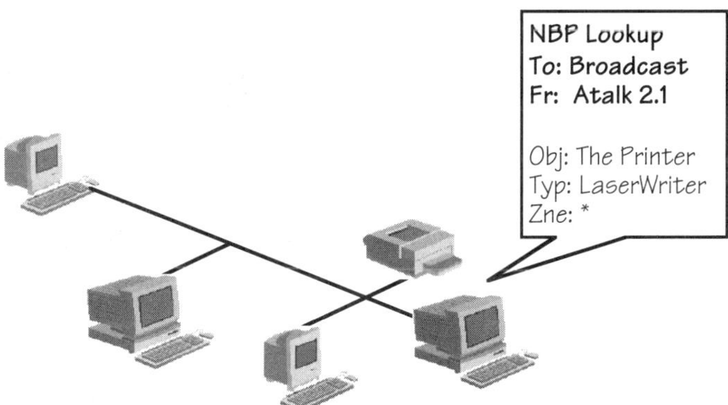

NBP Broadcast Request Being Issued

Step 2   The printer—and each other device—inspects the NBP Lookup packet. The printer obtains the sender's address for the reply and then replies directly to the sender, informing the sender that it is indeed the exact named device, as well as the exact type of device specified in the NBP Lookup packet.

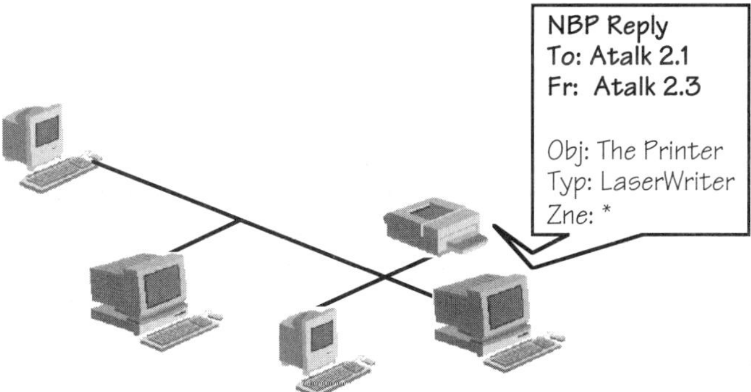

Printer Responding to NBP Lookup

Step 3   With the address in hand, or "in packet" I should say, the two networking devices open a session and the print job begins. After the print job finishes, the two devices close the session and life continues as usual.

Okay, that sounded pretty simple. Now let's look at what happens when the two devices that want to hold a conversation are on separate subnetworks. In the case of communicating between LocalTalk and Ethernet, the first problem encountered is that there are two types of addressing. While LocalTalk uses only a dynamically assigned protocol-based address, EtherTalk uses both the Xerox-assigned MAC layer address *and* a dynamically assigned EtherTalk protocol address. The second problem is that these two networks are just that: *two* different networks, each with their own network, or cable, number. Therefore, the two subnetworks' numbers must be managed so that each network can maintain its own individual identity while allowing other networks to access them. Since the router sitting in between these two networks must have a reconciliation scheme for the two subnetworks, as well as a connectionless, or invisible, methodology for relaying traffic between devices on the different subnetworks. Let's take a look at the same print job, but with a router in the middle of the two subnetworks.

Step 1   On a routed network, the host computer sends out an NBP Broadcast Request to a local router, requesting the same type of information that it would have requested on a non-routed network. In this case, it is looking for a specific printer in a specific zone that was previously selected in the Chooser. The name and type of the NBP request are the same as described previously. Zones are used to segregate devices in the Chooser, as well as limit some types of network traffic.

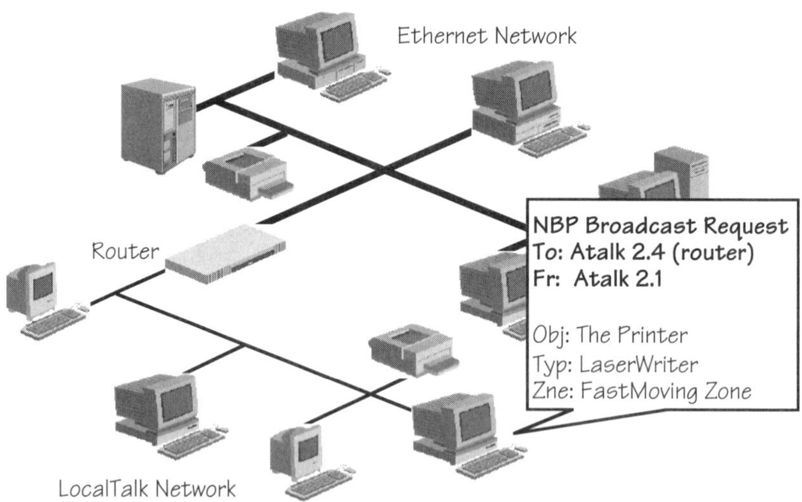

NBP Broadcast Request Sent by Originating Computer

Step 2 The router picks up the packet and examines its Zone Information Table (yes, a ZIT table. Don't you just love it?). It does this to determine which subnetwork is the home for the zone—in this case, the FastMoving Zone—in which the device being looked up is located. It then examines its routing table to determine which of its ports is the forwarding port to that network. Once it has determined the forwarding port to the network, it forwards the packet onto the network and performs the lookup in the appropriate multicast address. Multicast addresses are assigned to zones. If you didn't know that, refer to our *OpenTransport Primer* book for more information or to *Inside AppleTalk: Second Edition.* In this case, the router forwards the packet onto the Ethernet segment and then sends out the NBP Lookup in the appropriate zone on the EtherTalk side.

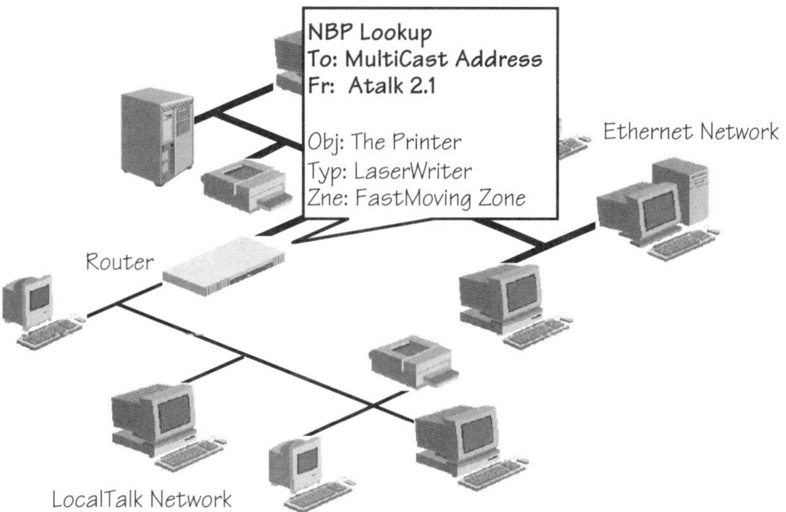

Router Forwarding the NBP Lookup

Step 3 On the Ethernet side of the network, all devices registered in the appropriate zone "hear" and then pick up the NBP Lookup request. The appropriate device then gleans the sender's address from the packet—in this case the router is the "forwarder" and not the sender—and formulates a reply. The reply will be sent directly to the originating computer much like what happens without a router. However, instead of sending it directly to that computer, the printer sends the reply *through* the router *to* the computer.

As the packets pass through the router from LocalTalk to Ethernet or Ethernet to LocalTalk, the appropriate Data Link layer addresses are formatted and the packets are reformatted from one type to another. Headers are stripped or added by the router as necessary to ensure that the packet is forwarded to the appropriate destination address.

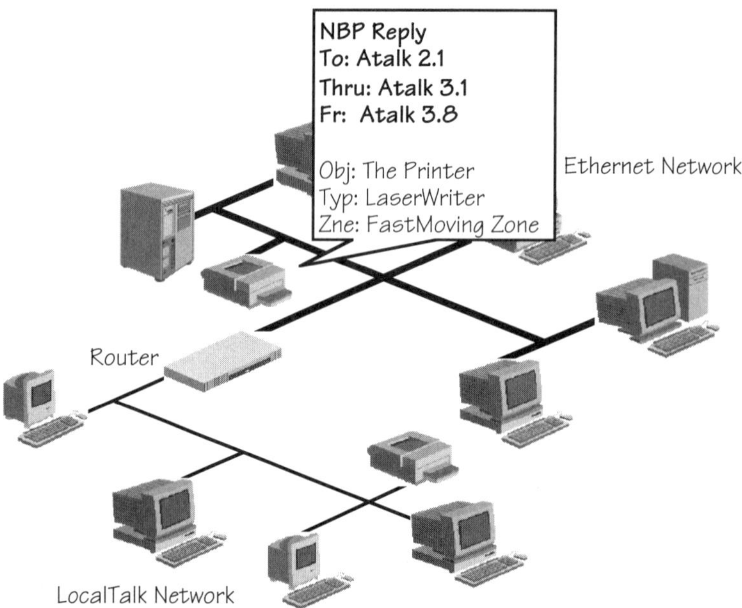

NBP reply is forwarded through the router to the originating computer.

Is That All?

Well, of course not, or this would be one of the shortest books on the market, right next to *Great Moments in Geek Sports History*. Heck, there is a whole book's worth of stuff you need to know. That is, of course, if you want your network to work correctly. There are folks out there who have routers and don't know what in the world these things are doing on their network. They don't know why they are there or what the network numbering scheme is all about. There is so much more that the router does with the packet, and a lot more to the connectionless relays of network traffic that we aren't going to go into. That is all well explained in both *Inside AppleTalk, Second Edition* and our own *OpenTransport Primer* book. In this section of the book, we first explain what routers do, where network numbers come from, and some basic numbering schemes. We also explain the mysteries of zones, and how they can serve your network design and management needs.

LAN-to-LAN or LAN-to-WAN Connectivity

One of the basic functions of routers is to connect different subnetworks together. Remembering that routers *route* packets of the same genre—as in AppleTalk to AppleTalk—between different subnetworks, they can be used to connect Local-Talk, EtherTalk, or TokenTalk together into one large internetworking system. This means that different floors within a building can have their own network and still be connected into one large network overall. Different buildings can be connected into a campus LAN, and through LAN-to-WAN connectivity, different networks from across town or across the country can be connected to form a *very large* internetwork.

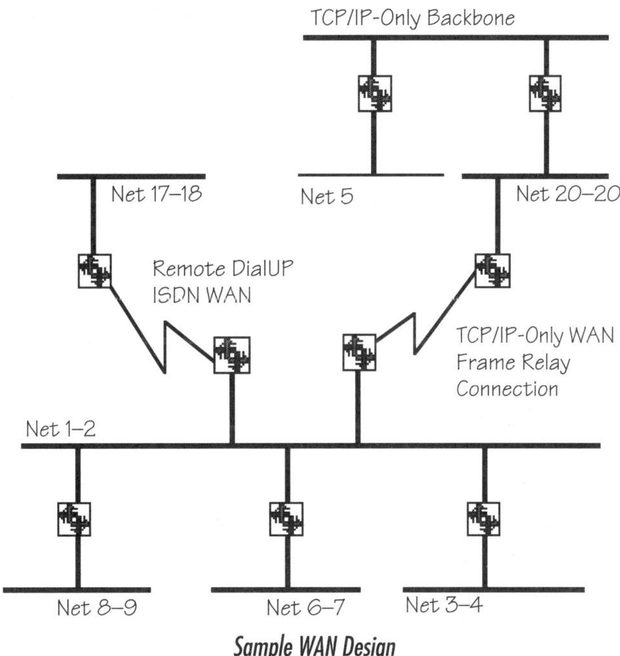

Sample WAN Design

AppleTalk Phase 2—the protocols we have been using since 1989—is divided into two different categories for routing information. One category is most commonly used on the LAN-to-LAN routing and is called Routing Table Maintenance Protocol, or RTMP. The other is used on widely populated WANs and is called Apple Update-based Routing Protocol, or AURP. These two protocols will be discussed in semi-detail later, and at great detail in our *OpenTransport Primer*.

Subnetwork Isolation

Along with subnetwork integration, routers also provide subnetwork traffic isolation. Without a router, every time a user sends out an NBP Lookup, the Lookup is sent as a broadcast packet. This means that *every* AppleTalk device on the network must actively listen to the traffic. As there isn't a way to segment broadcast traffic, the broadcast goes *everywhere* on the network, whether bridged or not. (Remember, bridges and switches by nature automatically forward all broadcast and multicast traffic.)

Once a router is added to the network, however, all broadcast traffic within one subnetwork *stops* at that port of the router and is *not* forwarded to other subnetworks within the internetwork. Therefore, it can be said that with the addition of a router, all broadcast or multicast traffic is subnetwork bound.

When dividing a large single network into two or more subnetworks, there are some rules to follow with respect to the numbers of computers allowed on each type of subnetwork and how the subnetworks are identified or numbered. One key rule is that networks should be numbered consecutively from 1–65,000. The numbers actually go slightly higher, but because of startup ranges of devices, at Network Frontiers we don't recommend going over 65,000.

Non-Extended Networks

LocalTalk is a networking type considered by AppleTalk to be a non-extended network system. By being classified as a non-extended network, the implication is that the non-extended network can have only a single network number. That network number allows up to 254 total nodes. Other non-extended subnetwork classifications are ARA dial-up networks (supported by the LANRover and Apple Muliport ARA series) and some WANs (as supported by Frame Relay implementations in Compatible Systems and other routers). Don't worry about the upper limit of 254 devices on these types of networks. There isn't a LocalTalk network out there that can support all 254 nodes without being clogged with traffic, and I haven't seen any 254-node Frame Relay meshes out there yet.

Extended Networks

Ethernet, Token Ring, and FDDI networks are considered extended network systems. These systems allow for far more than the 254 nodes allowed on a single non-extended network. Instead of allowing more devices per network number, the AppleTalk design engineers took the approach of extending the network numbering system from a single number to a range of numbers. Each number within the range of numbers supports a total of 253 devices per network number, with one more device number being reserved by extended networks. A good example of this is the network range of 1–5. Each of the numbers in this range—1, 2, 3, 4, and 5—equals a total number of 253 devices. Ergo, $253 \times 5 = 1265$ total devices allowable on that subnetwork 5's cable range.

The Golden Rule

One a network number has been identified within an internetwork, that number can no longer be utilized anywhere else on the system. That means that if there is a network range identified as 100–200, the administrator cannot identify a subnetwork elsewhere as 150, because 150 falls within the range of 100–200.

Another True Story

Sorry, Favian, I have to tell this one. One of our clients came to our network design class in San Francisco, and after listening to all of this, raised his hand and said, "I guess, then, that it's not a great idea to set the range of your backbone to 1–65,000?" Whoo, boy, and he wondered why he had problems?

If you don't know how each of the computers on extended or non-extended networks gain their network numbers, refer to our primer.

Multicast Isolation

AppleTalk routers provide a unique form of multicast addressing for each end user device within the subnetwork. When a router is set up for the first time, not only does the network manager identify the cable range, also called network number, for the subnetwork segment, but a multicast or several multicast addresses are identified as well. In AppleTalk parlance, these multicast addresses are called *zones*. When a workstation is started up, it requests the local zone list from its subnetwork router. The router returns the network number identification for that cable segment, as well as a listing of the possible zones for the network—on Ethernet or

Token Ring—or *the* zone for the network—on LocalTalk, ARA, and WANs. Where there are multiple zones, a single "home zone" is suggested by the router as well as the rest of the list. The end user can choose from the list of available local zones in which to place the device. As with subnetwork numbering, certain rules must be followed when creating zone lists. One of them is that zones, unlike subnetwork numbers, can be used over and over again. You can have one zone for all 152 subnetworks, although it's not advised. You could also have 152 zones for 152 subnetworks. Finally, if you have few extended subnetworks, you could feasibly have about 200 zones.

Non-Extended Networks

Non-extended networks can have only a single zone. Period.

Extended Networks

Extended networks must have *at least* one zone. If an extended network has more than one zone, one of the zones in the list must be identified as the default zone. This is often the first zone typed into the zone list by the administrator, although it can be changed easily. The reason I point this out is that when a device starts up on the subnetwork for the first time, it asks the routers which zone is the default zone. If different routers have different default zones, computers could potentially be placed into different zones unbeknownst to the administrator.

Spelling and Capitalization

According to Apple's definition of a multicast zone-based address, the multicast address for a zone is based on the spelling of the zone's name. According to some routers' implementations, not only is the multicast address based on the spelling of the name, it is based on the capitalization of the name as well. Therefore, *Acme Public* would have one multicast address, while *acme public* would have another. Ignoring this design rule could cause serious problems on a network.

Once a device is "placed" in a zone, it answers to NBP Lookups within that zone *only.* Let's say that there is an Ethernet segment on my network with three zones: Zone1, Zone2, and Zone3. I place a printer in Zone3. When a user opens the Chooser and searches the network for a printer, the user must select a zone to search. If the user selects Zone1 or Zone2, even though those zones exist within the same cable segment, the printer ignores the NBP Lookups, as they are not addressed to the appropriate multicast to which the printer belongs, Zone3.

Dynamic Learning of New or Changed Routes

Each router maintains a list of other routers on the network. Each router maintains a routing table by exchanging information about the routes it knows with other routers on the network. Routers on the LAN do this through RTMP and routers on the WAN do this through AURP. Routers are typically "aged out" of the routing table if they are not heard from within two minutes. When passing on the information about networks they are aware of, AppleTalk routers use what is called split-horizon routing. That means that they forward information about *one side* of the network they know about to the *other side* of the network they are connected to. This keeps the packets as small as possible while providing key connectivity information to the other routers.

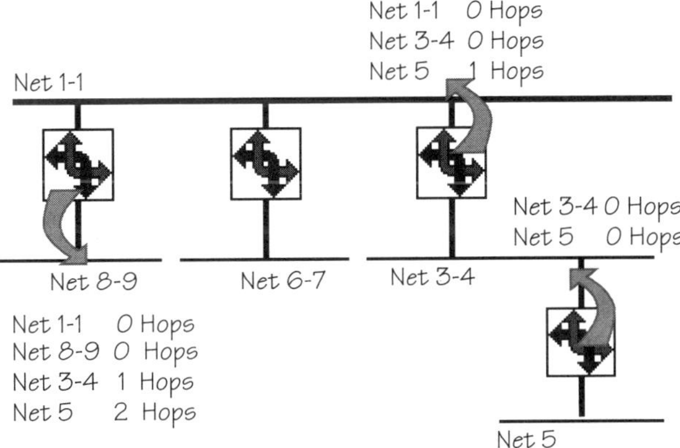

Sample of Split-Horizon Routing

While the general rule is that it takes approximately two minutes to pass information about a new route from one side of an extended internetwork to the other, we have worked on networks that take as long as 5–7 minutes to pass this information. The delay is caused by the speed of the interconnecting relay WAN lines. Some of them at the client are as slow as 14.4 modem lines, and they are several deep, so plan accordingly.

Best Route Algorithm

Each and every node on an AppleTalk network holds information about routers on the network in what is called the *RTMP stub*. This means that devices "listen" to the RTMP packets on the network. Each time a device on the network "hears" a router's RTMP packet, it files information about that router's address in its RTMP stub. It uses this information when sending a packet out to a distant network; it has to forward that packet through a router first before it reaches the next network, such as during NBP lookups.

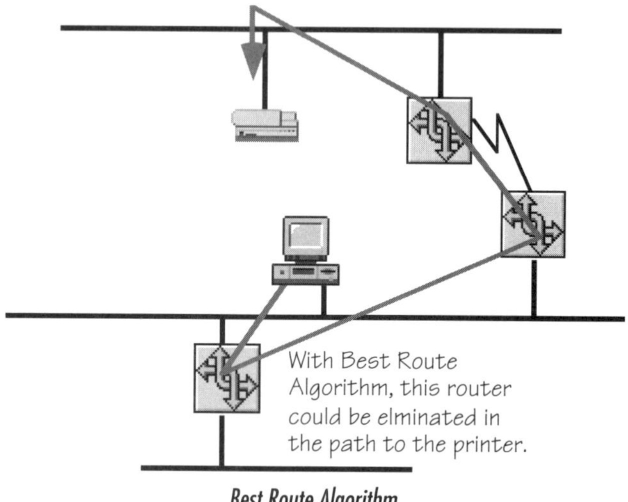

Best Route Algorithm

There could feasibly be times when, given a choice of routers, a device could send a packet through an unnecessary router in the path to the end node. However, using the best route algorithm, as the router receives packets back from the end node, it examines the address of the last router that forwarded the packet to it. It then stores this address in a table and uses it to reach that network in the future.

Tunneling and Encapsulation

Tunneling is the transferring of data between two routers across an "intermediate system" when that particular system does not support the protocols used by the end nodes transferring the data. In other words, a network could be designed with three segments. The two end segments could be AppleTalk segments and the center segment could be a TCP/IP segment. Because all three segments are not native AppleTalk, the only way a computer on one end segment could communicate with a computer on the other end segment would be if the routers connecting the three segments supported tunneling or encapsulation of AppleTalk within TCP/IP. That means that the router would receive a native AppleTalk packet and would put that foreign system's "wrapper" around the packet before placing it on the system's network. This also means that the router needs to support that system's addressing and packet formation routines. On the far side of the foreign system, the router then takes the wrapper off and forwards only the native AppleTalk formatted information to the appropriate destination.

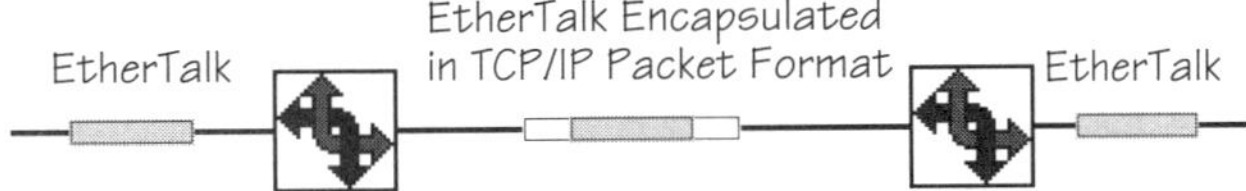

Packet Encapsulated Between Two Routers

Tunneling isn't limited to a single instance in which a router has to encapsulate data. AppleTalk routers can be configured at various points to tunnel information through as many routes as necessary in order to reach the final destination.

An AppleTalk router that connects an AppleTalk subnetwork to a tunnel is an exterior router. Exterior routers function as AppleTalk routers within the local subnetwork and as end nodes in the foreign network system that connects the AppleTalk subnetworks. There are two types of tunnels: dual end-point tunnels, or *point-to-point tunnels,* used to connect two halves of a WAN connection . . .

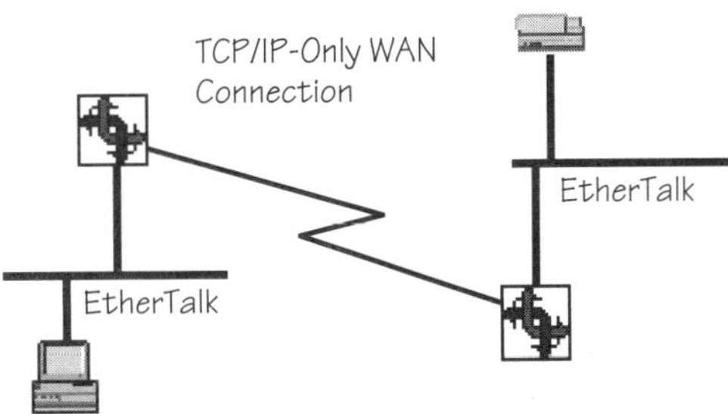

Point-to-Point Tunnel

. . . and multiple end-point tunnels, or *multipoint tunnels,* with more than two routers accessing the tunnels.

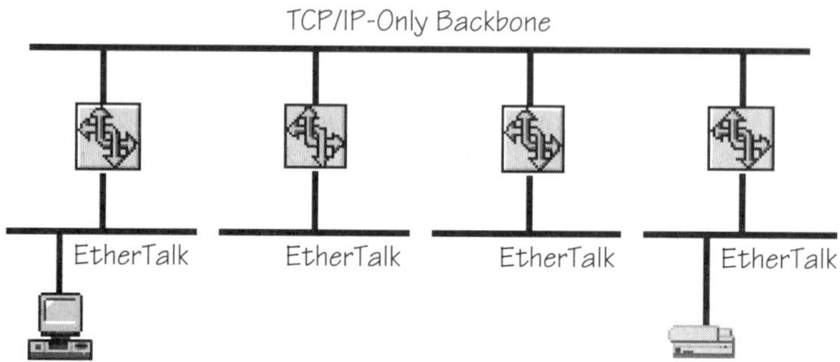

Multipoint Tunnel

These routers use RTMP to pass their routing information within the AppleTalk subnetwork to which they are connected. They then use AURP and the Network layer protocol of the system in which they must tunnel information when communicating with the other exterior routers connected to the tunnel. An exterior router always sends split-horizon routing information to the other exterior routers on a multipoint tunnel.

Some good examples of multipoint tunnels are Frame Relay meshed networks supporting only TCP/IP on the mesh, and, of course, the world's largest multipoint network, the Internet itself. Can you route through the Internet? You betcha. Would I suggest it for day to day operations? Probably not. If any of you out there want to try it, give us a call. We will set up a router to our training room to let you see what it's like. We need one or two days to get ready, and you need to be ready to communicate network numbering information (see renumbering in the next section). We have done this before, and it's kind of fun.

Subnetwork Renumbering

As networks grow in size, they become more complex. As networks grow in geographic proportion, they may be managed by people who don't necessarily communicate with each other. As this occurs, one of the biggest problems that faces network administrators is network number conflicts. AppleTalk network design states that there can't be any duplicates of network numbers within a given Apple-Talk internetworking system. AURP has the ability to resolve various network numbering conflict problems by remapping networks with potential numbering problems. While this is a good idea for initial network connections, good network management practices state that networks should be numbered correctly for a permanent solution.

When configuring exterior routers, the administrator or designer can specify a range of AppleTalk network numbers to be used for imported networks, meaning the *other subnetworks external to the home subnetwork*. The exterior router then maps the network numbers of incoming packets into the remapping range. It reverts remapped network numbers to their original numbering scheme when forwarding back out to the internetwork. When forwarding packets within the subnetworked system, packets containing remapped network numbers appear to have originated from networks in the remapped range.

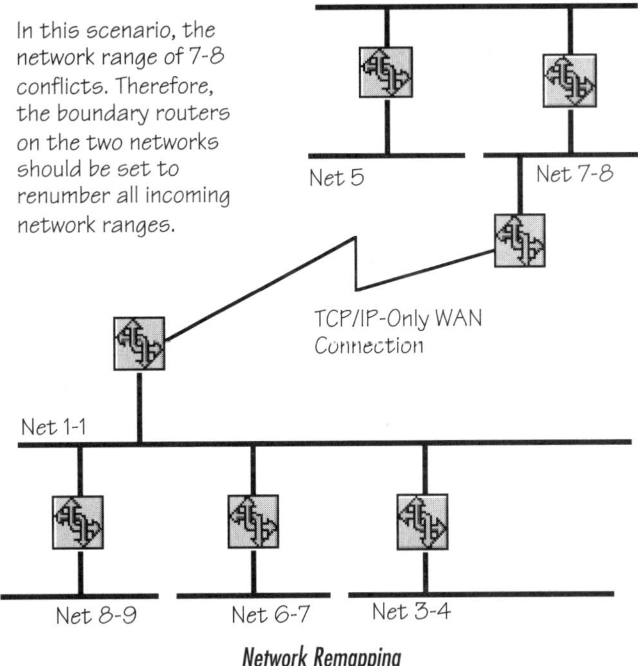

Network Remapping

When working with networks that have network number conflicts and when using network remapping to overcome those conflicts, the one thing that you **cannot** introduce into the equation is a redundant route, or multiple points of access to the networks being remapped. All networks being remapped should have a single point of access through an exterior router. If a redundant path to a renumbered network exists, the network range can loop back through the redundant path to the exterior router that originally remapped the network range. If this occurs, the networks in question will have two different ranges assigned: the original range and the remapped network range. The exterior router will remap the range again, which will loop back within the networking system and cause all sorts of havoc.

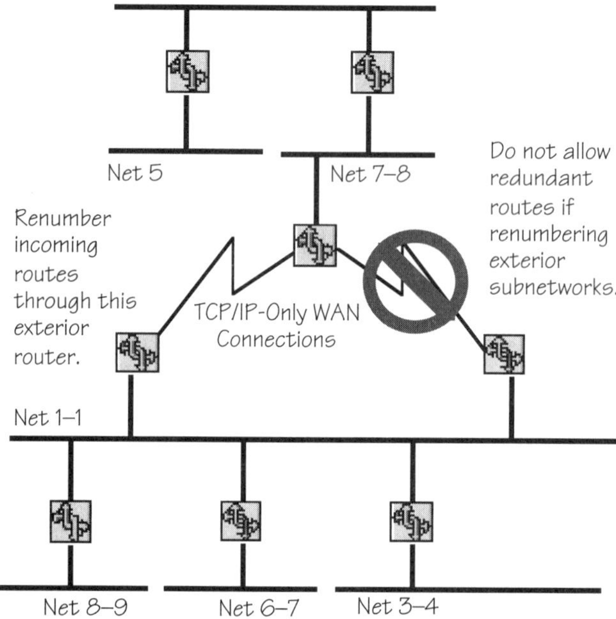

Redundant routes when renumbering a network are Bozo No-Nos.

Router Hop Count Reduction and Weighting

Normally, one of the design constraints of AppleTalk networks is that a packet may only traverse up to 15 routers. Each time a packet passes through a router, that packet's hop count is "upped" by at least one count—some routers weight the count and add more increments, but we'll go into that in a minute. In very large organizations, this limit can cause some connectivity problems that can't be easily overcome because of physical design issues, logical design issues, or political, religious, or budgetary issues within the corporation. One way to overcome this is to set an exterior router to automatically reduce the hop counts of packets as they traverse the router.

One of the things you can do with hop count reductions is to "weight" a route to another network. If you have multiple points of access to another network, called *redundant routes,* and you *are not* renumbering the far networks, you can set one of the routers to raise or reduce the hop count through that router to the next network. By doing this, you can force packets to take a single route to the far network. Why would you want to do this? Let's look at the following diagram. On the left there is a three-router path to the printer from the end-node computer. On the right is a four-router path to the printer from the end-node computer. Using the best route algorithm, the node would send its packets through the router on the left. But what if the router on the left is a 56K WAN connection and the router on the right is a T1 (1.5 MB) connection? Realistically, the path on the right would be *much* faster than the one on the left. By weighting the hop counts differently, you could force packets to the right instead of the left path.

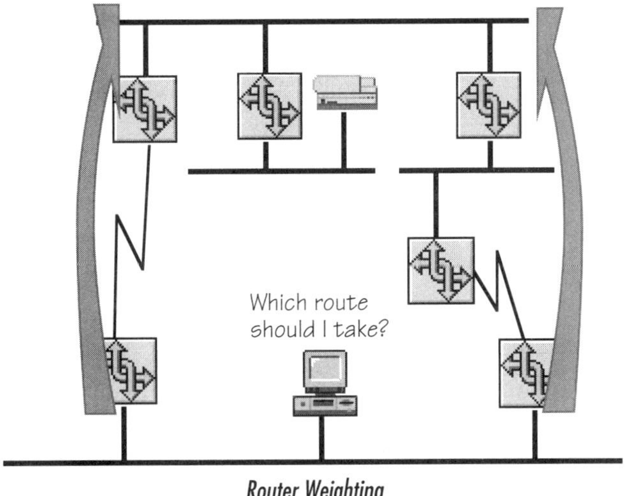

Router Weighting

To weight networks properly, you have to know a whole lot about the network connections with which you are attempting to work. Don't do this unless you have mapped your network with a product like LANsurveyor, and performed some packet analysis on the relative speeds of your connections. Further, ensure that the path you choose won't become overly clogged with traffic once you change everyone's routes through it.

Subnetwork Hiding when Tunneling

Network administrators can provide network-level security for a subnetwork by hiding that network from the rest of the internetwork system at the exterior router's access point. This prevents other subnetworks on the internetwork system from becoming aware of the presence of the hidden subnetwork. When exterior routers exchange their information about the routes that they know of, they simply don't export the information about the hidden subnetworks. You can hide a subnetwork on an internetwork from a specified few or from all exterior routers.

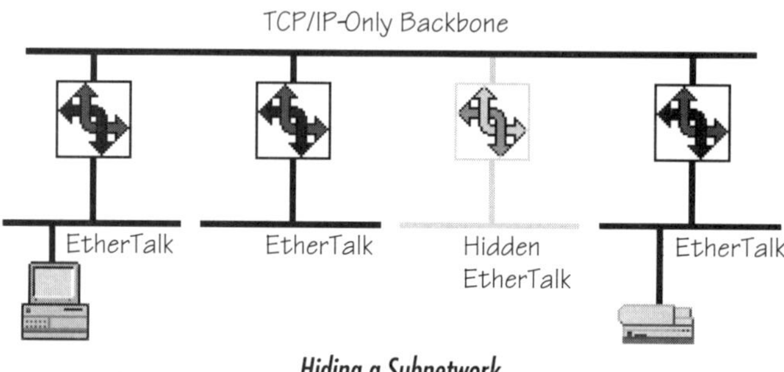

Hiding a Subnetwork

Device, Type, and Zone Hiding

Device hiding is another security mechanism that provides NBP layer protection. Routers can prevent devices within the local subnetwork from being visible to other nodes on *other* parts of an internetwork. They do this by not forwarding NBP Lookup Reply packets from that device *through the router* to other segments. This does not prevent devices *within* the local subnetwork from accessing the device, as the NBP Lookup Reply packets don't have to pass through the router.

 One warning: Never use device hiding as a full security measure. It only stops devices from forwarding NBP-type packets through the router. If a user wrote an application that didn't rely on NBP to establish a connection, it would bypass the device-hiding security.

Finally, whole *types* of devices and even entire *zones* can be hidden also. Most routers on the market implement hiding printers—type of "*LaserWriter*"—from those outside the subnetwork, as well as hiding the home zone of the router or whole lists of zones. Again, do some planning before you begin hiding devices.

Chapter 11: RTMP and the Basics of LAN Routing

The *Routing Table Maintenance Protocol (RTMP)* and *Apple Update-based Routing Protocol (AURP)* provide AppleTalk routers with a means of managing routing tables that forward packets from a node on one network to a node on a distant network. RTMP maintains a table called a routing table within the router itself. This table is used to determine the shortest path from the sending node to the receiving node within a large network. The Apple Update-based Routing Protocol is a newer version of RTMP that sends out its routing tables only when changes occur, such as the addition of another network segment. This makes AppleTalk routing more suited for Wide Area Networks, as they don't transfer as much information as often as RTMP does.

Although RTMP resides in the Transport layer, routers operate at the Network layer of the OSI model. They operate at the Network layer because they inspect the DDP protocol headers in each packet and base their forwarding decisions upon the network number ranges they find there. To do this successfully, each AppleTalk router must first build a routing table consisting of the networking information for the other routers on the network. This is built dynamically and continually using the RTMP or AURP protocols. We discuss RTMP in a page or two, and AURP is discussed in connection with backbone and WAN routing issues. Each router has to have at least two ports. Connecting two networks together via a router—one network cable per port—builds an *internet.* Thus, routers form a sort of wall between the two networks. Network traffic sent from one computer to another computer on the near side of the router will not affect computers on the far side of the router.

Routers can be used to connect multiple networks using the same protocol, such as AppleTalk. Connecting networks using different protocols, like AppleTalk running on one network and TCP/IP—a protocol that is *very* different from Apple-Talk—running on another, takes a different type of device called a *gateway*. Gateways and TCP/IP implementation are covered in Chapter 13.

Router Initialization: How Networks Obtain Their Numbers

There are many issues to consider before a router is added to the network. I don't want to sound like I'm trying to sell you training, but if you haven't done this before, take a good network design course. There are things you need to know that I just can't cover here. I will give you some of the basics, though. First of all, a router must contain at least two ports; many times one of these is Ethernet and the other is LocalTalk.

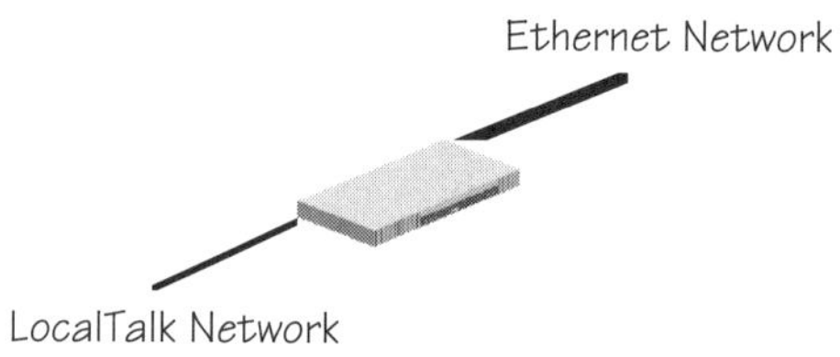

LocalTalk-to-Ethernet Router

When setting up the router, the network administrator must first assign a network number, sometimes called a cable number, to each of the networks being attached to the router. Without a router, the network number defaults to zero on LocalTalk networks and anywhere from 1-65000 on Ethernet or other extended networks. Each network on a router *must* have a different number. Having the same number would be like assigning all streets in your city the same name. Imagine the confusion for the Post Office if you had two addresses that were both Apt. 318 at 180 East 10th Street! The same thing applies to networks. It would be chaotic to have two or more computers with the same node number on different networks. The choices for network numbers range from 1–65,427. The administrator also has the opportunity at this time to assign zone names to the different network segments. In the following diagram, the upper network is network number **20** and its zone name is **Acme Admin**. The bottom network is network number **10** and its zone name is **Acme Production**. Computers in the upper zone would be members of the **Acme Admin** zone and their network numbers might be as follows: 10:10, and 10:128. Computers in the lower network belong to the **Acme Production** zone and their network numbers would be something like 20:42, 20:133, and 20:212.

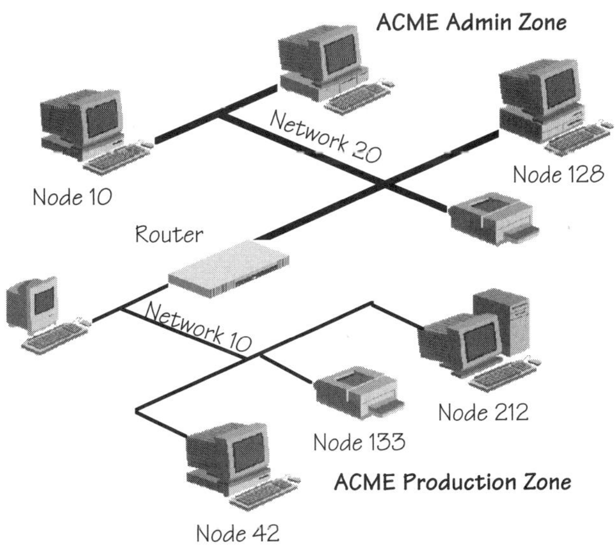

Small Network Diagram

This numbering scheme is implemented by the network administrator connecting his computer to the router and launching the router software to configure it. Once the software is opened, and a connection is made to the router, the administrator sees a window something like the one in the following screen shot. This particular router has two ports: a LocalTalk port and an Ethernet port. This window doesn't really belong to a router. I produced it to show the broadest characteristics of how a normal router can be configured. Let's go over the options as they appear in the window from left to right.

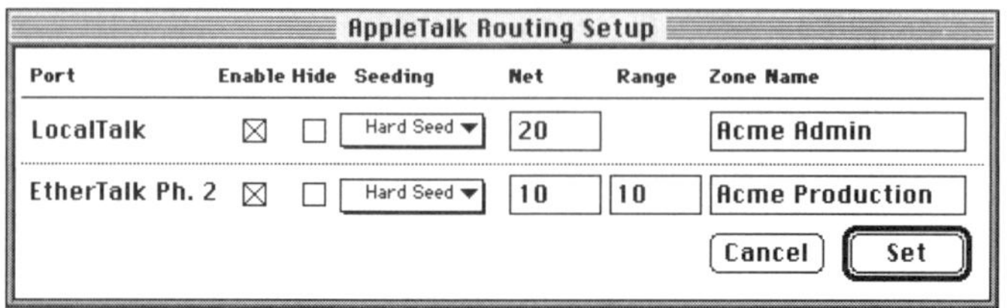

Sample Routing Setup

Port All routers have at least two ports or they couldn't route anything. This router has one LocalTalk port and one Ethernet port. Other routers, such as the Farallon InterRoute 5, can have as many as five ports—four LocalTalk and one Ethernet.

Enable Status Each router allows the administrator to enable or disable the port. This is useful, as networks can become corrupted and, in turn, can corrupt the router. Being able to shut off a network segment during troubleshooting is important.

Hide The administrator may "cloak" an entire zone from users on different networks. In this case, users within the network can see other networks. However, users outside the network are unable to see services or users within the hidden network.

Seeding There are three types of seeding for a router. The first type is **hard seeding**. This means that a router looks at what you typed into its network number and zone fields. It then checks the appropriate port to see if there are any other routers out on the network *on that port*. If the router finds another router on that port or no routers at all, and the network numbers match or do not exist yet, the router will enable the port. If they don't match, the router *will not* enable that port. After hard seeding, there is **soft seeding**. Soft seeding means that a router takes all the aforementioned steps except that when it finds a conflicting router on the port, it simply disregards what the administrator typed into the fields and enables the port, but with the other router's information. **Non-seeding** means that the router doesn't look for anything you typed in, and gathers network information from the other routers on that port. In the case of non-seeding, the router doesn't route information to a port where it finds no other routers because without a number or zone, the network doesn't exist to AppleTalk.

Network Numbers Theoretically, each LocalTalk network can handle up to 254 computers, because that's how many numbers are in the eight-bit LocalTalk node numbering scheme. That's fine for LocalTalk. However, for companies with tens of thousands of computers (Alf, Ron, I'm talking about you guys), most of those networks are running Ethernet. Ethernet networks allow more computers than 254, but to keep node numbering consistent between LocalTalk and Ethernet, Apple decided to allow Ethernet networks to have *extended addresses*. All Ethernet networks are numbered as *ranges*. A single range can be from 1–1, 1–500, and so on. Any set of contiguous numbers is acceptable. Within each number, there can reside 253 computers. So if you want to put 254 computers on an Ethernet network, you have to have a range of, say, 1–2. This would allow you a total of 506 computers. (Question: How many numbers would the range have to span if you wanted to put on 666 computers? Answer: A *hell* of a lot [Get it? 666, *hell* of a lot?].)

Zone Names

Hey, folks, your zone names come from here, as well! The network administrators tell the routers which zones to attribute to which networks. LocalTalk networks can have a single zone. Ethernet networks can have multiple zones, just like they can have multiple network numbers. There are whole sets of rules concerning zone naming etiquette, but the only thing you need to know right now is that you better spell your network zone names right each time you add a router. I've been to more than one network that has zones like "R&D" and "R & D" in the Chooser because the administrator spelled the same thing two different ways.

Routing Tables

Not only do routers separate traffic and tie networks together, they also act as traffic cops, directing AppleTalk packets from one network to another. Remember back in junior high school? Yeah, me neither. But I do remember my first day in high school. It was so much bigger than my rather small junior high. I remember reporting to home room for first period and being swamped by the much larger students who were everywhere. Luckily for me, we had hall monitors standing at the intersections of the corridors to help freshmen find their way. That's what routers do on the network. They maintain routing tables of network numbers and other routers on the network. Just like the hall monitors, who knew the school corridors and the shortest routes to take when navigating them, routers know the networks to which they are connected and how to reach the networks to which they aren't connected.

To make all these numbers, addresses, and naming conventions transparent to users, the routers maintain an internal table of information used for routing packets across the internet. The routing table lists all the other routers it finds on every connected local network in the internet. These tables are maintained and refreshed on a regular basis by the router. When a router is first turned on, it creates its routing table by examining each of its networked ports. RTMP must create an entry in the router's table for each network cable number. Then, periodically, the router broadcasts RTMP packets through each of its ports to notify all other routers of its ID and its current routing table. RTMP must also have a way to detect if other routers no longer exist on the network. If a router fails to respond with an RTMP packet after a certain amount of time, it is "aged out" of the routing table. The following picture is a sample router table. Not all information in the table is maintained by all the routers on the market. I'll point out the information *all* routers maintain.

Routing Table						Cumulative Traffic Received as of 9:45 PM 3/30/94	
Zone Name	Net Number	State	Hops	Router Port	Next Router Address	Percent	Packets
Acme Admin	30 – 40	Good	0	ET Ph.2	30.150	47	494
Acme Marketing	10	Good	0	LT 1	10.144	43	456
Acme Public	70	Good	1	ET Ph.2	38.157	0	0
Acme R & D	50 – 60	Good	1	ET Ph.2	30.137	3	41
Acme Senior Staff	20	Good	1	LT 1	10.190	0	4

Sample Routing Table

Zone I've already described zones. This is not a requisite part of the routing table, although it is a requisite for setting up a router's port.

Network Range This identifies the network cable address of the router. This number could also be the network number, depending upon the type of network.

Entry State Each routing table has an entry state for all routers in the table. This entry state can be one of three values: good, suspect, or bad. This has nothing to do with direct network connections. It is a process of routing table maintenance. The entire time they are in use, routers must publish their routing tables within a certain amount of time. If that amount of time has lapsed, the entry moves from good, to suspect, to bad, and finally out of the table.

Hop Count This is the distance in "hops" to the next router. The distance between nodes on an internet is measured by how many routers the packet has to hop through before arriving at the destination node. Each router represents one hop. The number of hops to a network directly connected to the router is always zero.

The maximum hops a message can take before it arrives at its destination is 15. Every time a packet reaches a router, the router checks its hop count. Every time the packet passes through a router, one hop is added to the hop count. If the hop count reaches 15 and the packet still hasn't reached its destination, the packet is not forwarded by the next router. The router reads the hop count to be 15 and then just disregards the packet. It will not be delivered.

 Some routers, like the Liaison software router from Farallon Computing, use low-speed modems to connect networks. When establishing a hop distance to the next router, on the other side of the modem, they advance the hop count to account for the time lag when sending a packet from 10 routers through a 19.2 modem. So, don't just think your routers are "x" hops away from each other on a wide area network; look at the routing tables before you plan your network expansions.

Port This is the port on the router through which the packet travels to reach its destination cable. There are at least two ports to a router, and many routers have multiple ports. Some routers show the port by name, and others show that port by number. It's the same thing. This is the port on which the packet *exits,* on its way to the network in question.

Next Router Address Routers don't maintain tables of information for nodes or sockets. All they maintain is a table of information for a network and the router that connects to that network. Therefore, the routing table has the address of the next router to which it would need to send a packet when forwarding that packet to a distant address.

IMPLEMENTATIONS OF LAN ROUTER/BRIDGES

There are a great many kinds of routers being built today. There are software-based and hardware-based routers. There are two-port routers, three-port routers, four-port routers, and routers on a card that can be set into a casing to be configured as many multiport ports. Because of the different types of routers and the plenitude of them, we are going to break them down into different groupings, and then give you what we consider to be the best of the breed in each grouping.

The first of these groupings is the basic hardware router. This is simply a router that connects other devices. However, because of the advanced nature of the routers being built today, these routers can also be configured as bridges or IP gateways. Only four years ago we were stuck with two-port routers, like the FastPath and the GatorBox. A couple of years ago there was a three-port router called the TCPII. However, router manufacturers today don't design routers unless they are three-, four-, or more ports, or are specialty routers like hub or switch routers. The two routers described in the following sections are both four-port routers. One is a two-port Ethernet and two-port LocalTalk router (3000E), and the other has four Ethernet ports but no LocalTalk ports (4000S). The text used to describe the routers comes from the home pages of the companies that built them and is unedited, except to clean up grammar or take out parts we thought were "marketing bullshit."

Compatible System's RISC Router 3000E Bridging Router

The RISC Router 3000E is a very high-performance dedicated Ethernet-to-Ethernet router that supports TCP/IP, IPX, AppleTalk, and DECNet network protocols. By relying on the latest RISC technology, packets are routed at Ethernet "wire speed," 14,800 packets per second, between its two Ethernet ports.

You can use the RISC Router 3000E to transparently isolate an Ethernet subnet from an Ethernet backbone network. Only the subnet traffic destined for the backbone will be routed to it, yielding lower network traffic and better Ethernet performance on both the subnet and the backbone.

Multiple RISC Router 3000E routers can also be used to create a high-performance "hierarchical" network structure, which isolates local network traffic in local areas, conserving network bandwidth for inter-area communications. Because of its wire-speed operation, the RISC Router 3000E introduces virtually no performance penalties in inter-area communications.

Devices that can communicate through a RISC Router 3000E include Ethernet connected personal computers and printers, laser typesetters, UNIX workstations, DECnet compatible minicomputers, and many other Ethernet devices. The RISC Router 3000E comes ready to connect to thick, thin, or 10BaseT Ethernet networks on both ports.

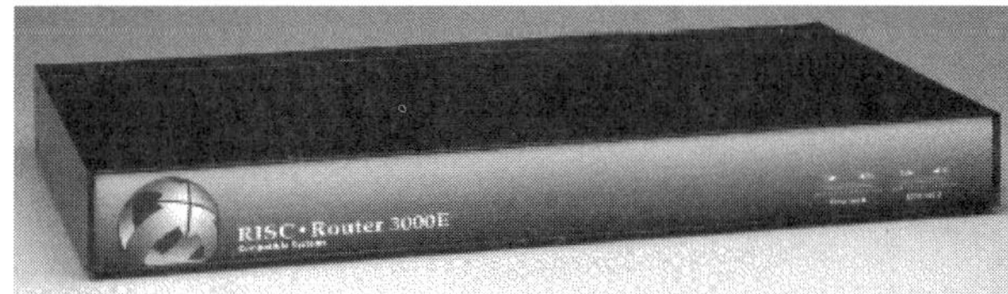

Front of RISC Router 3000E

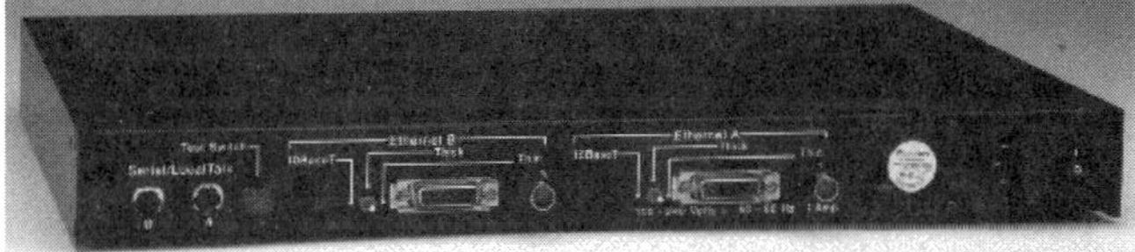

Back of RISC Router 3000E

The RISC Router 3000E can be set to bridge or route on any of its four ports, and acts as a DDP/IP forwarding gateway as well.

Compatible System's RISC Router 4000S Bridging Router

The RISC Router 4000S delivers simultaneous wire-speed routing and bridging between four local Ethernet segments. With all the benefits of network routing plus speeds as great as network switches, the 4000S provides a flexible, growth-oriented solution for interconnecting Ethernet networks. The RISC Router 4000S supports the TCP/IP, IPX, AppleTalk, and DECnet network protocols on all ports and also supports spanning-tree bridging for other protocols such as Net-BEUI and DEC LAT.

The RISC Router 4000S comes ready to connect to thick or 10BaseT Ethernet and features four auto-switching AUI and RJ-45 ports. A low-speed RS-232C connection supports out-of-band management and system event logging.

You can use the RISC Router 4000S to divide an Ethernet network into four individual segments for improved performance while still maintaining full connectivity between segments. Or use the RISC Router 4000S to transparently isolate up to three Ethernet subnets from an Ethernet backbone network.

The RISC Router 4000S's multi-protocol routing features provide the logical network segmentation that simple Ethernet switches lack—you can create IP subnets, AppleTalk zones, and IPX networks, and filter network packets based on these parameters. These features also protect your network from the Ethernet broadcast storms that can plague simple switched networks.

Front of RISC Router 4000S

Back of RISC Router 4000S

Much like the RISC Router 3000E, the RISC Router 4000S can also be set to bridge or route on any of its four ports, and can be enabled as a DDP/IP forwarding gateway as well.

IMPLEMENTATIONS OF LAN ROUTER/REPEATER AND ROUTER/SWITCHES

These devices are combinations of routers and multiport repeaters—also known as hubs—or multiport switches. Use these devices if you need to introduce a LocalTalk hub or switch into an Ethernet environment.

Farallon's StarRouter

Farallon's StarRouter is a 12-port intelligent LocalTalk hub and hardware router that gives users access to Ethernet and TCP/IP gateway services.

The StarRouter supports industry standards including SNMP and AURP for multi-vendor compatibility, easy configuration, and IP tunneling over AppleTalk. Performance is increased by Farallon's unique multibus architecture. StarCommand management software is included for control over the router on the network. This uses AURP to interconnect networks by tunneling AppleTalk through TCP/IP for easy configuration and added performance. For network managers running AppleTalk on IP backbones, it decreases traffic jams.

Hard seeding will allow you to control your AppleTalk internets by designating the exact zone and network numbers used on given routers. With network number remapping, you can communicate with any device without worrying about address conflicts. If a user sends a message to a remote device with a duplicate number, the StarRouter automatically reassigns a different number to ensure the information reaches its intended destination.

Farallon StarRouter

Farallon's InterRoute/5

Farallon's InterRoute/5 provides AppleTalk routing and full AppleTalk TCP/IP gateway services between one Ethernet and four LocalTalk (StarController-based repeater) networks with high performance integration. Ethernet and LocalTalk users can more easily share information between Macs, PCs, and UNIX systems.

The InterRoute/5 supports industry standards including TCP/IP, SNMP, and Apple standards such as AppleTalk and AURP for multi-vendor compatibility, easy configuration, added performance, and IP tunneling. Selectable seeding and remapping features are included for added control, and performance is even further increased by Farallon's unique multibus architecture, designed to ensure faster throughput than you'll find from any other network vendor. Reduce traffic and improve performance with the InterRoute/5 by logically segmenting larger networks into more manageable, smaller ones. Save time managing and troubleshooting those networks with StarCommand management software.

Farallon InterRoute/5

Tribe's TribeStar

As an AppleTalk switching hub with eight LocalTalk ports and one Ethernet port, TribeStar can handle eight simultaneous full-speed connections between LocalTalk users and Ethernet services. TribeStar's packet-switching technology allows up to 32 users on its eight LocalTalk ports direct access to Ethernet.

TribeStar, designed to integrate LocalTalk and Ethernet in the most powerful way, creates a path between the two systems eight times "wider" than a typical router.

Easier to administer than a router, TribeStar creates one AppleTalk network that encompasses both the LocalTalk and Ethernet segments. Utilizing packet switching among its LocalTalk ports, TribeStar handles concurrent LocalTalk signals (ordinary LocalTalk hubs handle only one signal at a time).

TribeStar

About the size of a hardback book, TribeStar is easy to install. The Ethernet side connects to 10BaseT, 10Base2 (ThinNet), or 10Base5 (ThickNet) via a standard Ethernet transceiver. The LocalTalk ports connect to the network via a patch panel or punchdown block.

TribeStar IP offers all the advantages of TribeStar plus it allows Macs connected to its LocalTalk ports to access TCP/IP services without the aid of a separate MacIP gateway. TCP/IP protocols and Internet connectivity offer huge advantages to almost any organization, and TCP/IP is gaining momentum as a connectivity standard. TribeStar IP offers a fast, inexpensive way to have full access to UNIX servers and IP services such as e-mail, FTP, and Telnet.

This device can be configured as a router, a bridge, or a DDP/IP gateway when in routing mode.

Implementations of Software Routers

Software routers aren't really our choice for high-performance routers. Because they are software-based, the computer on which they run should be the fastest possible computer. Putting a software router on something like a Mac IIsi with an Ethernet card wouldn't provide robust or fast Ethernet-to-LocalTalk connection. However, putting an Internet Router on an 8150 Workgroup Server that also has ARA would create one of the best Internet access servers for remote users.

Apple's Internet Router

The router offers you local and wide area networking flexibility. You can connect your local work groups over industry-standard network types, including Local-Talk, Ethernet, and Token Ring. As your network grows larger and more global, the Apple Internet Router lets you link remote sites to your network through a dial-up connection over a standard modem, or you can add one of the Apple Internet Router Wide Area Extensions (available separately) to link your Apple-Talk networks using X.25 or TCP/IP.

The Apple Internet Router features the AppleTalk Update-based Routing Protocol (AURP), a powerful wide area networking standard. AURP ensures that wide area links function efficiently, substantially reducing the traffic over wide area networks. With AURP, you can maximize the use of your network resources.

The Apple Internet Router software runs on a broad range of Apple Macintosh computers and Workgroup Servers—pretty much everything except the Power-Book series. Thus, you can tailor your router configurations to meet your cost and performance requirements. Like other Macintosh computer-based software, the router is easy to use, configure, and support. Even a network novice can have the router up and running and can begin to make use of its powerful features within minutes. In addition, the router has built-in support for the Simple Network Management Protocol (SNMP), so it can be easily monitored by any SNMP-based management station.

The router supports all the connectivity ports that the host computer has installed. This means, at the very least, that the host computer has an Ethernet port and two serial ports that may be defined as LocalTalk ports or dial-up ports.

By adding a Token Ring card or Ethernet card to the computer, you can increase the number of ports supported by the router. Realistically, I would never add more than one other card to the router, as that would significantly decrease the router's performance on a busy network.

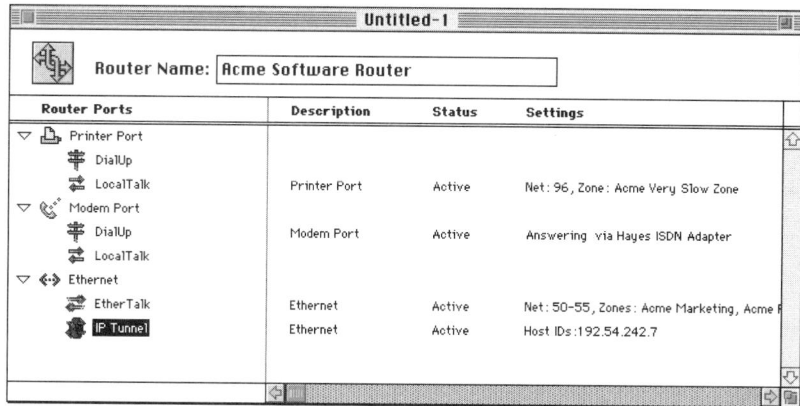

Apple Internet Router Setup Screen

With the Wide Area Network extension, you can set the router to tunnel through a TCP/IP segment, rather than to route through it. The router supports network hiding on the exterior routing ports, as well as device and type hiding on all ports.

If you are looking for an easily configured ISDN router, this is the one I recommend. The other one I can recommend is the Netopia Internet Router from Farallon, although its scope and access is limited to only ISDN as the WAN connection feature.

LAN Router Architecture Design Issues

This section is *just a little more* comprehensive than the sections on other architectures, such as hubs and bridges. There are seven major router architectures. Six of the seven are divided into two categories (LAN and WAN), and the seventh is the "putting it all together" category. The seven are as follows:

- Simple LocalTalk-to-Ethernet connectivity (LAN)

- Distributed backbone routers (LAN)

- Collapsed backbone routers (LAN)

- Point-to-point routing (WAN)

- Collapsed backbone—called *hub and spoke*—routing (WAN)

- Distributed—called *meshed*—routing (WAN)

- Combination of LAN and WAN routing architectures—the "putting it all together" category mentioned above

We will cover the LAN router architecture options in this section. See Chapter 12, "WAN Routing Basics," beginning on page 281 for the WAN router architecture options. In covering the WAN categories, we give you a *very* abbreviated breakdown on what is going on with ISDN technology and Frame Relay technology, and how the two of them operate. If you are interested, contact us and we will give you *much* more information about both subjects. Since the technology is changing rapidly, the best thing to do for more information is to e-mail us or look at our Web page for more information (www.netfrontiers.com). Each of our consultants maintains a personal page with references and links to cool places on the Internet with more info than we have at our fingertips.

Simple LocalTalk-to-Ethernet Connectivity

Corporations usually begin exploring connectivity because of the need to connect their LocalTalk-only computers to their Ethernet computers. Thus, it isn't so much of a design *strategy* as it is a design *need*.

There are two ways users on a LocalTalk subnetwork can access users on an Ethernet subnetwork: through a translational bridge or through a router. The diagram to the right shows a simple LocalTalk-to-Ethernet connection through a two-port router.

LT-to-EN Router

As we've mentioned before, these simple networks were commonplace a few years ago, with two-port routers such as the FastPath and the GatorBox proliferating. They aren't as common now, since most of the routers on the market these days are three-, four-, or more-port LAN-based routers. There are two notable exceptions still on the market: Tribe's TribeStar and the Farallon EtherRoute. Both of these routers are LocalTalk hub (EtherRoute) or LocalTalk switch (TribeStar) to single Ethernet port routers. While there is a single Ethernet port, the LocalTalk port is combined with a hub or a switch to provide added connectivity. Both of these routers are great for small office designs in which the users are on LocalTalk, as in classroom or mobile users, and need connectivity from one area to the rest of the office.

There is one caveat to using a router/hub or router/switch in a network design: Too many people use the multiple ports on the hub or the switch to connect whole LocalTalk subnetworks. I once was visiting a client site where the client had a TribeStar connected to their Ethernet network. They were asking why the performance of the computers on LocalTalk was so slow. When I investigated, I found that there were 238 total devices on the LocalTalk side of the TribeStar. They had daisy-chained close to 32 devices off each port! They thought it was a multiport (multiple LocalTalk routes) router!

Collapsed Backbone Routers

There are a lot of people who talk about the need for a collapsed backbone network, and don't even know that they have one. Simply put, the backbone of your network is the one place that all traffic must traverse if it is going to reach any other point. Well, if you have a single multiport router, guess what? You have just implemented a collapsed backbone network. Congratulations. Now you can amaze your geek friends at your local juice bar. The picture to the right depicts the network design you might end up with if you purchase a single RISC Router 3000E from Compatible Systems. It has two Ethernet ports and two LocalTalk ports, giving it the capability to create four networks when all ports are routed, or fewer if you choose to bridge some of the ports.

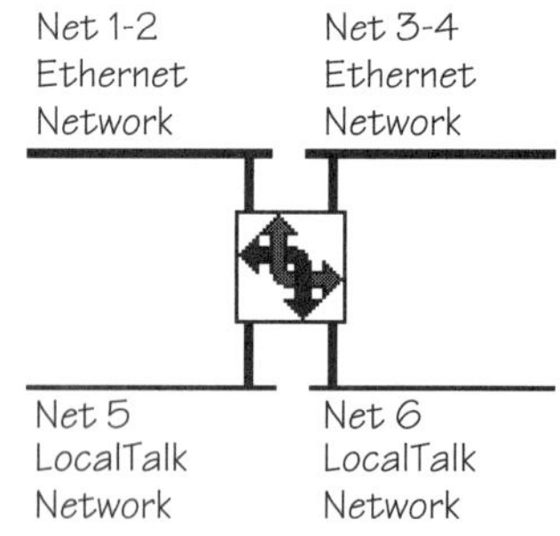

Collapsed Backbone Network

While a single router can create a small collapsed backbone, the implementation of several routers on the network creates a true collapsed backbone. The next picture shows a network design with five routers on it, creating a total of eight different subnetworks. This is a collapsed backbone. How can you tell? Easy enough: The central path that all other networks have to take when travelling from, say, subnetwork 10 to subnetwork 7 is through the router in the center of the design.

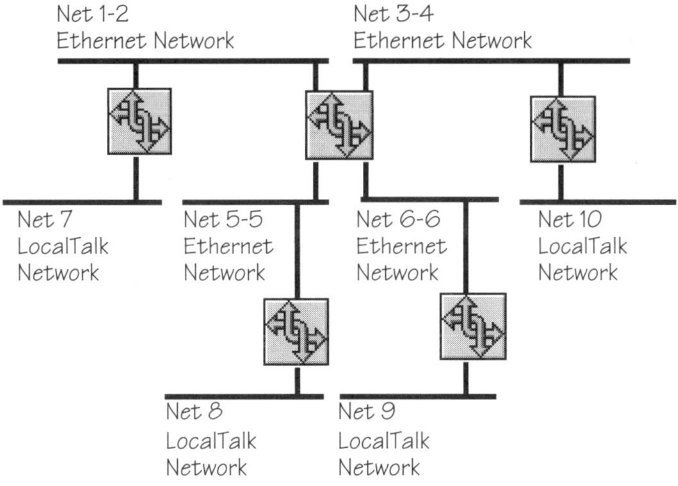

Larger Collapsed Backbone

 While this isn't a *bad* design, the design does have one major weak point—the central router. If that router goes down, the internetwork would be split into four different subnetworks that can't connect to each other. The other thing to keep in mind is that if you put a central router in the middle of your network, make sure the router is capable of handling the work load.

Another Amazing True Story

I was contacted recently by a corporation that wanted me to come over and take a look at their network design. I was told it was a collapsed backbone design that was mainly Ethernet, but included two LocalTalk segments. They said that once they segmented the network, their primary server (a Quadra 950) became slow. First, I scanned the network with LANsurveyor from Neon Software. I did indeed find a simple collapsed backbone design with six Ethernet segments and two LocalTalk segments. Since I had never seen an eight-port router that supported Ethernet and LocalTalk simultaneously, I asked to see their setup. "Surprise, surprise, surprise," to quote Gomer Pyle. I almost laughed myself silly. Here was their Quadra 950 file server with six Ethernet cards *completely filling* the NuBus slots in the computer. Two LocalTalk segments hung off its modem and printer serial ports. The file server was *completely* inundated by the routing processes of the Apple Internet Router and therefore wasn't functioning well as a router *or* as a file server. Incredible.

Distributed Backbone Routers

Take a piece of coax (10Base2) cable and connect your TribeStar's Ethernet port, an InterRoute/5's Ethernet port, and a FastPath's Ethernet port, and you have yourself a distributed backbone. A distributed backbone—some folks call it a *boundary router design*—is simply an internetwork design in which the connecting path for most transactions on the internetwork is a subnetwork in and of itself. Usually the subnetwork is some kind of extended networking system like Ethernet, Fast Ethernet, Token Ring, or FDDI. Of course, if your network isn't well designed, it might be LocalTalk (right, Don?).

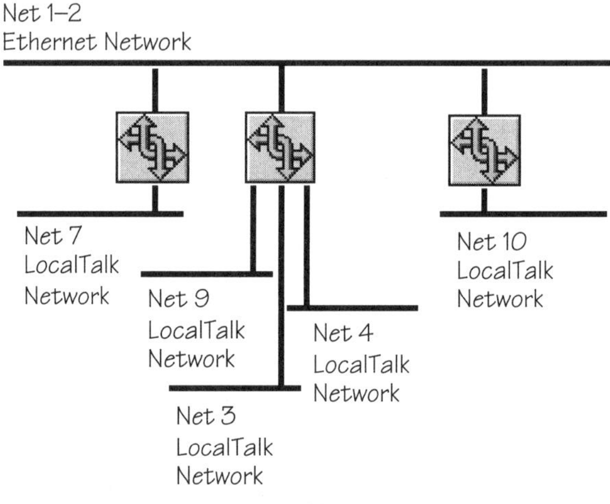

Distributed Backbone Network

Where a collapsed backbone's weight is placed on the backbone router, the weight of network traffic in a distributed backbone is placed on the relaying (backbone) subnetwork itself. This means that you need a subnetwork with the same utilization rate, or higher, than the other subnetworks it is connecting. LocalTalk subnetworks routing *up* to an Ethernet backbone network is one example. If you are running a 10-Mbps Ethernet network already, choose an FDDI network running at 100 Mbps, or a Fast Ethernet network as your corporate backbone.

If your network starts at 10 Mbps and ends at 10 Mbps, having a 100-Mbps backbone doesn't increase speed. Thus, while a faster backbone doesn't provide overall faster throughput, a faster backbone *does* provide higher utilization rates. A 10-

Mbps network with a utilization rate of 10% takes up much less utilization on a 100-Mbps system.

If all you have are two-port routers, a distributed backbone can be easy to build. But what happens if the routers with which you are working are multiport routers? The next diagram shows an internetwork of eight subnetworks. The subnetworks were made from a single two-port router and two four-port routers. When I arrived onsite, the network administrator proudly pointed to a whole bunch of servers on network 5–6 and told me that this was the backbone of their system. He wanted to know what I thought of the design. I ran LANsurveyor, and then sat him down and explained that a backbone isn't someplace you just *say* is a backbone. It is designed specifically as the connectivity *relay* between adjoining networks. He moved the servers. Remember, look at the logical layout of the network to determine where the backbone is.

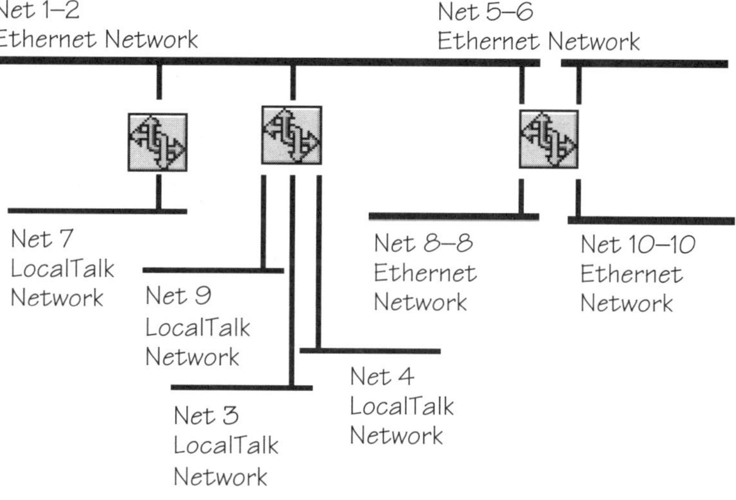

Which subnetwork is the backbone?

Rules to Route by

Okay, now let's put everything into one cohesive set of rules. These rules, in part, were taken [read *wholeheartedly stolen* here] from the folks at Neon Software, with their permission.

Rule Set 1: Network Numbers

AppleTalk can use the network numbers in the range of 1–65279. The range of 65280–65534 is called the *startup range* and should never be used as network numbers when configuring a router.

Extended networks can have network ranges (1–20 is a range; 1, 4, or 8 is not), while non-extended networks can have only a single network number.

Remember that a total of 253 nodes can "live" within any given network number in an extended network. That means that the network range of 100–101 will hold 506 computers. Since the maximum number of computers you can realistically place on an Ethernet network is about 800, you should never need a range larger than four numbers.

Once you have used a network number, you can't use it again. If you are using network number remapping on an exterior router, you could use a network number twice, in theory, but even then it's not a good idea.

All routers sharing a common network must have the port attached to that network assigned the same number. In other words, on a distributed backbone or on a fully meshed WAN, the backbone or the mesh is normally assigned a network number or a network range. All router ports connected to the backbone or the mesh should have the same number or range entered into the port configuration.

Rule Set 2: Network Zones

Just like network numbering, the physical medium determines the zone assignments. Just as there can only be a single network number for a non-extended network, there can only be a single zone for a non-extended network. Extended networks may have more than one zone.

Zone name lengths should be limited to 32 total characters.

The number of zones you can have is determined by the routers you have on your network. There are some routers that can hold no more than 256 zones per total zone list. There are some routers that can hold more than that, and some routers that can hold less than that. Don't argue about the rules when your routers are going to be the determining factor.

Extended networks can have a zone list, as well as a default zone. All router ports that share a common physical medium, such as a distributed backbone or a full mesh WAN, *must* have the same local zone names and defaults.

Spelling counts when creating zone names. Names with spaces are different from names with underscores. Capitalization isn't supposed to count according to the Apple design guidelines, but realistically it does. Work with reality.

Rule Set 3: Hop Counts

There can be no more than 15 hop counts per packet. If you have a network that is more than 15 router hops deep, reconfigure it.

Remember that each router counts as one hop count. When connecting two WAN half-routers, they are supposed to equal one hop count each. Realistically, some do, and then there are those routers that time packets as they cross the WAN and add a couple of extra hops to the hop count to adjust for the slower links. Others count each one as a full hop. Ergo, you'll need to get a good understanding of how the routers see the world.

If you are going to use AURP's ability to adjust hop counts, make sure that you don't have a loop, or *redundant path,* in your network, or you will really screw things up.

Rule Set 4: Seeding Your Routers

Some routers are hard seed routers and some are soft seed routers. Figure out which ones you have. You need to know this when planning which routers you will start first in case of a power failure.

Remember that some routers start much faster than others. Some of the larger Cisco routers take about seven minutes to load AppleTalk after they have loaded all the other protocols in the world, count the number of angels which fit on the head of a pin and get a cup of coffee. Make sure you know how long it takes to stop and restart the AppleTalk processes on your routers.

If you set up seed and non-seed routers on your network, plan to have at least two of your routers set up as seed routers. Just in case you lose the configuration file for one of them, you will be able to recall what you set up by reading the configuration file of the other.

Rule Set 5: AURP

Just because the WAN router is a WAN router doesn't mean that it supports AURP. If it supports AURP, that doesn't mean it *fully* supports AURP.

Whatever you do, try to prevent the propagation of RTMP packets on your WAN. RTMP can completely clog a WAN's utilization capabilities if there are a lot of routers on it.

If you hide or renumber networks, remove your redundant path. Renumbering and hiding go crazy if you don't do that.

Hiding a network, zone, or device isn't the best security—a baseball bat and a gorilla are much better.

Rule Set 6: WAN Links

When setting up your WAN connections, check for Annex D versus LMI for Frame Relay. Check on your DLCI port information for each router for both AppleTalk and TCP/IP. Test your CSU/DSU for local *and* remote loopback, test that you can "ping" with IP out of your WAN router, and test that you set your IP gateways correctly. This, then, brings us to the next chapter on WAN routing.

Chapter 12: WAN Routing Basics

A WAN is an internetwork that extends between two or more LANs located across geographic distances and connected by means of telephone, microwave relay, satellite, or some other long distance communications technology. WANs often connect local networks at different sites to allow such things as access to databases, messaging, and file transfer. Ideally, a WAN is invisible to the user; that is, the user does not recognize any differences when using local or remote resources.

Voice-grade phone lines, X.25, ATM, Frame Relay, SMDS, ATM, and ISDN are the most popular network standards for WANs. However, within these, voice-grade phone lines (called *POTS,* for Plain Old Telephone System), ISDN, and Frame Relay are by far the most widespread and readily available. We will be talking mostly about these systems. A brief description of each of these standards follows and after that, a description of the routers that support these systems.

> **Before you create a WAN, make some preliminary connections to the Internet to do some research and prepare yourself. Don't just connect your company to a WAN and the Internet; connect your own computer directly through an ISP using SLIP or PPP to do your homework and get a feel for what is out on the Internet, and what you are going to run up against when drafting your connection plan.**
>
> **I mean it.**

CONFIGURING MACPPP

This information will help you prepare for your initial Internet connection.

A remote or mobile Macintosh can access the Internet via MacPPP. Much as ARA provides network access over telephone lines to Macintoshes running AppleTalk, this freeware system extension distributed by the University of Michigan and Merit Network permits the same for Macintoshes running MacTCP. While ARA uses the AppleTalk Remote Access Protocol (ARAP) to provide a sort of bridge over which AppleTalk can travel, MacPPP uses the Point-to-Point Protocol (PPP) to provide the same for TCP/IP.

There are several pieces of information needed to configure MacPPP for your remote users. You need a dial-up telephone number to the ISP. It should be local. You need an IP address and a domain name for the remote computer. You need a login name and password for the remote user. You need the domain and IP addresses of the ISP's domain name server or servers. Finally, the user needs to be equipped with at least a 14,400 bps modem.

With MacTCP and MacPPP installed and with your login data in hand, go to the user's computer and open the MacTCP control panel. If it is not already selected, choose the **PPP** icon as the connection method, and then click the **More** button to bring up the Administrator window. If remote users are going to have a static address of their own, choose the **Manually** button in the **Obtain Address** field in the upper left of the window. Otherwise, select **Server** so the ISP's terminal server can assign the address.

Unless told to do so by the ISP, you can leave almost everything else alone. The variables to configure are in the lower right—**Domain Name Server Information**. Add the domain name and IP address of the domain name server(s) given to you by the ISP. After exiting the Administrator window, type the user's static IP address, if there is one, in the MacTCP control panel window.

To configure MacPPP, open its accompanying Config PPP control panel. Click **New** and give the connection a name in the resulting PPP Server dialog box. The PPP Server is the ISP's machine that acts as a proxy for the user's desktop computer. The new name will appear in the Config PPP window's pop-up screen.

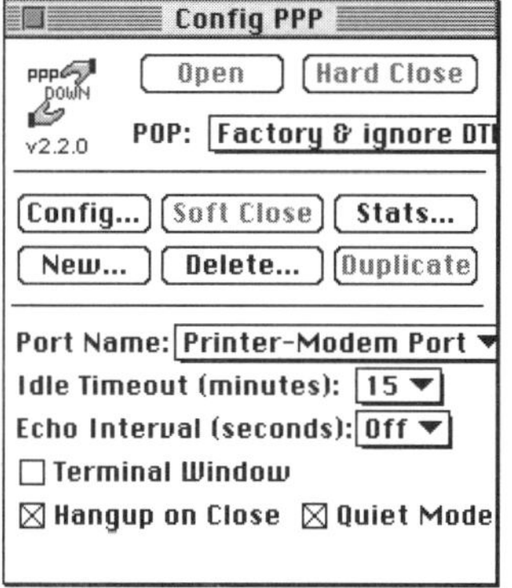

Config PPP Window

Next click the **Config...** button and enter the necessary modem information.

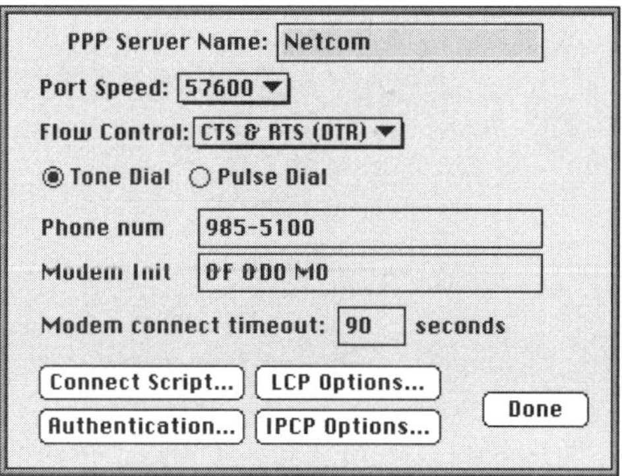

Entering Modem Information

In this window, you might as well choose **38,400** bps for **Port Speed**, as that is the fastest you can cram data through the Macintosh serial port. You are allowed to go as high as **230K** in case the particular Macintosh and modem are not hampered by this bottleneck. In the **Modem Init** field, the command **&F** initializes the modem with its factory settings. Use **&D0** to tell the modem to ignore the Data Terminal Ready (DTR) signal. This is necessary, as some high-speed modems will attempt to use the DTR wire in the modem cable to signal whether or not the device should hang up. The Macintosh wants to use this line for a Request To Send (RTS) signal instead as part of its flow control. Disabling DTR permits this. Finally, you might want to add **M0** to turn off the noisy modem speaker. Keep the modem manual handy, along with references to the AT command set. Generally, you want to end up with a modem set as follows:

- Hardware flow control (**CTS & RTS**) enabled, not software flow control (**XON/XOFF**)

- A fixed serial port speed, as in 38,400 bps

- Data compression enabled, as in V.42 bis or MNP5

- Error compression enabled, as in V.42 or MNP

- The "busy" message permitted

 It is hard to tell a hardware handshaking cable from a non-hardware handshaking cable without tracing the pinouts, so make sure the modem has one. They work with any Macintosh except the 128, 512K, and 512KE.

You may or may not need to create a special login script. If the network access provider has given you a login script, click **Connect Script** and enter its variables.

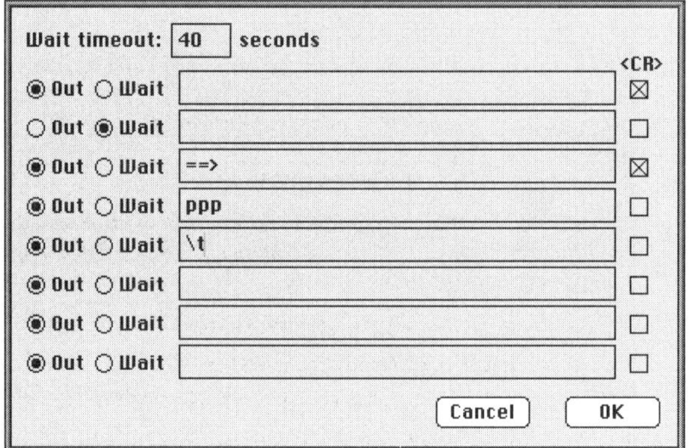

Entering Variables for a Login Script

As these vary by the provider, there is no point in going into it here. Be aware, however, that checking a **<CR>** checkbox adds an automatic carriage return after a command and the **\t** command causes MacPPP to enter terminal mode, in which the user can type a login name and password.

Whether or not you have entered a login script, if you want the user's login name and password information added automatically, enter this data in the fields accessed through the **Authentication** button.

Entering User Name and Password Preferences

Here, too, you may enter the number of times MacPPP tries to reconnect after a busy signal and at what intervals. If you need to statically assign an IP address, click **IPCP Options** (IP Control Protocol) and enter it in the **Local** field.

Entering IP Control Panel Information

If you were not given a static address by the service provider and you do this, PPP will not open a connection unless the terminal server can negotiate the address you typed in. If you have problems, try letting the terminal server provide the IP address by leaving the address with the default setting. Unless you are really cozy with Internet Request for Comment (RFC) series 1331, 1332, and 1334, you should leave the LCP (Line Control Protocol) and IPCP options alone. They relate to how PPP negotiates its connection with the local terminal server.

Once you have this all set, close out to the MacPPP control panel window and test the connection by clicking **Open**. A dialog box is generated to show the connection's progress. Once the connection is established, the Config PPP window changes to reflect it—**PPP up**. You may never need to use the MacPPP control panel to connect like this again. Once it is set up, all the user has to do is boot up an Internet application and the PPP connection will be established automatically!

Besides the **Open** button, which can be used to manually make the PPP connection, there are other useful commands in the main window:

- **Idle Timeout**: After the time specified in this pop-up menu has elapsed without there being activity on the connection, MacPPP automatically shuts it down. This means that you don't have to rely upon the user to open the control panel and close the connection when finished with it. If you want, deselect **Quiet Mode** and they receive a warning dialog box before it closes down.

Sometimes MacPPP will establish a connection out of the blue. Ghosts in the machine, I guess. Set the **Idle Timeout** to a fairly short time period to save money in case this happens when the user is not around. Also, using the **Hard Close** button in the control panel will prevent this from occurring, but the user thereafter needs to initiate a connection manually via the **Open** button.

- **Echo Interval**: The control panel uses a PPP packet called the LCP (Line Control Protocol) echo request to find out if its connection is still functioning or if it has been dropped. MacPPP sends out these requests at the interval specified here, assuming that the link is down if the terminal server does not respond after three tries. For dial-in connections, I suggest you make the intervals fairly long, or just leave this option **Off**.

- **Terminal Window**: This brings up a terminal emulator window when MacPPP is connecting with the local terminal server. For ease of use, leave this unchecked. Otherwise, the control panel ignores the telephone number and modem INIT fields and makes the user type in everything.

- **Hangup on Close**: This directs MacPPP to send the modem a hang-up command (+++ ATH) when the PPP session ends. Select this option.

Once you have your basic Internet connection up and running on your individual workstation, start doing some homework on the Internet.

BUYING YOUR CONNECTIVITY SERVICES

Doing the Homework

Because of the wide range in pricing and types of costs for ISDN, do your research before you decide that you are going to buy ISDN services for your network. Here are a couple of pages on the Web to check out *before* you make any other decisions. The page on the left is Bell Atlantic's ISDN pricing page and can be found at http://www.cicat.com/cicat/pricing.htm, and the page on the right is another ISDN pricing page found at http://www.essential.org/cpt/isdn/isdn.html. I like the right-hand page, as it is a part of Ralph Nader's site.

Business ISDN-BRI Pricing
Residential ISDN-BRI Pricin
ISDN-PRI Pricing

FROM NOW UNTIL THE END OF TH

FREE

Order your Bell Atlantic ISDN Business lines from
incredible discounts on your ISDN ha

CICAT Approved Solutions

Motorola BitSURFR (1 pots interface) $300
Motorola BitSURFR PRO (2 pots interfaces) $375

Adtran ISU Express $325
Adtran ISU Express (1 pots interface) $400
Adtran ISU Express (2 pots interfaces) $450

IBM WaveRunner $500 ($700 with NT1)

Ascend P25 $600 ($900 with compression)

Send us E-mail at cicat@cicat.com for pricing on products nc

(*)Restrictions:

Hardware discounts only valid on ISDN business lines
One ISDN product per line
Installation support extra
This offer is valid only for Bell Atlantic customers

ISDN pricing issues

This section of the Consumer Project on Technology web contains information about ISDN pricing controversies. For background on what ISDN is, or for other ISDN resources, try Dan Kegel's ISDN page. You may also want to checkout the archives of ISDN@ESSENTIAL.ORG, an Internet discussion list on ISDN pricing.

There are five main parts to this Web page.

Current Events and News on ISDN Tariffs

Information on ISDN pricing disputes by State

Notes on LEC pricing strategies

Useful Documents ISDN pricing

Additional ISDN links

Current Events and News on ISDN Tariffs

Comments on UTAH's US WEST tariff due by January 31, 1996

Washington State Rejects US WEST Rate Hike on January 9, 1995

Virginia Corporations Commission asked to investigate Bell Atlantic tariffs

California Public Utilities Commission Accepts Email Comments on huge Pac Bell Rate Hike

Washington DC PSC considers $32 flat rate tariff

Information on ISDN tariff battles by state

California | Delaware | District of Columbia | Maryland | New Jersey | New Mexico | Texas | Virginia | Utah | Washington State | West Virginia

Useful Documents on ISDN pricing

Contact information for all 50 state public utilities commmissions, and utility consumer advocates in forty states.

CPT's January 11, 1995 letter to Virginia Corporations Commision regarding proposed investigation into BA residential ISDN tariff.

A January 5, 1995 sign-on letter to the Washington State Utilities and Transportation Commission (WUTC) in opposition to the US WEST residential ISDN tariff.

CPT's January 4, 1995 comments to Washington Commission on US WEST tariffs

Sample ISDN Pricing Pages

Finding a Salesperson Who Actually Wants to Do Business

The following transcript is *real:* My voice is in plain text and the various Sprint representatives' voices are in italics.

Hi, Sprint? I'd like to buy some Frame Relay lines.

What's that?

It's a data communications line.

Oh, Frame Relay—Here's the number.

Hi, I'd like to buy Frame Relay lines.

Are you hard of hearing?

No. Why?

This is the voice relay service of Texas. We support hearing impaired customers.

Hi, Sprint, I'd like to buy Frame Relay lines.

We relay all of our calls automatically.

No, Frame Relay is a type of data line.

We only service voice calls. Would you like me to transfer you?

Yes, please, but don't send me back to Texas.

I wouldn't know how to even get you there.

Hi, I'd like to buy Frame Relay lines.

Didn't you just call?

Hi, Sprint, I'd like to buy Frame Relay lines.

I think that would be our business department. Would you like the number or would you like me to transfer you.

How about transferring me and holding on until we make sure I'm not back in Texas.

Hello, this is customer support. May I know the nature of your problem?

My problem is that none of you morons seem to be able to find your damned business sales department.

Sir, we cannot tolerate that kind of language. I'll transfer you if you are willing to hold.

(On hold for seven minutes.)

May I ask your name and phone number?

Do you sell Frame Relay lines?

No, sir. Sprint does not sell Frame Relay lines. May I ask your name and phone number, sir?

Yes, you do. I know you do, because I have your competitor's bid that says you do. Do you mind actually looking up something for me, like the name of someone who has more brain cells working today than you do?

May I ask your name and phone number first?

(I give him the Chinese take out number down the street. I dial (913) 624-6000, and get a very pleasant woman on the phone.)
Hi, do you know what a Frame Relay line is?

Sure, do you?

(I love her already.)
Yes ma'am, I do. I need to buy about seven of them.

Okay, I'll transfer you to Debbie.

Hi, I need to buy Frame Relay lines for my business data transmissions.

Does this have to do with data transmission?

Uh, yes. I just said that.

Okay, let me transfer you to Vance.

(I get transferred to Vance's voice mail and leave him an extended message, repeating my phone number three times and insisting that it is urgent. Here's his number: (800) 877-4646. He never called back. Why don't you call him and harass him a bit for me?)

This transaction is to clue you in on the frustration you had better be ready to deal with when purchasing Frame Relay or any other type of business communication systems. My advice? Hire a consultant. If you don't want to follow my advice, here's a sample bid that you can send out once you find someone at the communication provider who wants to receive it.

Know Your Services

The first thing that you should know is what type of services you want to run between your offices and the Internet.

- Is this system merely for dial-in services, like PPP or ARA? If so, would 28.8 kbps be fast enough? What about 28.8 kbps service to the Internet? Sometimes you don't have to go any farther than the phone lines you are using, especially in a small office setting.

- Are you going to run e-mail? File transfers? Web pages of normal or commercial usage? How about list servers and newsgroups? If you are running multiple mail servers, how are they communicating and updating each other's user databases?

- Are you running synchronicity-type applications between your WAN sites, such as Lotus Notes or Meeting Maker?

- Are you allowing cross-office printing and file serving? What about peer-to-peer file sharing amongst users across the WAN?

Know Your Locations

Next, figure out the area codes and prefixes of all your locations. This relates to the LATAs in which the users are located. You buy your telecommunications technology based upon the LATAs in which you and the rest of your users are located. In each and every instance of purchasing telephone communications, you need to break down the tables into these rough divisions during the bid process:

Location	Local Loop	Port	(Rate)	DLCI Costs	Monthly costs	Installation

Cost Table for Your Bid

Next, look up the person to whom you are sending the bid in your LATA map.

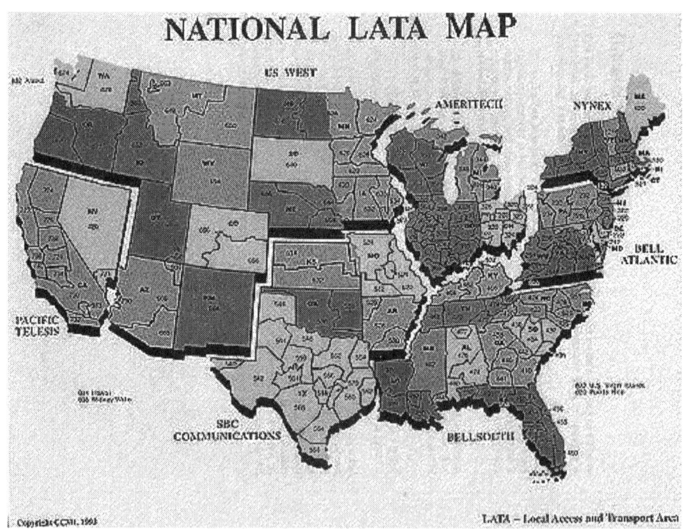

National LATA Map

Depending upon whose territory you are in, you will be sending your bid to a local service provider, or an international provider such as MCI or Sprint.

Some local providers, like PacBell in our area, work with international service providers of Frame Relay and ISDN lines. In this way, if the local provider is not able to help with the purchasing of the lines, they might have connections to another service or provider who can.

Sending off the RFQ isn't hard. You don't need a lot of information in it. In short, you need to know to whom to send the quotes, when you want them back, the parts of the country or countries to which you need connectivity, and perhaps some of the current services you are running. Like any other request for proposal or request for quote, make it clear that there is a single point of contact for *all* the locations. Otherwise, providers will try to negotiate *around* you if they sense that you are playing hard ball with them. Things can become really messy really fast when that happens. The following pictures show a sample from our files.

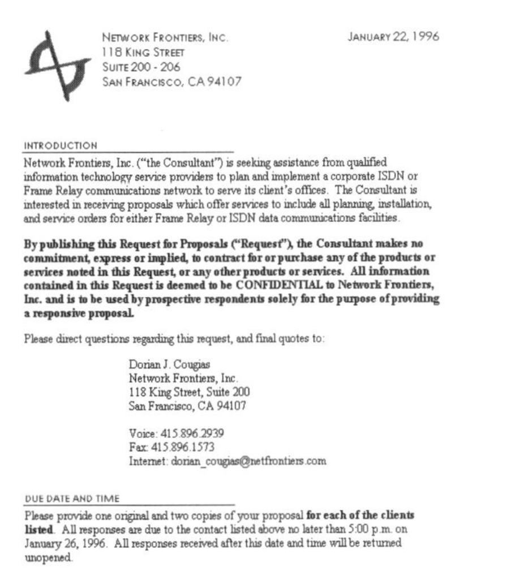

NETWORK FRONTIERS, INC.
118 KING STREET
SUITE 200 - 206
SAN FRANCISCO, CA 94107

JANUARY 22, 1996

INTRODUCTION

Network Frontiers, Inc. ("the Consultant") is seeking assistance from qualified information technology service providers to plan and implement a corporate ISDN or Frame Relay communications network to serve its client's offices. The Consultant is interested in receiving proposals which offer services to include all planning, installation, and service orders for either Frame Relay or ISDN data communications facilities.

By publishing this Request for Proposals ("Request"), the Consultant makes no commitment, express or implied, to contract for or purchase any of the products or services noted in this Request, or any other products or services. All information contained in this Request is deemed to be CONFIDENTIAL to Network Frontiers, Inc. and is to be used by prospective respondents solely for the purpose of providing a responsive proposal.

Please direct questions regarding this request, and final quotes to:

Dorian J. Cougias
Network Frontiers, Inc.
118 King Street, Suite 200
San Francisco, CA 94107

Voice: 415.896.2939
Fax: 415.896.1573
Internet: dorian_cougias@netfrontiers.com

DUE DATE AND TIME

Please provide one original and two copies of your proposal **for each of the clients listed**. All responses are due to the contact listed above no later than 5:00 p.m. on January 26, 1996. All responses received after this date and time will be returned unopened.

FORMAT

Please submit, for each client, a separate ISDN and a separate Frame Relay quote. The format should follow the following table as closely as possible:

Location	Local Loop	Port (Rate)	DLCI Costs	Monthly costs	Installation

EXISTING SYSTEMS

The Consultants clients are currently using PC-based systems (DOS/Windows and Macintosh based) in all of their operations. Each of the multi-user offices have an autonomous LAN linked by rudimentary remote access solutions (Apple Remote Access or Timbuktu Remote) and electronic mail (CE Software's QuickMail v. 3.0). Some employees in some locations are also using dial-up services to access specialized services or the Internet. All data communications are over POTS with standard analog modems (2400 to 14,400 baud). Included below is a list of locations and a summary of existing equipment and services.

AUTOMATIC CUT-OVER

In the case of clients which have pre-existing ISDN or Frame Relay services from other vendors, the cut-over to your services should be done within a single day, and if possible, have any installation fees waved.

CLIENTS & ASSOCIATED SITES

The Consultant is purposefully withholding the client's name and address so that all inquiries and proposals are propagated through the Consultant instead of directly through the clients. This is done at each of the clients requests. Therefore, here is a listing of each of client's main offices and desired remote offices by city location, area code, and prefix. In the case of offices overseas, the office's city will be listed.

CLIENT A	Menlo Park	415	854 xxxx
HEADQUARTERS: MENLO PARK, CALIFORNIA	Boston	617	478 xxxx
	New York	212	880 xxxx
	Houston	713	964 xxxx
	London	Richmond, Surry TW9 IPX	
CLIENT B	Kansas City, MO	816	324 xxxx
HEADQUARTERS: KANSAS CITY, MISSOURI	Dallas	214	630 xxxx
	Kansas City, MO	816	842 xxxx
	San Leandro	510	569 xxxx
	Kansas City, KS	913	362 xxxx
CLIENT C	19 sites in Antioch, CA	510	706 xxxx
HEADQUARTERS: ANTIOCH, CA	All sites have same area code and prefix		

Thank you very much for you time and consideration.

1

2

Sample RFQ for Buying Frame Relay Services

AN OVERVIEW OF WAN TECHNOLOGIES

POTS, ISDN, and Frame Relay are the most widely available and most widely implemented standards for WANs. Thus, we will limit our focus to them in this book. A brief description of each of these standards follows.

Voice-Grade Telephone Line Networks (POTS)

Voice-grade telephone lines are those lines that are already installed in your company and at your home. These are those often noisy, overused analog telephone lines. Our small company of about a dozen people has more POTS lines than we have employees—some for phones, some for ARA, some for FAX, and some for e-mail servers to dial-up systems like AppleLink, CompuServe, and America Online. PacBell loves us.

In a traditional telephone conversation between two points, data communication takes place over circuit-switched voice channels. Within the path of the call are network switches and circuits supported by the Local Area Exchanges and inter-exchanges. When a user places a long distance call, it is first connected through the Local Exchange Carrier (LEC), which then connects the call through an Inter-Exchange Carrier (IXC) to another LEC, and then on to the end-point destination. To signal the setup and clearing of the call, the system uses an audible tone, called an *inband signal,* over the same "talking-path" of the connection. We are all tired of hearing these setup signals squawking and squeaking on our modems, so this should be nothing new to any of us. The connections are established through a local carrier, are used during the call, and are then released by the local carrier once the call has been completed. Thus, the circuit connection is established only during the duration of the call. All session setup, data transfer, management, and tear-down are conducted over the same channel. The following are some of the basic characteristics and uses of voice-grade telephone line.

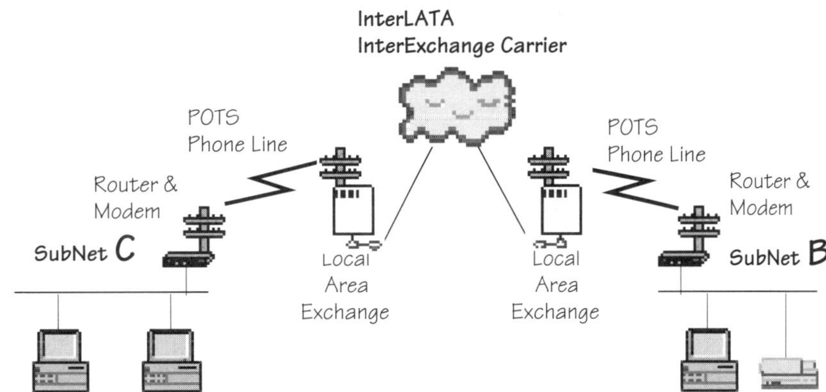

Path of a Standard Telephone Call Connecting PPP-Based Routes

Uses Voice-grade lines can be used for simple dial-in for e-mail, file transfer, and Web usage from home. They can be used for network-based FAXing and for point-to-point connectivity to your ISP for Internet access at speeds of around 28.8 kbps. Very *low end* network-to-network routing is possible using this type of communications system.

Speed Most modems labeled "slow" start at about 9600 baud and range up through 28.8 kbps. Using the standard data compression algorithms in these routers, you can actually reach up to 57.6 kbps or 115 kbps.

Connection Speed To connect, a handshake has to be established between each router. This could take anywhere from 1–30 seconds or longer.

Costs Costs are the standard phone costs you would normally incur at your business or home location. Typically, local calls are a flat rate and long distance calls are based upon a per-minute charge.

Advantages/ Disadvantages The ease of accessibility and the compatibility with modems and other serial-based routers on the market are the biggest advantages. The biggest disadvantages are the speed limitations, error correction and setup overhead, line noise, and long distance costs associated with regular phone lines.

Connector Hardware To utilize analog lines, you need an analog modem attached to your router or your remote access server. Modems convert digital data into analog signals that the POTS lines can interpret and then use to transmit the information across the carrier services from one location to the next. When a modem receives an analog signal, it converts it into the digital form that the computer systems can use. There are two main criteria to use when choosing your modems:

- **Error Correction:** Error correction provides the checking mechanisms not found in protocols such as ARA. Error correction filters out noise and other problems while allowing for the retransmission of lost or corrupted data. The error correction methodologies supported in today's modems include, but are not limited to, V.32, V.34, and V.42 defined by ITU-TSS, and MNP 1-4 and 9-10 defined by Microcom, Inc.

- **Data Compression:** Data compression provides faster throughput from modem to modem. It does this by compressing the data before it is sent across the analog line, and then decompressing it when it is received on the other end. Data compression can add up to 100% faster throughput between two modems on relatively error-free POTS lines. Data compression protocols supported today include but are not limited to, V.32 bis and V.42 bis defined by ITU-TSS, and MNP 5-7 defined by Microcom, Inc.

Integrated Services Digital Network (ISDN)

This is an international data communications networking protocol used to transmit not only digital voice communications but also data and video transmission across standard installed telephone lines. Although ISDN has a completely different method of organization for passing information over digital lines, one of its major strengths is its compatibility with most common telephone lines and national and international infrastructures. In other words, even though ISDN is designed for specialized communications equipment, it works over the same telephone lines that are run into your house today. In fact, in many places, ISDN is tariffed like a phone call, based on call duration, time of day, and distance. There is no volume data charge, as with X.25, and thus it is most cost-effective for file transfer. In other places, ISDN lines are billed at a flat rate, whether they are used or not.

When talking about ISDN lines, we need to make a few distinctions. The first thing to clarify is the term *bearer service*. The bearer service of network media transports end-user information from one location to another. With ISDN, this bearer service is placed with the "B" channel of the ISDN line. This distinguishes the bearer service from supplementary services and other functions. These supplementary services are placed into an ISDN "D" channel. With this in mind, we can then say that when placing an ISDN "call," there is a 64 kbps channel placed between two end-points. The Basic Rate Interface (BRI) is two 64 kbps bearer (B) channels, and one Delta (D) channel. If more information needs to pass between any two points at once, the ISDN Primary Rate Interface (PRI) is used. The PRI consists of 24 channels, divided into 23 B channels and one D channel, all of which run over the same physical interface as a standard T1 line. Of course, if you are in Europe or some other place that uses E1 standards with greater bandwidth, the PRI has 30 B channels and one D channel.

Let's get back to that BRI and those two B channels. Since there are two B channels, that means that the end-node can put through two voice calls at the same time. On the D channel it is managing incoming message reception, which is the ability to send a "busy" signal or the ability to tear-down one of the channels not being used at the moment. We can easily see that the advantage to ISDN lies in the existence of the two B channels that bear the data and the separate D channel supporting message management, all running over "conventional" telephone media and infrastructures. What this ultimately means is that a router connected to an ISDN line can simultaneously use both B channels to two destinations. It could also double the throughput to a single destination if both B channels are available for hookup, while the D channel is used for call setup, management, and breakdown independently from the data-bearing B channels. What this further means is that much like a phone line, ISDN connections are *not* permanently "up," like Frame Relay or asynchronous dedicated lines (ADN lines). ISDN is called a *dial-on-demand* system. These dial-on-demand capabilities give ISDN a broad flexibility for connectivity to multiple sites at will on one hand, while they create some networking problems on the other.

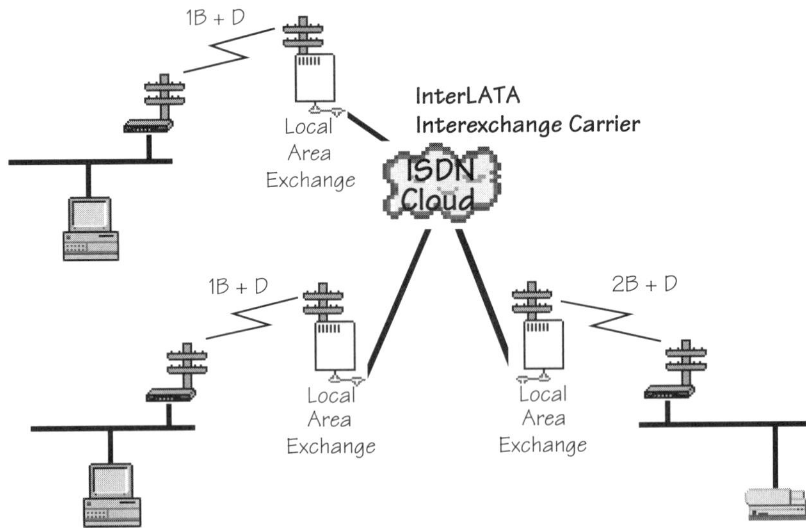

ISDN setup is much like that of a standard phone line, with a few enhancements.

Problems with Dial-on-Demand Routers

Let's go through two sample connection models and anticipate what could happen when four separate networks are trying to connect to each other. In the first scenario, there are four networks connected together through three networked sessions. Session 1 is established because subnetwork **D** has a single-channel connection to subnetwork **B**. Session 2 is established because subnetwork **A** has a single-channel connection with subnetwork **C**. Finally, session 3 is established because subnetwork **C** also has a single-channel connection to subnetwork **B**. Thus, subnetworks B and C are utilizing both channels of their ISDN lines, while subnetworks A and D are utilizing only a single channel. Assume that there aren't any contentions for a line, and therefore there are no problems. When users on a network open up their Choosers and select a server or printer on a far network, the ISDN session is opened and the requests and replies are sent. As soon as the users are finished printing or transferring files and have signed off the file servers, the session between the devices is closed. Soon after, the connections between the two networks are closed because no more traffic is moving between the two.

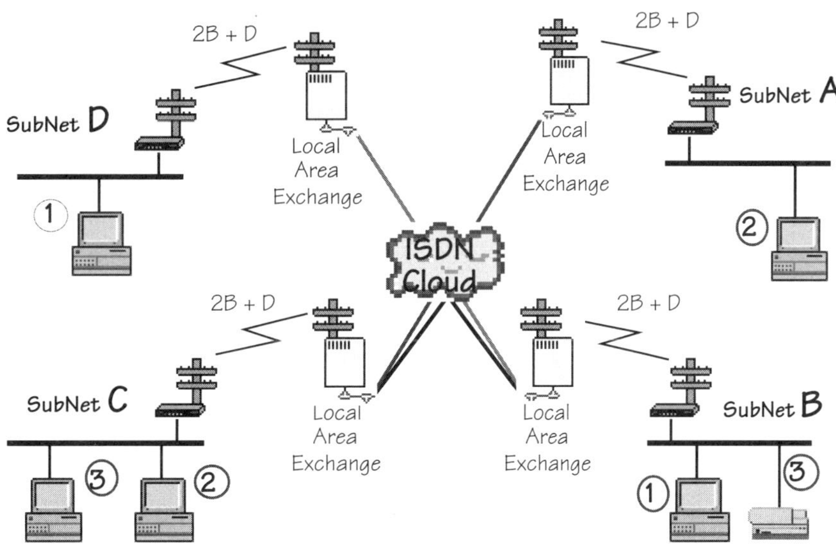

Four Networks and Three Different Simultaneous Sessions

Now let's look at the scenario wherein we have an ISDN contention problem. In this scenario, subnetwork B and subnetwork C have formed a connection to establish session 1, a continuous AppleShare server session. Subnetwork A and subnetwork C *also* form a connection to establish session 2, another AppleShare server session. So far, so good. The problem occurs when a user in subnetwork D decides to sign in to one of the two servers on subnetwork C. The router receives a busy signal from the ISDN carrier, because both of subnetwork C's bearer channels are in use with current connections. Each of the channels can support only a single communication session with another single site. Thus, the two networks cannot connect while the lines are busy. Depending upon the application that the user is running in subnetwork D, the user receives an error or a notification that the other network is not "up" at the present time and therefore cannot be reached for connectivity.

 ISDN connectivity contention is one of the primary drawbacks to ISDN networking. Therefore, ISDN and PPP dial-up connectivity are for situations in which there is a single connection point to another LAN, *or* for use in dial-up remote connectivity to end-user's homes. ISDN shouldn't be used as a multi-site connectivity methodology.

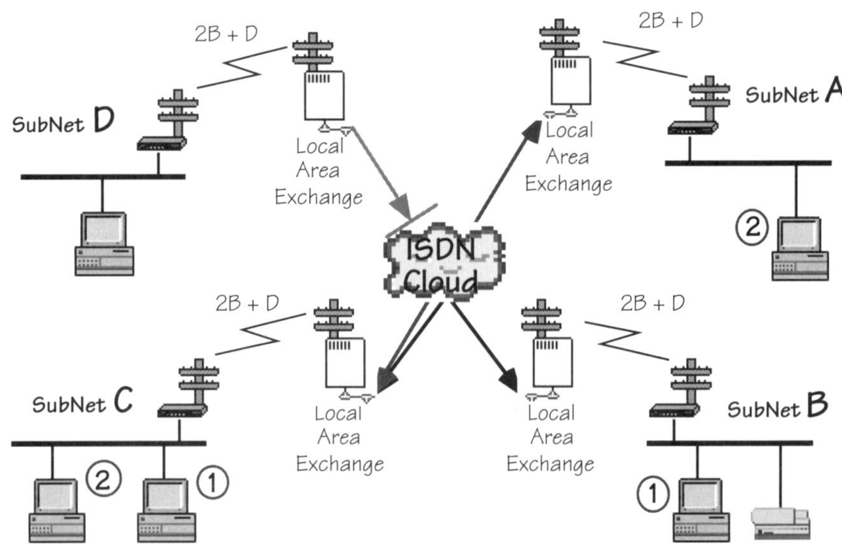

Four Networks and Contention for Connectivity

 ISDN is one of those networking systems that is a setup, manage, and tear-down system. In many areas of the country (like California, where we have our offices), you have to pay *by the minute* for ISDN connectivity. You are probably thinking that you would use it to connect your networks for file transfers, e-mail transfers, and printing, and then have the router disconnect when you are finished. However, what if someone signs in to a remotely connected AppleShare server and doesn't sign off? What happens if a user logs into a server, like a Meeting Maker calendar server or a Now-Up-to-Date server, and forgets to log off? You are going to be in pretty deep doo-doo. I know a guy over at a certain router manufacturer in the Bay Area who had a bill for $1,500 for the first month of ISDN. With ISDN, keep an eye on your expenses and network traffic, unless you have both ends of the line in flat-rate tariffed areas.

Here are some of the characteristics and uses of ISDN.

Uses One of the best uses of ISDN is ISDN routing between an office and an ISDN service provider. This keeps connectivity costs down between the office and the provider. It also doesn't cause as many headaches as network-to-network routing with ISDN, as there aren't any servers that can be left mounted by a remote user. Another great use for ISDN is point-to-point video conferencing between two individual computers. Dial-up routing from one point to another, such as from a home office to a *lightly* populated remote office is another good use for ISDN. Finally, use ISDN for multiplexed file transfer with customized software, like that available from 4-Sight.

Speed   In full-duplex mode, connecting both B channels together, ISDN has a through-put rate of about 128 kbps (64 kbps in each direction) when connected with a BRI. Multiply that by the number of open channels if both connections are using PRI services.

Connection Speed   Currently, the connection speed for ISDN is usually under two seconds for any line in use.

Connection Costs   If you do it right, connection costs range from $40 a month for a home user, through $400 a month for a corporate user. If you aren't watching and managing the system, you could receive that $1,500 bill that we mentioned. PRIs have monthly starting costs in the thousands of dollars for companies in most states. Believe me, do some homework about the costs and obtain solid quotes from your providers before you decide to purchase anything. This is one of those things that you had better do before you purchase a system, or you could be in deep trouble.

Advantages/ Disadvantages   One of the biggest disadvantages is the long distance costs associated with ISDN, as well as basic connectivity to all points of the globe. While most of us can connect ISDN everywhere, there are still many places that can't. Hopcfully, by the time it is necessary to revise this book, every location can have ISDN. The biggest of the big disadvantages is the up-and-down connectivity and the point-to-point nature of ISDN. While it is great for remote conferencing and remote dial-in or connection to a single point, it bites the big one in terms of full-time meshed connectivity for a corporation.

Connection Hardware   ISDN doesn't use an analog modem for connectivity between the router and the ISDN line or between the computer's ISDN card and the ISDN line. It uses what is called a *terminal adapter*.

Frame Relay

Frame Relay is a packet-switched WAN service. It is normally used to establish a permanent connection between one or more locations in what is called *PVC*, or Permanent Virtual Circuit. Frame Relay is actually a blend, or better yet, a new and improved version of X.25 statistical multiplexing, port sharing, and time-division multiplexing services. Once you have more than two sites that need connectivity, look to a Frame Relay network—especially if you want full-time connection. Frame Relay is a packet-based interface standard that has been optimized for protocol-oriented network traffic. Frame Relay has the ability to statistically multiplex the data moving through it to provide the same bandwidth-sharing and efficiency capabilities of X.25, with advancements that surpass X.25.

With a Frame Relay network, a path is established between two or more points within a circuit, or PVC. No bandwidth is allocated to a path until actual data needs to be transmitted between any two points in the path. Bandwidth is then dynamically allocated on a packet-by-packet basis. This statistical multiplexing is important because data transmissions are "bursty" by nature. If, for a short period of time, more data needs to be transmitted than is normally allocated, the switches within the LATA or interexchange can buffer the data until it can be transmitted.

How Frame Relay Is Set up and Works

Unlike ISDN, Frame Relay does not require a separate channel for every connectivity session between subnetworks. Instead, Frame Relay contains what is called a Data Link Connection Identifier, or *DLCI,* denoting which conversation "owns" the frame of information. Within a multipoint Frame Relay network, the frames are routed to their destinations based upon the circuit numbers in the frames. In a hub and spoke model, such as that shown in the following picture, one point on the Frame Relay network is the central point to which all the other Frame Relay routers must first send data. Let's look at the three different WAN sessions happening simultaneously in this internetworking scenario where subnetwork **D** is the hub, and **A** through **C** are the spokes.

- Session 1 is established between D and C directly for an AppleShare session. At the same time, a user in subnetwork B is routing through D to open another AppleShare session with the same server. Thus, there are simultaneous conversations between B, C, and D for AppleShare.

- Session 2 is established between subnetworks A and C *through* subnetwork D for a different file sharing session.

- Session 3 is established between subnetwork D and B, so that a user can print.

Users on each of the LANs see the connection to the other LANs as a dedicated point-to-point connection. There is no setup or tear-down of the network. It is *always* up (unless it crashes).

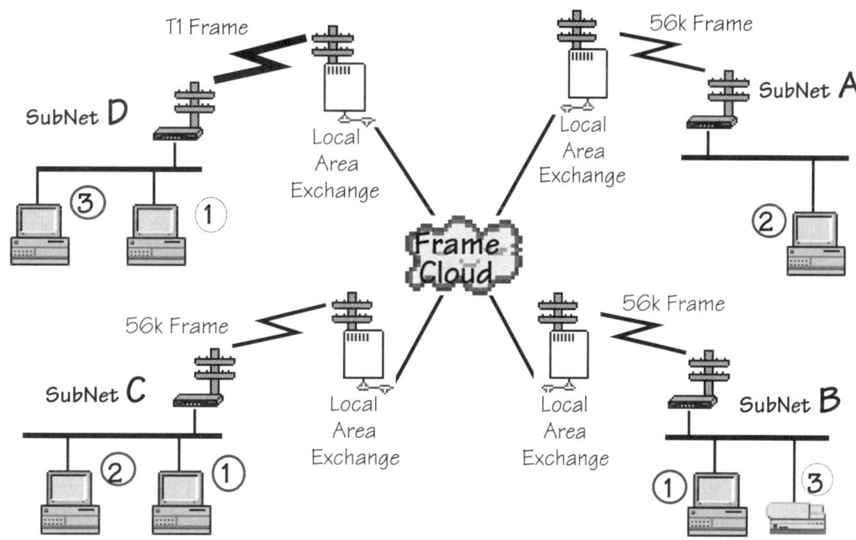

Hub and Spoke Design of Frame Relay

 The only major problem with a hub and spoke network design is that all traffic moving from point to point on the Frame Relay must first pass through the hub router. This isn't too bad if you have a router about the size of a battleship and a full T1 line to the hub router, so that it can handle the intranetwork traffic. Just note that instead of being one hop away, the next network is two hops away once you include the hub-router.

Meshed Exterior Routers

There is another way to set up a Frame Relay network, and that is with what is called a *full frame mesh*. The frame mesh is basically nothing more than establishing PVCs for all routes on all routers. What happens is that each router is set up with a DLCI map to every other router on the Frame Relay. The mappings of all of these DLCIs form a weblike infrastructure of connectivity so that a packet passing from one network to another doesn't have to stop off at the "hub" network first. A frame mesh for four networks (numbered 1–4) would look something like the following diagram, with each DLCI mapped to the other and the lines of interconnectivity showing connection paths.

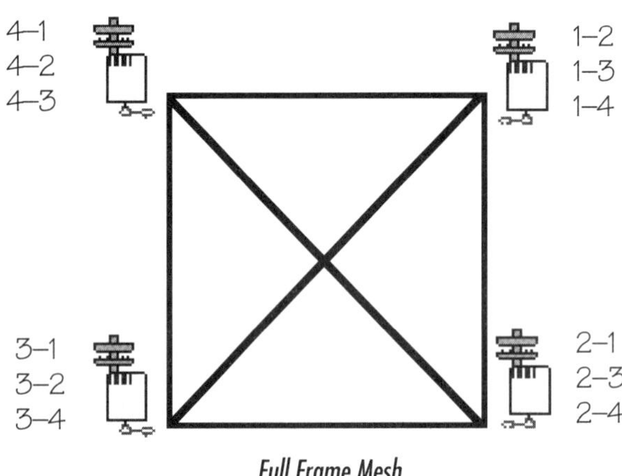

Full Frame Mesh

Let's go back and take a look at the same connectivity scenario we had with the hub and spoke model, but this time using a full frame mesh. While you might think that this is the same thing as a distributed backbone, where all traffic passes through the WAN and all routers "hear" it, it really acts like a collapsed backbone in a certain sense. Only traffic bound for a circuit will be heard on the circuit. Packets bound for other circuits are not transferred over to circuits not concerned with those packets. In this scenario, we'll have three subnetworks connected on the frame simultaneously supporting three different sessions.

- Session 1 connects subnetwork B and subnetwork C, and then connects subnetwork D and subnetwork C for two computers accessing a single file server. The file server traffic between B and C is not seen on A or D's Frame Relay circuits. The file server traffic between D and C is not seen on A or B's circuits. Therefore, the only circuit that holds traffic for both clients of the server is the one attached to subnetwork C.

- Session 2 is opened between a personal server in subnetwork A and an end-node in subnetwork C. Traffic from this session is not seen at all on subnetwork B or D's circuit.

- Finally, session 3 is opened when a device in D prints to the printer in B. This session's traffic is limited to D and B's Frame Relay circuits.

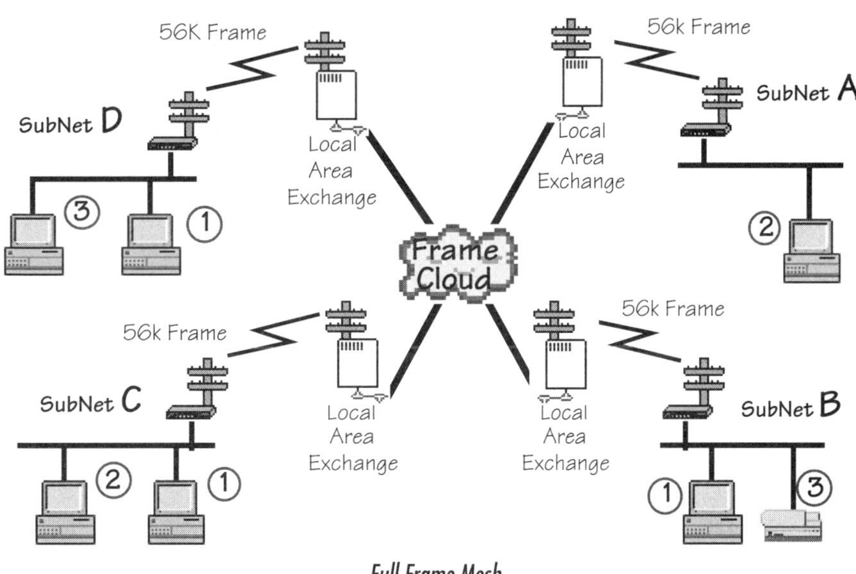

Full Frame Mesh

 When working with a full frame meshed network, there are a couple of things to watch out for. One is the pricing set up by your local phone tariff, and the other is the person or organization selling you the lines. These folks like to take the high road when it comes to prices. One of their favorite games is to charge an exorbitant amount per DLCI connection for a full frame mesh. Another is their favorite line, "We can't do that."

Yet Another Incredible True Story

When setting up a full frame meshed network, make sure that your routers can handle it. While working on a project for a school system in Pennsylvania, we set up a meshed network for our client that had fourteen schools on a primary mesh with around four or five clusters of 6–8 schools on secondary meshes. Two vendors, Compatible Systems and Wellfleet, bid for the hardware for the schools. The only problem with the winner, Wellfleet, was that their router of specification, the ASN, couldn't handle fourteen DLCIs on its Frame Relay port! It could handle only 6–7. The Compatible Systems routers, on the other hand, could handle 16 DLCIs per port on their MR1000 and 64 DLCIs per port on their 3400R series. The project ended up with Wellfleet not only eating crow after having "fibbed" about the capabilities of their router, but they also ate the cost of a higher-end router they had to supply to our client to finish the job. While it was great that the client received a better group of routers for the same price, it set the network implementation plan back about six weeks. That hurt more than anything else.

Uses
Frame Relay can be used for most WAN traffic for any multipoint networking system. It isn't to be used for remote access, PPP, or home users dialing in to the network. From 56 kbps to 2 Mbps, Frame Relay is actually more efficient than ATM WAN networking. The one thing that Frame Relay can't be used for is point-to-point audio traffic. However, this is a bit misleading, since Frame Relay *can* be used to support QuickTime conferencing and other network-based software that encodes audio traffic into normal data transmission packets.

Speed
Frame Relay works efficiently from 56 kbps to 2 Mbps. The lines, however, are purchased in many areas as a frame rate line (56 kbps) with a *committed access rate* that is normally between 25–50% of the full frame rate (16–32 kbps). Some areas, like areas covered by USWest or some AT&T lines, give the users the full 56 kbps line rate. It is wise to consider moving to ATM networking when you hit 2–45 Mbps, although ATM's overhead is too high for anything under that.

Connection Speed
If the systems aren't always fully connected (which they usually are), the connection speed is well under two seconds.

Connection Costs
Connection costs for Frame Relay depend upon the frame rate, committed information rate, number of DLCIs per port of the router, and any long range overhead charges you might incur for a DLCI going out of the country. Pricing Frame Relay is best accomplished after research on the Web and after submitting RFQs to at least three of your local providers and long distance providers.

Advantages/ Disadvantages
Obviously, Frame Relay's meshing capabilities combined with its "full time up" connectivity and relatively high throughput rates give it a remarkable advantage over other network connectivity options. The biggest disadvantage for Frame Relay is the phone companies themselves acting as service providers. Many of them don't even want to provide for full-meshed capabilities, and attempt to charge exorbitant rates for international networking connections. As one MCI sales representative put it, "I don't have to give your small client the same low rates as I give a larger client, so don't even try to bargain with me."

Connection Hardware
Frame Relay networks need to use devices that are called *CSU/DSUs*. A CSU/DSU is similar to an analog modem except that it is used to connect the networked router to a digital circuit, such as a switched 56 or T1 line. Simply put, the CSU portion is used to terminate the telephone company's portion of the line and provide diagnostics, such as local and remote loopback testing. The DSU portion provides the data transmission and receiving capabilities, as well as error correction, buffering, and flow control.

WAN ROUTERS AND REMOTE ACCESS SERVERS

Much like our LAN router section, many of these descriptions come directly from the vendors themselves. All we have done is check the grammar and spelling and debunk any marketing we thought was bullshit. This gives you, the reader, greater throughput and error-free communications.

Compatible System's MicroRouter 1000R

The MicroRouter 1000R from Compatible Systems provides an economical solution for companies connecting local area networks (LANs) in two or more remote offices. The 1000R routes the TCP/IP, IPX, AppleTalk, and DECnet LAN protocols from an Ethernet network over standard telephone lines, or over switched, leased, or ISDN lines, providing a link that can grow with your requirements.

The MicroRouter 1000R comes ready to connect to a thick, thin, or 10BaseT Ethernet network. It provides one high-speed RS-232 WAN port, which may be operated asynchronously or synchronously at rates up to 128 kbps. The MicroRouter 1000R supports both the Point-to-Point Protocol (PPP) and Frame Relay and will interoperate with other PPP and Frame Relay routers.

Front (left) and Back (right) of a MicroRouter 1000R

Compatible System's RISC Router 3400R

The RISC Router 3400R delivers high-speed remote routing and growth flexibility for organizations connecting to satellite office local area networks or to the Internet. The 3400R routes the TCP/IP, IPX, AppleTalk, and DECnet network protocols from an Ethernet network over multiple high-speed leased, switched, or on-demand communications lines.

The RISC Router 3400R comes ready to connect to thick, thin, or 10BaseT Ethernet and features four wide area (WAN) communications ports. The two primary WAN ports support high-speed synchronous communications from 56 kbps to T1/E1 (1.5–2 Mbps) speeds using the Point-to-Point Protocol (PPP) or Frame Relay over leased, switched, or ISDN lines. Two secondary WAN ports provide synchronous/asynchronous communications and support data rates of up to 128 kbps over standard analog or digital lines.

Front (left) and Back (right) of 3400R

The only problem with this router, as I see it, is that it supports only a single Ethernet port, meaning that you can't use it to establish a separate, secure Internet-only LAN subnetwork. This is why I suggest the Cisco 2500 series as an alternative router.

Engage Communication's ExpressRouter

The ExpressRouter from Engage Communication supports TCP/IP, IPX, and AppleTalk protocol suites. It does not support DECNet Phase IV, as some other WAN routers do. However, while this router supports only three of the four major protocol families, it does have built-in support for Frame Relay and PPP. It has its own CSU/DSU for 56 kbps Frame Relay connections and built-in PPP capability.

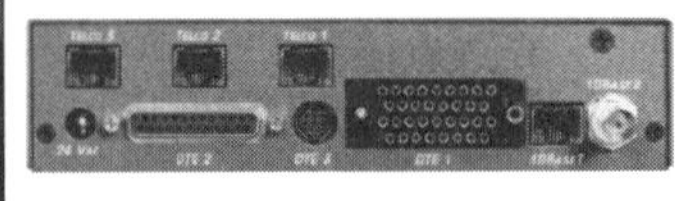

Front (left) and Back (right) of an ExpressRouter from Engage

The base ExpressRouter is available with 1–3 WAN ports for up to three simultaneous WAN connections via user-selectable serial port configurations: V.35, RS449, RS530, or RS232. Both Standard BNC and 10BaseT Ethernet connections are supported. LAN protocol support for IPX, TCP/IP, and AppleTalk is included, as is support for SNMP, Telnet, Frame Relay, and PPP. In the ISDN solution, Engage bundles the ExpressRouter with an ISDN terminal adapter with an internal NT1 unit. All ExpressRouter ISDN bundles include EngageDialer (Macintosh) for full Hayes AT command set and V.25 bis support.

Wellfleet's Access Node EN-to-WAN Router and WAN Router/Hub

Typical connectivity requirements of remote offices are supported by the AN's LAN interfaces (a single Ethernet, a single Token Ring, or both an Ethernet and a Token Ring), and serial interfaces (two synchronous interfaces or one synchronous and one ISDN BRI interface). If you want to combine your router with a multiport repeater, the Ethernet ANs are also available in fully managed (using Windows-based software or SNMP management software) eight-port or 12-port Access Node Hub (ANH) configurations, reducing equipment and management complexity. The eight-port ANH also features one AUI port, and both ANH configurations support two serial interfaces. In all configurations, the two serial interfaces provide remote office network design flexibility. For mission-critical applications, they facilitate dial backup and bandwidth-on-demand support. Also, dial-on-demand functionality enables ANs to extend network availability on an as-needed basis to small remote sites, minimizing WAN service costs. Optionally, one synchronous interface may be used for SDLC, allowing the consolidation of SNA and multiprotocol LAN traffic over one WAN link to the internetwork backbone. Most AURP protocols are supported in the AN and ANH configurations of this router.

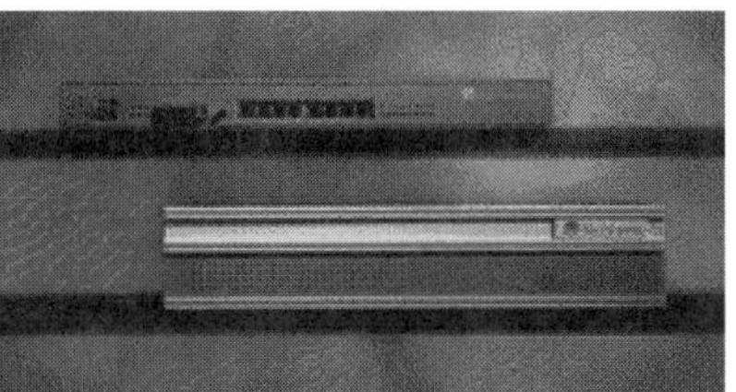

AN and ANH WAN Router and Router/Hub

Cisco's 2513–2515 Dual LAN Series

Cisco Systems has three Cisco 2500 models that double the local area network (LAN) interfaces of the original models. Based on the Cisco 2500 technology, each of these models features two LAN interfaces instead of one—either Ethernet, Token Ring, or one of each. They are designed for use in environments that need the increased density as a way to segment an existing LAN, or as a cost-effective way to link mixed-media LAN installations over wide area networks (WANs). All Cisco 2513–2515 models come standard with Frame Relay, X.25, X.25 DDN, and SMDS software, providing access to packet-switched networks and Permanent Virtual Circuits at remote sites. All models also come standard with V.25 bis and Integrated Services Digital Network (ISDN) signaling software for access to circuit-switched networks.

Cisco 2500 Series Router

The great thing about these routers is that they provide dual LAN and dual WAN connectivity. We'll discuss that in a bit, but believe me, it's a great idea!

Farallon's Netopia Internet Router

Netopia ISDN Internet Router

The Netopia Internet Router is a single-port ISDN-to-Ethernet WAN router. Netopia offers on-board LAN connections for 10BaseT, EtherWave, and AUI, so you can plug and play with virtually any existing LAN. Netopia offers a built-in NT1 with "U" interface, so no external ISDN device is needed. The Netopia comes in three flavors: 630, 640, and 440. The only difference between the 630 and the 640 is that the 630 supports up to five simultaneous LAN users while the 640 can support an almost unlimited number of users. For networks using Local-Talk, the Netopia 440 is a perfect solution. It integrates an AppleTalk-to-TCP/IP gateway with a router for Ethernet and LocalTalk connectivity. It includes MacIP for dynamic TCP/IP addressing, and it provides AURP tunneling that allows Apple-Talk file sharing and print services over the Internet.

Automated TCP/IP addressing with DHCP means a greater number of users can be served with fewer IP addresses. Netopia offers a built-in PC card slot for remote configuration with an analog modem, as well as full SNMP network management, so remote sites can be set up and monitored from a central location. Automated connection profiles and scheduled connections reduce costs and add Internet access controls. Comprehensive security includes IP firewall filtering, callback, PAP, and CHAP security protocols to prevent unauthorized use.

Shiva's LANRover and Integrator

The Shiva LANRover is one of the longest-standing ARA servers on the market. Shiva hasn't watched the competition pass it by, though. They have gone out and actively developed the LANRover so that it now not only supports ARA dial-in, but also dial-out and LAN-to-LAN WAN capabilities. The LANRover's LAN-to-LAN (two LANRovers are used as half-routers) capabilities over analog or digital lines include switched-56, modem and PPP, X.25, V.34, and ISDN. The LAN-Rover/E Plus supports a single Ethernet connection—the LANRover/T supports Token Ring connections—along with eight modular ports for analog or digital line connections.

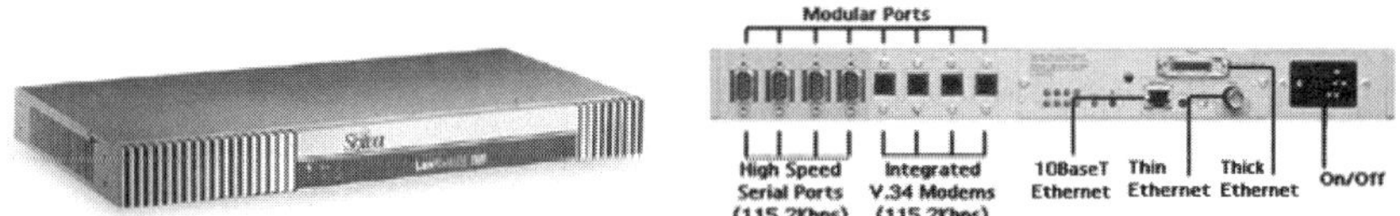

Front (left) and Back (right) of a LANRover/E Plus

Shiva also has a newer product called the ShivaIntegrator. There are two products in the ShivaIntegrator family. The 100 model is an ISDN access server that supports the Basic Rate Interface, providing two channels for interoffice connectivity. The 500 model is what they call a "central site concentrator" that supports Primary Rate Interface and provides up to 46 simultaneous connections. Both models offer what Shiva calls "Tariff Management" features to minimize costs, which are basically types of spooling and keep-alive auto-answering capabilities.

Global Village's OneWorld Network Modem Combos

OneWorld Network Modem Combo

With the OneWorld Combo telecommunication server, Global Village Communication introduces a product that provides the capabilities of a FAX server, a remote access server, and a network modem all in a single unit. With OneWorld Combo, everyone on the office network of Apple Macintosh (or clone) computers can take advantage of advanced telecommunication services, without needing individual dedicated modems and phone lines. OneWorld Combo supports the 28,800 bps PowerPort Platinum modems for the highest communication speeds currently available. OneWorld Combo lets people in the office FAX directly from their computers as quickly and easily as they print documents. Global Village includes its GlobalFax software that provides easy-to-use yet sophisticated FAX capabilities. The OneWorld Combo also provides Apple Remote Access (ARA) 1.0/2.0 services, so that remote users can dial in to access the office's AppleTalk network. With the OneWorld Combo server's network modem support, the staff in the office can also dial out directly from their Macintosh computers to connect to on-line services and access remote resources.

Tribe Computer Works' TribeLink8

The TribeLink8 is Tribe Computer Works' eight-port PPP remote access router. It uses standard phone lines with PPP connection software (as opposed to Apple's ARA connection software) or it uses ISDN lines. Not only is it a remote access router, it also provides full TCP/IP integration and IP gateways for AppleTalk remote users. It can be used as a remote access server and as a LAN-to-LAN router at the same time.

TribeLink8 PPP Dial-In Server

TribeLink8 provides multiple levels of protection. RADIUS, a server-based authentication system, gives network administrators enhanced accounting by providing detailed connection logs that can be stored on the RADIUS server. All sessions between the TribeLink8 and the RADIUS server are encrypted. Maximum connection times can be established for each user by day, week, or month, and users are informed when they have exceeded the allowed connection time. Two levels of PPP-standard authentication protocols prevent unauthorized users from accessing the network. The Challenge Handshake Authentication Protocol (CHAP) verifies connection requests using encrypted passwords. Password Authentication Protocol (PAP) confirms with clear-text passwords. AppleTalk filters allow zones or individual network devices to be hidden from remote access users on a per-user basis. Tribe's management tools track user connections, record the identity of all callers in a log, and allow the administrator to disconnect a user. When routing IP, administrators can further control network access by suppressing RIP and setting up static routes.

We think this is one of the best PPP dial-in routers available.

IMPLEMENTATIONS OF SOFTWARE ROUTERS AND SERVERS

Software routers aren't our choice for performance-based routers. Because they are software-based, the computer on which they are running should be the fastest computer possible. Putting a software router onto something like a Mac IIsi with an Ethernet card wouldn't provide a robust or fast Ethernet-to-LocalTalk connection. However, putting an Internet Router onto an 8150 Server that also has ARA makes one of the best Internet Access servers for remote users.

Apple's Internet Router

This router offers local and wide area networking flexibility. You can connect your local work groups over industry-standard network types, including LocalTalk, Ethernet, and Token Ring. As your network grows larger and more global, the Apple Internet Router lets you choose among several wide area options. You can link remote sites to your network through a dial-up connection over a standard modem, or you can add one of the Apple Internet Router Wide Area Extensions (available separately) to link your AppleTalk networks using X.25 or TCP/IP.

The Apple Internet Router features the AppleTalk Update-based Routing Protocol (AURP), a powerful wide area networking standard. AURP ensures that wide area links function efficiently, substantially reducing the traffic over wide area networks. With AURP, you can be certain that you're maximizing the use of your network resources.

Because the Apple Internet Router software runs on a broad range of Apple Macintosh computers and Workgroup Servers (pretty much everything except the PowerBook series), you can tailor your router configurations to meet your cost and performance requirements. Like other Macintosh computer-based software, the router is easy to use, configure, and support. Even a network novice can have the router up and running and can begin to make use of its powerful features within minutes. In addition, the router has built-in support for the Simple Network Management Protocol (SNMP), so it can be easily monitored by any SNMP-based management station.

The router supports all the connectivity ports that the host computer has installed. This means, at the very least, that the host computer has an Ethernet port and two serial ports that may be defined as LocalTalk ports or dial-up ports.

By adding a Token Ring card or Ethernet card to the computer, you can increase the number of ports supported by the router. Realistically, I'd never add more than one other card to the router, as that would really decrease the router's performance on a busy network.

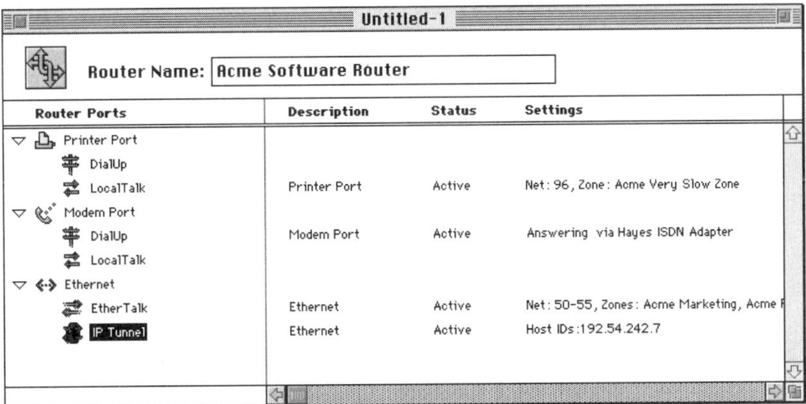

Apple Internet Router Setup Screen

With the Wide Area Network extension, you can set the router up to tunnel rather than route through a TCP/IP segment, if you desire. The router supports network hiding on the exterior routing ports, as well as device and type hiding on all ports.

If you are looking for an easy to configure ISDN router, this is the one I'd recommend. The other one that I'd be willing to recommend is the Netopia Internet Router from Farallon, although its scope and access is limited only to ISDN as the WAN connection feature.

Apple's Remote Access Server Software and Hardware

Apple's Remote Access server comes in two flavors—a single-port version called the ARA Personal Server and a four-port per card version called the Multiport Server. While you can have four ports per card, don't have more than two cards per computer. Tests we have conducted show that putting more than two cards in any given server can bog it down. By the way, these are NuBus, not PCI cards.

The Apple Remote Access Multiport Server is designed to streamline administrative tasks, while maximizing administrator productivity and control. The software installs in minutes and features AppleShare admin-based management capabilities, as well as industry-standard Simple Network Management Protocol (SNMP) support. This allows administrators to flexibly manage and maintain connections. Adding ports is simple, and the server features an automatically generated activity log that can be exported to a variety of programs for further analysis.

The Apple Remote Access Multiport Server offers a host of security features that allow administrators to maintain the integrity of the network. These features—such as password aging, location validation, and the ability to filter access to services—make it one of the most secure remote access servers available. Because its security architecture is supported by leading third-party security vendors, administrators can choose to augment the server's built-in security features with additional challenge-and-response security modules.

Apple's ARA servers offer only modem-based and POTS-based connectivity support. They do not support ISDN at this time.

GLOBAL VILLAGE'S INTERNET START-UP PACKAGE

Global Village has come up with a great idea: Not only do they provide a hardware connectivity device for Internet access, but they provide the Internet access as well. They call it the GlobalCenter Internet Service, and it consists of their box that provides a 28.8 modem or ISDN-based connection and all the software you need to connect your office to the Internet.

Here's the deal: You receive an Ethernet-based Internet box and management software that is used to connect your office to the Internet. This device and management software works hand-in-hand with CE Software's QuickMail server to allow everyone with QuickMail e-mail to also have Internet e-mail and other services access. The Internet connection is initiated through Global Village ISP (Internet Service Provider) POP (Point of Presence) on the Internet. Global Village provides the corporate user with Domain Name registration, as well as Internet Class C licenses.

Global Village takes this further by providing the corporation with a World Wide Web site, sample pages, tracking reports, and management tools. We cover the setup and integration of this system within the next two chapters.

CHAPTER 13:
MacTCP, Open Transport, and IP Gateways

Model of a TCP/IP-to-AppleTalk Gateway

Many of you are predominantly AppleTalk users who use TCP/IP only as a means to access information on the Internet. Then there are even more folks out in the real world who use TCP/IP as their sole or predominant networking protocol for everyday usage. Because of speed differences, larger packets, and other political or budgetary issues, many corporations are turning more and more to TCP/IP as a protocol methodology. Therefore, in any book about AppleTalk networking it is necessary to include a discussion about TCP/IP. This includes knowing how TCP/IP addressing works and how to route or gateway to TCP/IP protocols for Macintosh users utilizing both TCP/IP services *and* AppleTalk on their networks.

Before this instigates a lengthy discussion about whether TCP/IP can replace AppleTalk, think of this: how many printers do you have that support TCP/IP and AppleTalk, and how many support only AppleTalk? Are you willing to replace those printers *today?* How many computers can you load Open Transport onto and have it work? If you are willing to give up your AppleTalk-only printers and can load Open Transport onto all your other devices, then yes, you can remove AppleTalk from your network. If you are not ready for all of that, you will be a two or more protocol network for a while.

SELECTING YOUR ISP AND INTERNET CONNECTION

Since only part of your connectivity is going to be the WAN connection between your sites, make sure that the Internet service provider (ISP) you are choosing is right for your needs. Papers and magazines are full of horror stories about companies that chose the wrong ISP. Many of the books published about Web design and other Internet issues are full of statements like, "Your ISP is your friend." Take it from us: Our ISP is an arrogant so-and-so for the most part, and we *always* have to make things a federal case when changing a portion of our service.

Fortunately for us, the Web has some great pages that rate and list service providers. One of them is shown in the next set of pictures on the left, and its URL is http://www.iworld.com/. Another one, shown on the right, is maintained regularly and covers alternatives to straight ISP connections. Can you find this page on the Internet? Can you find other pages like these? As an exercise, I'm not going to give you this page's address—find it yourself!

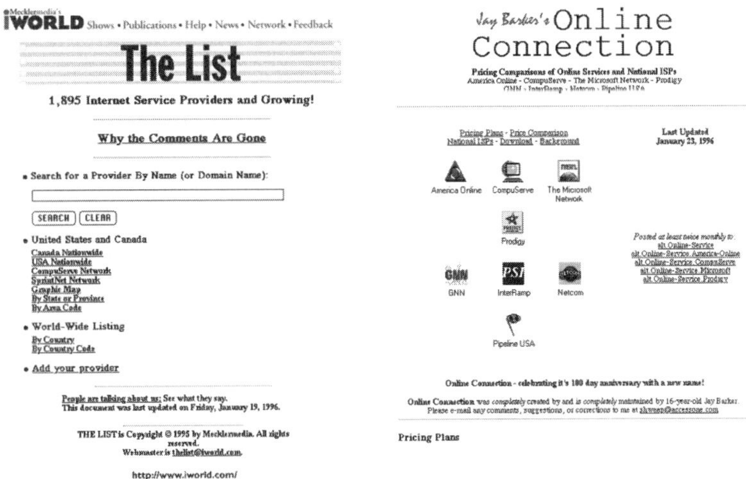

Sample ISP Rating Pages

Planning the Necessary Internet Connectivity

This is pretty simple. To reach the Internet, you have to have an ISP. The ISP can provide these services to you, or you can provide them yourself. The more you provide yourself, the more management capabilities you will have and the more "uptime" you will likely have. These services include the following:

- Domain name registration

- Domain Name Server

- POP3 mail server for e-mail

- Class license from the Internet

Domain Name Registration

For your organization to have a domain name, you need to register your name with the InterNIC. Registration for this name is around $150.00 for two years and has to be done through the InterNIC. You need a form for this, which can be obtained through your ISP.

Domain Name Server

You need a Domain Name Server running somewhere. This is mapped by the InterNIC so that people can find you. Your ISP can provide this service for you, or you can run the software yourself. Either way, plan for this and have a clear understanding of whose responsibility it is. If you are planning to use your own DNS, see the companion book to this one, *AppleTalk Network Services*, also published by AP PROFESSIONAL.

POP3 Mail Server

If you don't have a point of presence (POP) mail server, your ISP needs to provide that for you, or you need to install and run one yourself. If your ISP provides the mail server for you, you will need an SMTP gateway from your mail system to your ISP to send and receive e-mail on the Internet, or your own POP3 mail server. Again, gateways and mail servers are covered in *AppleTalk Network Services.*

Class License from the Internet

Obtain this class license from your ISP, or at least coordinate it with your ISP. Unlike AppleTalk numbers, you can't just make theses up and use your own. You have to play nice with the rest of the world, and to manage this, everyone obtains their numbers from the same place.

THE BASICS OF TCP/IP (THE SHORT COURSE)

This is the short course on TCP/IP protocols for you faithful AppleTalk users. If you need something more hardy, again, refer to our primer on AppleTalk and Open Transport.

TCP/IP networking is broken down into many different protocols, very much like AppleTalk, even though we hear about the Transmission Control Protocol (TCP) and the Internet Protocol (IP) most often. Even though IP is responsible for routing packets from one network to another, it doesn't guarantee that the packets will arrive intact or even in the proper order. It is TCP that breaks the data into the different packets and then verifies that those packets have arrived at their destination intact and in the correct order.

Whereas AppleTalk uses AFP for file sharing, TCP/IP networks use the File Transfer Protocol (FTP) for file transfer. Whereas AppleTalk networks have proprietary protocols and PowerTalk for e-mail, TCP/IP networks use the Simple Mail Transfer Protocol (SMTP) for universal e-mail.

Internet Protocol

IP handles routing datagrams based on destination address. It allows for the interconnection of multiple networks by routing datagrams across network boundaries when necessary. Higher-level protocols (such as TCP) pass data to IP for routing to a destination. The higher-level protocol must handle all the necessary tracking of datagrams, as in which ones belong together, which ones have been acknowledged, and so forth. IP does not need to know anything about a datagram other than where it is going. It may seem like the higher-level protocols do all the work. However, IP has quite a job in moving datagrams to their destination since they may be routed through several networks, including Ethernet, serial lines, phone lines, and even satellite links.

Transmission Control Protocol

TCP ensures reliable stream-oriented communications between cooperating processes. Because TCP calls on IP services, these processes can exist on machines in different networks. Since IP provides unreliable, connectionless datagram delivery, applications that use only IP can be error prone. Datagrams are lost, delayed, corrupted, accidentally duplicated, or delivered out of order. Rather than requiring every application program to check for such errors, TCP provides a general solution to the problem of reliable delivery of datastreams.

In keeping with the layered approach to networking, most systems that support TCP/IP provide a software interface to the TCP functions, allowing application programs to set up sessions with cooperating processes, listen for requests for sessions, send and receive data, and close sessions. The Application Program Interface (API) to TCP varies from machine to machine.

Setting up a session, also referred to as a *virtual circuit connection,* is analogous to dialing a phone call before starting to talk to a remote person. It is necessary before data can be sent. Once a connection is established, the upper-level application channels continuous datastreams through TCP for delivery to its peer process. TCP puts this data, along with any necessary control and addressing data, into units called *segments.* It then passes the segments to a lower-level protocol, usually, but not necessarily, IP. TCP is flexible enough to handle a variety of underlying delivery systems. IP divides the segments into datagrams and sends them across the internetwork. TCP, on the other end, checks for errors, acknowledges error-free segments, and arranges them for delivery to upper-level applications.

Internetwork Naming and Addressing

For in-depth information on internetwork naming and addressing, please refer to books written specifically about TCP/IP, such as *Internetworking with TCP/IP: Principles, Protocols, and Architecture* by Douglas E. Comer. These books cover topics such as addressing, Class A, B, and C networks, subnetting, domain names, and fixed versus server (RARP) addressing. We cover the basics of IP addressing here, but not in the depth in which these other books cover it.

TCP/IP Protocol Services

The TCP/IP networking environment provides your customers with a rich set of protocol services, including the following:

- **Telnet:** This is a remote access protocol that enables users to connect to remote systems as if they were directly connected.

- **FTP:** This enables your customers to transfer files across networks. Through FTP, users' host computers can connect to remote hosts, send or receive files, list directories, and implement simple commands across the network.

- **SMTP:** This protocol enables users to send and receive e-mail messages across the network.

- **SNMP:** This provides users with a unified standard for managing their networks. SNMP was developed by the Internet Engineering Task Force (IETF) to address network management of TCP/IP internets and to provide a simple, reliable network management protocol.

IP Addressing

AppleTalk uses a "network.node.socket" address, such as 154.27.54 to designate a computer on network 154 with a node address of 27 and a software socket address of 54. The network numbers are assigned by a network manager or designer, and can range from 1–65,000, while the node and socket IDs are dynamic. IP addresses are a bit different. They are 32 bits in length and are broken down into four segments of eight bits each. While the addresses are broken down into network and node identifiers, they are *assigned* in a completely different manner from AppleTalk addresses. Nodes are not assigned dynamically, and network numbers aren't made up by administrators. They are instead rationed out by the Network Information Center (NIC) directly or through a company's ISP. There are several address classes given out by the NIC, most notably Class A–C. By examining the first few bits of an IP address, you can quickly and easily determine the address class of the license and the rest of the structure of the address. Class A licenses reserve the first bit in the address as a 0, Class B licenses reserve it as a 1, and Class C licenses reserve the first bit as a 1 and the second bit as a 0. If you don't understand this now, you will after reading the next page or two.

Since some of you may not be used to working with bit-type addresses, we've included a small table to help you understand how the addresses work and how they convert to standard numbers. Basically, the table shows the four sets of binary numbers that make up an IP address in *both* their binary (bit) equivalents and, below that, in their decimal equivalents.

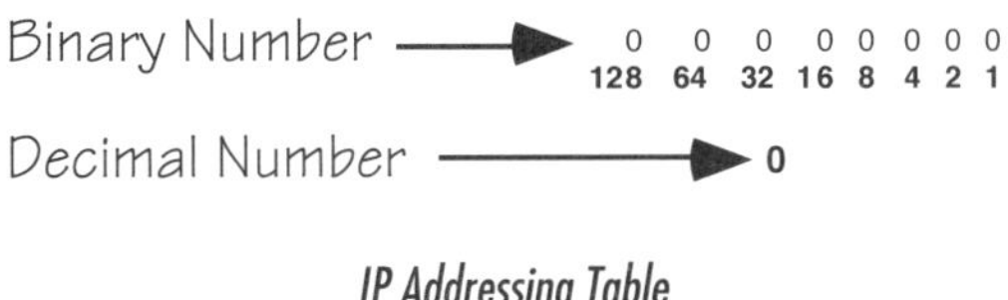

IP Addressing Table

In the binary system, each number is doubled as it moves from right to left. Hence, if the first digit in a binary number is 1, double that and you have 2 for the second number, and so on. IP addresses have four sets of binary numbers with eight bits each. If each of the bits in the binary number are set to "on" or 1, and each of the numbers with its bit "on" is added up, the total is 255. Therefore, the highest IP number is 255.255.255.255, which is a reserved number in the IP system used as the overall broadcast address. Likewise, if each of the bits in each byte is set to "off" or 0, the number would be 0.0.0.0, which is also reserved. Combinations of bits being "on" and "off" give us the rest of the ranges from 1–254 in each byte of an address.

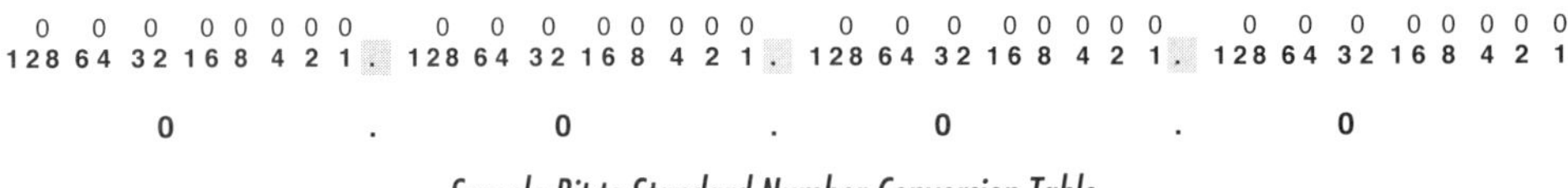

Sample Bit to Standard Number Conversion Table

Now that you know all of that (I know you already knew it—I just wanted to review it myself so that I don't get confused), let's look at how the addresses are classified and some general rules of addressing. The first and most important general rule of addressing is this:

As a network address becomes longer and takes up more bits, the possible number of nodes for that address is lessened.

There can be only so many bits and combinations of bits within an IP addressing system. If your network address takes up half of the bits in the addressing table, you are left with only half of the possibilities for creating node addresses. Everything costs something in life, and this is no real exception. To show how this works, we will add one bar on top of the addressing table to represent the reserved numbers, another bar with a dark border to represent the network address portion, and finally a gray bar to represent the node address portion.

Class A Addresses The *first bit* of a Class A network is reserved, since it identifies the address class. Class A networks use the *first byte* of an IP address to identify the network, and use the rest of the address space to identify subnets and individual nodes. The first bit of the address must be zero. Class A network addresses can be identified by the first set of numbers ranging from 1–127. Therefore, a computer numbered 120.8.2.67 identifies it as being node 8.2.67 on network 120. While this doesn't allow for many Class A networks, it does allow a lot of nodes on that network.

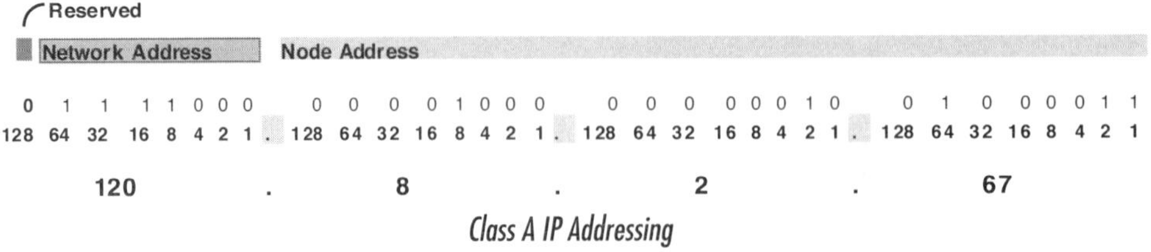

Class A IP Addressing

Class B Addresses

The first *two bits* of a Class B address identify its class. Where the first bit of a Class A network is zero, the first two bits of a Class B network are a one and a zero. Class B networks use the first *two bytes* of the address to identify the network and the last two bytes to identify the node. Notice in the following table that all we did to change the number from the original table was to change the reserved bits at the front of the address. This changes the initial decimal number from 120 to 184. Also notice that the number of bits reserved for node IDs has been reduced by one whole byte!

Class B IP Addressing

The network address range has shifted from an eight-bit network identifier to a 16-bit network identifier. The node identifier has shrunk from a 24-bit identifier to a 16-bit identifier. Therefore, the range for Class B networks begins at 128 and ends at 191. Thus, 184.8.2.67 identifies network number 184.8 and node 2.67.

Class C Addresses

Continuing on a theme, if the first *three bits* of the address are 110, this identifies the address as a Class C address. Class C networks use the first *three bytes* of the address to identify the network and the last byte to identify the node. The network address is now 24-bits long and the node address is now only 8 bits long. The range for Class C networks begins at 192 and ends at 255. However, network addresses with a first byte value greater than 223 are reserved for special Class D multicast addresses, which we won't cover at this time. Therefore, the identifier 210.192.52.10 identifies node 10 on network 210.192.52.

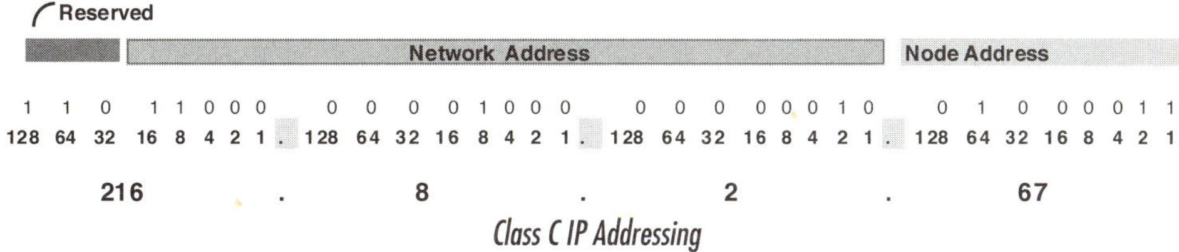

Class C IP Addressing

THE NEED FOR SUBNETTING AND MASKING

Now that we have covered the basics of network addressing, it's time to consider what has to happen to an address if you divide your network into subnetworks using routers. With AppleTalk, you would simply make up another number and assign your network that number. With IP, you have to play with all the rest of the network administrators in the world. Therefore, you have to learn a few rules before you decide to divide your network into its various realms of feudal power.

The IP Mask

IP masks are used to indicate which portion of an address is used for the network address and which portion of the address is used for the node address. Understanding how to mask is easy. For every segment of the address which is dedicated to the network number, place a mask. In other words, follow this simple table and you'll be fine.

Class	Network	Node	Mask
A	1	3	255.0.0.0
B	2	2	255.255.0.0
C	3	1	255.255.255.0

IP Masking Table

IP Subnets While the organization of IP network addressing per se allows the Internet a manageable and efficient routing structure, IP subnetting allows network designers and administrators to perform the same types of organization as the Internet. Just like dividing AppleTalk networks into subnetworks, subnetting an IP network performs the same management of traffic. It also limits the broadcast packets by using the node address bits as additional network address bits, and therefore the standard structure of an IP address can be modified to create a subnetwork. This moves the logical "dividing line" between a network address and a node address, thus creating more "networks" while losing a certain number of possible node IDs for the address. While this works "locally" in Company X's network, the Internet still interprets all the addresses within the license as standard IP addresses.

Defining the Subnet Mask

To define a subnetwork within any given license a bit mask, called the *subnet mask,* is applied to the IP address. Once a bit is "on" in a mask, that bit in the address is interpreted as a network bit instead of a node bit. Thus, as I warned you before, as you lengthen the network address you will have less node addresses possible. We are going to discuss the basics of subnetting here using the example of a Class C license, which is the most common of all licenses. Let's take the Class C address range of 216.8.2.0. If the network is not subnetted, all computers consider themselves to be on the same network and listen to the same broadcast packets.

The standard subnet for a Class C address is 255.255.255.0. In creating a common Class C subnet that divides the network into four subnets, the subnet mask would be used to extend the network portion of the address by one byte. The subnet mask would become 255.255.255.192. The *top two bits* of the last byte are used for the *subnetwork address* and the *last six bits* are used for the *node ID*s within those subnetworks, with the subnet incrementing by 64 each time.

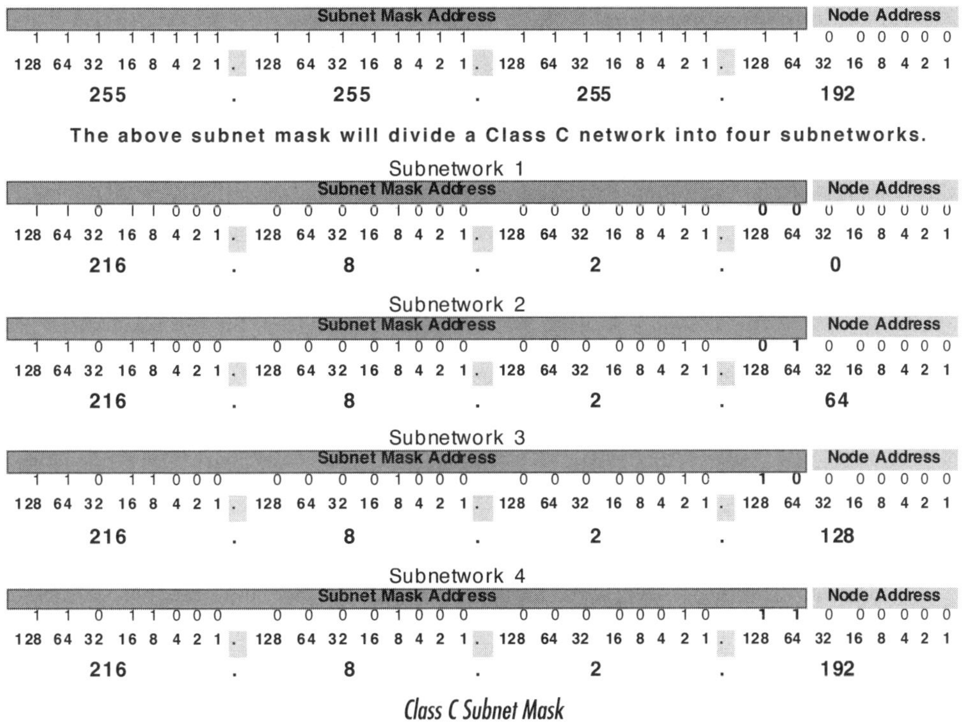

Class C Subnet Mask

If given a Class C license, the four subnetworks with their subnetwork numbers and masking would be broken down as shown in the following diagram.

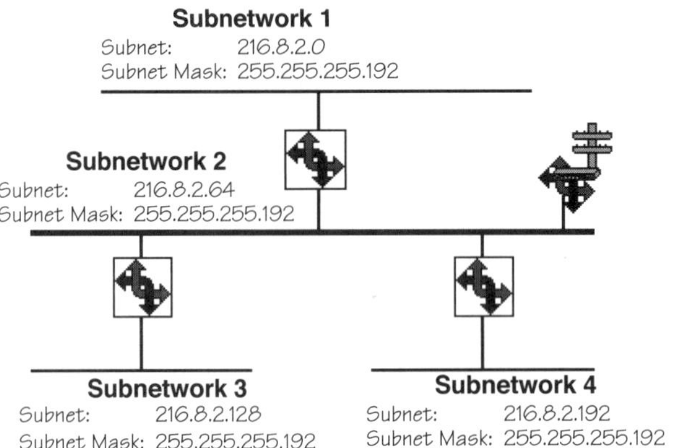

Breaking Down a Class C into Four Subnetworks

Setting the Broadcast Address

Whereas AppleTalk networks have a set broadcast address for every network, the broadcast address for IP has to be set per subnetwork and is usually set to all 1's. Therefore, the standard broadcast address for the Class C network 216.8.2.0 would be 216.8.2.255. However, that doesn't take into account subnet masking. The basic rule is that a broadcast address for a subnetwork should be the highest node address within the subnet.

Subnet	Mask	Broadcast
216.8.2.0	255.255.255.192	216.8.2.63
216.8.2.64	255.255.255.192	216.8.2.127
216.8.2.128	255.255.255.192	216.8.2.191
216.8.2.192	255.255.255.192	216.8.2.255

Broadcast Addresses for Each Subnet

Setting the Rest of the Addresses

Along with the network, subnet mask, and broadcast addresses to set for IP, there are a few more setting to configure before you are ready to roll. These include the name servers (along with the domain name), the default gateway, and how you are going to handle individual node addressing.

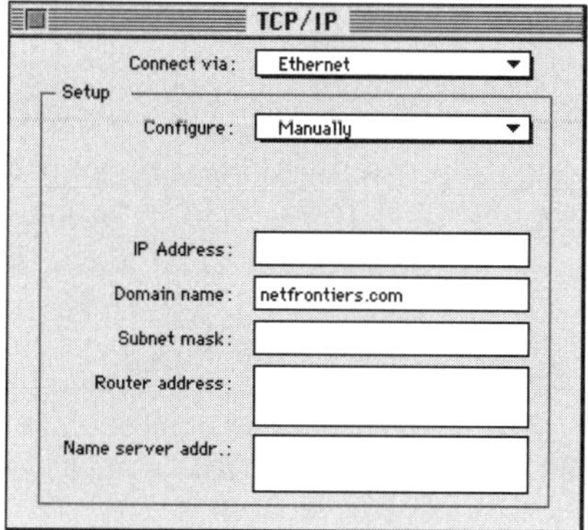

Open Transport TCP/IP Control Panel

IP Address

This is the node's IP address. This should be filled in using "dot" notation, meaning something like 157.22.252.17 (but please don't use this one, since it's mine).

Domain Name

Your domain name must be registered with the InterNIC committee. Once that is accomplished, your Domain Name Server (DNS) can be set within your network or at your Internet service provider. Enter that information into the **Domain name** field *exactly as it comes back from the InterNIC committee.* Somebody once asked me if spelling matters. Yes, of course it duz (that's a joke, folks).

Subnet Mask

This is the same subnet mask that you gave to the subnetwork router when you set up the network. This, too, needs to be filled in using dot notation. Again, here's a sample from our system which I'd rather you not use yourself unless you know why you need to use it: 255.255.255.192.

Router Address

Any time a packet must be sent outside of the local subnetwork, it must be sent through a router. With AppleTalk, each computer holds an RTMP stub that has the address of the last router from which it heard. With IP, you need to know the address of the router or routers that are the default gateways to the world outside of your subnetwork. Type in either *the* router's address in dot format or a list of router addresses in the same format.

Domain Name Server Address

Finally, you need to know the address of the Domain Name Server with which you are working. If this is inside the company, use that address. If it is outside the company, say at the ISP, guess what? You need that address, too.

CONFIGURING YOUR ROUTERS FOR TCP/IP

Now let's cover setting up your routers for IP. We take a small network with Ethernet and LocalTalk connectivity and show how the routers that are already set up for AppleTalk can be set up for IP as well. The following diagram shows the network I'm describing. There are a total of eight subnetworks, not including the network link to the ISP. AppleTalk Networks 1–1, 950–950, 1800–1800, and 2000–2000 are all Ethernet networks that can directly support IP. Networks 3, 4, 5, and 6 are all LocalTalk networks that *can't* directly support IP since their Physical layers do not match. Therefore, we need an alternative for setting up these users for IP traffic. We show the router names as well as the IP addresses for each subnet in the larger type, with AppleTalk information in smaller type.

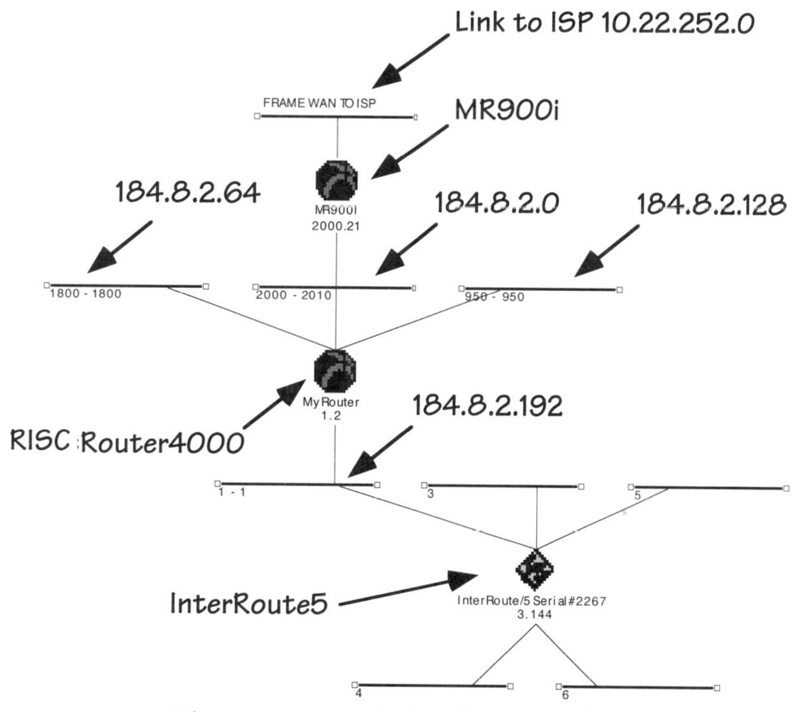

Mid-size LAN Showing AppleTalk and IP Network Addresses

Setting up the WAN Router

The WAN router for this network has two basic ports: a port to the WAN and a port to the Ethernet network. Both of these have to be configured before connectivity to the Internet can be established. When setting up your WAN port configuration, you need your IP address, subnet mask, broadcast address, and the remote node IP address from your service provider. These are all set by your ISP. Trust me, if they give you the wrong information, you'll never get configured. Make sure that you double-check everything with them before you launch into the nitty gritty of configuring your routers.

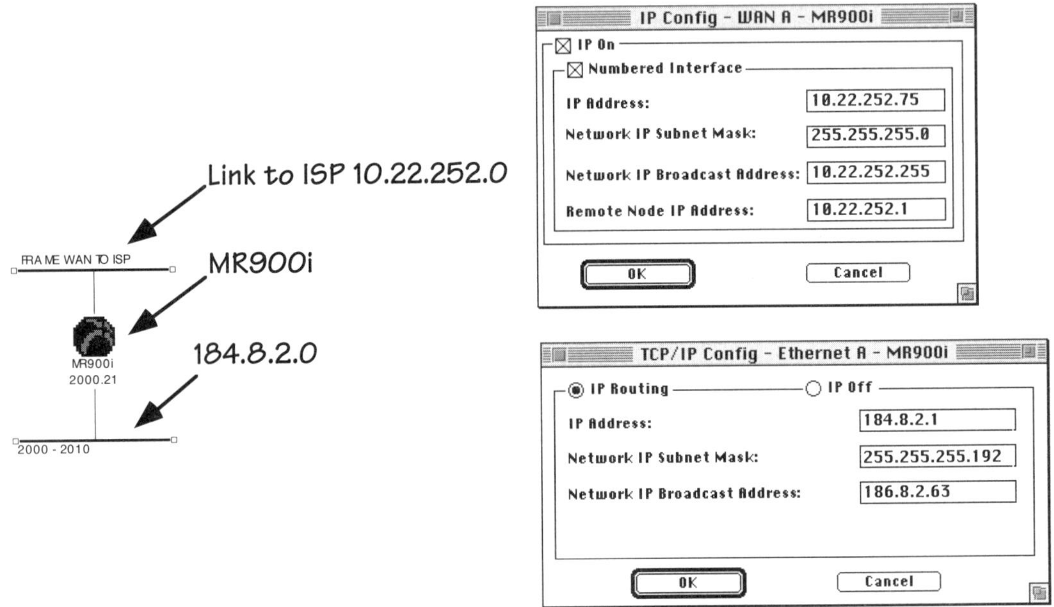

Setup Configuration for the Sample WAN Router

When configuring your Ethernet port for the router, you need to know the IP address for the *router port itself,* the network subnet mask, and the network IP broadcast address. The reason that I emphasized the router port's address is because each of your nodes can be set for static (manual) addressing or some type of server-based addressing. The routers and other fixed devices on your network, such as printers and servers, should all have manual addresses. Your routers *must* have manual addresses set for each port. When setting the address of a router, it is usually smart to set the address as the first couple of addresses for that subnetwork. Ergo, your first router should be 1, with the second router as 2, and so on. It makes management easier down the road.

If you use decent software, you should receive a suggestion for a subnet mask. Once that is set, the software should enter your broadcast address automatically for you. If your software doesn't suggest the correct broadcast address, remember that it is the *highest* number in the subnet range.

Setting up the LAN–LAN Router

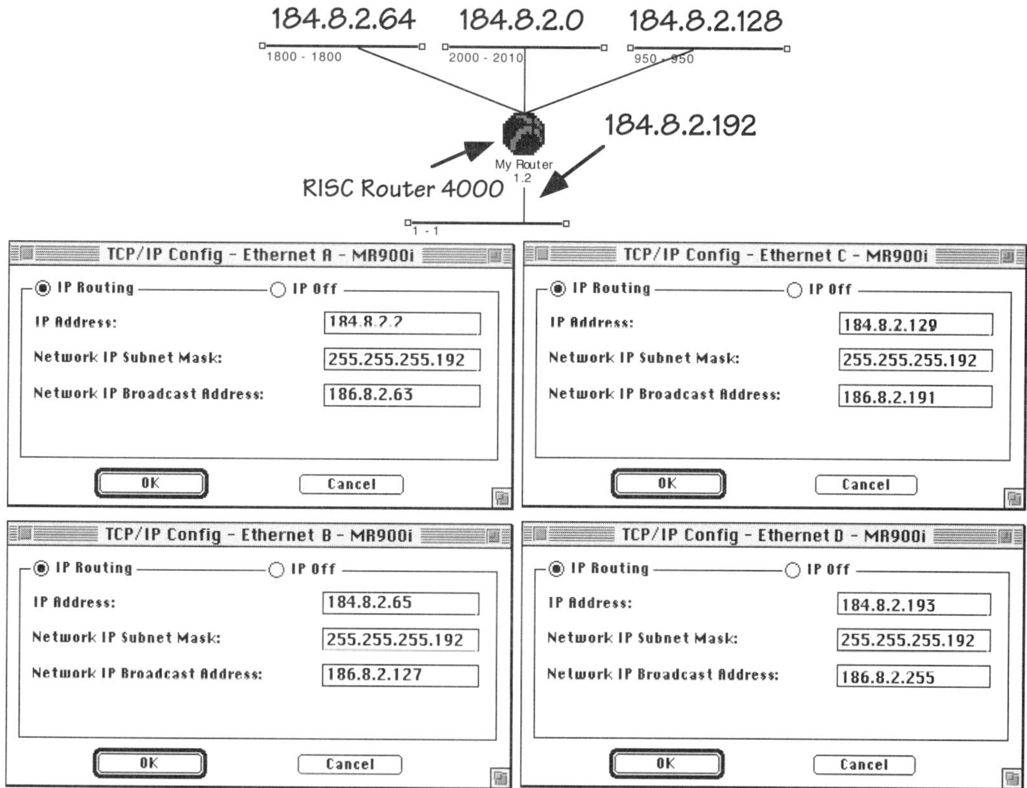

Setting up a LAN–LAN Ethernet Router with IP Routing

We have already configured one of the networks for TCP/IP protocols—the network that the LAN router shares with the WAN router. Therefore, one of the IP addresses for that LAN is in use by the WAN router's Ethernet port. When setting up the second router for that network, we know that the router's IP address has to be at least the second address in the range. Given the subnet masking that we have performed to create the four subnetworks, we set up each of the routers with the appropriate information and routing setups. It's not that hard to do.

Setting up Your Router as an IP Gateway

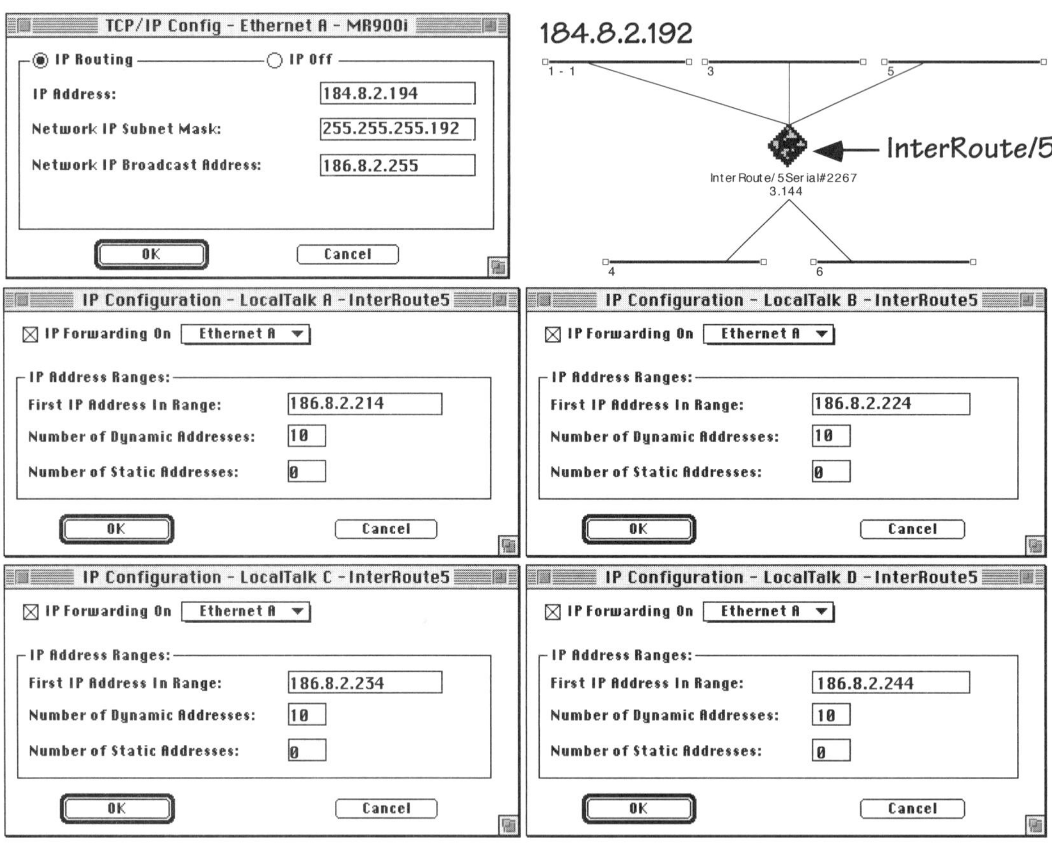

InterRoute/5 Acting as an IP Forwarding Gateway

Now that you have your IP routers set up, it's time to figure out how to give IP access to your nodes on LocalTalk (IR counts as LocalTalk, remember). If your router supports it, the easiest way to do this is to set up your router as an IP forwarding router. This allows LocalTalk or ARA users to access IP addresses over other-than-Ethernet Physical layers. At this point, you have tow choices. The first choice is to set up your router to use the address space for a single IP subnetwork address range. The second choice is to set the router to subnet down to LocalTalk.

IP Forwarding

The first choice, IP forwarding, reserves a combination of static and dynamic (server-provided) addresses within the given network range. Usually, all you have to do is provide the starting address, the number of dynamic addresses, and the number of static addresses within the range you desire.

You can have only one IP gateway per zone. Your users will need to know the AppleTalk zone in which the router is located so that they can find it during the setup of their workstation's IP addressing. Set up your users for a MacIP Server (the service the router registers) and select the router's zone in the user's TCP/IP control panel for Open Transport or MacTCP control panel for standard Apple-Talk users.

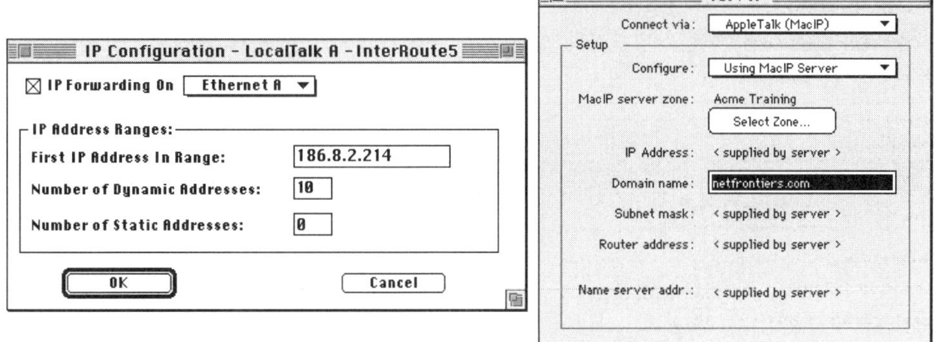

Router Setup (left) and Corresponding User Setup (right)

IP Subnetting

If your router is capable of subnetting your LocalTalk networks, then you can set your routers to route down to LocalTalk while creating a subnet mask for them. Open Transport supports both server-based and manual addressing of LocalTalk nodes as long as your routers are set up as shown in the following screen shots. Again, this is a generic routing diagram—actually taken from the screen of a Compatible RISC Router—but you'll get the idea. When subnetting down to LocalTalk, don't forget that you have to give the LocalTalk port of the router an IP address. Also assign the subnet mask and give some of the devices dynamic addresses. If you want to hide the LocalTalk subnet from the rest of your internetwork, don't turn on the broadcasting of IP routing. If this is on, the routers will know of the presence of this subnet. If it is off, it will be hidden from the rest of the network.

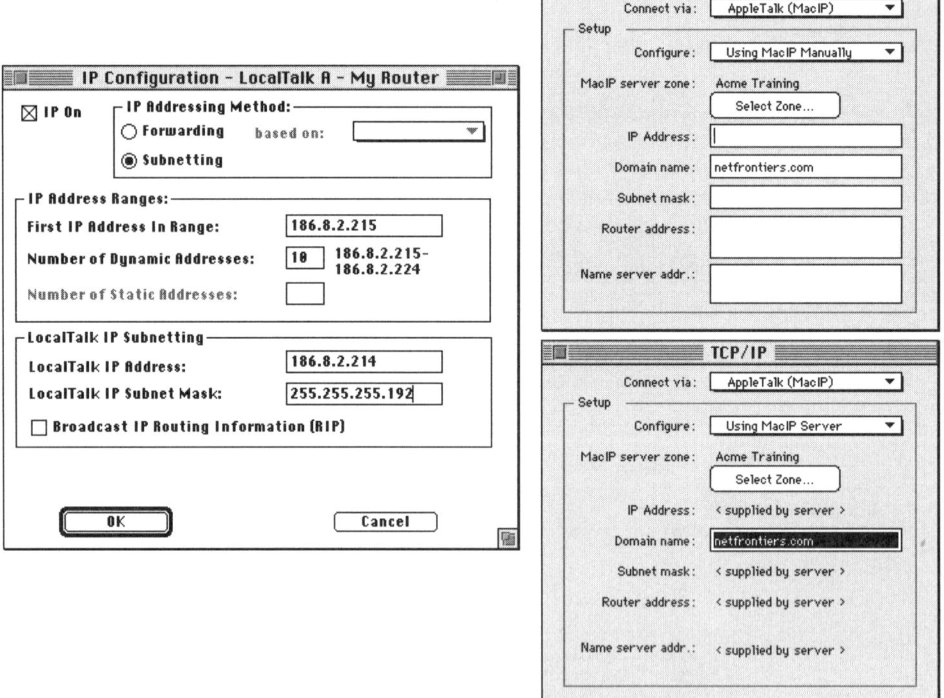

Router Setup (left) and Corresponding User Setup (right)

SETTING UP THE MAC IP GATEWAY

There is one last item on our agenda. If you don't have a router that is capable of acting as an AppleTalk-to-IP gateway, or you don't want to use your router as such, you need some way of using your IP services. One of the best ways is through the Apple IP gateway. This is a software-only product that resides and runs on any Mac which is capable of running Ethernet and IP. In reality, I wouldn't go putting it on my company's IIsi, but I wouldn't spend a bunch of money to put it on an 8100 either. Something like a IIci or a Quadra is a great computer for this gateway.

The sole purpose of the MacIP gateway is to deliver IP addresses over AppleTalk to users who need them. Configuring the user is simple. Set the Open Transport Control panel to MacIP and point it at the zone with the gateway.

There isn't much to configuring the gateway itself, either. The only real thing that you need to know about configuration is that the machine on which the gateway is running must be configured for a manual IP address. This, along with the routers, is one of those incredibly important machines on the network, and therefore should always be manually addressed. It doesn't work if you don't do that, by the way. The basic Gateway Information window for our network is shown in the next screen shot. It shows a few of the people that have signed in to it—probably Netscape surfers.

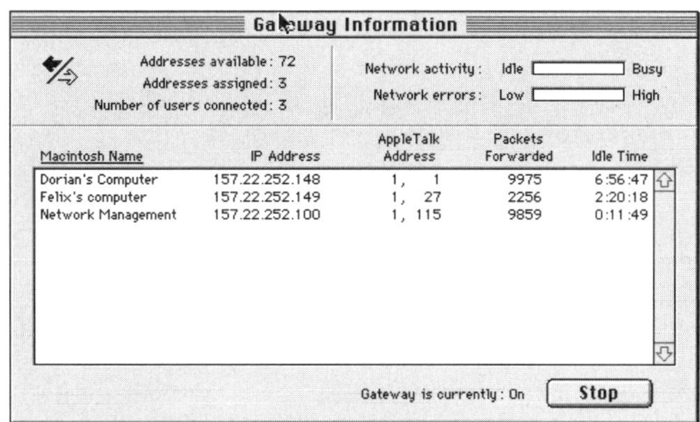

Gateway Window

Configuring TCP on the Gateway Computer

When setting up the MacIP gateway, first set up the TCP/IP configuration on the computer on which you are running the MacIP gateway. This will show the original MacTCP configuration. If you are configuring TCP using Open Transport, you will "get it" by looking at these screens.

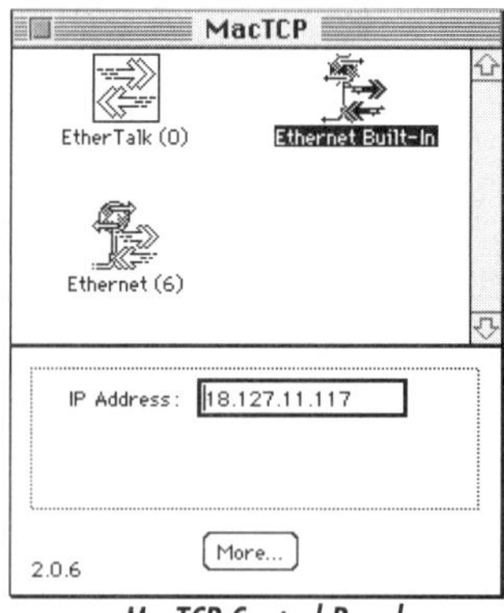

MacTCP Control Panel

1. Select the Ethernet port connected to the IP network. "EtherTalk" is not used in this case, since that refers to IP encapsulated in Apple-Talk. Here you are configuring the IP network connection, which is native IP.

2. If the gateway's IP address is manually obtained, enter its address in the **IP Address** field. Click **More...** to reach the next dialog box.

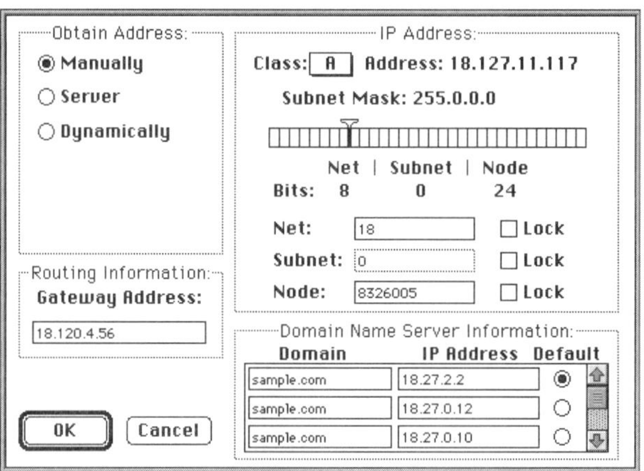

The "More" Window of MacTCP

3. Under **Obtain Address**, select **Manually** if the gateway has a fixed IP address. Select **Server** if it will obtain its address from a server. Most IP gateways will use **Manually** here.

4. Fill in the **Domain Name Server Information** fields as specified by the net-work manager.

5. If the gateway has a fixed IP address, first set the subnet mask to the value specified by the network manager. Next, in the **Gateway Address** field, enter the IP address of the subnet's IP router.

Configuring the MacIP Gateway Software

Once you have set the TCP/IP configuration for the computer itself, set the start-ing range for the IP addresses, how many there should be for server-based address-ing, and how many there should be for manual addressing, if you want that also. Finally, you can set individual node security for the gateway by setting a user restriction list. That's all there is to that, folks.

1. Select **Automatically assigned** in the **Addressing Preferences** field if the gate-way will assign IP addresses to clients. Select **Manually assigned** addressing if each client has a fixed address. Select **Both** if both methods apply.

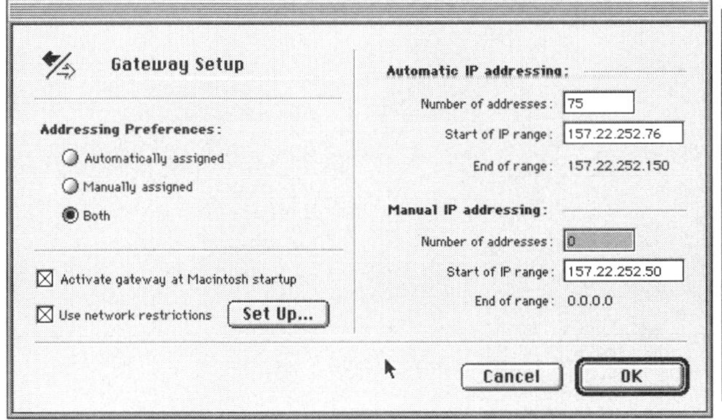

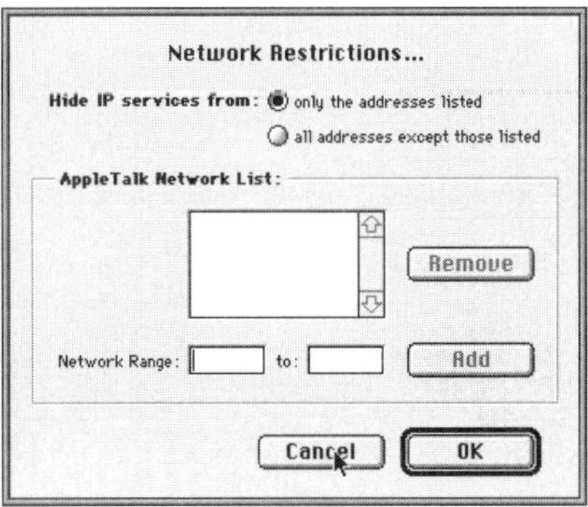

Gateway Setup Windows

2. Each mode can support up to 253 contiguous addresses. Enter the number of addresses and the first address in the range for each method that will be used.

3. Specify whether to activate the gateway at Macintosh startup.

4. Specify whether to impose network restrictions.

5. **Network Restrictions** can be used to restrict access to the IP network from certain AppleTalk networks.

6. Use the radio buttons to specify whether you are allowing or denying access to listed networks.

7. Enter the beginning and ending numbers of each AppleTalk network range to be included.

WHERE TO GO FROM HERE . . .

There is a lot more that you need to know to route TCP/IP properly. This is just the beginning. With the advent of Open Transport, Macintoshes will be able to become full IP citizens, with the ability to use BootP, DHCP, and other servers. Many vendors are beginning to make a move toward normal AppleTalk services running over TCP/IP because of packet sizes, so it might make sense for you to really invest some time in learning as much as you can about it.

In *AppleTalk Network Services*, we discuss which services might run better under AppleTalk and which might run better under TCP/IP. Understanding when to move to TCP/IP is just as important as deciding *how* to move there.

I hope we've been able to help. As always, if you need to get a hold of us, you can (our contact information is on page xv of the introduction to this book).

CHAPTER 14: PUTTING YOUR LAN AND RACK TOGETHER

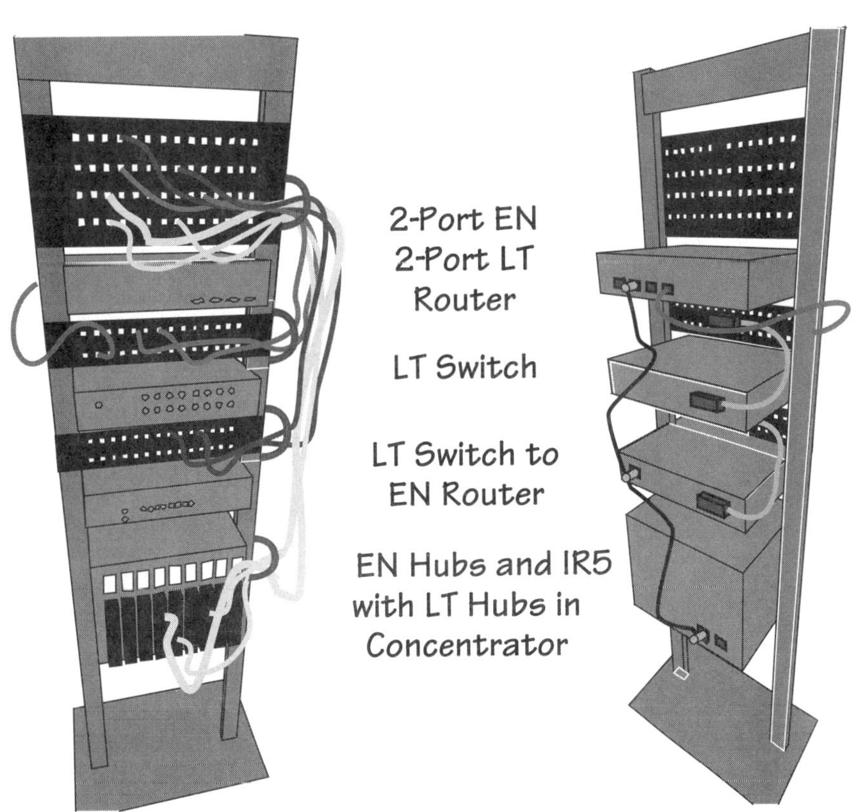

Front (left) and Back (right) of a Wiring Rack Populated with Routers, Switches, and Hubs

WORKING WITH A SINGLE RACK

With your wiring system in place, you need to build the rack that will house your Ethernet and LocalTalk hubs, your switches, and your routers. This chapter explains some of the concepts behind building a *single, non-extended rack*. We discuss a single rack only, because we merely want to show how to build one of them. The rack we work with has a multiport router, a LocalTalk-only switch, a Local-Talk-to Ethernet switch, and a Farallon Concentrator populated with both Ethernet hubs and an InterRoute/5 Ethernet-to-multi-LocalTalk hub router. This combination should give you a good idea of what you might expect in the real world when connecting systems together, along with the software you need when doing it.

Start with Interconnections

First, plan the interconnections of the wiring rack devices themselves. If you don't have a methodology for connecting them together, you will have a bit of a problem. Believe me, putting them together on a drawing board is very different than putting them together in the real world. I can't tell you how many of our students and clients plan their networks without realizing how they are going to connect all their devices together. To begin this process, take an inventory of the kind of interconnection devices you have on each piece of your rack gear. Taking an inventory of our rack gear, we find that we have the following:

- The four-port router has DIN-8 standard LocalTalk connections for the two LocalTalk ports and has switchable AUI/RJ-45/ThinNet connectors for the two Ethernet ports. With Ethernet, this means that we can connect any way we want. With LocalTalk, this means that we need StarConnectors for each port we want to use.

- The LocalTalk switch does *not* have a "backplane," meaning that if we want to connect it to something, like the LocalTalk port of the router, we need to use one of the ports on the front panel. That means that we have to *give up* that port and can not use it for end-user connectivity.

- The Ethernet-to-LocalTalk switch we are using has an AUI port on the Ethernet backplane. That means that no matter how we want to connect to Ethernet, we need to purchase a transceiver of some sort.

- The concentrator has two Ethernet channels that can be used for "upward" connectivity to the rest of the network. One of the Ethernet channels has an AUI port and the other has a ThinNet BNC.

Debate and Decision

We could connect the Ethernet-to-LocalTalk switch off one EN port of the router, the concentrator off the other EN port, and the LocalTalk switch off one LT port, thus using as many ports as possible. Another option would be to connect the concentrator *and* the EN-to-LT switch off one EN port on the router, leaving the other port free for future expansion. If we connect all three devices together, we need to use a common Ethernet connection methodology. The easiest way to do that is to connect them using ThinNet coaxial cables. Both the concentrator and the router have BNC connectors and transceivers built in, leaving the EN-to-LT switch as the only device for which we need to buy a transceiver.

We decided to put the three EN devices together on one ThinNet bus, thus leaving the router with a free port for expansion. Given that there aren't too many Ethernet computers, the network shouldn't become bogged down with traffic. To decrease the possibility of collisions due to NBP requests, we will segregate the network into several zones. Building this internetwork will create a total of nine different network segments—two Ethernet and seven LocalTalk. The planning diagram for this network is shown in the next picture, with the letters describing the following:

A. This is the connecting line for the ThinNet network. It connects from the router through the EN-to-LT switch and ends up at the concentrator. The concentrator's internal bus takes care of connectivity for the different hubs and the InterRoute/5.

B. This is the short connection from the LocalTalk port on the router to the port on the LocalTalk switch.

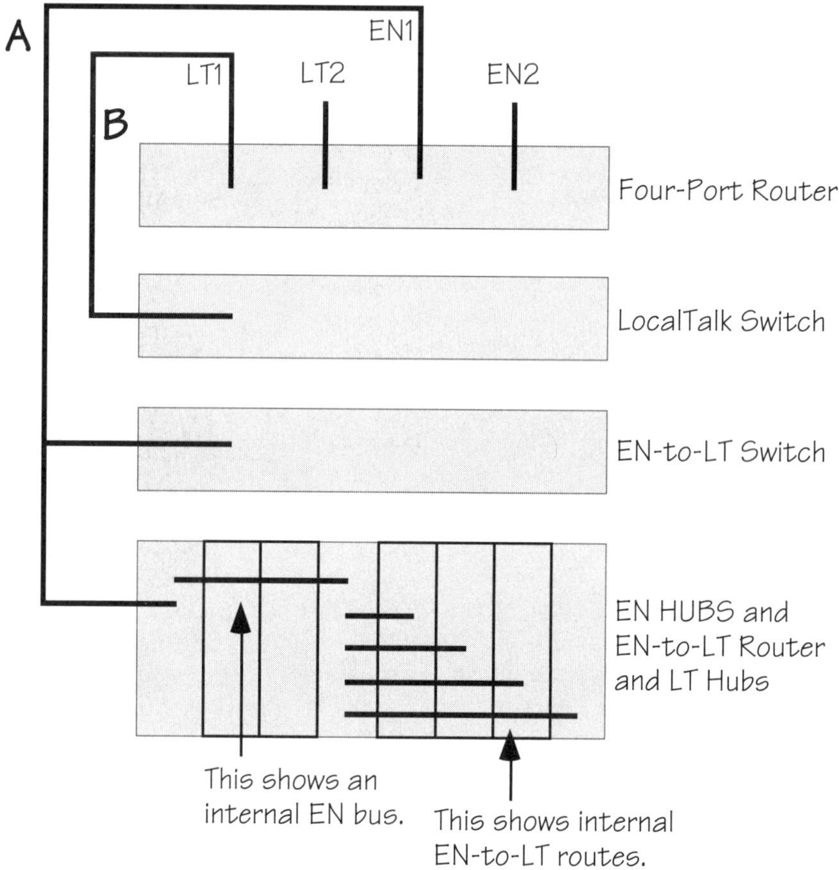

Planning Diagram for the Wiring Rack

The next picture shows what the back of the rack would look like with everything networked together. Sorry about not being able to draw a ThinNet transceiver, but hey, I build networks, I don't do art. We can't afford a great artist—except for our covers—so you'll have to use your imaginations a little bit, okay?

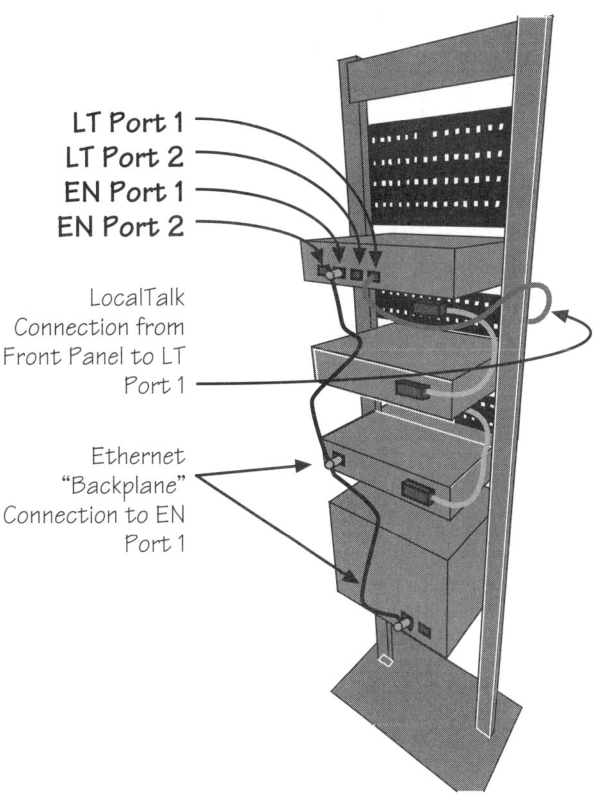

Back of the Rack

Logical Connections

Now that the routers, hubs, and switches are physically connected, create the "logical" network. In other words, create the AppleTalk network numbers and Apple-Talk zones that need to be configured in the routers before they can become operational. You really have three routers in this rack—one is the four-port router, another is the EN-to-LT switch, and the third is the InterRoute/5. However, in our configuration, you have only two Ethernet networks. Remembering our definitions of routers, that means that only one of the routers has to be a seeding router for the Ethernet side. The other two routers can take their cue from this first seed router, if necessary. You could seed all your routers. If you do, make sure that you enter the *exact* same information in each one of them, or you will have some real problems. Remember, management of routers should be accomplished at the port level, not the device level. Each port is a network or connects to a network, and you manage *networks* in the real world.

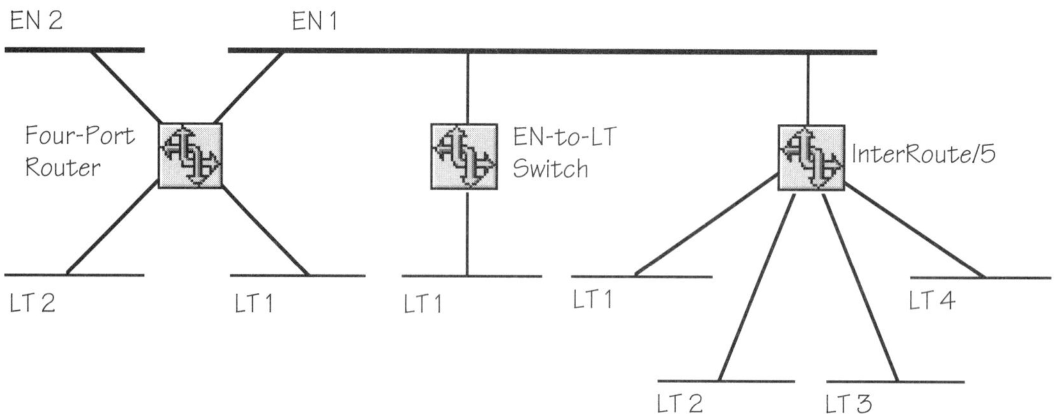

Logical View of the Network

Once you have planned your physical and logical network, create a routing table. Do this on paper first. In that way, you know exactly what to enter when you are in front of your computer actually setting each router's parameters. Our method of creating a table is simple. We include the router's name, port information, seed status, network number or range information, and the router's zone list. With Ethernet routers, there can be multiple zones, but one of those zones is the router's *default zone*. When creating our table, we usually list the default zone in boldface. Since there can be only a single zone on LocalTalk networks, there is no need for a default zone or typing the zone name in boldface. If your network already has routers in place, ensure that you have the network number/range and zone information for the existing routers. Life can get pretty weird if you decide to put up a router on your network with a network number that already exists elsewhere.

Review of Numbering

There can be 253 devices per each Ethernet network number. That means that if you have an Ethernet network range of 1–1, you can have up to 253 devices. If your range is 1–2, you can have 506 devices. Make sense? There are a lot of networks out there that have ranges of 1–5000, or an extreme of 1–65000 (right, Favian?). In actuality, you don't need that many numbers in a range. LocalTalk networks can have up to 254 devices per network. In reality, it is inadvisable to put more than 500 devices on any given Ethernet network and more than 36 per LocalTalk network. When creating a network numbering scheme, then, put into practice something that makes sense. We always number Ethernet networks so that they end with a 1–3, and LocalTalk networks so that they end with a 4–9. That way, when looking at a packet trace, if the originating computer came from network number 4021, I know that the computer is on Ethernet. Likewise, if it came from network number 1766, I know that it originated from a LocalTalk network. It's just our way of doing things. Here is our sample table:

Router	Port	Seed Status	Net Info	Zones
4-Port Router	Ethernet 1	Seed	1–2	Public, R&D, Senior Staff, Admin
	Ethernet 2	Not Used	–	–
	LocalTalk 1	Seed	4	Senior Staff
	LocalTalk 2	Not Used	–	–
EN/LT Switch	Ethernet 1	Non-Seed	Garnered	Garnered
	LocalTalk	Bridged	Garnered	Garnered
InterRoute/5	Ethernet 1	Non-Seed	Garnered	Garnered
	LocalTalk 1	Seed	5	Admin
	LocalTalk 2	Seed	6	Admin
	LocalTalk 3	Seed	7	Admin
	LocalTalk 4	Seed	8	Admin

Sample Router Table

Front of the Rack

Once you have everything figured out and installed into your routers, it's time to patch the cables together on your new rack.

The smart way to do this is to use colored cables from the incoming distribution patch panel at the top—where the wiring company terminated horizontal cable runs going to the computers—to the appropriate switch or hub on the bottom. This gives you a visual representation of where your cables are going and quickly helps you discover to what a computer is connected.

At the same time, *label* not only the patch panel positions, but the cables as well. What I tell people to do, and what they rarely do and always regret not doing, is to label the patch cable in two places. On the end going into the incoming distribution panel, place a label that says into which port and hub/switch the cable is plugged at the other end. Guess how you should label the end going into the hub or switch? How smart our readers are! Yes, label it with the position number of the cable at the incoming distribution panel.

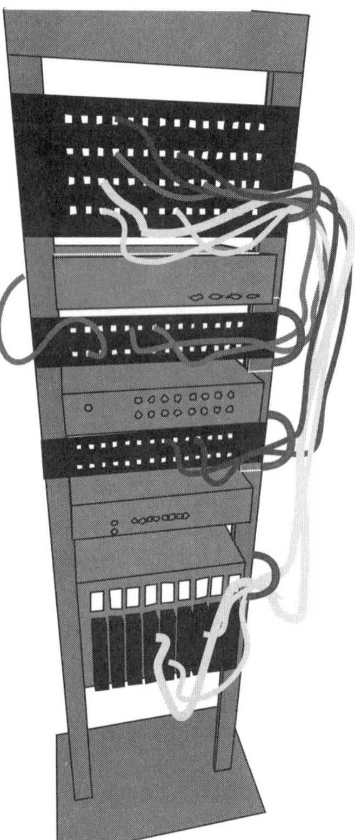

Front of the Rack

Once you have connected everything and checked the UPS (yes, Joe, you *do* need a UPS on your rack), you are pretty much finished with the rack. You can leave feeling good about yourself, knowing that when the time comes, you will be able to find and troubleshoot any of the computers.

CHAPTER 15:
STRUCTURING A SIMPLE LAN/WAN

Now that we have covered how to install a single wiring rack, let's take a look at network planning and installation a different way. We are going to look at what it took to build the network shown in the following diagram.

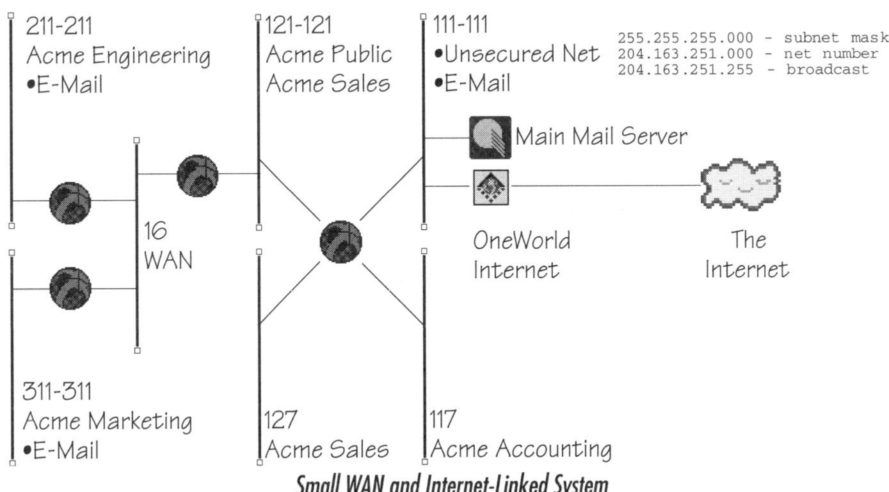

Small WAN and Internet-Linked System

This system has the following basic architecture:

- Internet feed

- Unsecured IP/AppleTalk networking area

- Secured router firewalls separating IP from AppleTalk

- E-mail server that links to the Internet

- IP gateway to dynamically assign IP addresses for Ethernet users

- IP gateway to dynamically assign IP addresses for LocalTalk users

- LAN and WAN routers

We will walk through how we conceived of and then installed the networking components and critical software configurations.

THE APPLETALK NETS

Let's discuss the original design concept of the networks and internetwork, and then we'll cover how that design changed as the needs of the network changed. Remember, the structure of your network is not only based upon your architectural needs, it is based upon your services as well. Since this book doesn't cover the implementation of services per se, we look at them separately in their own book, *AppleTalk Network Services*.

Building One

Building One's network combined two Ethernet networks and two LocalTalk networks. Building One is a two-floor building with approximately 75 computers on each floor. As there was a mixture of LocalTalk-based computers and Ethernet-based computers on each floor, the network architecture took that into account.

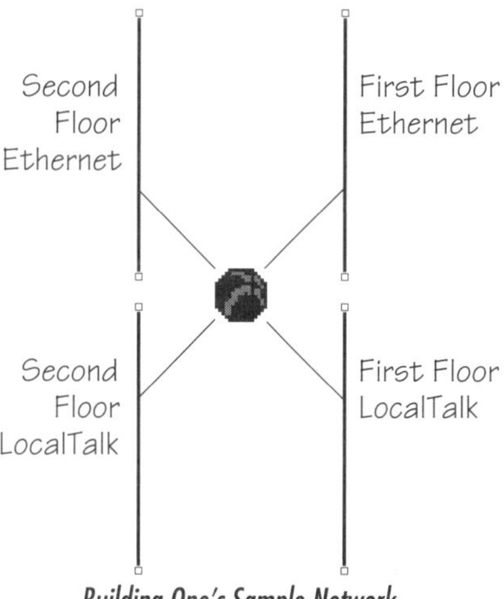

Building One's Sample Network

During the design phase of the network, it was decided that the LocalTalk users, who were spread out across the two floors of the building, would pretty much remain within their LocalTalk network. Mainly, they used limited FileMaker databases and printed to LocalTalk-based Hewlett Packard laser jets. Therefore, extended throughput to Ethernet wasn't needed. The LocalTalk users were segregated, with one floor dedicated to the sales staff and another floor dedicated to the accounting staff.

The Ethernet users, much like the LocalTalk users, were also segregated mainly by the floors on which they worked. The first-floor Ethernet users were made up of 30 sales staff members dedicated to selling to the computer geek-based market. They therefore all had Ethernet-based mobile computers. The second-floor Ethernet users weren't "users" per se. They were made up of the information services (IS) staff, the executive staff (who have computers on their desks that look "cool" to their golfing buddies), the main file server, the main application distribution server (FileWave), the main mail server (QuickMail), and a couple of high-speed HP5si-mx printers.

Thus, the original design of the network called for a single four-port router to be implemented: two ports for Ethernet and two ports for LocalTalk. This router segments the traffic and the floors themselves. The router selected was the RISC Router 3000E from Compatible Systems.

Buildings Two and Three

Buildings Two and Three are separated from Building One by about four miles. They are both in the same office complex. In the original design of the complex, Building Two was the first building, followed by Building Three, and finally Building One was built to be the company's corporate offices for MIS, accounting, sales, and executive staff.

Building Two houses approximately 50 Ethernet users. Building Two is mainly for the engineering staff that builds the Acme Widgets, and therefore it has many CAD workstations, high-speed printers, and a mix of high-end Macs and servers. It has its own e-mail system based on QuickMail.

Building Three has about 20 Ethernet users and contains mainly the marketing staff. They had their own e-mail server, along with all the color printers, RIPs, and other material needed to create the package designs and marketing material for their products and catalogs.

Original Network Design Plan

As originally designed, the networking plan called for three different networks: Building One's network, Building Two's network, and Building Three's network. The buildings would be linked only by the QuickMail-to-QuickMail bridges. Since only Building One's network had a router, it was the only one that would need network numbers and zones. The zones were basic. Sales and Accounting were the primary zones, with sales running over from LocalTalk to Ethernet to make it easier for the sales staff to find each other. The MIS staff and others in the executive department also shared a zone called Acme Public in which they placed the mail server and major services that all users could access from time to time.

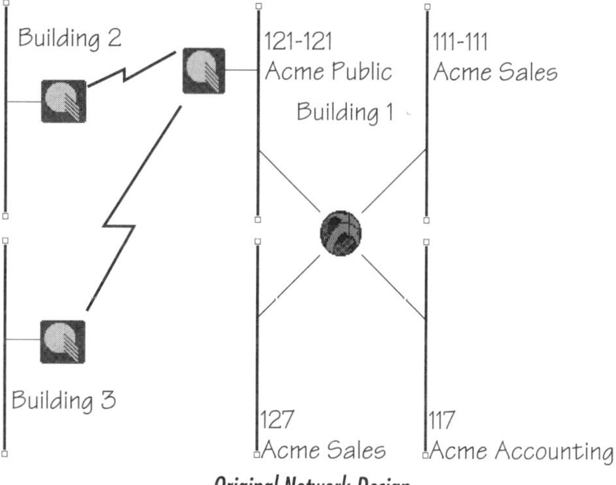

Original Network Design

The network numbers reflect a basic design philosophy for AppleTalk numbering. The numbering system is as follows:

- Each network number ends in 1–6 for Ethernet and 7–9 for LocalTalk.

- The second digit in each number represents the floor on which the network is physically located. In the event that a network is located across two or more floors, its number shows the originating or lowest floor.

- The rest of the numbers indicate the building.

Thus, network *127* would designate *Building One (1), second floor (2),* and *Local-Talk (7)*. This gives the network administrators an easy way to determine from which location a problem originated.

This plan worked well . . . for about a month. It worked until the marketing department decided that they needed direct Internet access for researching Web pages and, even more important, for Internet electronic mail to their customers. This meant a complete change of structure for the network. TCP/IP access would need to be added, as well as electronic mail gateways to the Internet itself.

New Network Design Plan

The new needs were for full access to the Internet from every workstation on the network, as well as security from the Internet and potential hackers, and security from abusers of the system within the company. Thus, the company was forced to restructure its LAN and WAN designs. When migrating from individual networks to a WAN, the connection methodology for the WAN itself had to be configured. The questions at hand were as follows:

- How do you connect all three buildings and the Internet together?

- How do you create a firewall for security to and from the Internet that is still easy to administer?

- How do you keep your WAN connection costs down while giving your users as much throughput as possible?

These questions come to a boil when you look at the two possibilities for WAN connections: Frame Relay and ISDN.

Frame Relay would provide for a three-way connection between the three buildings that could be left "open" and "running" at all times. Building Two could communicate with Building Three without having to be routed through Building One's router. Tariff management would not be necessary with Frame Relay, as there aren't line usage charges like ISDN's long distance charges. Frame Relay also provides a methodology for extending the WAN connections between any new buildings that might be built. Thus, Frame Relay was chosen for the building-to-building routing plan.

ISDN allows for bandwidth at the basic rate that is twice that of the 56 kbps Frame Relay lines chosen for the building-to-building connections. However, ISDN is a tariffed protocol that charges for long distance calls and thus couldn't be used for any building-to-building WAN routing. What ISDN offers, though, is a fast and efficient methodology for accessing Internet ISPs. Accessing the Internet only when needed, ISDN's up and down connection methods won't cause any network interruptions. Therefore, owing to twice the throughput and local calls being placed to the ISP, thus making it as inexpensive as an access system, ISDN was chosen as the Internet access methodology.

The WAN access methods were thus divided into Frame Relay for building-to-building access and ISDN for Internet access. The only thing left was to select an ISP. When selecting an ISP, the following was taken into consideration:

- E-mail POP3 server

- SMTP gateway to QuickMail, the company's e-mail system

- Basic security levels for different types of access

- Web page management and servers

- Domain Name Server and domain name management

Acme Widget was accessing the Internet for the first time and didn't want to manage its own POP3 server or any special QuickMail SMTP gateways. It also did not want to manage its own Domain Name Server or Web server. Finally, it wanted an easy way to manage basic Internet security. Acme Widget turned to Global Village for both the WAN router and basic Internet access service. Global Village would provide the ISP service, as well as domain name registration, class licensing for IP addresses, mail server presence, mail server gateway software, and even some basic security. Therefore, a new design was created, as shown in the next picture.

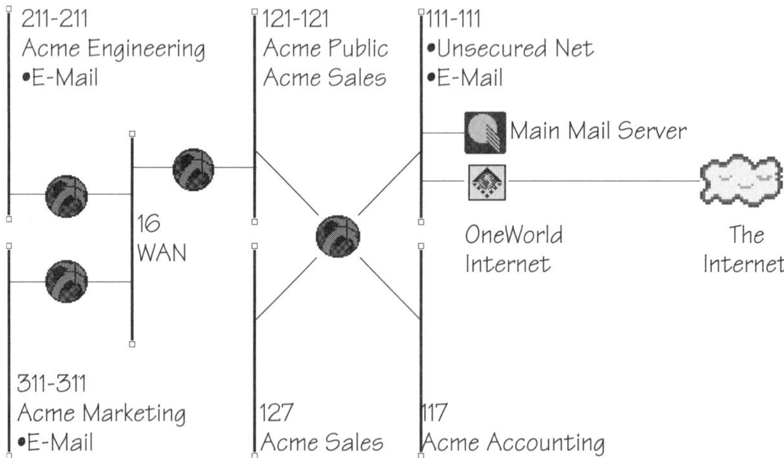

Final AppleTalk Network Numbering and LAN/WAN Architecture

Building One

For Building One, the Ethernet network that was previously split between floors was now consolidated into network 121–121, originating on the second floor with the MIS shop. Another router was added to the second-floor's Ethernet network providing access to the other buildings via Frame Relay. The first-floor's original Ethernet LAN, network 111–111, was converted into what Acme Widget called the *unsecured LAN*. This means that this LAN is the one that holds the Internet access router from Global Village. This is the only LAN with both TCP/IP *and* AppleTalk running on it. The two LocalTalk networks were left alone.

Buildings Two and Three

There weren't any major changes to Buildings Two and Three. The only changes were the addition of a WAN router for each of the buildings, and having the QuickMail servers now send data through the WAN using ADSP, which is *much* faster, instead of sending data between the routers over their modems.

WAN

The WAN between the buildings was given network number 16. This designates that the Compatible Systems' RISC Routers could handle 16 DLCIs to create a meshed architecture on Frame Relay, but with more than that, there would be problems integrating with other routers. The WAN used a non-extended network architecture and therefore only received a single network number and single zone.

Zones

Buildings Two and Three each gained a new default zone appropriate for the departments that were housed in the buildings. Acme Sales and Acme Public were both placed into network 121–121, as they were combined during the restructuring. Network 111–111's default zone became "•Unsecured Net." The bullet ensures that the zone name goes to the bottom of the list. The WAN was given the zone name WAN to ensure that it, too, would be at the bottom of the list.

Finally, another zone was added wherever there was a mail server. This zone was called "•E-Mail" and each of the e-mail servers on each of the LANs was placed into it. By designating the zone name this way, the name is at the bottom of the list *and* finding mail servers is easy. There is only one zone to search through. By *not* making it a default zone, most users won't accidentally be placed into it.

INTEGRATING TCP/IP INTO THE DESIGN PLAN

Once the company redesigned its standard AppleTalk networking setup, it had to deploy TCP/IP services to the users on the network, as well as for the purposes of Internet access. Before this could be accomplished, the company needed to connect its new Global Village OneWorld Internet router with Global Village's Internet Service Center. This was performed offline, meaning that the Global Village box was *not* connected to the rest of the network. This was primarily because of security. Also, since this was the first time that Acme Widget was connecting to the Internet, the network administrator decided to test the connection on a separate network. If something went wrong, there would be fewer pieces to consider in the problem-solving equation.

First Steps—Initiating the Connection

Before the connection to Global Village could be established, the administrator had to set up his own computer correctly. Global Village's server uses a standard TCP/IP number on the server box itself and on the user's computer when initially signing in or after you lose your connectivity information. Thus, to start, the administrator set MacTCP to the manual address mode and entered the node's IP address along with the gateway address for the router.

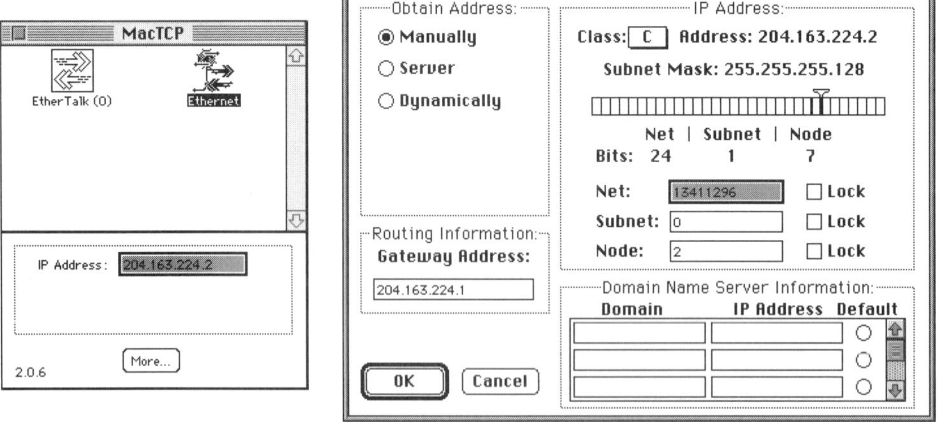

MacTCP Control Panel(left) and Setting up the Administrator's Computer (right)

Entering Registration Information

Once the computer was set the right way, the Internet router was turned on and the Global Village Management software was installed on the same computer running the QuickMail server. Global Village's router is easy to work with. A registration screen appears and prompts you through every step. The first and biggest step is figuring out how many TCP/IP addresses you need and filling out that information correctly.

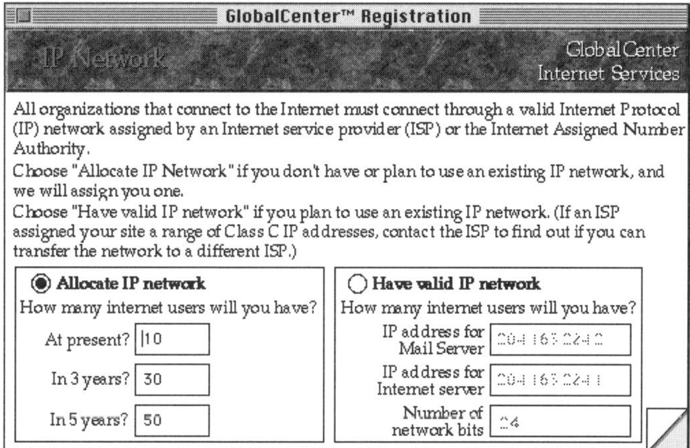

TCP/IP Address Information Window

After the address information is filled out, the next step is the domain name registration information. This is basically how others on the Internet will find you. Network Frontiers uses the domain name *netfrontiers.com*. Acme Widget Corporation filed for *acmewidget.com*. The administrator filled out his request and sent it in to Global Village. Global Village then obtained the required domain name for Acme Widget, which takes about 30–60 days.

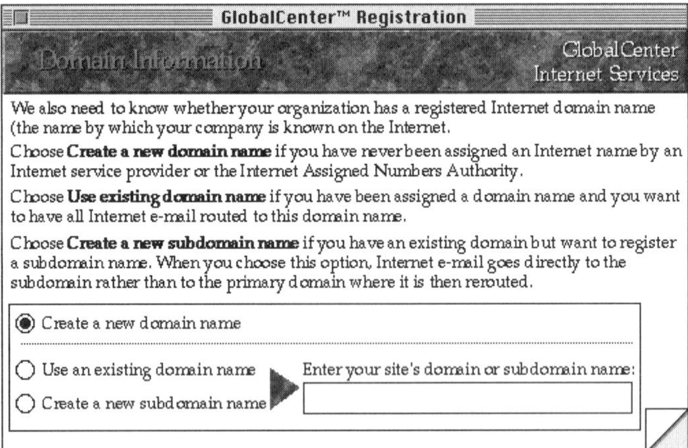

Domain Name Registration Window

After the rest of the information was entered, including billing information and contact point registration, the company sent the registration information to Global Village. The company was registered and running—albeit with a temporary domain name—within about 30 minutes. The network information that came back stated that the IP network number for Acme Widget was 204.163.251.000. They were assigned a Class C IP range.

Initial Security Decision

The initial decision to segment IP away from AppleTalk was security-based. Therefore, IP would be routed only into the networking system via the Global Village box, and then AppleTalk would be routed to the rest of the network. A MacIP gateway would be installed on network 111–111 to support users that wanted access to the Internet. Internet e-mail would be directly supported through QuickMail's Global Village Internet gateway.

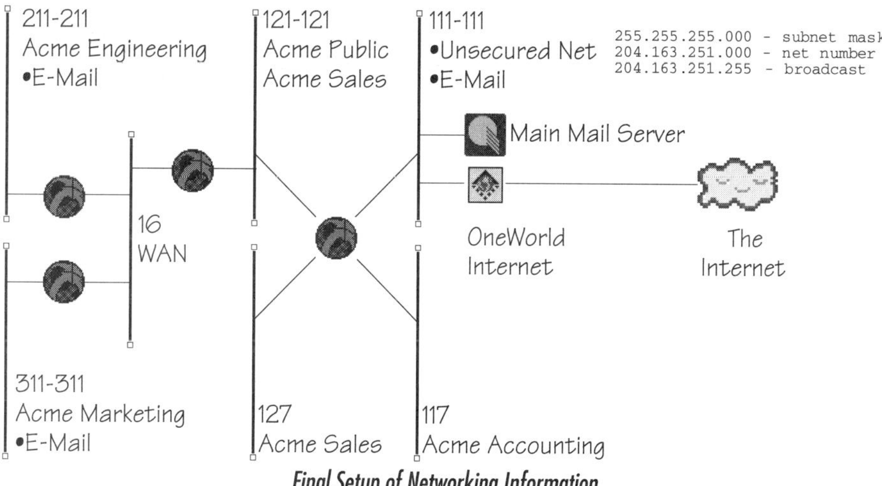

Final Setup of Networking Information

While this might not prove to be the best long-term solution, it's a great start. It uses AppleTalk's native ability to dissuade hackers to keep security tight during the initial network construction and testing phases.

Setting up QuickMail's Internet Gateway

The last thing to be done was to set up an Internet mail gateway to the outside world. Since Global Village installs the mail gateway software onto the QuickMail server during installation procedures, there was really not much to setting up the rest of the gateway itself. Within the QM Administrator application, the network administrator selected to create a new gateway called, appropriately enough, INTERNET. This was so that users could easily distinguish which MailCenter should be used when connecting to the outside world. The type was set to be GlobalCenter. They filled in the password, but we don't show you that because of security (so there! Thphphphpht!).

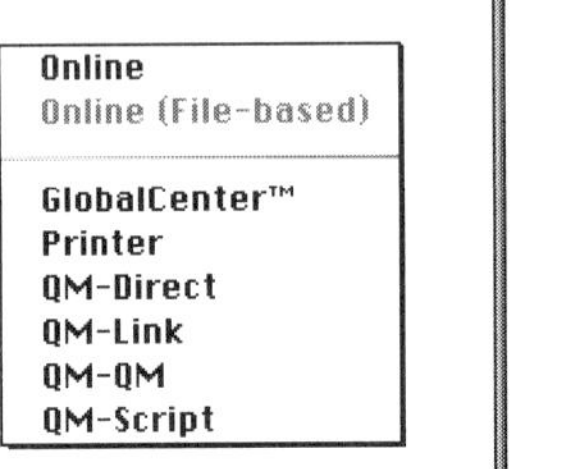

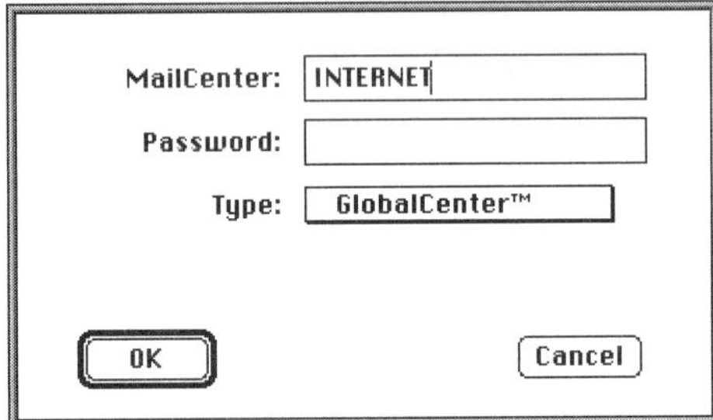

Possible Types of MailCenters (left) and Creating a New MailCenter (right)

Once the MailCenter was created, a custodian was chosen. In this case, it was the administrator, as he's the only one who manages any of the devices on the network. The mail logs were to be sent to the administrator every five days for review. Otherwise, the MailCenter is managed directly through GlobalCenter Manager.

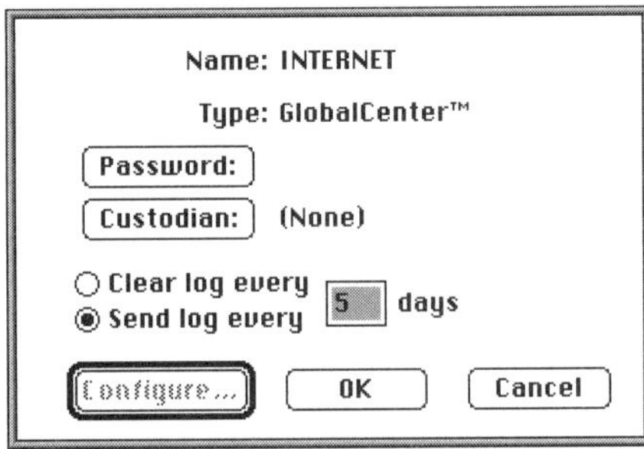

Setting up Housekeeping for the MailCenter

When finished, the QuickMail server had two MailCenters: one for the internal users and one for mail going to the Internet.

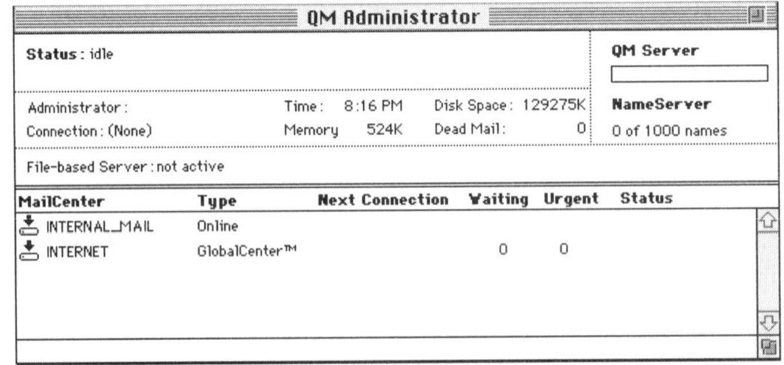

QuickMail Administrator Window Showing Newly Created INTERNET MailCenter

INDEX